Tony May

Italian Cuisine

Basic cooking techniques

First Edition

Italian Wine & Food Institute

TO THE READER

Although there are many cookbooks, this book fills a void. It not only deals with the basic techniques of Italian cooking but also serves as a manual for culinary students and faculty, as well as professionals who give Italian cuisine the attention, dedication and interest it deserves.

Italian cuisine is universally considered one of the healthiest, yet it is simple, pleasing and certainly one of the most liked. The diffusion of Italian cuisine is due to the determined contribution made by the Italians abroad who have been able to bring passion, knowledge and strength of a marvellous tradition to other lands. Today, Italian restaurants are among the most elegant, prestigious and popular in the world. The popularity of Italian cuisine is very flattering to us, but it also puts upon us responsibilities and duties. It is necessary that Italian cuisine be pure and faithful to its secular traditions and basic principles. This book ensures that.

Further, this book will contribute to spreading the knowledge of our gastronomy throughout the world. It is a book that attempts to set a discipline and that gives, to all those who are interested, a working instrument. After all, cooking is an art and Italy has always been a master of that art.

Calogero Mannino
Minister of Agriculture and Forestry.

ACKNOWLEDGMENTS

No book of this kind can be compiled by any one man, and whatever its value as a comprehensive and authoritative repository of informed opinion is due to the many people who have helped me pull all the elements together into a volume I hope is as readable as it is useful to the student. My gratitude to the following people is outweighed only by my respect for their knowledge, enthusiasm and energies in helping me bring this book out.

I wish first to thank Fernanda Gosetti, noted cookbook author, who helped me to write the first rough draft of La Cucina Italiana. For his dogged research into the origins, history, curiosities and regional differences of Italian cooking and for his review of the manuscript, I thank journalist and food writer Giorgio Mistretta. Without the helpful advice of my good friend and gourmet, Eugenio Medagliani, I might not ever have gone on with this project. And for their encouragement and help at every turn, I shall not soon forget the input of noted cookbook writer and television personality Vincenzo Buonassisi and journalist and food expert Stefano Milioni, and my good friend, anthropologist Alessandro Falassi.

When it came to compiling the recipes, chefs both in Italy and the United States, Valentino Marcattilii, Paul Bartolotta, Angelo Paracucchi, Carlo de Gaudenzi, Sandro Fioriti, and Pierangelo Cornaro offered enormous help and resources.

A smooth translation from the Italian into English was impeccably accomplished by Shelley Handler, assisted by Ada Cascone. From there it was taken over by John F. Mariani, whose editorial direction, from asking the simplest of questions to making the most insightful demands, has made what I once thought unmanageable into a work of authoritative cogency.

Many thanks go to my assistant Cynthia Brody and my secretary Marie Ioime, on whom I depended day after day and month after month to keep everything straight and in perfect form.

I must also offer my gratitude to Dr. Lucio Caputo of the Italian Wine and Food Institute for his help on this project, and to Mark Erickson of the Culinary Institute of America and his wife Lisa, who read through the recipes and gave me invaluable advice in the usage of consistant terminology and easy reading. I also wish to thank Ferdinand Metz and Tim Ryan of the Culinary Institute of America for their support. I hope they and generations of students enjoy this book and learn from it as much as I have in putting it all together.

Tony May
May 1990

PREFACE

Today's "cucina Italiana" *is the result of a slow process of integrating different regional traditions and experiences. To better understand this concept, we must consider that when Italy was unified, in 1861, only 600,000 Italians, out of a population of 25 million, were able to speak the national language. The remainder spoke regional dialects. This same disparity existed in the cooking of various regions. The use of pasta, for instance, was popular in the south, but fairly unknown in the north. In Lombardy, Piedmont and Veneto, for example, the most popular staples were rice and cornmeal.*

Italy's unification, the proclamation of Rome as its capital, and the development of national railroad lines all contributed to interaction of habits, language and cooking styles between the north and the south, from region to region.

As the 19th century came to a close, a formalized Italian gastronomy began to emerge in family-run businesses, the so-called osterie, *where the housewife prepared for her customers the same dishes, featuring locally grown products, she cooked for her husband and children. By contrast, the food served in hotels was far different in that it addressed a more select, sophisticated clientele who travelled for pleasure and business. They were provided with a continental, basically French, cuisine prepared by French chefs and Italian chefs trained in French cooking schools. In Naples, for example, where the Borboni family reigned,* "monzu", *a dialect word for* "monsieur", *was the name used to identify a chef who worked for the nobility.*

It was not until 1891 that Pellegrino Artusi, a banker and epicure from Romagna who relocated in Florence for business reasons, wrote and published a book (La Scienza in Cucina e l'Arte di Mangiar Bene) *in which he attempted to gather the most popular recipes of the period. The first edition contained 475 recipes; by the 13th printing the number had grown to 790, the additions suggested to the author by enthusiastic housewives from all over Italy. Only after 1945 did Italy, which had turned away from its cherished traditions during two world wars and twenty years of dictatorship, start to reclaim its gastronomic culture. It wasn't until the 1950's that the old values again emerged as the country rediscovered its deeply rooted traditions. Old cookbooks, once very popular among patrician families, came back into vogue. Texts by Platina, Scappi, Stefani, Cristoforo da Messisbugo, were once again consulted and their recipes adapted for modern usage. By 1960, in the city of Mantova, one thousand guests were served a 36-course banquet that replicated a banquet that took place four centuries before at the Gonzaga Court. Thus, it took less than thirty years for the Italian table to regain its former great-*

ness by the simple process of asserting its own style of tastes and flavors.

Although regional traditions still exist, a traveller to Italy may discover that they merge into one single entity, thanks to an interchange of information, new taste preferences, and a greater concern for nutritive values. These values constitute an age-old eating habit newly defined as the Mediterranean Diet, emphasizing pasta and vegetables, fish and white meats, such as veal, rabbit and poultry, and the use of olive oil rather than butter, which is still more popular in the northern provinces where agriculture and cattle-breeding, along with milk and cheese production, abound. The use of strutto *or* sugna *(liquefied pork fats brought to solid form), once considered major cooking ingredients in rural areas, and the traditional Neapolitan cuisine, have almost disappeared owing to increased concern over cholesterol, which doesn't exist in olive and other vegetable oils.*

Increased reciprocity between northern and southern Italy, consistent with the business and social demands of a major industrial nation, has forced the restaurants to keep pace with this cooking evolution. Today the traditional trattoria *offers a cuisine that represents the extension of* cucina casalinga, *«home cooking», one that can expand, modify and satisfy average and popular taste. The* trattoria *presents local, sometimes regional, dishes according to established custom. Its vocation is to preserve the traditional values. In the kitchen, more often than not, we find* Nonna *(grandma),* Zia *(an aunt) or* Mama. *The decor is generally casual, informal and rustic with checkered tablecloths, simple chairs, and displays of art and objects made by local artisans.*

The restaurant, in contrast to the trattoria, *has instead a distinct personality. The host is not* Papa, *but a professional; the decor is contemporary or classic, the service distinctive and personalized, and the menu and wine lists show a knowledge of local and regional traditions. The restaurant manifests the personality of the individual within, who follows an eno-gastronomic culture that is both cosmopolitan and elitist. The function of a restaurant is to keep up with its clientele, follow the changes in life-styles, and thereby rethink and renew the traditions and, if necessary, to apply to the future the teachings of the past.*

In addition, Italian wines have followed much the same path. Once limited by small archaic facilities, Italian vintners have achieved state-of-the-art production, resulting in more eminent vineyards and a quality of wine equal, and in some cases better, than any other in the world. Only recently have these wines begun to receive the recognition they deserve.

A NOTE ON ITALIAN USAGE

*The language of food in Italy incorporates dozens of regional dialects, which may or may not conform to standard Italian grammar, spelling and usage. Also, an individual food term may take more than one regional name. For instance, «*fettuccine*» is the word used in Rome to describe the flat noodles known more commonly in Italy as «*tagliatelle*». The word for the dessert* tiramisu *is a Venetian colloquialism meaning «pick me up», much the same way the American slang phrase «pick-me-up» refers to an early evening cocktail. These regional terms enrich Italy's culinary language as devil's food, dirty rice and hush puppy enrich American English.*

Italian is an inflected language; however, the standard rules for singular and plural forms are based on gender. While Italian does make distinctions between male and female animals of the same species (e.g., bufalo, *for a male buffalo, and* bufala *for a female), only a thorough knowledge of the Italian language will help to sort out (though never make clear) why some words are masculine and others feminine. In general, masculine nouns in the singular end in -o and feminine nouns in -a. Masculine nouns in the plural end in -i and feminine nouns in -e.*

Here are some examples:

MASCULINE SINGULAR PLURAL

scampo	scampi
piatto	piatti
sorbetto	sorbetti

FEMININE SINGULAR PLURAL

quaglia	quaglie
galantina	galantine
linguina	linguine
fettuccina	fettuccine

There are exceptions to these rules, especially those singular nouns ending in -e that might be either masculine or feminine, e.g., il padre *(«the father») and* la madre *(«the mother»), in both cases the plural ending is -i. There are even Italian masculine nouns that end in -o that become feminine in the plural, e.g.,* l'uovo *(the egg), which becomes* le uova *(the eggs). These and other exceptions fall well beyond the scope of this book, but the student may be alerted to them as he comes upon them.*

The Italian definite article for the English word «the» agrees in gender and number with the noun it modifies. The most common form for masculine singular nouns is il *(il* piatto, *il* sorbetto*); for plural,* i *(i* piatti, *i* sorbetti*). Lo (singular) and gli (plural) are also used in special cases (lo* scampo, *gli* scampi*).*

The form for feminine singular nouns is la (la quaglia*); for plural, le (le* quaglie*).*

Usage for referring to a food item in the singular or plural is, as in English, very much a matter of common sense. For instance, in English the words «oats» and «French fries» are always used in the plural. So, too, in Italian spaghetti, gnocchi *and* tagliatelle *are always used in the plural. This is reflected in the glossary to this book, which uses the plural when it makes sense to do so.*

John F. Mariani, Ph.D.
Editor

TABLE OF CONTENTS

ITALIAN BREAD

Bread has always been the basic nutrient for the entire Mediterranean basin. Unjustly undermined for a while, bread has returned to take its rightful place as man's basic nutrient, according to a study conducted by Ancel Keys, Professor of Physiological Hygiene at the University of Minnesota. The study reports on the importance of the Mediterranean diet, based on olive oil and wine, and claims that bread occupies the first place in order of nutritional value.

In Italy the traditions of bread making are very old indeed. Still today we find several types of bread, very different among themselves. The most representative perhaps are *michetta, rosetta, banana, biova, bovolo, ciabatta, ciriola, manina ferrarese and, of course, the pane casareccio,* the traditional large-sized, thick-crusted bread which is still a favorite from Tuscany to Sicily.

It is clear that every name given to an individual bread represents a historic or geographical event that in reality or fantasy has played a major role in the tradition of regional bread making. A typical example is the Tuscan bread. Tuscan bread, made without salt, is a classic example of enduring traditions.

During the period of papal dominance, an extremely high salt tax was imposed, so, as a form of protest, the Tuscan bakers decided to abolish salt in the preparation of their bread, a tradition that has been perpetuated until today out of a preference for the taste rather than as an historical imperative. Consequently, the Tuscan *prosciutto* is much saltier than its Parma or Friuli counterparts, the additional salt making up for the blandness of the bread which generally accompanies *prosciutto*.

However, in the panorama of Italian bread, we cannot forget *grissino,* the famous bread sticks from Torino, known the world over, thanks to the many commercially produced versions. Legend has it that *grissino* was invented by the personal Doctor of the Savoia Family, rulers of Piedmont and Val D'Aosta regions in the 17th century who, while caring for the Duke's health, instructed a baker to bake some *"gherse"*, a word from Piedmont dialect which indicates a very long, thin bread.

In 1643, another episode exists noted by the Florentine monk Vincenzo Bucellai. During one of Bucellai's trips, he stopped at an inn in Chivasso (Piedmont) and was served a bread *"lungo quanto un braccio e sottile sottile"*, as long as an arm and very, very thin.

Bread baking is based on a biological process that can be partially controlled by the baker. The quality of bread is based on optimal conditions of several factors: flour, water, temperature, fermentation and, finally, baking.

To coordinate these factors requires considerable skill. Fortunately today the baker can avail himself of several pieces of machinery that allow a more uniform production and standard of quality. In the northern part of Italy, today, we find that bread is being produced more and more on an industrial level, while in the south this development is much slower. It is therefore easier to find small bakeries that still produce bread on a traditional and regional level.

The new Italian restaurant has been making strong efforts to give bread more importance in the total structure of a meal, to the point of proposing breads which are more suitable with specific dishes. The following recipes are designed to help you make such breads. These are the most popular breads in Italy:

BIOVA OR BIOVETTA, a roundly shaped, slightly elongated white loaf with a fat (strutto) added. Only the size distinguishes the two names. The Biova may weigh up to 12 ozs., while the *Biovetta* is generally one to two ounces.

Also typical of the north is *MONTASÙ*, a name meaning "climbing up", because of the bread's shape, triangular and rising in a spiral. It is made of wheat flour; oil is added to the dough and so it has a fairly compact mollica. Its size varies from 7-10 ozs.

MICHETTA OR ROSETTA is always found on the table of the Milanesi. Its size is $1 \frac{1}{2} - 2$ ozs., it is round in shape, prepared with white bread, very crusty on the outside, almost completely devoid of a doughy inside because of the forced fermentation (achieved with the help of appropriate mechanical mixer) that puffs up the bread while it bakes. The same dough, made into rolls are called *MODENESE*. Softer and richer, more widely used for sandwiches is a bread called *BANANA*, made from a strip of dough rolled into an oblong shape similar to the fruit from which it takes its name. Another characteristic Lombardy bread is called *MICCONE*. Its center is compact yet soft, and the loaf is made in a variety of different shapes that may easily exceed two pounds and which can be kept relatively fresh for at least a week. It is a bread which should be used sliced.

In the most northern regions where there is a decided Austro-German influence, the most common bread is called *CHIFEL*. Weighing about an ounce, it is shaped like a half moon, much like a croissant. It takes its name from the pastry chef Chiffering, who came to Italy to the court of the Duke of Parma, as part of the retinue of Maria Luisa of Austria. It was Chiffering who first produced the croissant in Italy, as a mock reminder of the battle of Vienna and the Turkish symbol of the half moon. By eliminating the sugar from the dough used in a croissant we get *Chifel*.

Not only in Trentino but throughout the northeast and Venezia Giulia as well, the common, crusty bread is called *SALINO*, which refers to the rock salt on its crust. Weighing approximately 1-2 ounces, the crust is sprinkled with salt or cumin seeds and customarily eaten with beer and fresh, dry, or grilled sausages. Larger rye and whole wheat loaves are also spread with cumin seeds and weigh about a pound. Using the same kind of dough, a flat bread about 5" in diameter is made to be eaten fresh with speck, a cured porkpie,

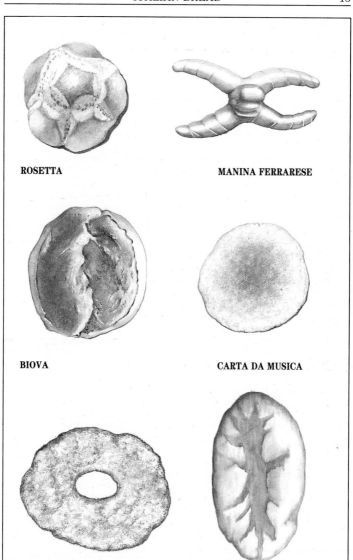

ROSETTA

MANINA FERRARESE

BIOVA

CARTA DA MUSICA

FRISEDDA

PANE TOSCANO

typical of the area. This bread may also be dried out and crumbled in soups and rich gravies.

Similar to the Piedmontese *Montasù,* the *BOVOLO* — a Venetian dialect name for snail, which describes its shape — has a firm dough with a delicate, soft crust and weighs about four or five ounces.

The most characteristic bread in Emilia-Romagna is called *FER-RARESE*, made with hard dough. The best example is called *MA-NINA* Ferrarese, shaped like a hand with thin strips of finger-like dough that remains soft inside while crusty outside after baking.

Heading south to Tuscany-Umbria, one more frequently finds *PANE CASARECCIO*, or "country bread", — large in size, round or oblong in form, ranging from one to three pounds and up (because it has to last more than one day). Made of white or whole wheat flour, the ingredients are no more than water and natural yeast, rarely animal or vegetable fats. In the past, because the bread was baked only once a week it was made of sufficient size to accommodate a large family. Because the women baked the bread in a communal oven, the loaves had personalized, distinctive cuts for easy recognition.

The *CIRIOLA*, from Rome, is a long shaped loaf, 3-4 oz., with a sharp cut in the center, and a golden, crispy crust.

Apulia has three definite bread traditions: *BARILE*, a 4 lb. loaf made with hard drum wheat with a thick, dark crust and a compact, porous dough; *SCHIACCIATA*, 4 pounds, is only allowed a single rise before being placed into the oven. It therefore remains a flat bread with a soft, porous dough.

FRISEDDA is a bread from Puglia shaped like a large doughnut. After an initial baking, it is cut into two disks and baked again until the bread becomes *biscottato* (dry and crumbly). It keeps for several months.

In Sicily the tradition of *PANE CASARECCIO* (country bread) is prevalent, and there are notable localized distinctions, such as using a pinch of saffron in the dough (of Arabic origin) or covering the dough with sesame seeds before baking. Even small loaves for average use run 8-10 ounces. *MAFALDA* is a typical Sicilian bread made with white flour, shaped like a braid. Another Sicilian bread is *FER-RO DI CAVALLO* made with hard dough shaped as a horse shoe.

The traditions of the island of Sardinia are exemplified in breads like the *CARTA DA MUSICA* (music paper) or *carasau*, a very thin sheet of bread made without yeast and left to dry before it is eaten in small pieces, simply flavored with a bit of olive oil. It is an essential ingredient in a very famous soup of the area called *pane frattau.* The bread is placed at the bottom of a bowl, covered with boiling broth, a fresh egg and grated cheese. Sardinia also produces the largest bread in Italy, made from the semolina of the area near San-luri and Cagliari, called Civraxiu; prepared with natural yeast, it can weigh up to ten pounds.

In addition to the better known regional breads, there is also *pan de frizze,* from Friuli, made with flour, eggs, cracklings of pork, butter and salt. *RAMERINO*, from Tuscany, with dough enriched by filtered warm olive oil strongly scented with rosemary. *PAGNOTTA DI SANTA CHIARA*, from Naples, is typical of stuffed, warm breads. This dough is made with potato and wheat flour, yeast, lard and pepper. It is shaped into two disks stuffed with tomatoes and anchovies, then rolled and baked.

RICETTE
Recipes

BASIC DOUGH FOR BREAD

4 cups bread-flour*
1 oz. brewers yeast or compressed yeast
pinch of salt
1 pt. of water
* high gluten flour

Method 1:
Place the flour on a wooden board and make a hole in the center. Dissolve the yeast in 1 cup lukewarm water and place in the middle. Work the mixture with the tips of your fingers, adding the rest of the lukewarm water a little bit at a time and the salt, until the dough no longer sticks to your fingers. Knead the dough for an additional 15 minutes. Form a ball, make a cross-shaped cut with a sharp knife on the top. Wrap in a dry cloth and let it rest in a warm place for half an hour, or until doubled in size.

Begin working the dough again, energetically, for another 15 minutes. Make a ball, cover it and let it rest for 6 hours. It should again double its volume and become elastic. It is now ready for baking, in any desired shape. (To obtain a darker color, there is an old fashioned custom of adding a teaspoon of sugar to the flour before mixing.)

Method 2:
There is also another, more elaborate method of preparing the dough. Dissolve the yeast in a cup of lukewarm water and work with a few teaspoons of flour until it forms a soft preliminary dough. Allow to rise in a warm place. When the dough has doubled in size, work in the rest of the flour with more lukewarm salted water, kneading continually until the dough has a smooth, even texture. Allow to rise until doubled in size once more, and work again, allowing it to rise a third, final time.

In the bakery, but also at home, when people used to make bread regularly, beer yeast was substituted with a special bread leavening agent consisting of a small piece of fermented dough watered down with lukewarm water to a fluid paste, which was then used to make the preliminary dough. This method takes much longer for the bread to rise, but the result is a particularly soft, fragrant and aromatic bread.

PANE INTEGRALE
Wholewheat Bread

Use the same quantities as in the basic recipe, but use 50% whole wheat and 50% white flour. (For better rising, dissolve the yeast in lukewarm water with few teaspoons of flour as in Method 2.) Mix together and form a small ball. Let rest, covered, in a warm place, for 20 minutes.

Prepare the flour on a wooden board with a center well. Add the dough prepared in advance, and work the dough energetically for 15 minutes. Once you have obtained a smooth, soft dough, form a ball, wrap it in a cloth, sprinkle with flour and let rest for one hour in a warm place. Place the dough on a greased sheet pan sprinkled with fine bread crumbs. For the first 20 minutes the oven must be approximately 500° F., then lower it to about 350° F. and keep baking until the bread is golden brown and crusty on the outside.

Tips: If you do not use a typical bread oven, to see that, the bread stays soft and retains a certain amount of humidity, place in the back of the baking oven a container full of water so that as the water steams, it is soaked in the dough and the finished product is soft, crispy and moist inside.

It is desireable to bake bread in a hearth oven. A hearth oven may be imitated by placing tiles in the oven and baking bread directly on the tiles.

GRISSINI
Breadsticks

2 lbs. flour	*1½ oz. brewers or*
2 cups lukewarm water	*compressed yeast*
	2 Tbs. salt

GRISSINI

Dilute ½ oz. of yeast in a cup of lukewarm water, combine with 3 oz. flour and let it rest in a warm place for 1½ hours, or until the volume doubles.

Add to the fermented dough, 1 lb.-3 oz. of flour, remainder of yeast, salt, and enough lukewarm water to form a dough which is soft and elastic. Work the dough until it comes away easily from your hands. Form the dough into a large ball, make a crosslike incision on top and cover with a towel. Let it rest in a warm place for 5 hours or until the dough doubles in size. Add the remainder of the flour and the water and work into the fermented dough until you achieve a smooth and elastic dough. Next, cut small pieces of dough and roll on a wooden board to form long, thin sticks and place into a baking pan. Let the dough sticks rest in a warm place until they double in size. Bake at 550° F. for 10 minutes.

NOTE: With the same dough, you can make the classic *michetta* or *rosetta*.

BRUSCHETTA
Garlic Bread

4 slices "homemade style"	*2 Tbs. olive oil*
bread $\frac{1}{2}$" thick	*salt to taste*
1 garlic clove	*pepper to taste*

Make a few shallow cuts across the surface of the slices then put the bread on the grill to toast, turning the slices 2-3 times. They should be golden and uniformly toasted. As soon as they are ready rub the surface with a garlic clove, drizzle with oil, salt, pepper and serve immediately. A variation of this recipe is to top the bread with a chopped fresh ripe tomato with basil.

CONDIMENTI
Fats for Condiments

Olive oil without a doubt is the most used vegetable fat in Italian cuisine. If it is utilized raw, to flavor salads and other dishes, extra virgin olive oil should be preferred. If it is used for frying, sautéeing, or other types of cooking processes, less priced types of olive oils may be used. It is however a fact, that olive oil or butter, lard or strutto, used to sauté onions, garlic, or other herbs and spices (*soffritto*), represent the authentic and the most important base for most sauces and condiments in Italian gastronomy. This is probably the very basic element that distinguished Italian cuisine, together with the simple oil and vinegar dressing for salads, from all others. In these chapters we propose to talk about the various Italian cooking fats. Cooking fats are called *condimenti* in the Italian kitchen.

OLIO D'OLIVA

Olive Oil

Olive oil is obtained by crushing olives, the fruit of a tree (Olea Europaea of the family Oleaceae) originally from Asia Minor, and from antiquity cultivated in the Mediterranean basin.

How Olive Oil is Made

The most classical method of oil extraction is crushing. The product obtained from the first pressing of the olives is the choicest quality.

The pressing of the olives to obtain olive oil has three stages. *Frangitura* is the process that breaks the olive pulp. The most common method is that of two large granite wheels turning on a gigantic granite platter. *Gramolatura* indicates the extraction of water from the crushed olives by a controlled temperature process. *Estrazione* is the actual pressing. The most common method is extruding by pressure, which allows the exit of

Frantoio, orci

the olive oil and any remaining vegetable water. The product after this pressing is called *mosto* (must). The solid remnants are called *sansa*. (*Sansa* is also used to produce rectified oils.)

Olive oil is clarified by placing it into large cone-shaped terra-cotta containers to rest, to allow for the heavier vegetable water to settle at the bottom. The oil is decanted into another container after 24 hours then again after 2-3 days, and once more after 5-6 days. With each transfer, more water is removed. At the end of the 9-10 days no vegetable water will be left in the oil. The color of olive oil varies, ranging from yellow to yellow green, depending on the olives and the processing. The clarified oil is filtered before bottling.

This method of decanting requires a lot of handling; nowadays it is done by a centrifugal process. Olive oil dislikes sunlight and it should be bottled in dark colored glass for house use and in tin cans for commercial use. Olive oil should be stored in a cool, draftless, dark room.

Classifications

Italian law provides a specific classification of olive oil, based on method of extraction and the acidic content. The law considers suitable for consumption all oils with an acidic content of not more than 4%. The presence of acidic fats in olive oils can change according to the tree, the climate, the pressing technique, and the length of time expired from picking to pressing. Olive oils are divided into three categories:

Virgin Olive Oil

The percentage of acidic fats content determines the classification of virgin olive oils.

EXTRA VIRGIN: Acidic content not more than 1%.

SOPRAFFINO VIRGIN: Acidic content not more than 1.5%.

FINO VIRGIN: Acidic content not more than 3%.

VIRGIN: Acidic content not more than 4%.

Rectified oil (*olio rettificato*): There are two types of rectified oil:

«A»: Olive oil with acidic content above 4%, or with organolectic imperfections, may be restored for consumption through a mechanical and chemical process.

«B»: The extraction of oil from sansa, (which still contains 5-6% of olive oil). Sansa is the solid residual that remains after the extraction of virgin olive oils from the olive.

All rectified oils must be devoid of any trace of the chemical substance used and must have an acidic content not above 0.5%.

Mixed oil (*olio miscelato*) Rectified oils are void of taste or color, they are mixed with virgin olive oil in quantities which vary according to the taste and color the producer wishes to achieve. The acidic content to be not more than 2% for type «A» and 3% for type «B».

NOTE: Rectified oils may also be sold as *olio raffinato* (refined oil).

Tasting

Olive oil can be tasted just like wine:

Visual: Clarity, density and color

Aroma: Varies according to region and type of olive: fine, pronounced, intense

Taste: The most important proof of a good quality product. It can be:

Pungente (pungent): typical of young oil

Armonico (harmonious): well balanced oil, so that no one factor dominates the other

Ossidato (oxidized): rancid, it becomes so when exposed too long to air
Rotondo (rounded): full bodied, well rounded, not too aromatic
Amaro (bitter): it is generally produced from unripe olives.

How To Use

The usage of olive oil is determined by the dish being prepared. A light preparation of vegetables or fish may require a light fragrant oil, while for dishes with definite strong flavors, more decisive, stronger oils are used. The extra virgin olive oils are always used raw.

Olive oil is often flavored by adding aromatic herbs, cloves of garlic or *peperoncino*. These flavored olive oils are used to dress salads, vegetables, or as toppings for *minestre, minestrone* and *zuppe*.

Olive oil is excellent for frying. For this purpose a rectified oil is recommended. Olive oil can only be re-used two or three times, because its usage adds to viscosity and highlights the toxic substances present in it. It is preferable to use young oil for frying and if virgin olive oil is used, it must not be used a second time. Also it is not advisable to add fresh oil to old oil.

Other oils

Other oils may be extracted by a mechanical and chemical process, that is, the extraction of the oil with chemical solvents. These oils can be made from peanut, corn, sunflower, flax seeds and other vegetables. It can be used as a condiment for various raw and cooked vegetables, as well as in the preparation of sauces.

It is generally used for frying, inasmuch as it gives a crisper texture — though the food will be lighter in color — than if olive oil is used. In comparison with olive oil, vegetable oil releases a lighter fragrance and boils at a lower temperature. Frying with vegetable oil at excessively high temperatures can be harmful because high temperatures release the toxicity of the solvent used to prepare the product.

BURRO
Butter

Among the animal fats butter is the least important in the preparation of Italian cookery; it is mainly used for the preparation of *risottos* and desserts. A good butter should have a whitish-yellow color, more yellow if produced in the summer, an aromatic flavor and a delicate, slightly sweet taste. If heated it melts into an oily yellow liquid, with whitish residues underneath (which may be dispensed with). In order to preserve adequately butter for a week or so, it must be kept in the refrigerator wrapped in wax paper or aluminum foil. It may also be frozen.

GUANCIALE
Hog Jowl

Guanciale consists of the jowl and the cheek of the hog. These pieces are placed in a corrosion-proof container, covered with a mixture of salt and pepper, and left in a cool place «to cure» for a month;

they should be turned once a week. The pieces are then hung in a dry, airy place for another month before being used. *Guanciale* can be used like lard or *pancetta*. It is most used in Central Italy.

LARDO
Lard (commonly known as back fat in the U.S.)
Lard is the layer of fat located along the back and underneath the skin of the hog. Hog-butchers prepare it during the slaughtering process and preserve it in salt. In Italy it is used mainly — either minced or in whole pieces — to prepare various kinds of sauces and soups, to cook vegetables and legumes, to lard beef or poultry. In order to remove any excess of salt, lard should be blanched by placing it in cold water, bringing it to a boil and then letting it cool entirely under cold running water.

MARGARINA
Margarine
Margarine is not a typical Italian condiment, but it has become popular since the 1950s as a less expensive substitute for butter in many dishes. It is an industrial product obtained by chemical and physical treatment of vegetable and animal fats, mostly of poor quality.
Contrary to most thinking, margarine has the same amount of fat as butter but seems lighter only because it doesn't have a taste or flavor of its own.

PANCETTA
Cured Pork belly
Pancetta is one of the most popular kinds of cured meats. It is made with the layer of fat and flesh located along the stomach, directly underneath the skin of the hog. The various versions of *pancetta* are all prepared with salt and pepper; some, such as round and stuffed pancetta, are prepared with cloves, cinnamon and other spices in addition to salt and pepper. *Pancetta* has a distinctive bright red color and ages for two months; smoked *pancetta* (better known as bacon) is smoked for at least two days with beech, oak or, less frequently, juniper wood.
Pancetta can be used to dress beef or game; it can be barbecued or baked. It can also be eaten sliced with country bread or roasted *polenta*.

RIGATINO
Lean Pancetta
This is a Tuscan word for a type of pancetta. It has more meat and less fat than typical *pancetta*. As with *pancetta, rigatino* can be used for *soffritto* and to dress various types of meat. It can also be sliced and consumed as a cold cut. *Rigatino* should not be sliced too thinly.

STRUTTO
Lard

Strutto is melted and reconstructed pork fat. When the fat is completely melted, it is strained through a large and sturdy cloth. The fat collects in the container underneath. (The strips of fatty meat are put through a masher to squeeze out excess fat, and refrigerated, to be consumed with bread or *polenta*. These very flavorful pieces of crispy fat go under the name of *ciccioli*.) *Strutto* is primarily used for frying, or to prepare crusts for savory pies. It is also called *sugna*.

Strutto can also be made with a combination of pork and other animal fats but it is less tasty and is slowly disappearing from usage. *NOTE:* Pork products must be certified by the U.S.D.A. for U.S. consumption.

ACETO
Vinegar

The product of the acetic fermentation of wine under the action of a fungus, the Mycoderma *aceti* first appears in the form of a light «veil», which penetrates the liquid more and more, forming a thick, folded, sticky skin, which is called in French *"Mere de Vinaigre"*, in Italian *"Madre dell'Aceto"*, and in English the "mother of the vinegar". A good vinegar must be clear and transparent, colorless if made from white wine, pinkish if it comes from red wine. It must have a distinctly acid taste and an aroma recalling that of the wine from which it comes. Vinegar may be made of any kind of alcoholic liquid. Alcohol vinegar is colorless, unless it has been tinted with caramel. Cider vinegar is yellowish, and always less acid than wine vinegar. Vinegar should be kept in dark, securely closed bottles or in a special vinegar cask, at ambient temperature: not too hot, not too cold. If kept too long, the vinegar may become cloudy: if this happens simply filter and transfer to a clean bottle.

Italian vinegar is also classified into various types:

ACETO ORDINARIO
Common Vinegar

Produced from non-vintage wine that is already slightly turned, or from grape must with less than 8 degrees of alcohol. Fermentation is rapid and finished within 2 to 6 months. Common vinegar is clarified and filtered before going on sale and has a moderately short life.

ACETO DI VINO
Wine vinegar

This is produced from quality vintage wines. Fermentation is fairly slow, and the vinegar is left to stand for about 8 months in special wooden casks before being transferred to bottles, where it remains for a similar period of time. When matured, the vinegar has a wine flavor and a clear color.

ACETO DECOLORATO
Decolored Vinegar

This is common vinegar that has been decolored and de-tanninized. It is primarily used for pickling vegetables, as it does not alter their color.

ACETO AROMATICO
Aromatic Vinegar

This is a quality vinegar with the addition of more aromatic herbs. Boil the vinegar, slowly reducing the quantity to half. Remove from fire and add into a container with the desired herbs or spices. Cover, and let marinate for a few hours. Filter and save in sealed bottles.

ACETO BALSAMICO
Balsamic vinegar

A traditional product of Emilia, particularly in Modena and its surroundings, this rare product is a culinary symbol of that region. It is made from *Lambrusco Solomino,* a full-bodied red grape, although in some areas outside of this region *Sangiovese* or *Trebbiano* grapes may be used. The wine is reduced by $\frac{2}{3}$ first, then aged for years in special barrels, in fact several barrels, each of a different wood. The vinegar is placed in a different barrel each year so that it may absorb the flavor of each of the woods from which the barrels are made. An authentic balsamic vinegar requires at least ten years to make, sometimes as many as thirty, the wood from which the barrels are made and the order in which the vinegars pass from one barrel to another are very jealously kept family secrets, which may only be passed from father to son. Some of the woods used may be oak, chestnut, cherry, ash, and mulberry.

The balsamic vinegar found in the market today is mostly a commercial, pasteurized product, the average age of which varies from 3 to 10 years; some of them are excellent. Balsamic vinegar is brown in color, more or less dark depending on its age, with an aromatic odor and sweet-acid taste.

True balsamic vinegar must be packaged in bottles of 100 grams, and must be at least 10 years old. The label must have the words *"Aceto Balsamico Tradizionale"* and must be stamped by the controlling agency, called the Consorzio *ABTM*.

Balsamic vinegar has in recent years become widely used in Italian cooking to enhance food flavors. It can be used straight or as an addition to sauces, in salad dressings or even fruits. In ancient times it was also used as a digestive. Balsamic vinegar is very strong and must be used sparingly. Balsamic vinegar can be used as a condiment in place of wine vinegar or to flavor various sauces for cold or hot dishes, or even fruits.

ERBE AROMATICHE
Aromatic Herbs

AGLIO
Garlic
   The pungent, segmented bulb of the perennial plant Allium sativum, a member of the Lily family, closely related to the onion. Among the oldest known cultivated plants and most universally popular cooking herbs, garlic appears extensively, both raw and cooked, in the cuisines of southern Europe and is considered essential to many dishes in Italy. The peeled cloves can be preserved for short periods in jars of oil.

ANETO
Dill Seeds
   Pungent and slightly bitter, dill seeds come from an aromatic herb (Anethun graveolens) with feathery foliage. In addition to being used to flavor salads, stuffings and sauces, they may also be used to flavor desserts and vinegars.

BASILICO
Basil
   An annual herb (Ocimum basilicum) of the mint family, this is the distinguishing ingredient of the Ligurian specialty *pesto*, its glossy, aromatic leaves are used to add tangy flavor and a mildly spicy bouquet to many dishes and sauces, especially preparations in which tomatoes play a prominent role.

CAPPERI
Capers
   The pickled or salted flower buds of the spiny, trailing Mediterranean shrub Capparis spinosa, capers add a tart flavor and mild astringency to uncooked sauces and cold dishes such as *vitello tonnato*.

CERFOGLIO
Chervil
   The scientific name is cerofelium, and it is a very aromatic plant. Chervil has been used since the Roman empire and is still widely used today. There are various varieties, the most common being the curly type used to decorate dishes. Chervil has a very pleasant aroma and should always be used fresh.

CORIANDOLO
Coriander Seeds
   Coriander seeds come from an Old World herb (Coriandrum Sativum), originating in the Middle East. The seeds are small and

spheric and have a strong, aromatic flavor. Coriander has many uses; it may be coated with sugar in confectionary or may be used in the preparation of salame and sauces.

CUMINO
Cumin
A low plant (Cuminum cyminum), long cultivated for its aromatic seeds. A classic flavoring used for sweets and to make the famous Kummel liqueur.

DRAGONCELLO/SERPENTARIA
Tarragon
Artenisia dracunculus is an herbaceous plant used to flavor salads and various sauces. Its leaves are thin, tapered and very fragrant; they are also used to flavor oils and vinegar. In Siena, where tarragon is very popular, it is also coated in batter, deep-fried and served as a side dish with fried meat entrees.

ERBA CIPOLLINA
Chives
A perennial plant (Allium Schoenoprasum) of grass-like appearance and a mild onion flavor, chives are usually finely minced and used to flavor salads and some sauces.

FINOCCHIELLA
Fennel seeds
These are the seeds of a wild plant; they are yellowish in color and very fragrant. Also known as «Alpine Fennel», the scientific name is menne athamanticum. Fennel grows spontaneously in the highland of Italy. The seeds are used to flavor roasts of meat and fish in the popular cuisine.

GINEPRO
Juniper
Juniper is an evergreen shrub or tree that grows in wooded areas. Juniperus communis in Latin, its berries are fleshy, very aromatic, blue-black in color and used to flavor or marinate various kinds of meat, especially game. It is also used as the base for the production of gin.

LAURO
Bay Leaves
The bitter, spicy, pungent leaves of Laurus nobilis, bay leaves are always dried before use. Extensively used as a flavoring agent for vinegars, and in pickling and marinating mixtures, they enhance stocks, soups, sauces, and almost any poached, braised or stewed dishes.

MAGGIORANA
Sweet Marjoram
The scientific name is marjorana hortensis and origanum majorana. It is a variety of oregano. Its leaves, with white flowers and tiny kernels, are stronger than oregano and more distinctive. They are used to flavor various dishes and in marinades for game.

MENTUCCIA
Wild Mint
Scientifically known as melissa officinalis, wild mint looks and smells similar to lemon leaves, but unlike the latter grows wild in meadows. It is used in the Roman specialty *Carciofi alla romana* and for marinades.

NEPITELLA
Catmint
The scientific name is satureja calamintha. It belongs to the family of labiate, the same family as mint. It grows wild, and is commonly used in salads, to flavor white meats or roasts. The aroma is similar to mint with scents of sage. It should not be confused with wild mint.

ORIGANO
Oregano
Origanum vulgare is a wild aromatic herb that is always used dried. It has a characteristic sauerkraut flavor, bitter and very aromatic. It is very common in the South of Italy and used in many tomato-based preparations, pizza, various salads, and sauces, e.g. *pizzaiola*.

PEPERONCINO
Chili pepper
Peperoncino's generic Latin name is capsicum. Widely used, especially in the South of Italy, *peperoncino* can be green or red, round or long, and more or less hot. Fresh peppers are used to add character to many dishes, soups and sauces, marinades or pickles. To preserve them for long periods, they should be dried. They can then be kept whole, finely chopped, ground or placed in a jar and covered with oil. Often they are threaded on a string by their stalks and hung. This process is called *"diavolicchio"*, a term used in Abbruzzese dialect, referring to the heat associated with the devil in the popular imagination.

PIGNOLI
Pine nuts
Also called *pinoli,* pine nuts are the edible kernels of several varieties of pine. Pinus pinea is used in sweet as well as in stuffings for various dishes. They are a traditional ingredient in pesto and commonly used in dessert cookery.

PISTACCHIO
Pistachio Nuts
Greenish, edible seeds of a small tree (Pistacia vera)of the sumac family. Used in sweets and gelati, as well as in galantines and *mortadella di Bologna.*

PREZZEMOLO
Parsley
Scientifically known as petroselium sativum, there are many varieties. Parsley is an aromatic, herbaceous garden plant, with smooth leaves. The curly type is less common and is particularly suitable for garnishing. Parsley is excellent as a countereffect to garlic's odor.

RAFANO
Horse-Radish
A large fleshy root, nasturtium armoracia is pungent in fragrance as well as in taste. It stimulates the eyes to tears and is used grated to prepare sauces or cut straw-like and served with cocktail sauce to be added at will. It is also known as *cren* or *barbaforte.*

ROSMARINO
Rosemary
Scientifically known as rosmarinus officinalis, rosemary is a bushy plant with needle-like leaves and a fresh piney fragrance. It is used to flavor various grilled roast meat, as well as sauces. It may also be used to prepare aromatic vinegar in Tuscany and is also known as *ramerino.*

SALVIA
Sage
Salvia officinalis has rough, silver-green leaves that are extremely fragrant. It is often mixed with rosemary to flavor roasts. It is also used to flavor sautéed fish and particular cuts of meat, such as veal, pork and liver. Butter and sage is a particularly good condiment for fresh stuffed pasta such as ravioli and *cappelletti,* and it is an essential herb for *saltimbocca alla Romana.* The broader leaves are often dipped in a light batter, fried in oil and served as an *antipasto* or side dish. It can also be used to prepare aromatic oils and vinegar.

SEDANO
Celery
The scientific name is Apimeu graveoleus. It is an aromatic plant with various varieties. The two most common types are celery with stalks (pascal) and celery root. Its characteristic is a large stem that resembles a tuber. The green type is used to lend aroma, the white for cooking. Only the stems are used; the leaves and filaments are

removed. Both types may be used for cooking to add flavor to soups and broths, or may be sautéed, marinated and used as a salad.

SEMI DI FINOCCHIO
Wild Fennel Seeds
Known as wild fennel (foeniculum vulgare) this is the seed of a wild flower that grows spontaneously in Italy. The flower is combed, and the seeds are then dried and peeled. They are dark yellow in color and have an intense, fennel-like aroma. The whole plant is used in cooking. For example, a broiled fish on a bed of wild fennel leaves gives the fish an exceptional flavor. The tips are used in Sicilian cookery. The seeds, highly aromatic, are used for baking, roasting and in chestnut boil.

SEMI DI SESAMO
Sesame Seeds
Sesamo is a plant that grows spontaneously in Africa and in India. The scientific name is sesamum indicum. In Italy it grows in small quantities in Calabria and Sicily. The major producer is China. Sesame seeds are used in the preparation of bread and biscuits. In the kitchen they may also be used as sesame seed oil, many times it is cut with olive oil.

TIMO
Thyme
Thymus vulgaris grows spontaneously in the arid areas of the Mediterranean. It can also be grown organically and is widely used in cooking. Thyme has very small leaves. The leaves are used dried to flavor sauces, marinades, certain roasts and varieties of fish.

SPEZIE
Spices

CANNELLA
Cinnamon
This popular spice is from the family of *cinnamomum* zeylanicom and it is the center part of a tree called *cinnamomo*. More precisely, it is the layer between the outer part, and the wood of the tree. Cinnamon has a pleasant, aromatic taste and can be bought in both sticks and powder. Cinnamon is employed to flavor various savory dishes as well as desserts.

CHIODI DI GAROFANO
Cloves
Cloves (Eugenia caryophillata) are stalks, petals and centers of a

flower that grow on a plant native to the Moluccan Islands in the East Indies and Philippine Islands. It is used to flavor stews, fish preparations, sauces, desserts, cooked fruit, marinades and brines.

MACIS
Mace
The lacy fiber that grows on the outside of the nutmeg. It is used to flavor fruits and desserts.

NOCE MOSCATA
Nutmeg
The solid kernel of the fruit of a tree that grows in Indonesia, myristica fragrans, is about half the size of a walnut, buff in color with a ridged exterior. It is pleasantly aromatic. Nutmeg is used dried and grated in small quantities to flavor stuffings, main courses and desserts.

PEPE
Pepper (White or Black)
A small and spheric fruit of the Orient, piper nigrum kernels are first green, then become red as it matures. Eventually it turns black as it dries. The white pepper is the kernel picked as it is maturing, still red, bathed in salted water and peeled, it is then dried. Pepper can be considered to be one of the oldest spices known to man. It is best when used freshly ground.

SENAPE
Mustard
These seeds come in three varieties: dark ones (Brassiga nigra), white ones (Sinapsis alba), and the Indian variety called Brassica Juncea; the strongest is the dark type and the mildest the white. The characteristic pungent flavor is released when the powdered seeds come in contact with water, which must be cold in order to promote a good mustard. Commercially prepared mustard sauce is used to season meat and as a flavoring for other sauces. Warm water would give the substance a bitter taste.

VANIGLIA
Vanilla
The vanilla bean is the fruit of a tropical climbing orchid plant. Dried, the fruit of this plant forms a pod, dark brown in color, about 12 cm. long. It has a very pleasant flavor that blends easily with any ingredient to which it is added. It is used mainly in desserts, such as custards and ice cream.

ZAFFERANO
Saffron
Crocus sativus is the stamen of a flower, originally from Asia Minor. In Italy it grows in the region of Abruzzo. It comes either

powdered or in threads and is used in various dishes, both to flavor and color the food, for example, *risotto alla Milanese*. It should be used in very small quantities, because if too much saffron is used it gives a medicinal taste. Generally, one gram can flavor five kilos of rice.

Saffron is one of the most expensive food ingredients in the world.

ANTIPASTI

The term *antipasto*, usually translated as "appetizer" in English, literally means «before the meal» and denotes a relatively light dish designed to stimulate the palate before the service of more substantial courses. In the hands of a creative cook or chef, the antipasto course can play much the same role in the orchestration of the meal that the overture does in the presentation of an opera: it can set the tone of, and heighten anticipation for, what is to follow,while establishing the author's style and outlook and the quality that may be expected of the whole performance.

Antipasti are not essential to the Italian kitchen; a formal Italian dinner without antipasti would not betray the traditions of Italian gastronomy. Today, however, it is difficult to imagine a formal dinner that would not include some dishes classified as antipasti. In the regional Italian kitchen, antipasti are an important element, not on a daily basis, but certainly on holidays and special occasions.

Many dishes, served as accompaniments to main courses, are today considered too rich for such use. So, through the years, many of these dishes have been adapted to serve as *antipasto*.

Antipasto take full advantage of all kinds of different foods not generally regarded as being substantial enough to be served as main courses. Cleverly used, they produce a wonderful variety of flavorful and unusual items.

VEGETABLES: Many vegetables used as salads, steamed, baked, stuffed or marinated, were at one time used as side dishes and today are used successfully as *antipasti.*

SALADS: Meat, fish, vegetables, legumes and starches can all be used as salad for starters, although they may be successfully served as a main course as well. The amounts served determine their role. Salads should be served well chilled at all times, although in recent times, we have seen the employment of lukewarm salads quite often as combinations of legumes or greens with fish or meat.

BREAD AND BISCUITS AS SALADS: Stale and re-baked bread as well as unleavened biscuits can be toasted, soaked and chopped together with vegetables, fish, greens and so on to make delicious first courses, and salads.

LEGUMES: Cooked beans can be used as salads or poured over bread or biscuits. These also are part of a wide range of foods that can be served as *antipasto.*

MUSHROOMS AND TRUFFLES: Fresh Mushrooms may be served as a salad with just oil and drops of lemon juice. White truffles can be used to add flavor to cheese, *antipasti,* or as toppings to toast or patés.

UOVA & FRITTATA: Eggs, either cooked soft, hard, stuffed or fried, like a flat omelet, accompanied by, or with the addition of a variety of meats, cheese, or vegetables, can make some interesting starters.

PIZZA: Regarded more as a snack than as an *antipasto. Pizza* has come a long way since its inception as poor people's food in Naples. Toppings can be as varied as your imagination. *Pizza* should be used as an *antipasto* only in small amounts; otherwise it would be too heavy to begin a meal.

FOCACCE AND FRITTERS: Focacce and fritters, as well as savory pies and *sformati,* can be served, like *pizza,* as starters. Some judgement must be exercised in selecting these foods as *antipasti* because they are rather filling. The amounts, shapes and stuffing can vary according to the ingredients used.

MARINADES: The term marinade refers to all types of food flavored with herbs, spices, liquids or fats, to be consumed raw or be cooked afterwards. At times certain foods are first cooked then marinated or preserved. The role marinades play in *antipasti* is very important, because in this category fall dishes such as *carpaccio,* marinated raw anchovies, vegetables marinated in vinegar (*sottaceti*) or marinated in oil (*sottolio*).

IL FRITTO: From vegetables to organ meats, frying is one of the most widespread forms of using bits and pieces of leftovers. The skill of frying should not be underestimated, as it requires perfect timing. Fried food may be served as *antipasto* or as a main course.

SALAME AND SALUMI: Salumi, such as *prosciutto* and *bresaola,* are quite often served as *antipasti,* often with fruit such as melon or figs, with greens like *rugola,* with a condiment of oil and lemon. *Salame* can serve as an *antipasto* as part of *affettato misto,* a term which implies that many types of *salami* and *salumi* are used in the same dish. *Salame* can also be served as a snack or as a stuffing for sandwiches.

CHEESE: Cheese leftovers can be very cleverly used as appetizers. Cheese such as *mozzarella* or *ricotta* are best served as *antipasto* when very fresh but are also excellent cooked when they are a few days old.

FISH: The Italian coastline provides a rich variety of fish that may not be appropriate as main courses, but would be excellent as an *antipasto.* Among the fish *antipasti,* one can list *bottarga* (dried fish roe), fish *carpaccio,* sea food salads, baked, sautéed or stewed fish, shellfish and mollusks or dolphin fillets (musciame), which can be served either alone or as a principal ingredient in a famous Ligurian recipe called *cappon magro.*

SALSE E RAGÙ
Sauces

What is a sauce? It is neither a food, nor a dish in itself, but it is a dressing, to add flavor.

As a matter of fact, centuries ago, in Italian civilization, sauces were called *savori* or "flavors", from the Venetian *word saor,* meaning they were used precisely to give flavor to meat, fish and other dishes.

There are hundreds of Italian sauces, many made by simply sautéeing oil and onions (*soffritto*); others by more complex means; and each has its own autonomy.

This is not true for sauces of other recognized cuisines, which represent a "system". In fact, these basic sauces are developed by mixing them, adding something to them, or creating variations "on the theme". The result is a succession with wide variety.

Italian sauces, on the other hand, do not have a common system. With the exception of a basic tomato sauce, each sauce represents an original creation.

Ragù is a condiment very typical of Italy. There are many variations, but basically it is a sauce made by slowly braising one or various pieces of beef or fish with a *soffritto* of vegetables and herbs and in many cases with the addition of tomatoes. There is not a region of Italy that does not have its own *ragù.*

RICETTE
Recipes

AGLIATA
Garlic Sauce

Agliata, along with *Porrata,* are some of the most interesting condiments in Italian cooking. The first is prepared with garlic, the second with leeks. Their existence dates back to ancient Rome. The following version of *Agliata* is still used today.

6 garlic cloves	*2 cups olive oil*
3 oz. fresh white bread crumbs	*2-3 Tbs. vinegar*
salt	*pepper*

Finely pound the garlic in the mortar. Add the bread crumbs, which have been soaked in vinegar, then drained and squeezed. While beating constantly, add in a very slow steady stream of olive oil into the mortar, add a pinch of salt and black pepper, until obtaining a smooth emulsion.

Agliata is recommended on boiled or broiled fish, meat and vegetables. In a *porrata* leeks are used in place of garlic.

AGRODOLCE
Sweet and Sour

Agrodolce is a preparation based on the combination of two elements, sour and sweet. Although vinegar and sugar are commonly the two basic elements, these can be accompanied or replaced by many other ingredients with the same characteristics, e.g., candied citrus, raisins, chocolate, balsamic vinegar, lemon. It is believed that this sauce was first introduced in Sicily by the Arabs, who have long favored sour-sweet condiments.

Basic recipe:

8 oz. vinegar
4 oz. white wine
2 Tbs. Sugar

Simmer vinegar and wine till reduced by one third, add sugar, mix well until dissolved, and remove from fire. (The sugar can be reduced to one tablespoon if less sweetness is desired.)

Usually this sauce goes well with meat, fish, several vegetables, particularly for pearl onions, or as an addition to beef, venison, or lamb reductions, to be afterwards used as sauces.

DOLCEFORTE 1
Sweet Mustard Sauce

This recipe comes to us from the Renaissance, today it is very seldom used. This sauce is similar to *Agrodolce;* instead of using vinegar, mustard is used, and frequently honey replaces sugar. Unsweetened chocolate may be added for strong meats such as wild boar.

1 oz. butter   *juice of ½ a lemon*
1 cup red wine   *1 lb. sugar or honey*
2 Tbs. dry mustard   *salt*

Melt butter in a casserole. When melted add wine, let simmer for a few minutes, then add the sugar, combine well, add in lemon juice and salt. When the sauce is reduced by one third, add the mustard, mix well and remove from heat.

This sauce is excellent with boiled meats or venison.

DOLCEFORTE 2

9 whole walnuts, shelled   *7 oz. honey*
¼ cup broth   *1 tsp. dry mustard*

Scald the walnuts in boiling water. Peel and pound them in a mortar until you have a paste. Mix the walnuts with broth, mustard, and honey. Stir until you achieve a smooth emulsion. The sauce will keep a couple of days in the refrigerator.

SALSA VERDE
Green Sauce

Salsa verde was originally known as *Bagnet Verd,* (the Piemontese word for green sauce). The basic ingredient for this sauce is parsley and it is used for boiled meats or fish.

3 salted anchovy fillets	*1 Tbs. vinegar*
3 oz. parsley	*2 cups oil*
2 oz. fresh white bread	*pepper*
crumbs	
2 garlic cloves	

Thoroughly wash and cut anchovy fillets into small pieces. Chop the parsley, soak bread crumbs in the vinegar and drain. Mince the garlic. Place all ingredients in a mixing bowl, add the olive oil in a slow steady stream while stirring continuously until you obtain a dense sauce. Add pepper to taste. The addition of capers, onion, and hard boiled egg yolks is optional.

This sauce is excellent with boiled mixed meats (*bollito misto*).

BAGNA CAUDA
Anchovy and Garlic Dip

The literal translation from the Piemontese dialect is for "warm bath". The ingredients suggest it is a farm style food, because all ingredients are garden grown. Even the oil was probably produced on the farm. The exception is anchovies, which were widely used as a substitute for salt.

4 cloves crushed garlic	*1½ oz. butter, melted*
4 oz. chopped anchovies	*pepper*
1 cup olive oil	

Sauté the crushed garlic and chopped anchovy fillets in the oil, stirring constantly until the anchovies disintegrate. Add butter and mix. Add pepper to taste.

This sauce is served in a pot, for all to dip the vegetables in, or in individual terra-cotta bowls. The garlic's flavor can be somewhat diminished by leaving the cloves to soak in milk for a few hours or by adding a small amount of heavy cream at the last minute. Bagna cauda must be placed on warmers, as it must simmer constantly. It is usually served with cardoons, fennel, peppers, celery and carrots, in the same way as for *Pinzimonio*.

MOSTARDA DI FRUTTA 1
Fruit Mustard

This is not technically a sauce but preserved fruits. The ingredients, particularly the ground mustard seeds, used to preserve the fruits, give the pungent flavor characteristic of this specialty. The best are considered to be made in Cremona.

Fruit mustard is very good with boiled and white meat.

2 lbs. 3 oz., mixed fruits	*3 cups honey*
(apples, peaches, pears,	*1 lemon*
apricots, citrus)	*¼ cup ground mustard seeds*
	1 cup white wine

Wash and dice all the fruit. In a casserole, cover the fruit (first the ones which take longer to cook) with water and add 1 tablespoon of honey, the grated rind and the juice of a lemon.

Cook the fruit for 30 minutes over medium heat. Remove from fire and cool. In a second casserole, warm the wine and the rest of the honey, reduce by one third the syrup and mix in the mustard. Remove from heat and cool. Combine the fruit (not drained) and the syrup. Mix well and refrigerate.

NOTE: It may also be preserved, for this a sterilization process must be used.

SAVOR DI FRUTTA
Fruit spice

Savor means "flavor" in Venetian dialect. This is a very old recipe from central Italy, usually prepared in autumn.

6 lbs. grapes	3 oz. walnuts
5 lbs. fruit (pears, apples, peaches, quinces)	

Remove the grapes from stems, wash well, then press out juice. Let the juice sit for 24 hours. Clean the fruit and cut into pieces. Chop the nuts. Put all the fruit and nuts into a large pot, add the grape juice, cover and let cook on low heat for a two hours, stirring often. The *savor* is ready when the volume is half of what it was initially. Cool and refrigerate.

Savor is served with boiled meat, but can also be used as a filling for sweets, with squash *tortelli* and with *polenta*. If only must (grape juice before fermenting into wine) is used, the resulting syrup is called *sapa* (or *saba*) and is used for fillings or as a mix for cocktails.

NOTE: This spiced fruit may also be preserved, for this a sterilization process must be used.

AGLIO, OLIO E PEPERONCINO
Oil, Garlic and Peperoncino

One of the oldest ways to dress pasta was with raw oil and garlic. Later ingredients like *peperoncino* were added.

1 lb. spaghetti	parsley
3 oz. oil	peperoncino to taste
3 garlic cloves	salt

In a skillet, sauté the garlic in oil with the peperoncino until they become a golden brown.

You may remove the browned garlic, if desired. Mix cooked spaghetti briskly in the same skillet, add a generous tablespoon of finely chopped parsley, toss and serve.

NOTE: The spaghetti should be undercooked before tossing with the sauce. If they prove to be too dry add a ladle of the water in which the pasta has cooked in.

As a variation on this recipe, add some anchovies (6 salted fillets, washed and cut into pieces) to the garlic and oil, add a handful of black or green olives cut into pieces, and sauté together until golden brown.

Another version of this sauce which is commonly used in Southern Italy, is made by browning 3-4 Tbs. of bread crumbs in oil and garlic and adding some more *peperoncino* to taste just before sautéeing with the pasta.

SALSA ALL'ARANCIA
Orange Sauce

Lemons and oranges became very popular in Southern Italy in the Middle Ages. Only in the Renaissance did the Florentines began to use and trade them in Northern Italy and throughout Europe.

Florentine chefs were the first to use orange and lemon juices in their recipes, the most famous being *"Il Papero al Meloarancio"*, today known as duckling with orange sauce.

Basic Sauce:

$\frac{1}{2}$ cup oil	2 Tbs. grated orange peel
$\frac{1}{4}$ cup red wine	salt
1 cup orange juice	

Combine wine and oil and bring to a simmer. Add the orange juice, drop by drop, add a pinch of salt, simmer until reduced by one third, then add 2 Tbs. of grated orange peel. Stir well and remove from heat. This basic sauce is ready to serve as is or it may be used as a condiment for beef, poultry and venison.

SALMORIGLIO
Olive oil, Lemon and Garlic Sauce

This is probably the most interesting of the Mediterranean sauces, inherited from Sicilian cuisine.

To achieve a good emulsion it is advisable to whip *salmoriglio* in a double boiler, or just combine all the ingredients, mix well and use as a sauce over grilled fish, meat and poultry.

Basic Sauce:

1 oz. fresh lemon juice	2 garlic cloves
4 oz. olive oil	1 tsp. oregano

Add lemon juice to a bowl, whip vigorously and add oil in a slow steady stream. Finish with minced garlic and oregano.

There are many variations, some replace oregano with parsley, others add crushed tomatoes and many replace lemon with vinegar.

SALSA PEVERADA
Spicy Sauce
Peverada is a sauce that always contains pepper — *pevere*. Since the spice was once rare and expensive, it was fashionable for rich families to use it on or in everything, from soups to sauces, to broths. *Peverada* was also referred to as "the water in which beef has been cooked in" or "peppered broth". It was called *piperatum* in ancient Rome, and it was prepared by adding *garum* to pepper. *Peverada* is a sauce used as a common condiment in today's Italian cookery. The most popular is the recipe used in the Veneto.

Basic Sauce:

4 fillets of anchovies	2 oz. olive oil
2 garlic cloves	salt to taste
1 bunch parsley	1 tsp. fresh ground black pepper
1 slice soppressa (about 3 oz.)	2 cups beef broth
	1 Tbs. lemon juice
1 lb. duck liver	1 Tbs. pomegranate juice
	1 Tbs. wine vinegar (or wine)

Mince anchovies, 1 garlic clove, parsley, *soppressa* and duck liver. In a casserole, heat the oil and the remaining smashed garlic clove. Remove when well browned. Drop in the minced ingredients, minus the liver. Stir constantly and, when golden brown, add the liver, a pinch of salt and the pepper. Sauté briskly for 2 minutes then add the broth and simmer for 15 minutes. Then, add the lemon juice, pomegranate juice and wine vinegar; reduce for 5 more minutes and remove from heat. This sauce should be rather thick but fluid.

This sauce is excellent with duck, or other game, poultry and roasted meats.

FINANZIERA
Chicken Liver and Sweetbread Sauce
Although it is said that *finanziera* is a French sauce introduced in Piedmont two centuries ago, the Piedmontese claim it is one of the most traditional condiment of their regional cooking.

Basic Recipe:

7 oz. chicken combs	1 oz. mushrooms
3 oz. veal sweetbreads	1 oz. lean veal
½ cup Marsala	2 oz. butter
3 oz. chicken livers	salt and pepper to taste

Simmer the combs and sweetbreads into a pot with cold water for a few minutes. Drain and cool under cold running water. Peel the combs and chop the sweetbreads. Chop the combs, chicken livers and veal and brown in butter with the mushrooms. Add the sweetbreads and cook on low heat for twenty minutes adding some water or broth if necessary. Add salt, pepper to taste, add the Marsala and let reduce a few minutes.

This sauce is usually served with *risotto* or sweetbreads.

SALSA DI NOCI
Walnut Sauce

Walnuts are widely used in Italian cookery in a variety of ways, best known being preparations from Liguria.

½ lb. shelled walnuts	1 Tbs. fresh marjoram
2 oz. fresh bread (without crust)	salt
	1 clove garlic
3 Tbs. oil	1 cup cream

Scald the walnuts, and peel off the skins. Dip the bread in water and squeeze out most of the it. In a mortar pound the walnuts together with the bread, garlic, marjoram and salt to achieve a smooth paste. Place the mixture into a mixing bowl, drip in the olive oil, stirring constantly. Add the cream, stir well.

This sauce is ready to use. In the original Ligurian recipe, soured milk, called *Prescinseua* in dialect, is added instead of cream.

This sauce is very good with stuffed pasta *"pansotti"* or with roasted or boiled white meats.

SALSA AL POMODORO
Tomato Sauce

In a book by *Pellegrino Artusi, La Scienza in Cucina e L'Arte di Mangiar Bene* (Science in the kitchen and the art of eating well), written in 1891, in a preface to a recipe for tomato sauce, he emphasizes its popularity with this anecdote: "There was a priest of a small village who had the bad habit of sticking his nose into everything and into everybody's family affairs. He was, however an honest man, and more good than bad came from his meddling and his people would let him be. But the villagers, sharp as they were, renamed him 'Don Pomodoro' because, just like tomatoes, he could enter and be welcomed everywhere".

A good tomato sauce is the basic condiment of many wonderful dishes.

Basic Sauce:

2 lbs. ripe tomatoes	1 small diced onion
5 Tbs. very good olive oil	salt
1 crushed garlic clove	10 fresh, basil leaves, washed and chopped.

Scald the tomatoes in boiling water. Cool, peel, seed and either dice or crush them.

Heat oil in a skillet and sauté the garlic. Remove when brown. Add the onion and sauté over medium heat until the onion begins to get tender (do not let it brown), stirring occasionally. Add the tomatoes, salt to taste. Cover and let simmer for about an hour, stirring now and then. Add the basil at the end.

The sauce is now ready to be used. If fresh tomatoes are not available, canned peeled tomatoes may be used, provided they are of good quality. If the tomatoes are not very ripe, add a small carrot, finely diced, to the *soffritto*. This will help to tone down the acidity of the unripe tomatoes.

NOTE 1: This basic sauce may be used as a condiment for pasta or for all preparations requiring tomato sauce.

NOTE 2: To achieve a creamy consistency it may be passed through a fine sieve.

NOTE 3: If instead of basil oregano is added, the sauce is called *"Pizzaiola"*.

NOTE 4: Add 4 anchovy fillets, peperoncino, a spoonful of capers, two Tbs of Gaeta olives to the basic recipe, and the sauce is called *"Puttanesca"*.

SALSA AMATRICIANA
Spicy Tomato Sauce

7 oz. guanciale	*peperoncino*
1 onion	*broth (if needed)*
1 lb., 2 oz. ripe tomatoes	*salt*

Slice the *guanciale* in thin slices and put in a pan. Let brown slowly, then add the chopped onion and cook until wilted. Discard all the liquid fat, add the peeled, seeded and chopped tomatoes and a piece of *peperoncino*. Salt and pepper to taste and cook for about 40 minutes over medium heat, adding a ladle of broth (if needed) occasionally and stirring often. This is used as a condiment for pasta, preferably *bucatini* or *perciatelli*. *Guanciale* may be replaced with *pancetta* or bacon.

PESTO
Basil Sauce

Pesto comes from the verb *pestare,* meaning to crush or beat. *Pesto* is a very old sauce, especially in cities on the sea, often hedged in by mountains and enemy fleets that might prevent access to food. In fact, all ingredients used in *pesto* can be kept for long periods while the basil could be easily grown on the window sills and preserved in oil for a long time. *Pesto* is most associated with Genoa, on the Ligurian sea, where this very popular condiment is said to have been created. The basil here has a particular scent and is not too reminiscent of mint.

Basic Sauce:

8 oz. very fresh basil (if possible,	
use the leaves of a basil plant	
which is in flower)	
½ cup pine nuts	
(or toasted walnut kernels)	
2 peeled garlic cloves	
1 Tbs. Parmigiano	*1 cup of extra virgin olive oil*
1 Tbs. Pecorino cheese	*salt*

Wash the basil leaves and dry with a clean cloth. Place in a mortar. Add pine nuts, the garlic and a pinch of salt. Pound these ingredients with a circular motion of the pestle, adding the two cheeses a bit at a time. Continue the operation until you achieve a soft green paste. Put the paste in a bowl and gradually drip in the oil. Mix well and set aside. The preferred pasta with *pesto* is *trenette*. Boil the water with the addition of a finely sliced potato. Cook pasta in the usual manner, drain, reserve a small amount of the water, toss the pasta with the pesto (the potatoes will have disintegrated, they will have formed a grainy

Mortaio

texture on each string of pasta so, the sauce will cling better to it.) Add a little of the water if the pasta is too dry. Toss well and serve immediately. *Pesto* may also be used for *minestrone Genovese*. Note: 4 oz. of *pesto* should be enough for 1 lb. of pasta.

SALSA TONNATA
Tunafish Sauce

Tuna sauce has become popular in various regions of Italy, and has several variations, some suitable for pasta, others for roast or boiled meats. One of the best known tuna dishes is a Piemontese tradition — a sliced roast of veal with tuna sauce (see meat chapter). Following is a recipe for tuna sauce for pasta:

1 lb. spaghetti	few pine nuts
2 Tbs. olive oil	5 oz. tuna in oil, crumbled
½ oz. dry porcini mushrooms	1 cup peeled tomatoes
1 small onion, cut in thin	salt and pepper
slices	1 Tbs. butter
garlic, chopped	parsley, finely chopped
celery, diced	
1 carrot, finely chopped	

Reconstitute dry *porcini* in lukewarm water, chop, and set aside. Sauté onion, garlic, celery and carrot in oil. When vegetables are wilted (not browned), add mushrooms, pine nuts, and tunafish. Sauté briskly, add the tomatoes, let cook for few minutes, salt and pepper to taste. Simmer for 5 more mins. and remove from fire. Boil the pasta in the usual manner, spaghetti would be preferable, drain and place the spaghetti in a large skillet together with the butter, the tuna sauce and the parsley. Toss well and serve.

RAGÙ BOLOGNESE
Bolognese Meat Sauce

3 oz. pancetta	⅓ lb. ground veal or
1 stalk celery	pork

1 small carrot	$\frac{1}{2}$ cup dry red wine
1 small onion	1 cup broth
1½ oz. butter	1 lb. peeled tomatoes
⅓ lb. ground beef	pepper, salt
1 oz. cream	

Prepare a *battuto* with *pancetta,* celery, carrot and onion. Melt butter in a saucepan, add the battuto and the ground meats, brown well, then add the wine and half the broth. Continue to cook until the liquids are reduced, then add the remaining broth. Reduce again, then add the peeled and seeded tomatoes, a pinch of salt and pepper to taste. Cover saucepan and let cook over a medium heat for 2 hours. Add the cream, and correct salt and pepper to taste.

The sauce is ready to serve over fresh or stuffed pasta.

NOTE: Variations of this sauce may include the addition of *prosciutto, porcini* or chicken livers.

RAGÙ NAPOLETANO
Neapolitan Ragù

Naples has its own *ragù,* with as many variations as you might imagine. Its nickname is *guardaporta* which means "doorman" because a doorman supposedly having nothing else to do but watch the main entrance, could watch the slow cooking of the *ragù* as well.

Neapolitan *ragù* has been written about in poems, such as that penned by journalist Giuseppe Marotta:

What an aroma
How delicious! And you, Maria, dip the fork in.
No, wait! Let us examine our conscience first!
I love you and I am faithful to you!
And you, Maria?
Let us think, well ....
ARE WE REALLY WORTHY OF THIS RAGÙ?

1 onion, thinly sliced	1 lb. whole veal shank
2 oz. oil	8 oz. pork short ribs
1 oz. lard, chopped	3 lbs. peeled, seeded and
1 carrot	chopped tomatoes
1 celery stalk	20 basil leaves
8 oz. whole top round	salt and pepper to taste

Sauté one onion in oil and lard in skillet. Add chopped carrot and celery. Sauté them until wilted but not browned, add the meats and sauté until browned on all sides.

Add the peeled, seeded and chopped tomatoes, basil, and season with salt and pepper to taste. Stir well and cook over very low heat with the pot covered for about 3 or 4 hours.

When the *ragù* is ready, remove the meat from the casserole and set aside. Use the sauce as a condiment for maccheroni, and serve the various meats with it or as a second course.

Other variations of *ragù* may include fresh pork sausages, *bracio-la* stuffed with raisins, pine nuts and spices, and pork skins stuffed in the same manner. These meats may be used in addition or instead of other cuts; in any event, the less choice cuts are more suitable for this long cooking *ragù*. If meats require less time to cook, they may be added halfway through the cooking process.

GENOVESE
A Sauce of Braised Onion and Beef
Despite its name, this is a recipe from Napoli and is used as a condiment for pasta. The origins seem to go back to the 16th century, when a group of immigrants from Genoa used to cook meat in this fashion; hence the name *"Genovese"*.

2 lbs. onion	*3 oz. olive oil*
1 garlic clove	*2 oz. pancetta, chopped*
1 celery stalk	*1 oz. tomato paste*
1 carrot	*1 lb. lean round beef*
1 oz. lard	*1 cup white wine*
1 oz. salami	*salt, pepper*
1 oz. prosciutto	*beef bouillon, as needed*

Cut onion, garlic, celery and carrot into julienne. Coarsely chop lard, *salami* and *prosciutto*. Put the whole into a baking pan, add oil and pancetta. Sauté slowly, over low heat until the vegetables are soft but not browned. Brown it all around, add the beef and dilute the paste into ½ cup of lukewarm water and add to the pot together with the wine and place the roast into the oven at 350 F. Cook for 3-4 hours, adding beef bouillon as necessary. Salt and pepper to taste. The final result should be that of a rather dark, glazed sauce.

This condiment is good for *ziti* or any other type of *maccheroni* with a large hole. The meat can be served together with the *ragù* or as a separate course.

SALSA DI FUNGHI
Mushroom Sauce

1 oz. parsley	*2 oz. butter*
1 small rosemary sprig	*2 Tbs. olive oil*
1 garlic clove	*2 anchovy fillets*
⅔ lb. ripe tomatoes	*a little broth*
14 oz. fresh porcini	*salt*
mushrooms	

Prepare a *battuto* with parsley, rosemary leaves and garlic. Peel the tomatoes, remove seeds and cut in small pieces. Clean and slice the mushrooms and set aside. Place butter and oil in a casserole, add anchovy fillets and the *battuto,* and let brown, stirring to dissolve the anchovies. Add the tomatoes. Moisten with the broth and add salt. Stir well and let cook at a very low heat for about half an hour. Add the mushrooms and cook another 5 minutes. Use over any kind of pasta or gnocchi.

RAGÙ DI PESCE
Fish Sauce

The most suitable fish for this *ragù* is octopus, squid, cuttlefish, prawns, clams and any fish with a firm flesh.

⅔ *lb. ripe tomatoes*	*1 oz. parsley*
1 lb. fish	½ *cup olive oil*
1 small onion	½ *oz. dried mushrooms*
1 small carrot	½ *glass dry white wine*
1 small celery stalk	*salt*
1 garlic clove	*pepper*

Peel the tomatoes, remove seeds and chop in small pieces. Clean the fish carefully and cut in strips or small pieces. Prepare a *battuto* with onion, carrot, celery, garlic and parsley. Heat the oil in a saucepan, add the *battuto* and mushrooms. Let brown over a medium heat, until the vegetables begin to get tender. Add the wine. When the wine has evaporated, add the tomatoes, the rest of the ingredients and let cook over a very low heat for about 40 minutes. Add the fish and cook till done (time varies according to fish used). Stir occasionally, adding spoonfuls of water if the sauce becomes too dry.

This sauce is best used with medium *spaghetti* or *linguine*.

SAUCE FOR CARPACCIO

2 Tbs. minced baby onion	*6 Tbs. parsley, finely chopped*
2 Tbs. minced gherkins	*1 cup virgin olive oil*
2 Tbs. minced capers	*salt*
2 Tbs. vinegar	*pepper*
2 anchovy fillets	

Mix all the vegetables in a bowl, then add the anchovy, vinegar and the oil, slowly working it, adding a little oil at a time until the consistency is thick but light. Add parsley and salt and pepper to taste. Cover, but do not drown, the thinly sliced raw meat with the sauce and serve.

INSACCATI
Salame and Salumi

SALAME

The term *salame* refers to ground meat which has been packed into a casing. The generic term for *salame* in Italian is *insaccati* (encased). The casing can be natural (intestine) or synthetic.

There are three types of *salame*, fresh, dry-aged, and pre-cooked. All fresh salame must be cooked before eating. Dry-aged can simply be sliced and consumed. Pre-cooked and preserved must be consumed within a limited period and kept refrigerated.

The production of *salame* is also covered by special guarantees and regulatory bodies to check ingredients and procedures followed in making and storing preserved foods.

There are four basic stages in preparing *salame*: preparation of the meat, marinating, packing, cooking, or aging.

It is impossible to generalize about the preparation of *salame* because each type requires a specific method. This holds true for the marinating process as well. Salt is the element common to all *salami*; pepper is frequently used. The list of ingredients may also include cinnamon, nutmeg, cloves and mace, whose use is recorded in the most ancient treatises on how to make *salame*. Other ingredients are coloring agents and nitrates, which are allowed by law and used as preservatives.

One of the crucial ingredients is the casing. It must be strong, flexible, and porous enough to allow the meat inside to age without rotting or becoming moldy. It must also be pointed out that *salame* cooked or smoked must be packed into heat-resistant casings.

There are two types of casings: natural and artificial. Natural casings are obtained by treating certain animal parts, such as bladder, intestine and pigskin, in order to achieve adequate strength and texture. Artificially produced casings can be divided in three categories: casings obtained from animal skin, casings made with cellulose fibers, and casings made of polyvinyl. Synthetic casings are mainly used for products that are cooked or smoked.

There are many varieties of *salame* for aging, and every pork-consuming region has its own delicacies. The choicest varieties are: *salame di Felino, salame di Varzi, salame di Milano, salsiccione, salame di Fabriano, salame toscano, soppressa calabra, salsiccia napoletana stagionata, salame mantovano, salame abruzzese, salsiccia sarda, finocchiona, coppa, cacciatore, bondiola, salama da sugo ferrarese, mortadella di Bologna* and *salame cotto*.

These salami are all made with pork, mixing three parts of meat and one of fat. Salt is always added; pepper, either ground or in peppercorn, is also usually present. Nitrites and nitrates, necessary preserving agents, are added in quantities allowed by law. Occasionally some coloring agent is also added.

Dry aging is done in well-ventilated, semi-dark cool rooms, specifically created for this purpose or in well-ventilated, not too humid, cellars or attics.

In good quality *salame* the filling must be compact and bits of fat must not separate from bits of meat when sliced.

SALUMI

The term *salumi* refers to whole cuts of meat that are either cured in salt, then dry-aged, or cured in brine (salamoia) and then preserved. Some *salumi* are cooked and later preserved.

All *salumi* can be employed as classic appetizers. *Salumi* must be cut into thin slices shortly before being served. It is best to remove the skin before slicing the *salumi* to prevent the meat from being contaminated by mold, which usually forms on the skin during the aging process.

The following types of cured meat may be included among the aged *salumi: pancetta, guanciale, speck,* various kinds of *prosciutto.* Another delicacy to mention — made with beef, not with pork — is *bresaola,* a specialty of the Valtellina area.

SALAME FRESCO
Fresh Salame

COTECHINO
Fresh pork sausage

Cotechino and *zampone* form the most classic fresh *salami* of the Emilia Romagna region. *Cotechino* is priced less than *zampone,* mainly due to its casing, which can be either natural or synthetic. *Cotechino* may be used as an *antipasto* or as a main course, with a starch or a legume, or added to a *bollito misto.*

COTECHINO

8 lbs. pork shoulder, whole
2 lbs. lean shoulder pork
8 lbs. pigskin
8 lbs. jowl or neck
1 ½ lbs. Salt
4 Tbs. black pepper
3 oz. saltpeter
cloves and cinnamon
natural casing (if possible)

Clean the pigskin, pass it over a flame, and scrub it. Grind it together with the rest of the meat and blend the resulting mixture with the other ingredients. Using a funnel pack the meat into the casings. Take care not to leave air bubbles while stuffing. Avoid pressing too much, however, to prevent the casing from breaking. Tie the upper end of the casing with several knots, cut the string and tie a single knot about every 10 inches, leaving one loop to hang each *cotechino.* Cut the casing and repeat the operation, creating several *cotechini.* Hang them by their loops and let them dry at least one day. When dried, *cotechino* may be stored for up to one month in the refrigerator. It is then boiled before eating.

COOKING PROCEDURE: Put the *cotechino* in cold water and let stand for a few hours. Then prick it with a fork all over (so that it does not explode while cooking), change water and bring to a boil over medium heat. When it begins to boil, lower the heat, cover the pot and cook one hour for each 10 oz. Let it stand in its cooking water for about 15 minutes before serving. *Cotechino* can be served sliced as an *antipasto* or with mashed potatoes as a main course.

ZAMPONE
Stuffed Hog Foreleg

The ingredients to make *zampone* are the same as those used to make *cotechino,* but instead of intestine casing, the skin of the hog's foreleg is used The boning is done from the top open end, not by cutting the skin down the side. The preparation is also very similar to *cotechino,* the difference being that the open end of the hog's foreleg is sewn up with thread.

COOKING PROCEDURE: Soak the *zampone* in water for about 12 hours, to soften the skin. Prick the foot in between the nails with a skewer. Lay it on a thin wooden board the same size as the zampone, and wrap with a clean towel or cheese cloth, to protect it while cooking.

ZAMPONE

Tie well and boil over a medium heat, without changing the water. When it begins to boil, lower the heat and cover; cook for about 3 hours. When ready, let stand in the pot for 15 minutes before serving. The classic accompaniment for zampone is stewed lentils. *Zampone* is served in the same way as *cotechino.*

SALAMELLE
Sausage rolled in *pancetta*

Use the same ingredients as the ones listed for the *cotechino,* substituting pancetta for the pigskin and white wine for red wine. Also, grind the meat more coarsely. In some Italian regions the white wine is flavored with a few cloves of crushed garlic, then strained. The making of *salamelle* is also very similar to that of *cotechino,* except that *salamelle* are smaller.

Salamelle generally are always eaten split and grilled.

SALSICCE
Pork sausages

The ingredients are the same as in *salamelle,* the difference being that less choice cuts of meat and more fat is used (60% lean meat and 40% *pancetta* fat). Garlic, fennel seeds and *peperoncino* can also be added to the mixture for added flavor. To make *salsicce,* follow the procedure outlined in the *cotechino* recipe, tying the sausages with

SALSICCE

knots. If the sausages are prepared without tying knots between them, they are called *luganiga* or *salsicce* by the yard.

Salsicce may also be consumed fresh, in this case 70% pork meat and 30% fat is used. They may be pan fried or cooked in sauce.

SALAMA DA SUGO
Liver, Beef and Tongue Sausage

Made with liver, beef, tongue and lard seasoned together with salt, pepper, nutmeg and sangiovese wine. Once encased, it must first be dried then aged in well-ventilated chambers; during this stage *salama da sugo* is periodically coated with a mixture of oil and vinegar. The aging process requires at least a year.

COOKING PROCEDURE: Wash the *salama* well, let it soak in cold water for 12 hours, then put it into a cloth bag. Tie the top of the bag to a wooden stick that reaches across the top of the cooking pot so that the *salama* hangs in the middle of it. Cook the *salama* in a large quantity of warm water over moderate heat for at least 4 hours. When ready, cut it open along the seam, and remove the meat from the casing with a spoon. Serve with mashed potatoes in winter and melon in summer.

SALAME
Dry-Aged salame

Dry-aged *salame* are made with raw pork (with or without beef), salt and various spices. The degree to which the meat is ground is different for various types of *salame,* as is the length of the aging period. The name of town on the labels of different salame specialities does not refer to where they were made but to the method of production. Large *salame* are sliced by machine (Milano, for example), whereas the smaller ones are cut by hand (i.e., *Felino* and *cacciatorino*.)

Most of the time, the various preparations differ only in how the sausage is tied, the proportion of lean meat to fat and the seasonings used. Following is the preparation of the most popular dry-aged *salame*.

CACCIATORE
Hunter Salame

This is a rather small *salame* usually made with half pork and half beef, with the addition of fresh *pancetta*, black pepper, garlic and

CACCIATORE

optional spices. *Cacciatore* is approximately 5-7" long and weighs about 6-8 ounces. It is knotted at each end (just like a regular sausage). The aging has to be for at least 30 days. This *salame* is also called *cacciatorino*.

SALAME DI VARZI
Salame from Varzi

The name comes from the small town of Varzi in Lombardy. This *salame* is made strictly with lean hog meat and fresh *pancetta*, both coarsely ground and seasoned with white wine and salt. No other spice is used. The standard length is approximately 12" and it is knotted lengthwise, then across with intermediate loops. *Salame di Varzi* must be aged for at least 6 months.

SALAME DI MILANO
Salame from Milan

This is a *salame* typical from Tuscany made with very very finely ground pork, beef and fat in equal quantities, spiced only with salt

SALAME DI MILANO

and pepper. The *salame* can weigh up to 3 lbs. and is aged for at least 3 months. It is knotted lengthwise then across with intermediate loops. *Salame di Milano* should be sliced fairly thin, either by hand or by machine.

FINOCCHIONA
Salame with fennel seeds
Made with pork and finely ground, it is seasoned with salt, pepper, garlic and, as indicated by its name, with *semi di finocchio,* (fennel seeds), dry-aged for about 3 months. It is rather thick in diameter and it is 8-10" long. *Finocchiona* is knotted lengthwise with intermediate loops across. It should be sliced fairly thick for consumption.

SALAM D'LA 'DUJA
Preserved salame
A small *salame* made with less choice cuts of lean pork meat seasoned with salt and pepper. *Duja* is a Piedmont dialect word for a *terra-cotta* jar used to cook or to preserve foods. This *salame* is typical of the eastern part of Piedmont in the provinces of Vercelli and Novara. It is a rather small *salame,* which is kept soft and fresh in a *terra-cotta* jar totally filled with liquefied pork back fat, then sealed. This particular method of preserving the *salame* is necessary in this region because the humidity in the air does not permit a normal dry aging. *Salame D'La Duja* is kept for three months in its jar before being eaten.

SALAME NAPOLETANO
Neapolitan salame
This *salame* is prepared with relatively finely ground lean pork meat mixed with a small quantity of fat and heavily spiced with ground *peperoncino,* which gives it its familiar red color. The mixture is then stuffed into a 1" wide, 20" long casing simply folded in half and tied at each end. There is also a much less peppery version of this *salame. Salame Napoletano* is dry-aged for a minimum of six months.

FELINO
Salame di Felino
This *salame* comes from the village of Felino, in the area around Parma. It is made of excellent quality, relatively finely ground pork mixed with a small quantity of pure pork fat and a few spices. It is put in natural casing, and once it has been stuffed and tied, it is about 15" long and bigger at one end than the other. It is knotted vertically with alternate loops across, and aged for at least three months. Felino is actually a village outside of Parma, on the hills below the Appennini (a chain of mountains that goes all the way from the north to the south of Italy) a few kilometers from Langhirano, the traditional *prosciutto di Parma* area.
The dry climate and crisp air allows for an exceptional aging of the

salame, which is particularly sought for it's excellent quality.

SOPPRESSATA
Head Sausage

Soppressata, not to be confused with *soppressa* (*a salume*), is made with lean meat taken from the head of the hog. This is then coarsely chopped, mixed with lard, pepper and spices and then stuffed into a natural casing. It is then flattened down (compressed), knotted with intermittent loops across, and pulled very tightly so as to form several squares, each attached to one another). *Soppressata* is aged for at least 40 days. This *salame* should be served rather soft, therefore, after 40 days, if *soppressata* is not consumed, it is kept under melted back fat. It is sliced by hand.

SALAME COTTO
Cooked and preserved salame

For cooked and preserved salame, it is intended to refer to *salame* which is pre-cooked and then preserved. They are mostly prepared with pork meat or beef or a combination of both. The meat is ground rather coarse and flavored with spices which vary from one type of *salame* to the next. The casing is generally synthetic, as it adapts better to the heat while cooking. These *salami* have a limited shelf life and must be kept in cool rooms and refrigerated after being cut.

MORTADELLA

MORTADELLA
DI BOLOGNA
Cooked salame
with pistachio

The preparation of *mortadella* goes back to the Middle Ages, when the seasonings included myrtle berries.

Mortadella is made in different sizes. The choicest being the larger ones. *Mortadella* uses the poorer cuts of meat that cannot be used for any other type of *salame.* The meat is ground very finely and mixed with coarsely ground backfat, plus the usual preserving agents, salt, finely ground white pepper, black peppercorns, coriander seeds, mixed spices, shelled pistachios, and wine.

The mixture is packed into a beef bladder for large *mortadella* and into a hog bladder for smaller *mortadella. Mortadella* is then hung in an oven and cooked at about 225 F. (2 hrs. per 2 lbs.). The finished product must be kept in a cool room at all times and refrigerated after being cut. The particular taste of this product is very different from any other type of *salame.*

GALANTINA
Galantine

Galantina is made with *pancetta,* lean veal, pistachio nuts and black truffle. The mixture is placed into a desired type of mold, soaked in a salt, spice and *Marsala* solution for up to 50 days, then wrapped in a veal membrane or cheese cloth. It is boiled for 35 minutes for each 2 lbs. of meat. Once cooked and cooled, *galantina* can be served sliced. It must be kept refrigerated and consumed within a short period of time.

SALUMI
Cured Meats

PROSCIUTTO
Cured hog leg

Prosciutto is made by salting, aging and dressing a pork leg, then preparing it according to local usage. The choicest varieties come from: Parma, San Daniele and Tuscany.

The *Parma prosciutto* is cut with a short shank or, as the native say, a *coscia di pollo,* "like a chicken leg". The hog leg should maintain the same shape as when butchered, that is fairly round.

The *prosciutto* from *San Daniele* is different in two ways. First, the leg is kept whole up to the hooves. Second, the leg is somewhat flattened. Therefore, the leg is worked in such a manner that it remains stiff. It is then salted and

SAN DANIELE   **PARMA**

placed under weight, a method that allows the leg to discard more moisture and, thanks to the particular climatic conditions of the area, allows for a particularly sweet flavored product.

Prosciutto from *Tuscany* has a very different production method from that of Parma and San Daniele. First of all, Tuscan production is limited to an artisan level. It is much saltier, because traditionally the Tuscans do not salt their bread. Consequently, the additional salt in the *prosciutto* compensates for the lack of salt in the bread. The *prosciutto* from Tuscany is, therefore, drier and much more red in color. It is traditionally sliced by hand and not by machine.

The basic method of making *prosciutto* is as follows: After having cut and cleaned the leg, let it lie flat for a day in a cool place. Then cover it with salt and let it lie flat on one side for 4 days, then, again, for 4 more days on the other side. When the salting period is over, rub it vigorously with fresh salt and let it stand for a few more days without salt. Wash the leg several times with cold water in order to remove the remaining salt and hang in a dry, airy, ventilated place.

This stage is very important since the air plays a primary role in the quality of the final product. It is not possible to set the length of this stage in advance; it depends on the local climate. The *prosciutto* will be ready when entirely dry. It generally takes 12-18 months to achieve a fine quality prosciutto. The production is supervised and approved by a local board, in charge of controlling and preserving the quality of the product.

NOTE: Prosciutto can be made anywhere that has moderate climatic conditions. The fact that prosciutto is so distinctive, in terms of aroma (fragrant) and taste (sweet) is because the climatic condition in Italy allows for a subtle aging. It is a natural phenomenon that cannot be easily explained or duplicated.

CULATELLO
Home-made cured hog leg

Culatello is a very particular type of *salume,* produced in a small area around Parma in the villages of Soragna, Zibello, Colorno and Busseto, all along the Po River. The most singular aspect of culatello is that it has the same characteristics of prosciutto but is aged into a casing. Only the best part of the hog leg is used, which is boned and rubbed immediately following the slaughter with a compound of salt and other herbs and spices. It is then wrapped into a layer of fresh hog fat, and stuffed into a natural casing of the hog and securely fastened with a strong thread.

Culatello is hung in the cellar and slowly aged for at least a year and, at times, eighteen months. When the

CULATELLO

time comes to use the *culatello,* it is placed into a bath of white wine for a few days (some prefer to wrap it into a cloth soaked in white wine). The thread, casing and protective fat is then removed and the sausage is eaten sliced like *prosciutto,* though *culatello's* taste is much smoother and sweeter. One of the main characteristics of *culatello* is its soft texture, which is due mainly to the climate of the area, particularly the morning mist around the river Po, which permits the phenomenon that provokes the slow disintegration of the enzymes of the product. *Culatello* is strictly home-made, and does not have real possibilities for industrial production. *Culatello* is one of the most prized and expensive cured meats, but is not easy to find.

COPPA
Cured pork neck

The best known *coppa* is prepared in the Piacenza area.

Coppa is known as *capocollo* in the central and southern part of Italy and as *bondiana* in Lombardy.

Coppa is made with pork neck trimmed to a desired shape. The whole neck is rubbed and then marinated with a seasoning mixture of salt, black pepper, cloves and wine. The marinating process takes at least 20 days, as this is done in stages. During every stage (in 5 day-intervals) it is rubbed again and again with the seasoning and turned over.

When the marinating is finished, the pork neck is rubbed dry with a cloth and wrapped into a casing. It is hung in a warm place for 2 days,

COPPA

then aged in a cool place for at least 3 months. It is sliced fairly thin and eaten with country bread.

SOPPRESSA
Cured pork shoulder or leg
This is a speciality of the Veneto region, particularly in Treviso. Made with lean pieces of meat such as the shoulder or leg and the meat around the throat, following the same method as *coppa*. Red wine is used, in addition to the usual seasonings. *Soppressa* is hung in a warm place to dry, and aged in a cool place for over a year.

SPECK
Cured hog leg (Boned and flattened)
Speck must not be confused with the German word speck, meaning lard. Italian *speck* is a specialty of the Upper Adige area, prepared by

SPECK

stretching and boning the hog's leg. The specifics of the process to prepare *speck* can only be described in general terms, since this is a homemade delicacy, and the methods used vary from family to family.

The meat is seasoned with salt, pepper, bay leaves and juniper berries, then placed on a tilted surface so that the meat juices can be collected and used to moisten the meat daily. The meat is then smoked with juniper wood and other aromatic woods.

PROSCIUTTO DI CAPRIOLO
Roe-Buck prosciutto
This is deer's leg treated with salt, pepper, finely minced garlic and *peperoncino*. It ages for about 50 days. It is usually thinly sliced, and served with oil and lemon, salt and pepper. It is typical of Val D'Aosta and Valtellina. It is also called *violino* (violin), referring to the elongated shape of the capriolo leg.

PROSCIUTTO DI CINGHIALE
Wild boar prosciutto

Wild boar *prosciutto* is typical of Tuscany, a region with a large extension of wooded land, an ideal habitat for wild boar. Basically the leg of the boar is processed with the same method as for all *prosciutto* — the only difference is that from the shank up to the hooves the skin is kept on. This allows for the dressed leg to absorb all the indispensable quantities of salt and spices only through the skinned portion of the leg, therefore the final product remains rather gamey, and not too salty. In the past, wild boar *prosciutto* was very rare, but today they are farm grown and more readily available. This *prosciutto* is rather lean, and it is thinly sliced by hand.

**PROSCIUTTO
DI CINGHIALE**

MOCETTA
Cured deer thigh
This is a characteristic product of the Valle D'Aosta made from the thigh of a chamois deer or mountain goat, (*stambecco*). It is made in the same way as roe-buck *prosciutto,* has a very distinctive, game flavor, and is served thinly sliced as an *antipasto.*

BRESAOLA
Dry aged beef

Bresaola is an Italian counterpart to the Swiss speciality called Viande de Grisons. *Bresaola* is typical of Valtellina. *Bresaola* is made from beef cuts (generally the fillet) treated with a mixture of salt and spices, then

BRESAOLA

wrapped in thin nets and aged for at least one month. When ready for consumption, *bresaola* is a bright dark red color and is softer than its Swiss counterpart and more aromatic. It is generally used as an *antipasto,* sliced very thin and briefly marinated in oil, lemon and pepper.

SALUMI COTTI
Cooked Salumi

PROSCIUTTO COTTO
Ham

Success in making hams depends entirely on the quality of the meat chosen. Begin with a medium-sized pork leg with the bristles, bone and fat removed. Put the meat in an adequate container in a brine of heavily salted water, a bit of sugar, bay leaves, cloves, cinnamon, and saltpeter. Let it stand for about 20 days. Wash the ham in cold running water, dry it and put it in a mold for cooking ham. The meat is pressed into the desired shaped mold.

It is sealed and immersed in a pot, covering it with water. While cooking, the temperature of the water should be 425 F. The ham should cook 1 hour for each 2 lbs. of meat. Let it cool in the cooking water then keep it in the refrigerator. Let it rest for one day and then the ham is ready to be eaten. This product must be refrigerated all the time and should be sliced only when ready to eat, otherwise it gets dark.

MARINATE E CONSERVE
Marinades and Preserved Foods

Marinades are known in Italy as *marinate* or *conce*. They are used to preserve, flavor or tenderize. Marinating time varies according to season and ambient temperature. There are two major kinds of marinades: quick marinade and long marinade.

MARINATE CORTE
Short marinade

The more delicate the food, the milder the marinade. Short marinades are suitable for *carpaccio* and small or thinly sliced fish or vegetables served either raw or previously cooked. The ingredients for short marinades may vary from just salt, pepper and oil to the addition of an acid liquid such as lemon, vinegar or wine, as well as herbs and spices. This varies according to the foods and the recipe being executed. These types of marinades are frequently used as *antipasto*.

MARINATE LUNGHE
Long Marinade

A long marinade is suitable for large cuts of beef, hare, rabbit, and other game.

Long marinades usually contain vegetables and wine. A common preparation is as follows:

Make a *battuto* with carrots, scallions, onions, celery and parsley (include the stems) and place it in a bowl together with some thyme, some crumbled bay leaves, a few peppercorns and some pounded (not ground) cloves. Add good white or red wine and vinegar, the amount depends on the size of the cut of meat being marinated. Arrange the meat in a bowl and pour the marinade over it, turning the meat over so that the ingredients can distribute evenly. Cover the bowl and let stand in a cool place for 2-3 days or as indicated in the recipe. If the meat is in small chunks, one day of marinating is enough; if it is a large piece and also tough, more time will be necessary. If marination time is going to be for more than two or three days the marinade must be cooked then cooled and poured over the food being marinated. Strain the marinade before using for cooking. The ingredients for cooked marinade are the same for those in the raw marinade, but the vegetables are sautéed briefly in a small amount of oil. When soft, not brown, add the wine or vinegar according to the recipe.

The marinade is brought to a boil and cooked over low heat for 5 minutes. The cooking for long marinades is necessary in order to avoid fermentation.

MARINATE CORTE
Short Marinades

ZUCCHINE IN SCAPECE
Marinated Zucchini

1 lb. zucchini
2 Tbs. extra virgin olive oil
2 Tbs. vinegar

1 sprig, finely chopped mint
salt and pepper to taste

Wash, slice, pat-dry and fry the *zucchini* in the oil. When golden brown remove from oil and rid of excess fat on paper towel. Arrange in a serving platter and flavor with vinegar mixed with chopped mint. Salt and pepper to taste.

SARDELLE IN SAOR
Sardines in Saor

2 lbs. sardines
flour
1 cup olive oil
salt

1 lb. white onions, sliced
2-3 cups vinegar
2 Tbs. pine nuts
2 Tbs. raisins

Gut and remove the head and bone of the sardines. Wash and pat dry, coat with flour and fry in olive oil. Drain them, remove the excess oil with a paper towel, salt and set aside.

Prepare a cooked marinade: Fry the onions in olive oil over low heat, and, when golden brown, add the vinegar. Keep over low heat for a few more minutes to reduce the vinegar slightly. Remove from pan, and set aside.

Fill a terra-cotta dish with alternate layers of sardines and the marinade and add pine nuts and raisins. The top layer should be the marinade.

Cover and let rest for 1 or 2 days before eating. This is a very good appetizer.

PESCE IN CARPIONE
Fish in Carpione

2 Tbs. olive oil
8 lb. any firm fish fillet
1 lemon, sliced
1 lb. onion
2 garlic cloves

1 sprig rosemary
1 sprig parsley
few sage leaves
1 cup vinegar
salt to taste

Flour and sauté the fish in hot oil over low heat on both sides. Place a paper towel to remove excess fat and arrange in a ceramic platter. Cover with slices of lemon. Prepare the marinade: In a sauté pan, heat the oil, add the onions, herbs and spices. When the onions are soft (not browned), add the vinegar and reduce slightly. Remove from heat, cool and pour the marinade over the fish fillets. Let stand in refrigerator for one day before serving.

INSALATA DI BIANCHETTI
Salad of Whitebait

Bianchetti are tiny fish, the spawn of sardines or anchovies, these can be fished only during certain and limited times of the year so as not to endanger the fish population.

The fish must be absolutely fresh for this dish.

1 lb. whitebait (dressed)	*lemon juice*
salt and pepper	*olive oil*

Wash the whitebait well in cold salt water (in Italy, where possible, they are washed in sea water), drain and season with salt, pepper, lemon juice and some olive oil. Let stand refrigerated for 1 hour and serve.

ACCIUGHE MARINATE
Marinated Anchovies

1 lb. very fresh anchovies	*2 cloves of garlic*
6 lemons	*parsley*
peperoncino	*olive oil*

Remove the scales, innards and bones (except the spine) from the fish without damaging them too much and leaving the fillets attached along the back. Wash and pat dry and place on a platter with a sliced clove of garlic.

Squeeze 3 of the lemons over the fish, cover and let sit in the refrigerator for 24 hours. After this period, drain the anchovies, squeeze the juice from the remaining lemons over them, then drain again.

Place on a platter and season with extra virgin olive oil, chopped parsley and garlic. Add *peperoncino* to taste. Let stand refrigerated for one hour and serve.

PESCE SPADA NEL PANE PROFUMATO ALLE ERBE
Swordfish marinated with herb bread

For curing process
1 lb center cut swordfish	*2 lemons, quartered*
8 oz. coarse sea salt	*1 Tbs. crushed peppercorns*
1 cup sugar	

Drying Process in Bread Crust
1 loaf day-old bread Casareccio	*oregano*
basil	*1 tsp. coriander*
tarragon	*2 cloves garlic*

bunch dill
chives
parsley
thyme

½ cup olive oil
½ cup balsamic vinegar
5 oz. white wine
1 Tbs. juniper berries

Dressing
1 cup olive oil
1 clove garlic
1 Tbs. balsamic vinegar
1 Tbs. white wine vinegar
pinch each of basil, chives,

tarragon, thyme, oregano
coriander seeds, dill, parsley
salt to taste
black pepper to taste
1-2 slices day-old bread

Herb Bread Crumbs
1 shallots
1 clove garlic
1 loaf day-old bread, cubed

a few sprigs parsley, basil,
chives, tarragon, thyme
oregano

Garnish
2 tomatoes, peeled, seeded
and chopped

julienne of 1 celery heart

Curing Process: Place the center cut piece of swordfish in a container and cover with coarse salt, sugar, black peppercorns and pieces of lemon. Turn 3 times per day in this marinade or at least 48 hours or until the swordfish has let out all its natural water and juices, obtaining a very firm, solid piece.

After the curing process, rinse the swordfish carefully and discard all of the marinade.

Cut the day-old bread into cubes and place in a large bowl. Add all coarsely chopped herbs, crushed garlic cloves, oil and vinegars. This should produce a moist bread compote, which is then pasted around the piece of swordfish, set on a rack, then into the refrigerator.

Allow to rest for 48-72 hours. At the end of this period, remove the bread crust and wrap the swordfish in plastic wrap. Keep refrigerated.

Dressing: Blend all the ingredients in a high-speed blender. Pass through a coarse sieve and set aside.

Herb Bread Crumbs: Cut the day-old bread into large cubes. Place garlic, shallots and herbs in a food processor and chop until semifine, then incorporate the day-Old bread. NOTE: The bread should be dry, as the herbs contain water and when chopped become moist. If the bread is too soft or too fresh, it will become pasty instead of becoming green colored bread crumbs.

Pass through a fine sieve and place on a sheet pan to air dry. Set aside. Slice the swordfish very thin using an electric slicer and cover the bottom of a dinner plate. Mix dressing and slightly cover the swordfish with it. Sprinkle with green bread. In a small bowl, season the julienne of celery heart with salt and pepper. Toss with the dressing and fresh parsley. Arrange around the outside of the plate. Garnish with cubes of tomato and serve.

MARINATE LUNGHE
Long Marinades

LEPRE AL VINO ROSSO
Hare in civet

1 hare	*2 sprigs of marjoram*
1 carrot	*4 cloves*
rosemary sprig	*2 celery stalks*
pinch of cinnamon	*clove of garlic, finely chopped*
3 sprigs, parsley	*2 bottles of good red wine*
pepper to taste	*salt*
5 juniper berries	*4 Tbs. lard*
2 bay leaves	*4 Tbs. butter*
	2 onions

Hang the hare, unskinned, by the back legs in a dark place for 3 days. Skin and clean the hare and cut into pieces. Put the pieces of hare into a large pot with an onion, a carrot, the celery chopped into pieces, parsley, rosemary, bay, cloves, juniper berries, cinnamon and marjoram. Add enough wine to cover the hare completely and let marinate for at least 12 hours.

Pound the lard, put into a large pan with the butter and brown with a finely sliced onion. Remove the hare from the marinade, cut it into eighths, reserving the liver. Pat dry and brown with the *soffritto* on medium heat for 20 mins. Add 2 cups filtered marinade liquid and cook for a couple of hours on low heat, adding more filtered marinade occasionally. When the hare is nearly tender, sauté the hare's liver, chop finely, then mix in with finely chopped garlic. Add the liver mixture to the hare and simmer for an additional 10 minutes. Serve with *polenta*.

LINGUA SALMISTRATA
Pickled tongue

Step 1: Marinade

1 veal tongue	*1 carrot*
1 lb. coarse sea salt	*2 celery stalks*
1 tsp. curing salt	*½ large lemon*
½ cup sugar	*2 leeks*
1 bunch thyme	*1 garlic head*
	1 tsp. peperoncino

Marinating: Wash tongue thoroughly and marinate with all spices, herbs and vegetables, for 6 days. Turn the tongue over every day.

Step 2: Cooking
2½ qt. veal broth
1 cup white wine
1 cup vinegar
Plus the same vegetables and spices as for the marinade

Cook the tongue in plain water for 1 hour. Remove tongue, skin and cook it again for 2 hours in the veal broth with wine, vinegar, vegetables, spices and herbs. Cool and refrigerate. Pickled tongue can be kept refrigerated for up to one month.

CONSERVE
Preserved food

Cooked and preserved, marinated in brine and preserved or salted, air-dried and packaged. These foods are meant to be kept for long periods of time. They are suitable for meat, fish, vegetables and fruits as well. Many of this type of conserved foods may be served as *antipasto,* sometimes simply by adding a few drops of oil.

SOTTACETI
Vegetables marinated in vinegar
This preparation is suitable for new onions, carrots, turnips, small cucumbers, peppers, string beans, celery. The vinegar has to be very good but not too strong, and preferably white so as not to change the color of the vegetables or render them too acidic to eat.

2 ¼ lb. mixed vegetables	*1 garlic clove*
(onion, turnips,	*1 clove*
celery, cucumbers,	*5 white peppercorns*
carrots, cauliflower)	*salt to taste*
1½ qt. vinegar	*pinch of tarragon*
1 bay leaf	*1 cinnamon stick*
pinch of sugar	*1 Tsp. olive oil*

Clean, wash and cut the vegetables according to the various types. Boil half the amount of vinegar, let cool and set aside. In a large saucepan bring to a boil the remaining vinegar with ½ bay leaf, a pinch of sugar, the garlic clove, the clove, 5 peppercorns, and a pinch of salt. Add the vegetables and let cook for at least 3 minutes, depending on their type. Remove the pot from the heat and, when the vinegar becomes cool, drain the vegetables and place them in a jar. Add the remaining bay leaf, peppercorn, tarragon, the cinnamon, oil and the vinegar which had been set aside. Cover the jar with an air tight cover. Store for later use.

SOTTOLIO
Vegetables marinated in oil
This preparation is suitable for small artichokes, mushrooms and eggplants. Prepare the vegetables in the same manner as for *sottaceti.* Cook them in 3 parts vinegar to 1 part water with pinch of salt until they are tender, but still crisp. Drain and let dry on a clean towel. Then place in a jar with few peppercorns, a few bay leaves, and a piece of cinnamon. Cover completely with extra virgin olive oil, close the jar with an air tight cover and save it for later use.

POMODORI ESSICCATI
Sun-dried tomatoes
This preparation is best done at the end of July or on the first 20 days of August, when the sun is very hot, so the tomatoes will be very dry and perfectly ripe.

ripe, firm tomatoes,	*basil leaves*
medium size	*salt*
virgin olive oil	

With a wet towel clean the tomatoes, cut them in half vertically, remove the seeds, put them with the open side up over a grate, and sprinkle liberally with salt (if they aren't salted enough the tomatoes become moldy).

Leave them in the sun for 4-5 days, turning occasionally, and taking them inside during the night. At the end of each day, drain the exuded water. On the last day, wash the basil leaves and let them dry over a cloth in the shade. Put the half tomatoes back together, placing a basil leaf in between the cut, and press well. Then place them in layers in a clean, dry jar. Press well, add some *peperoncino* and a garlic clove if you wish, cover the tomatoes completely with oil, close the jar with an air tight cover and save it. They will be ready for consumption in 2 weeks. The tomatoes prepared in such manner can be served as part of an *antipasto* or as side dish for boiled and broiled meats. If you cannot dry the tomatoes outside because of the weather, you can dry them in a warm oven (pre-heated and then turned off).

OLIVE SCHIACCIATE
Crushed Green Olives

5 lbs. green olives	*4 Tbs. oregano*
not too ripe	*1 sweet pepper, minced*
5 garlic cloves, sliced	*salt to taste*
1 bunch basil	*1 cup virgin olive oil*
peperoncino	*1 Tbs. vinegar*

Pound the olives with a mallet without crushing completely. Wash and let soak in water for about 10 days, changing the water frequently. Drain the olives, squeeze them and make a layer on the bottom of a jar which can be hermetically sealed. Cover each layer with a little garlic, basil, *peperoncino,* oregano and sweet pepper cut into thin strips. Salt each layer. When the jar is full, push down on the olives to squeeze out as much liquid as possible and discard. Fill the jar with virgin olive oil mixed with a few drops of vinegar. They are ready to eat after a couple of months.

OLIVE AL FORNO
Baked Black Olives

5 lb. black olives	*2 tsp. oregano*
½ tsp. salt	*3 cups olive oil*
1 tsp. peperoncino	

Make two or three small cuts in the pulp of the olives. Soak in cold water for a week, changing the water three times a day. Drain, let dry and cover the olives with salt. Bake at 225 F. until wrinkled. When cool, put into a Mason jar with the *peperoncino* and oregano, then cover completely with oil and save for later use.

PASTA DI OLIVE
Olive Pâté

This is served as an *antipasto,* spread on toast rounds brushed with olive oil. It can also be used as a sauce for pasta. Olive paté will keep in the refrigerator for about a month.

½ lb. black olives	1 Tbs. bread crumbs
half a lemon	4-5 Tbs. olive oil
4 Tbs. butter	salt and pepper to taste

Pit the olives and chop them very fine so as to make a homogeneous mixture. Add the strained juice and grated peel of half a lemon, the butter, softened and cut into pieces, the bread crumbs and 4-5 Tbs. oil. Salt, pepper and mix thoroughly.

Put the mixture into a jar, cover completely with oil and seal. It can be used immediately.

ACCIUGHE SOTTO SALE
Anchovies preserved in salt

5 lbs. anchovies	5 lbs. rock salt

Gut and clean the anchovies. Cover the bottom of a *terra-cotta* jar with rock salt, then arrange a layer of anchovies and a layer of salt again. Repeat the process until all the anchovies have been used. Finish with a layer of salt. Put a wood disk inside of the jar on top of the last layer. On top of the disk place something to act as a weight. The weight will cause the excess liquids to surface to the top. Remove it with a clean cloth. The anchovies will be ready after 2 to 3 weeks.

TONNO SOTTOLIO
Tuna in oil

2 lbs. fresh tuna, sliced 1" thick	4 garlic cloves
1 cup white vinegar	few bay leaves
1 onion	1 cup extra virgin olive oil
	10 peppercorns

In a large pot, place 2 qts. of water, the vinegar, the onion, 2 cloves of garlic and the bay leaves, and let the liquid simmer and reduce by one third. Add the tuna and continue simmering for 45 minutes. Drain and dry the tuna. Put it in a jar, cover with oil and add peppercorns and remaining garlic cloves.

Keep in a cool place. It will be ready to eat after 20-30 days and can be saved for as many as 5 or 6 months.

PIZZA E FOCACCE
Pizza and Focaccia

This text will not delve into the particulars of how and where *pizza* originated. The history of *pizza* is rather controversial, and it is difficult to reach an agreement on dates and origins. The widely accepted facts are that *pizza* is popular throughout the world and that Neapolitans created it.

Pizza always consists of a thin disk of leavened dough covered with various ingredients, such as tomato, cheese (especially *mozzarella),* seafood, small fish, mushrooms, and so on. The following recipes always refer to specialties within the culinary tradition of the various regions of Italy.

BASIC DOUGH RECIPE
Serves 6

> *9 oz. white flour*
> *½ oz. brewers or compressed yeast*
> *pinch salt*
> *water, as needed*

Crumble the yeast in a cup and dilute with several tablespoons of warm water (not hot, otherwise the yeast organisms die and their leavening power is lost); mix with about 2 oz. of flour, cover the cup with a cloth and keep it in a warm place so that it can leaven. Pour the remaining flour on the pastry board, add a pinch of salt and knead with warm water (the resulting dough should not be too soft).

Add the leavened dough and continue to knead vigorously until the dough achieves an elastic texture.

Shape the dough into six even balls, then place them on a flat wooden board, lightly coated with flour, cover with a cloth and keep it in a warm place until the rising dough becomes twice its initial size. The pizza dough is now ready to be punched down, made into disks of approximately 8" in diameter, and used for pizza with any topping you wish.

PIZZA NAPOLETANA
Neapolitan Pizza
Serves 6

> *pizza dough (basic recipe)*   *pinch of oregano*
> *12 oz. firm ripe tomatoes*   *salt and pepper to taste*
> *2 garlic cloves*   *white flour*
>   *8 Tbs. olive oil*

Peel, seed and crush tomatoes. Add basil, garlic, oregano, 2 Tbs. olive oil, salt and pepper to taste and set aside. Prepare the dough, following the basic recipe. When ready, punch each of the dough balls into a disk of about 8" in diameter, slide the pastry disk on to an edgeless peel (*pala*), coated with flour.

Spread the previously prepared sauce over the pastry disks and add 2 basil leaves on each.

Drizzle each with 1 Tbs. olive oil on top and slide the *pizza* with a brisk backward move into the floor of a wood burning oven and rotate it occasionally to allow for even cooking. Cook till done (a few minutes), remove from oven with the same *pala* and serve.

NOTE 1: The dough on the edges should be slightly thicker in order to prevent the ingredients from sliding off the dough while cooking.

NOTE 2: A wood burning oven should be lit at least three to four hours in advance; it will be ready for baking when the temperature is about 650 F.

NOTE 3: If you do not have a wood burning oven, cook the pizza on an oiled baking pan in the oven preheated at 550 F. or on a preheated sheet tray lined with ceramic tiles.

PIZZA MARGHERITA
Pizza with Mozzarella and Tomatoes
Serves 6

pizza dough (basic recipe)	*½ lb. mozzarella cheese, diced*
12 oz. firm, ripe tomatoes	*4 oz. olive oil*
2 garlic cloves	
12 fresh basil leaves	*pinch oregano*

The procedure is the same as in Neapolitan *pizza*. Simply spread the diced mozzarella over the tomatoes. Place two basil leaves over the *pizza* as it comes out of the oven.

There is also a variation of this *pizza* where the tomatoes are omitted.

PIZZA QUATRO STAGIONI
Pizza Four Seasons
Serves 6

pizza dough (basic recipe)	*tomato sauce*
7 oz. clams	*2 salted anchovy fillets*
7 oz. mussels	*10 black olives*
12 artichokes in oil	*6 Tbs. olive oil*
salt to taste	

Wash and shell the clams and mussels. Quarter the artichokes, prepare the tomato sauce as in Neapolitan pizza. Prepare and stretch the dough and prepare the sauce as in Neapolitan pizza recipe. First spread the tomato sauce on each disk of dough and then each of the ingredients into four different sections: mussels, clams, artichokes, olives with anchovies.

Drizzle generously with oil and bake as in the basic recipe.

PIZZA ALLE VONGOLE
Pizza with Clams
Serves 6

Pizza dough (basic recipe)　　*1 cup tomato sauce*
2.2 lb. unshelled　　　　　　*6 Tbs. olive oil*
littlenecks

Clean and shell the clams. Stretch the dough, cover with the tomato sauce as in Neapolitan pizza recipe and then sprinkle with the clams. Drizzle generously with oil and bake as in basic recipe.

Chop the clams if they are very large.

PIZZA CON CICENIELLI
Pizza with Whitebait
Serves 6

Pizza dough (basic recipe)　　*2 cloves garlic*
9 oz. whitebait　　　　　　　*6 Tbs. olive oil*
1 cup tomato sauce

Clean, wash the fish and let drain. Flatten the dough into 8" disk. Add tomato sauce as in Neapolitan *pizza* recipe and then top with the whitebait, add garlic and sprinkle generously with olive oil. Bake as in the basic recipe.

CALZONE
Stuffed Pizza with Ricotta
This is a type of *pizza* in which the dough is folded over and sealed, making a half moon shape enclosing the filling.
Serves 6:

pizza dough (basic recipe)　　*1 egg*
⅓ lb. mozzarella　　　　　　*3 tsp. grated parmigiano or*
⅓ lb. salame (or prosciutto)　*pecorino cheese*
⅓ lb. ricotta　　　　　　　　*salt and pepper to taste*
12 Tbs. olive oil

Dice the *mozzarella* and cut the *salame* (or *prosciutto*) into strips. Sieve the *ricotta,* let it fall into a bowl and mix in the *mozzarella, salame,* egg, grated cheese, a pinch of pepper and a little salt.

Stretch the dough with your hands (lightly coated with oil), forming a disk 1 foot in diameter and ⅛ inch thick. Coat the stretched dough with oil; cover half the dough with the mix previously prepared and fold the other half over. Pinch the edge of the two halves together sealing thoroughly. Coat generously with oil and bake in a wood burning oven until it achieves a golden color.

CALZONE FRITTO
Bite-sized Fried Calzones
The preparation is the same, with the difference that the disks of dough are 4 inch. in diameter and instead of being baked they are deep fried in oil or *strutto*. They are served hot with a tomato sauce.

FOCACCIA
A type of savory bread that may have various toppings such as onion or cheese. *Focaccia* are generally baked in a flat sheet pan, and then served cut in various sizes and shapes.
Serves 6:

pizza dough as in basic recipe
½ *cup olive oil*
¼ *oz. coarse salt*

Prepare the dough as for *pizza* dough basic recipe. In a well greased baking pan, flatten out one half of the dough and drizzle with oil; roll over the remaining dough and drizzle generously with oil, adding a pinch of salt (preferably coarse salt) and bake for about half an hour at 360 F. This is best eaten warm. Often, *focaccia* is topped with other ingredients; such as fresh sage, rosemary, chopped black olives, lightly salted onions, cheese or a combination of similar ingredients.

PIADINA
Pasta Disks
Piadine are a specialty of the Romagna. These are disks of pasta which can be substituted for bread. They can be eaten with a soft cheese (*squaquarone,* a delicacy of Romagna, or with either *prosciutto* or cooked ham.) They are best served warm, and must be cooked on the proper earthenware plate called a *testo* (or iron pan), placed on a lively flame.

1.2 lbs. white flour
1 oz. fresh strutto
fine salt

Pour the flour on the *spianatoia* (pastry board) forming a *fontana*. Add the *strutto* and knead the dough using just enough luke warm salted water (which must not be hot) so as to obtain a rather firm dough. Knead vigorously for ten minutes and divide the dough in pieces to be rolled out or stretched by hand to make piadine, each 8" in diameter.

Heat up the *testo* on burning coal, or on a stove, and lay on a disk of dough (do not brush with oil). Let cook well on one side and then turn it over; when you notice little charred bubbles forming on the disk, the dough is ready. Continue cooking several *piadine* in this manner, placing the ones which are ready in a pile so that they stay warm.

Serve the *piadine* either plain as a bread substitute or folded over with a filling such as: cheese, *mortadella, prosciutto,* or a cooked green vegetable such as cicory, or bitter *broccoli*.
NOTE: Piadine can also be cooked into an 8" round cast iron pan.

TORTE SALATE E SFORMATI
Savory Pies

Savory pies are common throughout Italy, and like many other preparations their beginnings are due to the needs of the poor to conserve food, meaning pies made it easy to use leftovers as stuffings. The dough used for the crust is very similar throughout Italy, but certain types of savory pies are made without a crust.

TORTINO DI CICCIOLI
Ciccioli Pie

½ lb. white flour	7 ozs. butter
1 oz. compressed yeast	3 eggs
⅔ lb. fresh ciccioli*	salt

Make a cone of flour on the pastry board with a cavity on the top. Dissolve the yeast in a few tablespoons of lukewarm water, pour into the cavity, add a pinch of salt, the butter at room temperature, the eggs and half of the *ciccioli* coarsely chopped.

Knead the ingredients together until the dough is no longer sticky, adding more flour if necessary. Butter an 8" cake pan with high edges, stretch out the dough until it covers the bottom and the sides, then sprinkle with the remaining *ciccioli*. Cover and set in a warm place until risen. Cook in a preheated oven at 400 F. for half an hour.
* Ciccioli are the solid particles which remain when one melts lard or bacon which have been pressed through a potato ricer to remove excess fat. When melting, lard or bacon should always be chopped.

TORTA PASQUALINA
Artichoke Savory Pie

Dough:
  2 lbs., 4 ozs. flour
  4 oz. olive oil
  water
  salt

Stuffing:

12 artichokes	1 lb. ricotta
1 cup olive oil	¼ lb. grated parmigiano
1 sprig parsley	2 oz. butter
1 small chopped onion	salt
9 eggs	pepper

With flour, oil, a pinch of salt and cool water prepare a soft dough. Knead well until the dough becomes elastic. Set aside wrapped in a wet cloth. Meanwhile prepare the stuffing as follows:

Clean the artichokes and cut into thin slices; cook in boiling salted water for 2-3 minutes, then drain. Sauté the onion and parsley with oil; add the artichokes and cook for 15 minutes. Let cool. Then combine with 3 whipped eggs, *parmigiano, ricotta,* salt and pepper and mix with the vegetables, set aside.

Divide the dough into 8 to 12 balls, the size of an egg, keeping each one in a wet cloth. Flatten each piece of dough, one at a time, making each a very thin disk, larger than the baking pan you are going to use. Place the first circle of dough in a greased 12" baking pan and brush the surface with oil.

Then place another disk over it and repeat the process until you have used 4 disks. Pour the stuffing over and make 6 small cavities close to the border. Pour a raw egg into each cavity and sprinkle each with salt, pepper, *parmigiano* and butter flakes. Cover with all the remaining disks of dough, each brushed with oil. Pinch the borders and trim the excess dough, prick the top of the pie in a few places then brush with oil. Instead of artichokes these can be prepared with other greens. Bake for about 1 hour and serve hot or cold (it is better warm).

ERBAZZONE O SCARPAZZONE
Savory Pie with Chards

A type of savory pie with a rich double crust, most often filled with greens, eggs or cheese.

Dough:

9 oz. white flour	3 Tbs. olive oil
1 oz. lard	salt

Stuffing:

2.2 lb. chard leaves	2 eggs
2 oz. lard or pancetta	2 Tbs. olive oil
1 oz. parsley	6 Tbs. parmigiano
1 small onion	pepper
1 garlic clove	salt

Clean, wash and drain the chard well and dry thoroughly.

Knead the flour with the lard, the oil and warm water to obtain a rather stiff dough. Knead for about 10 minutes, wrap in a sheet of wax paper and keep in a cool place for about 1 hour.

Make a *battuto* with lard, parsley, garlic, and onion. Chop the chard very finely. Lightly sauté the *battuto* with 2 Tbs. of oil and when the lard melts, add the chard and cook for about 5 minutes. Put this in a bowl and let cool. Add the eggs and, if necessary, a pinch of salt and pepper. Lightly coat a springform pan with high sides (9-10" in diameter) with olive oil.

Divide the dough in two batches, one twice the size of the other. Roll out the bigger batch with a rolling pin and make a disk large enough to line a 12" baking pan (bottom and sides). Arrange the chard in layers, sprinkling each layer with grated cheese. Roll out the remaining batch of dough, making a disk larger than the diameter of the baking pan. Roll the resulting disk around the rolling pin and unroll over the chard.

Since the top disk is larger than the baking pan, it will have a bumpy surface. Pinch the edges of the two disks of dough together, drizzle with a little olive oil and bake at about 360 F. for 40 minutes. In Emilia, a piece of hard lard is sometimes used instead of oil to dot the dough. The *scarpazzone* can be served either hot or cold.

TORTINO DI CARCIOFI
Artichoke Crust

4 artichokes	4 oz. olive oil
flour	salt
6 eggs	pepper
⅔ cup grated parmigiano	

Clean and cut the artichokes in quarters. Coat with flour and fry them in hot oil. Drain off excess fat and set aside. Beat the eggs with salt, pepper and *parmigiano* and mix with the artichokes. Grease an 8" pie pan and bake in the oven for about 20 minutes at 325 F.

TORTINO DI FUNGHI
Mushroom crust

4 slices white bread	4 eggs
½ cup milk	grated parmigiano
1 garlic clove, chopped	pinch of oregano
5 Tbs. olive oil	salt
1 lb. mushrooms, sliced	pepper
⅔ lb. tomatoes, peeled and chopped	

Remove and discard the crust of the white bread and moisten the rest with milk. Sauté the garlic with oil; stir in the mushrooms for few minutes and then add the tomatoes. Cook for 10 minutes. Let this cool for a while.

Whip the eggs; mix in the cheese and the moist bread; combine with two thirds of the sautéed mushroom and tomatoes, then place this mixture in a buttered baking dish — top with a layer of remaining mushrooms. Sprinkle with oregano, salt and pepper. Bake for about 10-15 minutes in oven at 325 F.

SFORMATI
Molds

This attractive dish is usually made with vegetables, but it is also possible to use meat, fish or many leftovers. *Sformati* are not to be confused with soufflés.

For more elaborate presentations various types of sauces may be poured in the center of the finished *sformato* — such as tomato sauce, chicken liver or beef *ragù,* etc.

The mold

In order to cook any kind of *sformato* you need a shallow, smooth-walled ring mold. The mold should have a capacity of $1\frac{1}{2}$-2 quarts. Butter the mold well, especially at the bottom, before pouring in the sformato mixture.

The baking

Sformati should be cooked in a bain-marie (*bagnomaria*) either on the stove or in the oven; in the latter case, it is advisable to cover the *sformato* with aluminum foil halfway through the cooking process, to *prevent* the surface from drying. It is ready when the *sformato* is firm (but not hard) to the touch. Remove the *sformato* from the bain-marie, let stand for about 5 minutes; remove from mold and serve.

Any kind of mild flavored, boiled green can be used to make a *sformato*. The greens must be quite dry, otherwise the sformato will turn out too soft (this cannot be compensated for by longer cooking: it will remain soft). The chopped textures can vary from very fine to rather coarse consistencies.

RICETTE
Recipes

SFORMATO DI VERDURE
Vegetable Mold

$\frac{1}{3}$ lb. string beans	1 small bunch of asparagus
3 artichokes	$\frac{1}{2}$ lb. butter
2 potatoes	salt
2 carrots	2 eggs
1 small cauliflower	6 Tbs. grated parmigiano
$\frac{1}{2}$ lb. sliced prosciutto	

Clean, wash and cut the vegetables according to the types. Then boil separately the cauliflower and the artichokes and, all together, the remaining vegetables. Sauté lightly in butter all the vegetables. Salt to taste and blend to a coarse consistency.

Whip the eggs, combine with *parmigiano,* a pinch of salt and mix with the vegetables. Line the inside of a buttered new 2" mold with *prosciutto* and fill it with the vegetables. Cook in a bain-marie in preheated oven at 350 F. for about 30 minutes.

SFORMATO DI POMODORI
Tomato Mold

1 celery stalk	*1 clove chopped garlic*
few leaves parsley	*1 cup bechamel*
1 small onion	*pinch of sugar*
1 carrot	*salt*
2 oz. prosciutto	*pepper*
¼ lb. butter	*5 eggs*

1 lb. ripe tomatoes, peeled, seeded and diced

Chop celery, parsley, onion, carrot and *prosciutto* and sauté with 3 ozs. of butter. Then add the tomatoes and the garlic. Salt and let cook for about ½-hour, stirring frequently. Blend to a coarse consistency (the mixture should not be very liquid) and set aside.

Pass the tomato sauce through a fine sieve, combine with the bechamel, adding a pinch of sugar, salt and pepper. Let cool, stirring frequently; then blend in the beaten eggs.

Mix all the mixtures together and pour in a buttered 12" mold and cook in bain-marie in a preheated oven at 350 F. for about 1 hour.

SFORMATO DI FORMAGGIO
Cheese Mold

¼ lb. diced, mild cheese	*1 cup bechamel*
¼ lb. grated parmigiano	*2 Tbs. butter*
4 eggs, salt and pepper	

While the bechamel is still hot, blend in the cheeses. Let cool, then incorporate the egg yolks and the whipped egg whites. Adjust seasoning.

Pour into a buttered 8" mold and cook in bain-marie in pre-heated oven for about 1 hour.

SFORMATO DI PATATE
Potato Mold

1 lb. potatoes	
¼ lb. butter	*¼ lb. grated parmigiano*
vegetable for garnish	*3 eggs*
(peas, artichokes)	*salt*

Boil the potatoes and mash them through a potato ricer or a sieve. Combine with butter, salt, *parmigiano,* egg yolks and whipped egg whites.

Pour the potato mixture in a buttered 10 " mold, and cook in bain-marie in a preheated oven for about 20 minutes. Garnish with buttered green peas or artichokes.

SFORMATO DI UCCELLETTI
A Mold of Thrushes

12 thrushes
½ lb. butter
2 bay leaves
1 cup bechamel

3 eggs (separated)
salt
pepper

Clean, bone and sauté the thrushes with half the amount of butter and 2 bay leaves for 35 minutes. Crush them in a mortar and pass through a sieve. Then combine with bechamel, yolks and whipped egg whites. Pour into a buttered 12" mold and cook in bain-marie in the oven for about 35 minutes at 375 F.

NOTE: all *sformati,* once unmolded, may be presented onto a serving platter, or may be used as an accompaniment to meat or fish preparations.

IL FRITTO E LE FRITTELLE
Fried Foods and Fritters

One of the best known and appreciated Italian culinary specialities is an assortment of fried foods; even though today, it is less popular in home kitchens because of the time it takes to prepare and because it is considered difficult to digest. *Il fritto,* however, is one of the basic foods of Italian regional cuisine and includes not only the traditional *fritto misto,* which is a platter with a wide variety of foods, but also various other fritters, which are listed in this and other chapters.

Instructions for Successful Frying:

Frying should be done by cutting, trimming or shaping into the same form and size, the food to be fried so that the cooking is done evenly. The food to be fried should always be dry. Some items are floured so as to remove any trace of humidity which would prevent a crust from forming and cause the fried foods to absorb oil.

Most foods can be simply floured and fried. If a thicker crust is desired, they should be dipped in beaten egg and then again, if desired, into bread crumbs. They can also be dipped into a batter, which can add flavor or can enclose the flavor of the food being fried. It may also be a binding agent when frying foods that are rather small and crumbly. Small fish or thinly sliced vegetables are usually only floured. Fillets and larger fish can be breaded. While some vegetables can be boiled first, fish must always be raw before it is fried.

Frying is always meant to be done by using a pan, but using a deep fryer is an alternative. When frying, do so by not crowding the pan, fry the food (floured, breaded or dipped in batter) in the oil a few at a time, so that they can be carefully watched and the temperature of the oil remains constant. Turn the pieces 2-3 times so that they fry uniformly. If it is necessary to add more oil while frying, make sure to wait until it reaches the correct temperature before continuing. Once the fried food is ready, remove them with a slotted spoon and set on paper towels to drain off the excess fat, then keep in a warm, dry place until serving time. Never cover fried foods or they will become soggy.

LA PASTELLA
Batter

Batter can improve the taste of fried foods in addition to increasing the volume of the food. It can also make it look more appetizing. Small and crumbly foods that fall apart easily are well suited for frying in batter. A standard batter is made by whisking flour into lightly salted cold water until the mixture is smooth and fluid. An egg or egg yolk may be added. A softer batter can be prepared in the following manner.

2 Tbs. white flour   *2 Tbs. olive oil*
2 egg whites   *6 oz. water*
salt

Whisk the flour into the water quickly, so as not to form lumps, bring to a simmer and cook for 20 minutes. Then mix in the oil and salt, remove from fire, and let cool. Just before using, fold in the beaten egg whites, then dip the pieces to be fried one at a time. Batter should always be put aside to rest for about 30 mins. before it is used.

The Pan

Ideally the pan should be made of light iron and be rather deep, so that it holds a lot of oil. It doesn't need to be very wide because it is better to fry a few pieces at a time. An iron pan should never be washed, but should be wiped out with paper towels after each use. Occasionally it should be rubbed with salt crystals then wiped again with paper towels. An electric pan fryer can produce excellent results, because it cooks evenly and the temperature can be regulated with the thermometer.

The Oil

There should always be plenty of olive oil in the pan (See "Olive Oil — How to Use" in *CONDIMENTS* Chapter). The temperature of the oil is very important. If a thermometer is not handy, the "frying point" can be determined by putting a piece of bread into the oil when hot. If bubbles begin to form around it, the oil is ready for frying. The temperature of the oil must remain constant. It should be low for vegetables containing a lot of water. For fish and meat pieces of larger dimension a low temperature is advisable because these require a longer period of time to cook. Foods which have previously been cooked (such as vegetables and croquettes) should be fried at medium-high temperature. The oil should be very hot for frying small fish, cheese and any kind of food in small or thin pieces. If pieces of food or batter collect in the bottom of the pan and turn black, it is better to filter or change the oil and to clean out the pan with paper towels before continuing to fry.

Fried-Raw: Cut the vegetables thinly and pat dry. Just before frying, flour the vegetables, then fry them in olive oil. The same procedure applies to small fish; clean, dry, flour and fry.

Batter-Fried: Par-boil the vegetables, drain and let cool. Cut into the desired shapes, pat dry, flour and coat with the desired batter and fry in very hot oil. Fish is always raw when it has to be fried, whether or not a batter is used.

Breading for Frying: Bread crumbs should be made from bread which is not too stale; do not use breadcrumbs which have been oven-dried. The breadcrumbs should be made out of 2-3 day-old white bread. If the crumbs are too dry, they can be sprinkled with a little water and rubbed between the hands to moisten them evenly. If you wish, you can add a small amount of grated *parmigiano* to the bread crumbs.

Breading Procedure: Dry the meat or fish thoroughly, then dredge lightly with flour, shaking to remove excess. Once coated with flour, the food must be immersed in beaten, unseasoned egg. Some chefs mix the egg with a teaspoon of oil to obtain a crisper crust. When well coated with the egg, cover the food thoroughly with breadcrumbs, pressing with the palm of your hand so that the crumbs adhere well. Do not dip in the egg a second time: the resulting crust will be too thick and the meat will not cook properly.

How to Cook Breaded Foods

Both oil or butter can be used (although the crust will come out tastier using oil, or a mixture of both). Heat the fat in a shallow frying pan and cook the breaded foods over a medium flame, turning once, so both sides are golden brown. Add salt and pepper to taste after cooking.

RICETTE
Recipes

FRITTO MISTO
Mixed Fried Foods

6 oz. veal sweetbreads	*1 sliced eggplant, salted*
6 oz. veal brains	*and drained for 1 hour*
6 oz. veal marrow from spine	*2 sliced zucchini*
3 oz. cock's combs	*6 zucchini flowers*
3 oz. chicken dumplings	*6 oz. sweet semolina*
6 pair frog's legs	*6 mushroom caps*
flour	*10 oz. breadcrumbs*
milk	*6 eggs, beaten*
butter	*olive oil*
salt	

Clean the meats, vegetables and bone frogs' legs. Cut the meats into thin slices then flour the meats, and frog legs, cut *zucchini* and eggplant into thick strips. Keep *zucchini* flowers and mushroom caps whole. Dip each into the beaten eggs, coat with breadcrumbs, pat the foods to get rid of excess crumbs and set aside.

For chicken dumplings, mix 6 oz. already cooked chicken with 1 tsp. parsley, 4 Tbs. breadcrumbs and 1 egg. Combine well to achieve a smooth mix. Then form small slightly elongated and flat dumplings. These are then floured, dipped in egg and in breadcrumbs and set aside. To make a *semolina:* bring a pint of milk to a boil with 1 tsp. sugar and 2 Tbs. butter, sprinkle in 6 oz. *semolina* flour and cook while stirring for 20 minutes. Add more milk if necessary, until *semolina* is cooked. Roll out the *semolina* into a 1'' thick rectangle on a greased plate then let cool and cut into triangles — dip in flour, egg, and breadcrumbs and set aside.

Fry each of the foods separately as each will require different cooking time. When golden brown on both sides remove from frying pan and place on paper towels. When all the frying is finished, arrange the various foods on a serving platter. Salt to taste. Serve very hot.

Speed is of utmost importance in a *fritto misto* and the amount will vary according to the number of people to be served. A good rule of thumb is always to use one piece of each kind of food for each person. Remember, for speed's sake you can also limit the types of food to include *in fritto misto*. *Fritto misto* can also vary according to seasonal foods availability.

CHIZZE
Small packets of rich dough filled with cheese and fried.

1.2 lbs. white flour
¼ cup butter
pinch of powdered yeast
vegetable oil (for frying)
salt to taste

1 lb. soft cheese
(i.e., ricotta, mascarpone
or robiola)
2 Tbs. fresh strutto

Knead the flour with a pinch of salt. Add the yeast, previously diluted in lukewarm water, and *strutto,* and enough luke warm water (or milk if you wish) to obtain a rather firm dough. Knead for ten minutes and then roll out with a rolling pin, the dough should be about ⅛ of an inch thick. Cut the dough in a rectangular shape, 3" by 2". Place the cheese in the center of one side together with a curl of butter, fold the other edge of the dough over the cheese and butter, pressing the dough firmly around the stuffing to seal the "packets" well, if not tightly sealed, the *chizze* will open when frying.

Repeat the process until there is no dough or cheese left. Then deep-fry the *chizze* in peanut or vegetable oil. The frying oil should not be too hot, otherwise the dough may remain raw on the inside. As they are ready, remove and drain with a skimmer, place on paper towels and keep in the front of the oven with door open, set at low temperature so they may dry a little.

CHISOLINI
A rich leavened dough that is folded and rolled to create many layers which are then cut in shapes and fried.

1.2 lbs. white flour
9 oz. milk, approx.
2 oz. butter

1 tsp. powdered yeast
vegetable or frying oil
teaspoon of salt

Place the flour on the pastry board with a cone in the center together with the yeast previously diluted in lukewarm water, 1 tsp. of salt, the butter (softened and cut in pieces) in the center of the *fontana* and start to knead with enough luke warm milk to obtain a rather soft dough. Knead for 15 minutes and then roll it out with a rolling pin, making a disk (or a square). Fold it in quarters, then roll out the dough again, and fold it again, repeating the process a total of five times. Roll the dough in jelly-roll fashion and slice the resulting dough in 1-½" pieces (you can also cut each slice in half) and stretch it with the rolling pin so as to obtain a piece of dough ¼" thick. Then cut into shapes each side 4" long (if you wish, you can alter the size).

When you have finished cutting all the dough, heat the vegetable oil for frying in a large frying pan and then begin frying the pieces of dough. Brown well on both sides. They will puff up and be an even, golden color. Drain, remove the excess fat by placing on paper towels and serve hot. They can be served with various ingredients such as *parmigiano* cheese, *prosciutto, salami,* etc.; they can also be eaten for breakfast with coffee and milk.

CARCIOFI ALLA GIUDEA
Deep-fried Artichokes

8 tender artichokes	*salt*
1 lemon	*pepper*
Plenty of olive oil	

Remove the outer leaves of the artichokes and leave about 1½" of stem. With a sharp knife trim off the hard part of the leaves. Open the leaves and remove the beard from the center. Place in cold water and lemon juice, to avoid discoloration.

Drain the artichokes and press them upside down until the leaves open completely.

Salt and pepper the inside of the artichoke, then place them still upside down in a deep terra-cotta or iron pot with 1 pt. olive oil. Over a medium-high flame, fry the artichokes for 18 minutes, with the pot covered. Remove from frying pan and place on paper towels to drain excess fat and cool. Reheat the same oil, this time making sure it is very hot. Immerse the artichokes into the oil stem up and cook till the artichoke opens up like a a flower. Remove from oil, pat the artichokes dry from oil drippings, and serve hot.

This is a very old recipe named *"alla Giudea"* because it was prepared in the Jewish ghettos of Rome.

SUPPLÌ DI RISO
Rice Dumplings

1 cup long-grain rice	*4 eggs*
4 Tbs. butter	*nutmeg*
3 cups chicken broth	*salt*
5 Tbs. grated parmigiano	*pepper*
2½ oz. diced mozzarella	*flour*

2½ oz. diced prosciutto	breadcrumbs
1 oz. parsley chopped	olive oil for frying

In a skillet, sauté the rice in the butter, then add the hot broth slowly, stirring frequently. The rice should be cooked in 15 minutes. When ready, mix in half the cheese, then spread the rice out on a board to cool.

Mix the *mozzarella* and *prosciutto,* the remaining cheese, chopped parsley, 1 egg, nutmeg, salt and pepper. With slightly damp hands, take a handful of rice in one hand, and a pinch of stuffing with the other. Push the stuffing into the middle of the rice. Squeeze the rice all around the stuffing and mold it into an egg shape. When all of the mix is used, flour the croquettes, dip into beaten eggs, then roll again in bread crumbs. Fry the *supplì* in very hot oil and serve immediately.

CRISPEDDI
Anchovy and Dill Fritters

1 oz. yeast	dill
2 lb. flour	salt
2 Tbs. olive oil	peperoncino
anchovy fillets	oil for frying

In a bowl dissolve yeast in lukewarm water and mix in about ¾ cup of flour, until a soft mixture is formed. Cover the dough and put in a warm place for about an hour. When the dough has risen, punch it down and knead in 2 Tbs. oil, the remaining flour, and enough warm water to make a soft dough, similar to bread dough. Shape the dough into a ball and put it into an oiled bowl. Cut a cross on the top with a sharp knife and leave covered in a warm place for about 3 hours. When the dough has doubled in bulk, knead again briefly, then divide into pieces the size of walnuts. Stuff each of the bits of dough with an anchovy fillet and a sprig of dill, then seal well.

Place the balls on a clean, floured towel in a warm place for about half an hour. Heat oil, but not to boiling point. Fry the balls, turning them often so that they expand and brown evenly on all sides. Let dry on paper towels, salt, pepper and serve hot.

BACCALÀ FRITTO
Fried Salt Cod

1 lb. salt-cod	approx. ½ cup white flour
olive oil	salt

Let the salt-cod soak in cold water for 2-3 days, changing the water frequently. Cut into even rectangular pieces removing any fins or bones. Dry well. Prepare the batter as in basic recipe, excluding egg white. Coat the cod in the batter and fry in hot oil. Place on paper towels to get rid of the excess fat and serve very hot.

NOTE: Other types of batter may be used.

ACCIUGHE IN PASTELLA
Anchovies Fried in Batter

2-3 Tbs. flour	*½ lb. anchovies*
3 oz. white wine	*salt*
3 egg whites	*oil for frying*

Prepare a batter whisking the flour in the wine. Cool and rest the batter. Beat egg whites until stiff but not dry. Gut, remove the head and bones and wash the anchovies. Leave them split open. Pat them dry with a paper towel. Fold the stiffened egg whites into the batter just before frying. Dip the anchovies in the batter and fry in hot oil.

CIECHE FRITTE
Fried Baby Eels

2 lbs. cieche	*sage*
2 oz. oil	*salt*
2 cloves garlic, crushed	*pepper*

This is an example of an uncoated food fried in relatively small amounts of oil. Warm the oil in a frying pan, add garlic and remove when brown. Add a few sage leaves and let the oil get very hot. Throw the *cieche* (previously washed, rinsed and patted-dry) into the hot oil, toss and mix the cieche gently. Fry till golden. Remove from pan, place on paper towels to rid of excess fat. Dust with salt and serve.

CALAMARI FRITTI
Fried Squid

1 lb. baby squid	*oil*
flour	*salt*
2 lemons	

Clean the squid well by removing the ink bladder, the bone, the eyes and the yellow liquid from the head. Wash and pat them dry with a paper towel. Cut them diagonally into strips to form small rings, leaving the tentacles whole. Roll them in flour and fry in hot oil until golden.

Place on paper towel, salt and serve garnished with lemon wedges.

FRITTELLE DI BIANCHETTI
Whitebait Fritters

1 lb. whitebait   *1 Tbs. chopped parsley*
4 Tbs. olive oil   *2 cloves garlic*
2 cups batter as in basic recipe

Wash and pat dry the whitebait. Prepare the batter as in basic recipe but add 1 Tbs. parsley. Dip the fish into the batter and mix so that the fish are evenly distributed.

Heat the oil with the garlic. Remove garlic when brown. When oil is very hot, take a spoonful of the batter with the fish and fry until golden brown. Place on paper towels to rid of excess fat and serve very hot.

EGGS & FRITTATE

Eggs are particularly suitable for making simple as well as sophisticated *antipasti*.

Boiled eggs may be sliced or cut in wedges and placed on a dish, alternating thin slices of tomato, *mozzarella* and scallion rings and drizzled with virgin olive oil.

Boiled eggs may also be served with anchovy fillets, capers, pitted green or black olives, chunks of tuna fish in oil, fresh lettuce leaves, celery strips and pepper preserved in oil.

Another way to prepare boiled eggs is to cut them in half, remove the yolks and sieve them together with either tuna in oil (or liver pâté), anchovies, caper, parsley or basil, and to fill the shells of the egg with the resulting stuffing.

Frittata is made with beaten eggs, mixed with vegetables or other ingredients, and cooked in a frying pan. Using no more than 6 medium-sized eggs, and a frying pan of about 10 inches in diameter will make the cooking process rather quick — a necessary condition to obtain good results.

How to Make a Frittata

Preparing a frittata is rather simple. The most difficult process is turning it. The eggs should be beaten just enough to mix the yolks with the whites. As an appetizer, *frittate* are always prepared with vegetables, such as asparagus, artichokes, peppers, onions, mushrooms, and tomatoes; cheese cut in small pieces, or meat such as livers, sweetbreads, kidneys and sausages. Frittate are served either hot or at room temperature.

The Pan

An aluminum pan with a heavy bottom is ideal for cooking *frittate* so that the temperature of the pan can be easily controlled. The bottom must also be completely flat, neither convex nor concave, and quite smooth. It must also be of proper size; it is preferable to use a slightly larger pan than a smaller one. If the pan is too small for the amount of eggs being cooked, the *frittata* will be too thick and consequently will take too long to cook, and the final result will be too heavy. For a *frittata* with 6 eggs (and no other ingredients) the frying pan should be 8" in diameter. It is best to have a frying pan that is used exclusively for frittata. Do not wash it after using, but simply clean it with absorbent paper. Every so often, it is a good idea to clean it thoroughly — the best way to do so is to heat the pan on a flame, rub it with coarse salt and then wipe with paper towels.

Mixing the Eggs

The eggs, at room temperature, should be broken into a bowl and beaten with a fork shortly before cooking. They must be beaten just long enough to mix the yolks with the whites; otherwise they form a kind of foam which will make the frittata heavier. A spoonful of milk or cream may also be added.

Cooking Procedure

You may use either oil or butter: for three eggs you need 3 tsp. oil or 2 Tbs. butter. Place the fat in the frying pan and turn the heat on. Break and beat the eggs into a bowl. When the butter is foamy or the oil is hot (it is important that the fats be hot, otherwise they will mix with the beaten eggs rather than cook them), pour the eggs into the frying pan, and with a wooden spoon, briskly mix the eggs, bringing the cooked parts to the center. Repeat the operation until the eggs achieve an even, semi-solid texture. Spread the eggs evenly on the bottom of the frying pan and let cook, shaking the frying pan now and then to prevent the *frittata* from sticking to the bottom. Then flip or turn the *frittata* over to cook the other side. To do so use a plate, or anything flat that covers the pan, turn the pan upside down with a very fast movement and slide the *frittata* back into the pan. Cook as long as necessary to allow the *frittata* to cook through. Remove from fire and serve immediately. The thinner the *frittata,* the better.

How to Serve Frittate

Generally speaking, *frittate* are served hot for breakfast, as a second course, or for a light meal. *Frittate* leftovers can also be used in sandwiches, or cut in strips and served as part of a country-style *antipasto.*

Frittata leftovers are also very tasty when cut in small strips, placed in a baking dish, covered with cheese (e.g., *mozzarella, taleggio,* etc.), drizzled with tomato sauce and baked for a couple of minutes at a low temperature, or topped with cheese slices and baked until the top layer becomes crispy. *Frittate* may be diced and served in a broth. *Frittata* leftovers can be used to either accompany or garnish various dishes.

RICETTE
Recipes

FRITTATA CIPOLLE
Onion Frittata

Sauté sliced onions in 2 Tbs. butter. Do so slowly over low fire so that the onions get golden. Let cool, mix with the eggs and cook as described in basic recipe.

ROGNOSA
Frittata with Cured Meats

This is a Piedmont specialty, probably created to use the leftover bits of cured meats too small to cut and serve as cold cuts but large enough for *frittata*.

Skin and mince 3 oz. *salam d'la 'duja* (see Salame and *Salumi* chapter). Mix the eggs with grated *parmigiano* (3 Tbs. for 6 eggs) salt and pepper. Heat 2 Tbs. butter and 2 Tbs. olive oil in a large frying pan and fry *salami*. Add eggs and cook the *frittata* as in basic recipe. The resulting *frittata* should be ¾" thick and tender. Various types of leftovers may be used for this preparation.

FRITTATA CON ZUCCHINE
Frittata with Zucchini

Wash, dice and sauté *zucchini* till golden brown. Place on paper towels to rid of excess fat and set aside, then mix with eggs. Make the *frittata* following the basic recipe. Use 1 small *zucchini* for each 2 eggs. Option: You may add some sautéed onions and/or grated *parmigiano*.

FRITTATA CON CARCIOFI
Frittata with artichokes

Remove the hard leaves with spiny tips from artichoke. Slice the tender leaves very thinly and place in acidulated water. Remove from water, dry and sauté the artichokes lightly; set aside. Mix artichoke and eggs and make *frittata* following the basic recipe.

FRITTATA CON LE RANE
Frittata with Frog's Legs

Use small sized frog's legs and poach them first in broth for 5-7 minutes. Remove meat from bone, sauté lightly in butter and set aside. Mix frog's legs and eggs and make *frittata* following the basic recipe.

FRITTATA CON FIORI DI ZUCCA
Frittata with zucchini flowers

Clean the *zucchini* flowers, cut into strips and sauté in oil with a few tablespoons of warm water. When cooked, drain and set aside. Beat eggs with chopped parsley, salt and pepper, add the *zucchini* flowers, then make the *frittata* following the basic recipe.

UOVA AL TARTUFO
Truffled Eggs
Serves 4

6 eggs	*2 Tbs. butter*
1 white truffle	*salt*
3 Tbs. grated parmigiano	*pepper*
4 Tbs. olive oil	

Beat the eggs in a small bowl, add salt, pepper, and *parmigiano* cheese. Brown the butter and 1 Tbs. oil in a frying pan, pour in the egg mixture, and stir.

Let the egg lightly scramble, keep soft, salt and pepper to taste. Dish it out and serve with shavings of white truffles.

UOVA FRITTE CON POLENTA E TARTUFI
Fried Eggs with Polenta and Truffles
Serves 4

8 slices of yellow polenta	8 eggs
3 Tbs. oil	salt
2 Tbs. butter	pepper
1 white truffle	

Prepare *polenta,* cool and cut into large ½" thick slices. Grill the *polenta* and place into serving dish. Brown the butter and oil in a frying pan, then fry the eggs two at a time. Slide 2 eggs onto each serving of *polenta,* add salt and pepper, then cover with plenty of very thinly sliced truffle. Serve immediately.

UOVA ALLA PROVATURA
Eggs with Provatura
Provatura is a cheese characteristic of Rome. It is fresh, has a stringy texture and is made exclusively of *bufala* milk. It is very similar to *mozzarella,* which can be used in its place.
Serves 4

4 oz. provatura	grated parmigiano
(or mozzarella)	salt
2 Tbs. butter	pepper
8 eggs	

Dice the *provatura* or *mozzarella* and put it into an 8" pan with the butter. Heat until the cheese melts then break the eggs on top, salt to taste and cook over a low flame, making sure not to break the yolk. Sprinkle with grated *parmigiano.*
NOTE: it is advisable to cook two eggs at a time.

UOVA AFFOGATE COL POMODORO
Poached Egg with Tomato

8 eggs	2 cloves garlic
1 lb. peeled tomatoes	few basil leaves
1 medium onion	

Sauté the onion and garlic, remove garlic when brown. Add the tomatoes and simmer for 15 minutes until a very light, fairly liquid tomato sauce is achieved. Add salt and pepper. Poach the eggs in 1 qt. boiling water and 3 Tbs. vinegar. Cook for 3 mins., remove from water with a perforated spoon and place in serving place. Spoon over the prepared tomato sauce, top with basil leaves and serve.

UOVA TRIPPATE
Eggs in tomato Sauce

Eggs *trippate* means a thin *frittata,* cut in strips that look like the way tripe is cut and subsequently prepared with a sauce.

8 eggs
4 Tbs. grated parmigiano
1 sprig parsley
8 leaves basil
4 leaves mint

1 small onion
12 oz. tomatoes peeled,
seeded and chopped
2 Tbs. olive oil

Prepare 4 very thin *frittate* using a larger pan than the usual 8" pan. Cool and then roll and cut them across into strips. Set aside.

Sauté sliced onions with oil till golden brown. Add the tomatoes, reduce by one third, add salt, pepper and basil and set aside. In a buttered baking dish, arrange layers of eggs, tomato sauce, cheese and basil and mint. Keep layering until all the ingredients are finished. The last layer should be the tomato and cheese. Bake in oven at 375 F. for 10 minutes. Serve.

VERDURE E INSALATE
Vegetables and Salads

Vegetables

It is most important to always choose vegetables in season. Early vegetables, in addition to being more expensive, have less nutritive value and are less flavorful.

Like all cuisines originating in farm communities, Italian vegetable cookery is based on accessibility. They are prominent in *antipasti* and are used as a variety of side dishes. The utilization of vegetables in the Italian tradition are from raw (for salads) to boiled, baked, braised, sautéed and pan-fried. The most traditional recipes are offered in the following pages.

ASPARAGI
Asparagus

This is a spring vegetable. There are different varieties of asparagus: green, white, purple, fat and thin. Another, less common but excellent variety, is that grown wild in damp woods. The stalks are long, thin, green and tender. The thin ones are called *mangiatutto* (literally "eat all"), in that even the stems can be eaten. For most other varieties, only the tips are edible. They must be washed and steamed. To prepare *Milanese* style they are dressed with butter, sprinkled with *parmigiano* and their tips covered with a fried egg.

To serve them in the *parmigiana* style, steam first and place them in a baking pan, cover with *parmigiano,* sprinkle with melted butter and bake at 350 F. until the cheese has melted.

BARBABIETOLE
Red Beets

Beets are red roots and are sold all year long. They must be cooked for they are never eaten raw. They are usually used in salad and can be mixed with boiled potatoes and onions. In dishes like *insalata russa,* beets improve the flavor, and their red color brightens the other ingredients.

BROCCOLI DI RAPE
Bitter Broccoli

This winter vegetable, very popular in Southern Italy, grows in bunches with slightly indented green leaves that have small green broccoli sprouts in the center. For most preparations, boil first to lessen broccoli's rather bitter taste. It can be included in soups, sautéed with oil and garlic, or simply seasoned with oil, lemon juice, salt and pepper. As a side dish, *rape* is generally served with pork meat or sausages.

CARCIOFI
Artichokes

Artichokes are available from November through May. They are the flowers (not the fruit) of a plant about 1 yard in length with large, tapered leaves. The best are those that grow at the top of the stem. In late spring the plant produces the last artichokes, which are only as big as an egg and ideal for canning. The artichokes may be with or without thorns (i.e. either prickly or Roman "unarmed') varieties, respectively). The soft parts can be eaten raw, sliced, with oil, pepper and salt. If boiled, they can be dipped in a sauce made with oil, garlic, and parsley, or stuffed and either baked or braised. They can be used to make *frittate, risotti* and other dishes.

Artichoke hearts without leaves can be boiled, fried, baked or filled with one of a variety of stuffings and served either cold or warm.

CARDI
Cardoons

Available in the fall and throughout the winter, cardoons look like large celery stalks and can reach 1 yard in height. It is a domestic variety of the wild thistle in the artichoke family. Since only part of each plant is edible, be sure to buy a sufficient quantity of cardoons when preparing them. Some are hollow (and thus suitable for stuffing), and some are solid.

Whatever the final preparation is to be, boil the cardoons first. Since cardoons darken easily, it is advisable to keep them in water acidulated with lemon juice. After having separated the stems, dispose of the woody stalks, slice the tender stalks and the heart, and cook them together. Once cooked, cardoons may be served with one of a variety of sauces or may be either breaded and deep-fried or cooked in the *parmigiana* style. Cardoons can also be eaten raw, with a sauce such as *bagna cauda,* or simply with virgin oil.

CICORIA
Chicory

This salad is on the market the year round, but the flavor is best in winter. Known variously in Italy as *catalogna, cicoria cimata,* or *cicoriella,* it looks like a big bunch of long, thin green leaves with a large white vein. *Catalogna* must always be cooked. In February and March, especially in the Lazio region, they make a salad of the buds (called *puntarelle)*

CICORIA

which come up in the middle of the heads of smooth-leafed *catalogna.* Before dressing them it is better to slice them thin and cover them with cold water for about half an hour. In this way they will lose a bit of their bitter flavor and will curl.

COSTE
Swiss Chard
The main season for Swiss chard is the spring. The variety with big leaves and thin veins, can be used instead of spinach, while the ones with large veins are usually used to prepare gratins, or for frying or stewing.

FINOCCHIO
Fennel
Available in winter, fennel has a delicate anise flavor and can be eaten raw — either sliced or whole and seasoned with oil, lemon juice, pepper and salt — or cooked in various ways (e.g. braised, fried, boiled, etc.). Fennel is usually served as a side dish to compliment meat courses. It can also be served as a salad.

FIORI DI ZUCCA E DI ZUCCHINE
Squash and Zucchini Blossoms
Available in spring and summer, squash blossoms are slightly bigger than those of the *zucchini*. Both are cooked in the same way. They are never eaten raw, but can be stuffed and fried, cooked in omelettes, and fried with a special batter or simply with flour. Always choose the freshest ones. When cleaning them, remove the pistil and check the insides to make sure that there are no insects.

LAMPAGIONI
Muscari bulbs
Also called *lampascioni* or *cipollacci,* these are often used in Southern Italian cuisine, especially in the Puglia region. They are a kind of bulb, similar to an onion, with a rather strong, bitter taste. After cooking they become reddish. Prior to cooking, the outer leaves must be removed and the bulbs should soak in cool water (which should be changed occasionally) so that some of their bitterness is lost. Otherwise they can be half cooked, drained, and cooked in fresh water until they are done. They are used in salads, fried, and marinated in oil or vinegar.

LATTUGA
Lettuce
Lettuce is the most popular of all salads, and there are at least 150 varieties. The most common is the *lattuga cappuccio* (iceberg) with a round shape and leaves that form one upon the other. *Lattuga romana* (romaine) has long ribbed leaves and *lattughina* lettuce is a variety with a fast cycle found mostly during the summer: Its leaves are very tender, light green in color, with red shades occasionally. Its taste is mild.

PORRO
Leek
Available almost all year round, leeks belong to the garlic and onion family. They may be substituted for onions in soups, *risotto,* and various sauces; they may also be baked.

MELANZANA
Eggplant
Available in summer, eggplants come in many varieties, according to size and color: they may be various shades of violet or white; they may also be long or round. All are cooked in the same way: fried, stewed, thinly sliced and cooked with oil, garlic and basil or oregano, or stuffed and baked. They can also be used in savory pies and cakes. It is advisable to slice, salt and place a weight on top of them one hour before cooking to remove the bitter flavor most often found in less mature eggplants. Before cooking the eggplant, it is necessary to wash off the salt, and squeeze dry.

PATATA
Potato
Available all year round, potatoes can be divided into two categories: white starchy ones (suitable for purées and *gnocchi*), called in the U.S. Idaho or russet, and yellowish ones with a more compact texture (suitable to fry and stuff), called in the U.S. red or white rose.

PEPERONE
Pepper
Available in summer, there are many kinds of peppers, varying in hotness (sweet or hot), color (most often green, yellow and red) and shade (light to dark). They can also vary in shape (round or long) and in size. Mixed with tomatoes, olives and onions, they are delicious. They can also be peeled, roasted and served in oil.

POMODORO
Tomato
Tomatoes arrived in Europe from central and northern America. The first mention of tomatoes in Italy is dated 1544 by Pietro Andrea Mattioli who gives an accurate description and calls them *"pomi d'oro"*. At the beginning, the tomato plant was not accepted so readily, as it was believed to be poisonous — so much so that in 1820 the state of New York passed a law banning the consumption of tomatoes. This belief was proven to be false by Mr. Robert Gibbon Johnson who took a bagful of tomatoes in a courtroom in Salem, New York and ate the entire bagful before an incredulous public.

Another gentleman, Mr. Michele Felice Corne did the same thing in Newport, R.I. In Italy, the tomatoes entered into popular use in the 17th century. In 1778 Vincenzo Corrado published the book *"Il Cuoco Galante"* in which he had several recipes with tomatoes. But the boom of tomatoes' popularity in Italy began in 1875 when Mr. Francesco Cirio started the industrial production of tomatoes first with the famous *"salsa cirio,"* followed later on by the canned, peeled, tomatoes. With this success, experimentation with the tomato plant began, and we now have many different varieties. Among the better known variety is the San Marzano, a type of tomato that takes its name from the area of its origin.

RAPA
Turnip

Available from fall to spring, according to variety, turnips are very digestible roots with a delicate taste. They can be cooked in various ways — in soups, baked or *sottaceto*.

SEDANO
Celery

Green Celery: available all year round, this is used to flavor soups and various sauces. The largest varieties are cooked like white celery. Both the stalks and tender leaves can be eaten raw.

White Celery: available in fall and winter, this comes in sizable bunches. The outside stalks are yellowish while the insides are white. White celery can be eaten raw, as an appetizer, seasoned with an oil-salt-pepper *Pinzimonio* dressing, or with *bagna cauda* sauce. It can also be cooked and served as a side dish.

Celery Root or Verona Celery: Available in winter, only the root of this celery is eaten, while the stalks may be used to flavor soups. It can be eaten raw, cut in match sticks and seasoned with oil, vinegar, pepper and salt. If served as an appetizer, it may be dressed with a mixture of mustard and mayonnaise, or cut in wedges or slices that are sautéed or fried (with or without breading). It is an excellent accompaniment for meat courses.

VERZA E CAVOLO CAPPUCCIO
Savoy Cabbage and Head Cabbage

These belong to the same family as broccoli and cauliflower and are primarily a winter vegetable. Savoy cabbages have compact heads of wrinkled, curly leaves, dark green on the outside and lighter in the inside. Head cabbages also have compact heads, but with smooth, light green leaves; they are more delicate in taste than the Savoy. The leaves of the head cabbage can also be russet or violet in color (known in Italy as *cavolonero* or Tuscan cabbage).

Both of them may be eaten raw, cut in thin strips and seasoned with oil, vinegar, salt and pepper, or may be stewed or cooked in savory pies and soups.

ZUCCA
Gourd Squash

The most common Italian squash of this type is the *zucca* — a squat, round, very bumpy-skinned squash, whose flesh resembles that of a pumpkin in color and texture. Available in late fall and winter, *zucca* can vary in shape and size.

They are heavier and much fleshier than common pumpkins and their flavor is a bit more like banana squash.

The *zucca* must be of the best quality, as it is impossible to improve the taste of a bad one. It may be baked, boiled, steamed, fried or sautéed. It may also be used in *risotto* or as a stuffing for *tortelli,* and *gnocchi.*

ZUCCHINE
Zucchini

Available in the summer, there are many varieties of this kind of vegetable, according to size and shape (straight or curved). Give preference to the small, very firm ones. Choose the shape according to how they are to be prepared (i.e. choose straight ones to make stuffed *zucchini*). They may always be sliced or diced, regardless or shape. They can be fried, steamed or baked.

RICETTE
Recipes

PEPERONI RIPIENI CON PANE
Peppers stuffed with bread

8 Bell peppers, small size	*3 salted anchovies*
3 Tbs. olive oil	*1 oz. capers*
2 cups bread crumbs	*2 oz. green olives*
parsley	*salt*
2 garlic cloves	

Clean the peppers, remove the stem and the seeds. Prepare a stuffing with 1 $\frac{1}{2}$ Tbs. oil, bread crumbs, parsley chopped with garlic, anchovies, capers and olives. Stuff the peppers without packing too tightly, place them in a baking pan, pour over the remaining oil and bake for about 1 hour at 350 F.

POMODORI RIPIENI CON RISO
Tomatoes stuffed with Rice

4 large round tomatoes,	*1 garlic clove, finely chopped*
ripe and firm	*basil, finely chopped*
salt	*pinch of oregano*
pepper	$\frac{1}{4}$ *cup boiled rice*
2 Tbs. parsley, finely	*virgin olive oil*
chopped	$\frac{1}{2}$ *cup breadcrumbs*

Wash, dry and cut the tomatoes in half horizontally, remove the inside, sprinkle with salt and set them upside down over a sieve for about 30 minutes.

Add parsley, garlic, basil, oregano and salt and pepper to taste to the rice.

Blend all the ingredients well, then fill the tomatoes with the mixture and level off the top with a spatula. Preheat the oven to 400 F. Coat the inside of a large baking pan with oil. Place the tomatoes side by side in the pan, cover the surface with bread crumbs, sprinkle with a small quantity of oil, and bake for about 30 minutes.

Serve warm, but they are also very good served at room temperature as a side dish or antipasto.

MELANZANE RIPIENE CON CACIOCAVALLO
Eggplant stuffed with Cheese

1 lb. eggplants, medium size	½ onion, chopped
olive oil	2 oz. caciocavallo, diced
1 garlic clove, chopped	(or semi-soft cheese)
1 lb. tomatoes, peeled,	1 Tbs. chopped parsley
diced	pinch of oregano
1 oz. capers	salt, pepper
3 anchovies, chopped	basil leaves

Cut the eggplants in half lengthwise, scoop out the pulp, and arrange the eggplants side by side in an oiled baking pan. In a saucepan heat 2 Tbs. of oil and brown the garlic, then add tomatoes, the pulp of the eggplant, capers, anchovies, onions and cook for 10 minutes at medium heat. Next, mix in the *caciocavallo,* parsley and basil. Adjust the seasoning with salt and pepper. Blend all the ingredients well and fill the eggplants with this mixture. Sprinkle with salt and oregano. Bake for about 1 hour at 325 F.

CAVOLO RIPIENO CON POLLO E SALSICCIA
Cabbage stuffed with Chicken and Sausage

1 cabbage	4 oz. butter
¼ lb. sausage	4 Tbs. grated parmigiano
⅔ lb. cooked chicken,	salt
chopped	pepper
2 eggs, beaten	

Boil the cabbage in salted water, remove from the pot when still firm, and let cool. Remove the outer leaves of the cabbage and set aside. Brown the sausage and remove from its casing. Prepare a stuffing with the chopped chicken and the sausage, mix with beaten eggs, *parmigiano,* and salt and pepper to taste. Place the cabbage in a greased baking dish and open the leaves with your hands, paying attention not to break the stems. Begin with a small ball of stuffing and rebuild cabbage head placing a small amount of stuffing between each layer of leaves. Finish with outer leaves of cabbage and tie the cabbage with a string to keep it together. Sprinkle with butter and grated *parmigiano* and bake for 30 minutes at 325 F.

ZUCCHINE RIPIENE CON FORMAGGIO
Zucchini stuffed with cheese

1 lb. zucchini	2 eggs, beaten
6 slices white bread	3 oz. bread crumbs

3 oz. milk   1½ oz. butter
1 cup ricotta   salt
4 Tbs. grated parmigiano

Boil the *zucchini* in salted water for about 5 minutes (they should still be firm). Let cool and cut lengthwise. With a spoon, scoop out some of the pulp, being careful not to cut into the shell, and set aside. Remove the inside of the bread, soak it in milk, then squeeze out the moisture. In a bowl mix *ricotta, parmigiano,* the pulp of the *zucchini,* eggs, and the bread and adjust seasoning with salt. Stuff the zucchini shells with this mixture. Sprinkle with bread crumbs and thin pats of butter. Place the *zucchini* side by side in a greased baking pan. Put in the oven at 325 F. for about 30 minutes or until they brown on top.
You may substitute a different cheese for the *ricotta.*

POMODORI RIPIENI AL PANE ED ERBE
Herb-Stuffed Tomatoes

4 round, ripe, firm tomatoes   ½ cup bread crumbs
1 sprig parsley   1 Tbs. oregano
8 basil leaves   1 Tbp. capers, chopped
1 clove garlic   salt
4 Tbs. olive oil

Cut the tomatoes in half horizontally and remove the seeds. Salt and leave upside down for half an hour on a towel.
Chop parsley with basil and garlic, add bread crumbs, oregano and the capers. Salt and mix well. Place the tomatoes on a greased baking dish and fill them with the stuffing. Drizzle them with oil and bake at 350 F. for half an hour or until a golden crust forms on top. These are excellent both warm or cold and can be served as a side dish or as *antipasto.*

INVOLTINO DI MELANZANE
Involtino of Eggplant

1 medium eggplant   6 Tbs. olive oil
salt, pepper   8 slices mozzarella
flour   8 fresh basil leaves

Cut 6 thin slices of the eggplant, leaving skin on. Salt lightly and let sit for ½ hour to draw out the water. Then wash the eggplant slightly and pat dry with paper towel.
Dust eggplant with flour and brown both sides in a saucepan with olive oil. Remove eggplant from pan and top each with a slice of *mozzarella* and basil leaf, salt and pepper and roll up to form an *involtino.* Place in pot, sprinkle with oil and pepper, and put in a low heat oven for about 5 minutes, just until cheese melts and the flavors are blended.

ZUCCHINE AL FORNO
Baked Zucchini

2 zucchini	*1 Tbs. grated parmigiano*
2 Tbs. parsley, finely chopped	*1 Tbs. olive oil*
1 Tbs. basil, finely chopped	*½ cup pine nuts, toasted*
1 clove garlic, finely chopped	*salt*
¼ cup fresh bread crumbs	*pepper*

The *zucchini* used in this recipe are cut across to about 1" in length. Scoop out and discard, only ¾ of the center.

Combine all ingredients, adding the pine nuts last. Mix well.

Cook *zucchini* rounds in boiling salted water until *al dente,* then cool in ice water. Drain on paper towels.

Fill *zucchini* with stuffing without packing too tightly and place in a casserole pan with a little oil. Let it bake for 5-10 minutes at 325° F.

CARCIOFI ALLA ROMANA
Artichokes braised with mint

8 small artichokes	*salt*
juice of 1 lemon	*pepper*
1 sprig wild mint, chopped	*8 Tbs. olive oil*
1 garlic clove, chopped	

Remove the tough outer leaves of the artichokes. With a sharp knife trim off the tips of the leaves and the skin off the stem. Do not cut off the stem. Open the leaves and remove the beard from the center. Place the artichokes in cold water and lemon juice, to avoid discoloration.

Wash and chop finely the wild mint and garlic. Remove the artichokes from the water, open the leaves and fill the center with mint, garlic, salt and pepper.

Then place them upside down tight against each other (with the stem up) in a pot at least as tall as the artichokes. Salt and pepper to taste, sprinkle olive oil, add as much cold water as needed to just cover the artichokes, cover and let cook over medium heat for about 1 hour.

Cool and place them in a deep dish and cover with the cooking juice (If there is too much liquid, first reduce over a high flame). They are best served warm, but may also be served at room temperature.

Caution about seasoning liquid before cooking, if it is to be reduced later, or it may be over salty.

MELANZANE ALLA PARMIGIANA
Eggplant Parmigiana

3 firm eggplants	*½ lb. mozzarella, sliced*

1 small onion, finely sliced	basil leaves
1 garlic clove, crushed	6 Tbs. parmigiano
½ cup olive oil	flour
½ lb. ripe tomatoes	salt, pepper
	pinch of sugar

Wash the eggplants, remove the stems, and cut into slices lengthwise, not thicker than ¼". Place the slices on a large platter, slightly on an angle. Sprinkle them with salt, place a weight on top, and let stand for about 1 hour.

In the meantime, brown the onion and the garlic in oil over a very low flame, then add the tomatoes and let simmer for about ½ hour, stirring frequently. When this is done, pass through a sieve and add a pinch of salt.

Cut the *mozzarella* into very thin slices and let them dry on a cloth. Chop the basil and mix it with the *parmigiano*.

Wash the salt off the eggplant and dry them. Dredge in flour and fry in very hot oil, turning them to brown and when both side are done, lift them out and drain on a paper towel.

Preheat the oven to 375 F. Coat a deep baking dish with olive oil and put in a layer of eggplant. Sprinkle with *parmigiano,* pour on a a layer of tomato sauce, and cover with slices of *mozzarella.* Repeat this layering until all the ingredients have been used, then cover with tomato sauce, sprinkle with more grated *parmigiano* and bake for about 30 minutes. This dish is very good hot or at room temperature and makes a good antipasto. *Zucchine alla parmigiana* can be made in the same way, substituting *zucchini* for eggplant.

FINOCCHIO CON FONTINA
Fresh Fennel with Fontina

4 heads fennel	nutmeg
2 oz. butter	broth
¼ lb. fontina cheese	salt

Clean the fennel and cut lengthwise. Boil for 5 minutes in salted water and drain. In a buttered baking dish, alternate a layer of fennel with slices of *fontina* cheese and butter. Sprinkle with salt, very lightly with nutmeg, and a ladle of broth and put under the broiler. The dish is done when the cheese has melted.

PEPERONATA
Peppers sautéed with oil and capers

2 lb. firm and sweet peppers	8 oz. ripe tomatoes, peeled,
1 small white onion, chopped	seeded and diced
1 garlic clove, chopped	8 basil leaves
8 Tbs. olive oil	salt
	pepper

Clean and cut the peppers into strips. Prepare a *soffritto,* by sautéeing the onions and garlic in a saucepan with 2 Tbs. oil. When golden brown add the tomatoes. Cook for 10 minutes over low flame, remove from fire and set aside.

In a large sauté pan, heat 6 Tbs. of oil, then add the peppers. When the peppers are slightly soft, add the *soffritto* and continue to cook until the peppers are tender but still crisp. Adjust seasoning. Remove from fire and serve. Do not overcook the peppers, otherwise the skin will fall off. You may add some pitted black olives. *Peperonata* is also served at room temperature.

MELANZANE A FUNGHETTO
Sautéed Eggplant

4 medium eggplants	8 Tbs. virgin olive oil
1 onion, chopped	salt
6 oz. ripe tomatoes, peeled	pepper
seeded and diced	

Cut the eggplant into very thick slices and place in platter. Cover generously with salt. Place a weight on top for one hour, then mash and set aside.

Prepare a *soffritto* with onion and tomatoes cooked in a saucepan with 2 Tbs. oil, (about 7-8 minutes) and set aside. Heat the remainder of the oil, add the eggplant, cook till almost done, and add the *soffritto,* toss well and continue to cook till the eggplants are tender but still crisp. Salt and pepper to taste. Serve warm or at room temperature.

CAPONATA SICILIANA
Eggplant and Tomato Stew

2 lbs. eggplant	1 tsp. capers
8 Tbs. olive oil	basil leaves
1 lb. onion, chopped	salt to taste
2 oz. green celery, chopped	2 Tbs. vinegar
1 lb. ripe tomatoes, peeled,	3 oz. green olives
seeded and diced	

Slice and salt the eggplant. Place a weight over and let them drain for one hour to rid them of the bitter water. Next, wash, dry, and dice the eggplant and sauté in olive oil. Cook until tender but still crisp and set aside.

Sauté the onion and the green celery in 4 Tbs. oil. When the onion-celery mixture is golden brown, add the tomatoes, olives, capers, and let cook for 10 minutes. Combine the whole with the eggplants, add chopped basil and salt to taste. Toss and serve.

This dish can be served warm or cold (room temperature) and as an *antipasto. Caponata* is also served in a sweet-and-sour version, in which 1 Tbs. raisins and 1 Tbs. pine nuts are added to a dressing of ½ cup vinegar and 1 Tbs. sugar, reduced by one third. Add dressing to *caponata,* toss well and serve.

BROCCOLETTI ALLA ROMANA
Braised Bitter Broccoli, Roman style

1 lb. broccoli di rape	*1 peperoncino*
2 spoonfuls olive oil	*salt*
2 garlic cloves	

Wash the *broccoli,* removing the large stems and larger leaves. Cook in salted boiling water for a few minutes, then drain and set aside.

In a large skillet, brown the garlic in the oil. Add the *peperoncino* and, when the garlic is brown, remove it and add the *broccoli.* Salt to taste and cook until tender but still crisp. Serve as a side dish to any white meat courses, such as fowl or pork.

CICORIETTA SALTATA CON PANCETTA
Chicory sautéed with Pancetta

2 lb. chicory	*1 oz. chopped parsley*
¼ lb. pancetta, diced	*½ cup dry white wine*
olive oil	*salt*
2 garlic clove, chopped	*pepper*

Clean, wash and boil the chicory. Drain, let cool and set aside. Sauté the *pancetta* until browned and set aside. In a large frying pan, brown the garlic and remove when brown. Add the chicory, sauté briskly, then add *pancetta* and parsley. Stir well for a few minutes. Pour in the wine and let simmer until the wine has evaporated. Remove from fire and add salt and pepper to taste. Serve.

CARCIOFI TRIFOLATI
Sautéed Artichokes

12 artichokes, cleaned and	*½ cup beef broth*
thinly sliced	*chopped parsley*
1 lemon	*½ cup white wine*
6 tsp. extra virgin olive oil	*salt and pepper to taste*
4 garlic cloves, chopped	

Clean, remove the tips and thinly slice the artichokes lengthwise and immediately dip them in water acidulated with the juice of the lemon. Brown the garlic in oil and remove when brown. Add the artichokes and sauté on moderate heat, stirring frequently. Add the broth and the wine. When artichokes are done, add the chopped parsley, salt and pepper to taste, toss well and serve.

Prepared in this manner, the artichokes can be served as a side dish for beef or for veal. With the addition of beaten eggs and *parmigiano* cheese, this becomes the basic ingredient for a wonderful *tortino di carciofi* (see Savory Pies).

BROCCOLI DI RAPE ALL'AGLIO E PEPERONCINO
Bitter Broccoli, Garlic and Peperoncino

2 lb. bitter broccoli	peperoncino
2 garlic cloves	salt
8 Tbs. virgin olive oil	pepper

Wash the *broccoli,* discard the larger stems and leaves, and put them in cold water. In a large skillet, sauté the garlic and *peperoncino* in 6 Tbs. oil. Remove garlic when brown. Remove the *broccoli* from the water but do not dry, place in the heated skillet and cook over a low flame. Let cook until tender but still crisp. Add salt and serve.

INVOLTINI DI CAVOLO
Savoy Cabbage Rolls

12 large Savoy cabbage leaves	pepper
⅔ lb. cooked meat	2 oz. pancetta, diced fine
¼ lb. mortadella, diced	1 small onion, chopped
1 egg	2 Tbs. butter
2 Tbs. parmigiano	2 sage leaves
2 Tbs. parsley, chopped	1 garlic clove
salt	½ glass dry white wine
1 cup chicken or beef broth	

Boil the cabbage leaves for about 3 minutes in salted water, being careful not to break the leaves. Drain and place them in cold water for 20 minutes. Drain again and lay them on a cloth. Cover with another cloth and let them dry. In the meantime, grind finely the meat and *mortadella.* Combine them with 1 egg, *parmigiano,* parsley, salt and pepper to taste. Blend well and top each cabbage leaf with this mixture. Roll tightly and fasten with toothpicks.

Finely chop the onion and the pancetta together. Brown them in butter over a low flame, along with sage and garlic in a baking pan. Remove garlic when golden brown. Add the cabbage rolls, continue to brown for few minutes, then sprinkle with wine, pepper and the broth. Cover and let cook for about 30 minutes over low flame Serve hot.

CIPOLLINE AL DOLCEFORTE
Sweet and Sour Pearl Onions

1½ lb. pearl onions	3 oz. very good white vinegar
¼ lb. butter	salt
2 spoonfuls sugar	

Peel the onions. Cook them in boiling water for 3 minutes, then drain and set aside. Melt the butter in a large saucepan and add the onions. Stir in the sugar and allow it to dissolve. Add the vinegar and stir well. Cover and simmer gently over low heat for about 1 hour. If the sauce becomes too thick, add some hot water, as needed. Pearl onions prepared in this manner can be served with braised meats or venison.

CARDI TRIPPATI
Cardoons Trippati

2 lb. cardoons	¼ lb. butter
pinch of flour	salt
1 lemon	pinch cinnamon
1 onion	4 Tbs. parmigiano
broth	

Cut the cardoons into julienne about 3" long. Cook until tender but still firm in boiling water with a pinch of flour and few drops of lemon juice. Drain and pat-dry. Chop the onion and sauté with half the butter. Add the cardoons and let cook gently over low flame for 4 minutes. Before removing from the heat, salt to taste. Add some chicken broth if necessary to keep moist. Sprinkle with a pinch of cinnamon, mix in the remaining butter and salt to taste. Top with parmigiano and serve hot.

INSALATE
Salads

In Italian culinary terms an *insalata* is any dish consisting of single or mixed greens, vegetables or legumes flavored with salt, oil and vinegar and served cold. More precisely, in addition to vegetable salads, Italians enjoy egg, meat, fish, seafood, cereal and even fruit salads. The following classification is meant to include various types of salads.
1) Simple green salads
2) Salads with vegetables
3) Various salads with meat, fish, rice and other ingredients prepared in diverse proportions and mixtures.

While the first type of salad can be considered as a side dish, the second as cold appetizers, the third category can be viewed as a cold main course. For example, a *panzanella* can function as an appetizer, or a salad with tuna in oil, onions and potatoes as a light main course.

INSALATA VERDE
Green Salad
This may refer to either a single kind of green or several types of greens mixed together.

Wash repeatedly in a generous amount of water, then drain well without crushing. If they are not to be used immediately after draining, keep in a covered container and refrigerate.

CONDIMENTO
Dressing
The typical dressing for raw salads is olive oil, wine vinegar, salt, pepper. The standard proportions — adjustable, of course to individual taste — are 3 parts oil to 1 part vinegar.

It is advisable to choose among the various types of oil (see Condiments chapter) and vinegar to make the most suitable dressing for the type of salad being served. Remember that white vinegar is strong and aromatic, while red vinegar is milder and fruitier in flavor. There are also aromatic and balsamic vinegars; the latter is particularly strong and should be measured out drop by drop (see chapter on Condiments).

Lemon cannot always be substituted for vinegar, as its acidity content is less than that of vinegar. Lemon-based dressing is suitable to flavor raw celery, fennel, artichokes, mushrooms and carrots.

For an emulsified dressing, pour the vinegar in a dish, mix it with the salt and pepper, slowly add the oil, whisking constantly. If you wish to add a light garlic flavor, do one of the following: rub the garlic on the inside of the bowl in which the salad will be tossed, or pierce a clove of garlic with a fork and use this to mix the dressing.

In dressing salads many combinations of ingredients may be used:
oil, wine vinegar, pepper and salt
oil, lemon juice, pepper and salt
oil, balsamic vinegar, pepper and salt
oil, grated horseradish, lemon juice, pepper and salt
pancetta or lard — browned to a crisp and together with its melted fat, mixed and boiled for a minute with vinegar: ideal with *radicchio*. This dressing is generally used with high fiber vegetables and served still slightly warm.

In addition to lemon, oil, salt and pepper, the following ingredients can be included in dressings to flavor all kinds of salads:
finely minced parsley
chopped or shredded basil
finely minced, raw scallions
chervil
mustard
oregano
crushed garlic
anchovy paste (obtained by pounding the anchovy fillets in oil to a paste)
capers, usually used together with anchovies.

COMMON VARIETIES OF GREENS

CICORIA RICCIA
Curly Chicory
    The leaves, joined together in a bunch, are curly on the edges as well as in the inside. Light green in color, some varieties have a slightly brown edge. As a salad it is always mixed with other greens and seldom used for cooking.

RADICCHIO
    Radicchio Trevisano is leafy and slender, while the *Castelfranco Veneto radicchio,* also known as *radicchio di Chioggia,* is more rounded, resembling a rose.
    The leaves of both types are white at the root, and a reddish overall color. *Radicchio trevisano* is the more traditional variety. *Radicchio* is a salad with a bite, and its taste is pleasantly bitter. *Radicchio trevisano* is also very good grilled.

RADICCHIO   **CHIOGGIA**   **TREVISO**

PUNTARELLE
Roman Wild Chicory
    From the same family as the chicory, this very special salad is typical of Central Italy and only available in the winter months. *Puntarelle* must be washed and the green leaves are dispensed. The white-greenish tips are split with a knife lengthwise and dipped in cold water.
    This will allow the leaves to curl and lose some of their bitter taste. They are best eaten with an anchovy dressing.

INDIVIA O CICORIETTA
White curly Chicory
    These are large bunches of curly, wrinkled, off-white colored leaves, becoming lighter in color at the center of the bunch. They can be served as a salad or boiled and dressed with virgin olive oil.

RUGOLA/RUGHETTA/ARUGOLA/RUCOLA
    There are many names for one very popular green which is oak-leaf shaped with a pungent, radish-like flavor. Because *rugola* has such a definite taste many times it is mixed with milder greens as a salad. Oil and vinegar is the most suitable dressing. *Rugola* is also served with a pasta dish from Puglia called *Orecchiette con rucola e pomodoro.*

DANDELION GREENS

Dandelion greens are the long, pointed, dark green leaves of the dandelion plant. The young spring greens are preferable, as they are less bitter in flavor. They can be eaten raw when young, or blanched or wilted with a hot dressing.

PINZIMONIO
Raw Vegetable Salad

The most simple dressing for raw vegetables in undoubtedly *Pinzimonio,* a dipping sauce of oil, salt and pepper. *Pinzimonio* is used as a dip for raw celery, artichokes, leek, scallions, fennel, sweet peppers, etc. The vegetables must be cut rather large so that they may be picked up by the stem and dipped in the dressing at the tip. Another popular raw vegetable salad is *bagna cauda* (see chapter on Sauces).

RICETTE
Recipes

PUNTARELLE CON SALSA DI ACCIUGHE
Roman Chicory with Anchovy Dressing

2 lb. puntarelle	1 lemon
2 garlic cloves	salt
3 anchovy fillets	pepper
3 oz. olive oil	

Let the *puntarelle* soak in cold water for half an hour.

In the meantime, crush the anchovies and garlic in a mortar until they become a paste. Blend in the oil, the lemon juice, a pinch of salt and pepper. Drain the *puntarelle,* place them on a large bowl, toss with the sauce, and serve.

INSALATA DI CAVOLFIORE CON SOTTACETI
Cauliflower Salad with Sottaceti

1 cauliflower	vinegar
¼ lb. Gaeta olives	4 oz. mixed sottaceti
1 spoonful capers	salt
8 anchovy fillets	pepper
8 Tbs. virgin olive oil	

Boil the cauliflower in salted water, without overcooking. Drain and let cool. Cut the cauliflower, or actually break up the flower from the stem, chop up the stem and place on a large platter. Combine with olives, capers and anchovies. Scatter the marinated mixed vegetables over the cauliflower and dress with oil, salt and pepper. Serve cool. This salad in the Neapolitan region is called *Insalata di Rinforzo* meaning it is a salad that gives a lot of "pep". It is traditionally served on Christmas Eve.

INSALATA DI FAGIOLI BIANCHI DI SPAGNA
Salad of White Spanish Beans

2 lbs. fresh white Spanish	1 garlic clove
beans	2 Tbs. chopped parsley
1 leek	salt
virgin olive oil	pepper
1 small celery stalk	
1 small onion	
1 bay leaf	
1 small carrot	

If using dry beans, soak them overnight. Cook the beans in boiling water (if fresh), or start with cold water (if dried). Tie the aromatics (celery, onion, bay leaf, carrot, leek) together in a bunch and add to the boiling water just after the beans. Cook the beans for 1½ hours. When done, drain, remove the vegetables, and place the beans in a salad bowl (not wood) and season the beans with oil, salt, pepper, chopped parsley and, if desired, garlic.
NOTE: Two lbs. of fresh beans are equivalent to ¾ lb. dry beans.

INSALATA DI TONNO E FAGIOLI
Tuna and Cannellini Salad

1 lb. cannellini beans	2 Tbs. extra virgin olive oil
6 oz. tuna in oil	pinch of pepper
1 medium onion finely sliced	salt

Soak the beans overnight and cook for 1½ hours, starting with cold salted water. Drain and cool. Combine in a bowl the beans, coarsely crumbled tuna and the onion. Add the olive oil, a pinch of white pepper and salt to taste. Toss well. Serve at room temperature.
VARIATION: The same recipe can be made with smoked herring instead of tuna.

INSALATA DI CARCIOFO CON PARMIGIANO
Artichoke and Parmigiano

6 artichokes	pinch salt
1 lemon, squeezed	pinch pepper
3 Tbs. virgin olive oil	6 Tbs. parmigiano reggiano

Remove the stems, the outer leaves and all the hard parts of the leaves, leaving only the bottoms of the artichokes. Remove the choke, cut in thin slices and set in cold water and lemon until ready to use. Drain the artichokes, dress with salt, oil, pepper and cover with *parmigiano* sliced thinly using a truffle cutter or a potato peeler so that the *parmigiano* will curl up. Serve in dinner plate.

INSALATA DI FUNGHI
Mushroom Salad

> 1½ lb. of ovuli or porcini   1 lemon, squeezed
> mushrooms   pinch tarragon
> 6 Tbs. extra virgin olive oil   salt and pepper

Clean and slice the mushrooms very thinly. Add olive oil, lemon, tarragon, salt and pepper to taste and toss delicately so that the mushrooms do not crumble. Serve.

VARIATION 1: Add very thin shavings of *parmigiano reggiano* on top.

VARIATION 2: The addition of thinly sliced *parmigiano* and white truffle shaving.

INSALATA DI FRUTTI DI MARE
Seafood Salad

> ½ lb. each of: squid,   6 Tbs. olive oil
> cuttlefish, octopus,   2 oz. chopped parsley
> scallops, lobster, fish   3 garlic clove
> fillets   2 lemons squeezed
> 8 oz. mussels   pepper, salt
> ½ glass dry white wine

Clean, poach and dice all the fish. Steam the mussels in 2 Tbs. olive oil, 1 garlic clove and the white wine till open. Shell and mix with the rest of the fish and refrigerate. Prepare a *battuto* with parsley and garlic and set aside.

Prepare the dressing with 4 Tbs. olive oil and the juice of the lemon, add salt and pepper to taste and set aside. Mix the dressing with the fish and toss well, top with a generous sprinkling of the *battuto* and serve.

INSALATA DI POLIPETTI
Baby Octopus Salad

> 3 lbs. baby octopus   2 garlic cloves
> 1 cup olive oil   2 Tbs. fresh lemon juice
> ¼ cup chopped parsley

Clean the octopus well by turning them inside out and removing the eyes and the small bone at bottom of the head. Boil them in a small amount of salted water from 25-45 minutes, according to their size. Drain, peel, skin and cut the octopus in small pieces. Season with chopped garlic, olive oil, lemon juice, salt, pepper and all the parsley.

Let stand for a few hours before serving to allow the octopus to become tender by absorbing the condiments. This salad is also excellent served immediately, while still warm.

INSALATA DI NERVETTI
Calf's Foot and Veal Shank Salad

1 veal shank	3 oz. olive oil
1 calves foot	2 Tbs. vinegar
1 large onion	pinch pepper
1 carrot	pinch salt
1 celery stalk	1 Tbs. chopped parsley

Clean the veal shank and foot well, scraping and scorching them if necessary. Bring a large pot of salted water to a boil. Add the carrot and celery, half the onions, all chopped in pieces. Add the veal shank and foot, cook for about two hours or until the meat begins to pull away from the bone.

Drain, let cool, then cut the meat into long, thin equal strips.
Season with oil, vinegar, salt, pepper and the remaining onion finely sliced. Do not put the *nervetti* into the refrigerator or they will toughen. Keep them in a cool place. Top with chopped parsley and serve.

INSALATA DI RISO NOVARESE
Rice Salad

3 Tbs. long grain rice	4 anchovies, chopped
1 cup dry white wine	2 lemons
6 Tbs. olive oil	salt
1 truffle	1 cup dry white wine
1 clove garlic	1 Tbs. chopped parsley

Cook the rice for 8 minutes in a large pot of boiling salted water. Drain and place in an oiled baking dish. Cover with the wine.

Bake until rice is tender, about another 6 mins., then drizzle with a small quantity of oil. Spread the rice out on a tray, let cool, then put it onto a large platter.

Sauté the garlic in oil, remove when browned, add anchovies.
Cook until the mixture becomes well blended. Add the lemon juice and chopped parsley. Remove from heat and cool. When ready to serve pour the sauce on the rice, toss well, cover with a finely sliced layer of truffle and serve at room temperature.

INSALATA DI ARANCI
Orange Salad

6 tarocchi (blood oranges)	3 Tbs. olive oil
1 onion	pepper
parsley	salt

Peel the orange and cut the fruit into thin disks. Slice the onion very finely into rings and place over the oranges. Sprinkle with chopped parsley. Dress with olive oil, salt and pepper, then let rest for 10 minutes. This is served as a side dish for meat, especially boiled or particularly fatty ones.

SALADS WITH BREAD OR BISCUITS

The most appropriate bread for *antipasti* is usually a large simple loaf called "homemade *casereccio* style" which should be neither too fresh nor too stale (day-old bread is ideal). This is so that it will absorb the juices of whatever is put on it without breaking. Regional specialty breads are frequently used *biscottate*. (After the first baking the bread is sliced and baked again). The toasted through bread lasts a long time and is very flavorful.

Some specific dishes such as *Cappon Magro* are made using *gallette* (sea biscuits), which are made without yeast and shaped like a bagel. Generally, all breads used for *antipasto* are soaked briefly either with water, water and vinegar or just with their own dressing.

FRISEDDA ALLA PUGLIESE
Frisedda with Tomato Salad

3 frisedde	*pinch oregano*
3 ripe tomatoes	*3 Tbs. olive oil*
salt	

Soften the whole *frisedde* in water for 10 seconds, then squeeze dry making sure not to break them. Lay *frisedde* on a plate and spread with a salad prepared with the peeled, seeded, coarsely chopped tomatoes, oregano, salt, and extra virgin olive oil. No pepper is necessary with this preparation because the *frisedda* has pepper in it.

CONDIGGION
Sea-Biscuits with Smoked Fish Salad

4 gallette (sea-biscuits)	*3 bottarga, thinly sliced*
4 Tbs. olive oil	*2 cloves garlic*
8 oz. tomatoes, peeled and	*1 head leafy lettuce*
seeded, (not sliced)	*1 Tbs. vinegar*
6 oz. sweet peppers,	*few basil leaves*
cut in strips	*salt*
1 fresh cucumber, sliced	

Drizzle the sea-biscuits with water and vinegar.
NOTE: They should not soak through entirely, just get them wet to soften. They will therefore become soft and not soggy.
Remove the excess liquid and place into a salad bowl, sprinkle with a few drops of oil. Wash and cut up the vegetables, keeping them separate, and set aside. Chop the garlic and basil and set aside. Slice the *bottarga* or *musciame* into fine slices and set aside. Now place lettuce leaves on top of the *gallette,* season with oil, vinegar, the chopped basil and garlic, and salt. Add a layer of *musciame,* a layer

of tomatoes, a layer of cucumber and a layer of sweet peppers. Add oil and vinegar again. Repeat operation starting from lettuce seasoning each layer as you go along. The last layer should be the air dried fish. Cover the bowl and refrigerate for at least an hour before serving.

PANZANELLA OR PAN MOLLE
Bread and Vegetable Salad

8 slices of 1-2 day-old
Italian bread
1½ lbs. ripe tomatoes,
cut in cubes
1 large white onion,
thinly sliced
virgin olive oil

white vinegar
salt
pepper
handful of basil (cut into strips)
1 bell pepper

Soak the bread slices in water, making sure they are not soggy, and keep their shape. Squeeze out excess water and place in a large serving dish. Prepare a salad with the tomatoes, onion, oil, pepper, vinegar, salt and pepper. Toss and spread over the bread, drizzle with more olive oil, add a few basil leaves and keep cool until ready to serve. There are several variations to this, in each one the author declares that his is the original. Whatever the case may be, they all contain the same basic ingredients: bread, tomatoes, other vegetables and olive oil.

CAPPON MAGRO
Ligurian Seafood Caponata
This is the original recipe which is still applied today if one wants to prepare true *cappon magro*.

Step 1:
¾ lb. sea biscuits
1 clove garlic
2 Tbs. vinegar

pinch of salt
water

Brush the sea biscuits with salt, dip in water with vinegar and salt for a few seconds, pat-dry excess water. Set aside.

Step 2:
1 cauliflower
12 oz. string beans
4 celery stalks
2 carrots
1 bunch red beets

½ lb. potatoes
2 bunches bitter root
1 cup olive oil
2 Tbs. wine vinegar
6 artichokes

Cook separately all the vegetables whole, except the artichokes. when done, remove from fire and cool. Peel and slice the beets and potatoes; dice the rest of the vegetables. Slice and cook the artichokes. When done, remove from heat and cool.

Dress all the vegetables separately with oil, vinegar and salt. Set aside.

Step 3:

1 lb. lobster	*juice of 1 lemon*
1½ lbs. sea bass	*salt to taste*
14 oz. olive oil	

Poach, bone, and crumble the bass and dress with oil, lemon and salt. Do the same with the lobster and set aside.

Step 4:

24 medium sized shrimps	*2 oz. musciame of dolphin or*
8 eggs	*Tuna (or another air-dried fish*
12 anchovy fillets	*fillet that is not salty)*
8 oz. mushrooms sottolio	*24 large green olives*
24 oysters	*2 Tbs. capers*
	6 Tbs. olive oil

Poach the shrimps and set aside. Hard boil the eggs, cool and quarter.
Prepare 12 skewers interchanging each with 2 olives, 2 shrimps, 2 anchovy fillets. Set aside.

Slice the air dried fish very thinly, mix separately the capers and the mushrooms, open the oysters and take them out of the shell. Set all the ingredients separately aside.

Step 5 — The Sauce:

1 bunch parsley	*2 hard boiled egg yolks*
1 clove garlic	*3 slices crustless bread*
4 Tbs. pine nuts	*6 large black olives, pitted*
1 oz. capers	*1 cup olive oil*
4 anchovy fillets	*6 Tbs. wine vinegar*

Place all the ingredients into a food mill, mix well and achieve a fluid consistency. Set aside.

Step 6 — The Preparation and Presentation:
Take a large round or oval platter and start with the sea biscuits, layered flat on the platter. Sprinkle with olive oil, add a few thin slices of *musciame* and dress with a 2-3 Tbs. of the sauce.

Next, with some of each ingredient, continue with layers of each of the vegetables and continue with layers of some of each of the fish, capers and mushrooms. On each layer add some sauce, continue until all ingredients are used. As you build up, the final shape should be like a *cupola* or pyramid.

Top the whole with sauce and decorate with the skewers previously prepared. Circle the base of the mold with oysters topped with green sauce. Serve.

LEGUMES

FAGIOLI
Beans
Beans were imported to Europe (from Central America) in the 16th century by the Spaniards and the Portuguese. In archeological research, beans have been found to be used as early as 4000-5000 B.C. In Italy, beans were introduced through Spain, and today they are grown in almost every region, particularly in Campania, Veneto, Lazio, Lombardia and Piemonte. The experience and development of industrial techniques have allowed for the creation of different types of beans. The most common bean in Italy is *borlotto,* oval in shape with white stripes or color that varies from white to red, coffee, gray and dark blue, which then become a uniform dark brown as it goes through the cooking process.

Another type of bean is *bianco di spagna,* a much larger bean. It can be as long as 1 to $1\frac{1}{2}$" and the same size in width. The bean is white or off-white in color. Finally, the most well known beans are *cannellini* or *toscanelli,* which are white or cream-colored and rather small in size. They are grown almost everywhere, particularly in Toscana.

Beans can be bought in season either fresh or dried all year round. The number of varieties tends to increase continuously because beans are particularly suitable for genetic combinations. Nearly every region in Italy has its preferred variety of beans.

To use dried beans, soak in cold water overnight. To cook fresh beans, start them in boiling water, contrary to dried beans which are started in cold water. In both cases, bring to a boil, then cook over a very low heat for approximately $1\frac{1}{2}$ hours for dry beans and 30 minutes for fresh. The ratio of water to beans is four to six to one by volume.

CECI
Chick peas
These are round, slightly dented, beige seeds. They are only sold dried and are cooked in the same way as are dried beans. Before cooking, make sure there are no stones mixed in with the chick peas. *Ceci* can be used for soup, either whole or mashed as a side dish for pork, or simply boiled and seasoned with oil. Their flavor is enhanced by the addition of rosemary, bay leaf and garlic.

FAVE FRESCHE
Fresh Broad Fava Beans
Fava beans are a springtime legume. It is preferable to choose the medium-seized pods, since they have a small seed with a more delicate flavor. If the seeds are too big, you might want to peel them to make them more digestible. If the seeds are too small, you can serve

them raw with salt, with fresh *pecorino* cheese or *salami* as *antipasti*.

If *fava* beans are boiled, it is desirable to season them with summer savory leaves, (the typical herb used with broad beans). *Fava* beans may also be stewed and cooked with *prosciutto*. All recipes used for green beans can also be employed to cook *fava* beans.

FAVE SECCHE
Dried Broad Fava Beans

Before being cooked, these should soak for a day or two. The skin can be removed to make them easier to digest or they can be purchased without the skin. Make sure that there are no small holes (caused by larva) in the *fave*. Throw away any beans with these marks. Dried *fave* are cooked in the same way as other dried beans and are used for soups and side dishes, as well as in a purée.

LENTICCHIE
Lentils

Dried lentils are usually served in winter. They are sold in several different qualities. It is important to buy lentils that have been dried only a few months in advance, since older ones are more susceptible to insects. Soak lentils in water for several hours before cooking. They are usually stewed and served with cuts of pork (i.e. *zampone* or *cotechino*). The best quality lentils come from Castelluccio (Umbria), where they are very tiny in size. Lentils are cooked the same way as dry beans.

PISELLI FRESCHI
Fresh Peas

These are green springtime legumes, which have a green pod containing small round seeds. Depending on their size, fresh peas are sold as "extra fine", "fine", or «medium» peas. The seeds may be green or white. There are two principal varieties of peas: "real" peas, those which must be removed from the pod, which can be eaten fresh or dried, and those consumed whole (see *taccole*), pod included, which must be eaten fresh. Tender, fresh peas are very sweet and can be cooked in a sauce, boiled, or added to soups. They make a very delicate side dish for white and red meats. Peas should not be shelled until just before cooking or they will become tough.

PISELLI SECCHI
Dried Peas

Two kinds of dried peas are sold in Italy: whole peas with the skin intact ("new peas"), and split peas which are dried when the pea is fully ripe and, the skin removed. These can be used in the same manner as dried beans but they cook much more quickly.

SNOW PEAS

This is a variety of pea eaten with the pod after cutting off the two ends. They should be cooked in boiling salted water, then sautéed in butter and served as a side dish with *parmigiano* cheese. They can also be used in soups or sauces.

RICETTE
Recipes

CANNELLINI ALL'UCCELLETTO
Stewed Fresh Beans

4 lb. fresh white beans	1 lb. tomatoes, peeled, seeded
2 garlic cloves	and diced
4 oz. olive oil	salt, pepper
few sage leaves	peppercorns

Shell the beans, wash and boil in salted water. Drain. In a saucepan brown the garlic in the oil together with sage and a pinch of pepper. Add the beans, and mix until well coated. Add the tomatoes, cover and let simmer for about 20 minutes. Season with salt and pepper.

CANNELLINI AL FIASCO
Cannellini Beans Cooked in Flask

⅔ lb. cannellini beans (dried)	pinch of fresh rosemary
2 garlic cloves	8 oz. oil
2 sage leaves	salt, pepper

Soak the beans in cold water overnight. Drain and place them in a flask-like container of flame-proof terra-cotta, together with garlic, sage, rosemary, oil and 2 cups of water.

Place the flask over the flame and let cook gently for 3 hours so that the water will evaporate and the beans absorb the oil.

Place them in a tureen, add some more oil, pepper and salt.

NOTE: The cooking can be in a glass flask in bainmarie.

FAGIOLI CON LE COTICHE
Borlotti beans with pigskins

1 lb. fresh pigskin	2 small onions
1 cup borlotti beans, soaked	2 small carrots
overnight	2 cloves garlic
1 Tbs. lard, chopped	pinch pepper
1 Tbs. butter	1 cup beef broth
2 Tbs. olive oil	¼ cup peeled tomatoes
2 celery stalks	

In a large pot, place the pigskins, one onion (cut in large pieces), and the garlic cloves. Cover with cold water, bring to a low simmer, and cook for 2 hours or till the pigskins are tender. Boil the beans starting with lightly salted cold water for 1 hour or till tender. In a casserole over medium heat, prepare a *soffritto* with lard, butter, oil and the onion, celery and carrots finely chopped. Add a pinch of freshly ground pepper. Let cook till tender but not brown, add the strained beans and pigskins cut into 2" long strips. Add the peeled tomatoes and broth and cook for a half hour. Serve very hot.

FAGIOLI ALLA VENETA
Beans and Salted Anchovies

1 lb. fresh shelled	1 cup white wine vinegar
Borlotti beans	1 Tbs. chopped parsley
2 garlic cloves	salt
2 Tbs. olive oil	pepper
10 anchovy fillets	

Boil the beans with very little salt for 45 minutes or till tender. Sauté the crushed garlic in oil and remove when golden brown. Add the chopped anchovies till they combine with the oil. Add the vinegar and pepper and let reduce at a low simmer for 10 minutes. Add the chopped parsley, mix well and pour this sauce over the strained beans. Serve.
NOTE: Dry beans may be used instead of fresh beans.

FAVE STUFATE
Braised Fava Beans

2 lb. fresh fava beans	1 cup beef broth
2 Tbs. prosciutto fat	6 slices stale bread
2 new onions, finely sliced	2 Tbs. butter
1 oz. mortadella	salt and pepper to taste

Shell the fava beans and set aside. In a casserole place the chopped *prosciutto* fat and the onions and sauté till tender but not brown. Add the *fava* beans, chopped *mortadella* and the beef broth. Salt and pepper to taste. Cover the *casserole* and cook over low flame for 45 minutes, adding more broth if necessary. The final dish should be fairly moist.

Sauté the slices of bread in butter, browning on both sides. Place them on a serving platter and pour over the *fava* beans. Serve very hot.

FAVE FRESCHE CON PANCETTA
Fresh Fava Beans With Pancetta

4 lbs. fresh fava beans	1 Tbs. oil
¼ lb. pancetta, diced	1 cup beef broth

1 onion, thinly sliced   salt, pepper
1 celery stalk, sliced   2 Tbs. chopped parsley

Shell the *fava* beans (remove the skin if they are very big). Sauté the *pancetta,* the onion and the celery in a saucepan with the oil, stirring frequently. When the fat of the *pancetta* has melted, add the *fava* beans, moisten with hot broth and continue to cook. When the *fava* beans are completely done (about 20 mins.), salt, pepper and sprinkle with chopped parsley. (Fresh peas can be prepared the same way.)

LENTICCHIE IN UMIDO
Braised lentils

1 lb. lentils   few sage leaves
2 oz. pancetta, chopped   salt
1 small onion, thinly sliced   pepper

Soak the lentils in lukewarm water overnight. In a casserole sauté the thinly sliced onion with the chopped *pancetta* and sage leaves and cook till tender but not brown. Add the strained lentils and cover with lukewarm water. Salt and pepper to taste and cook one hour over medium heat, or till the lentils have absorbed all the water. Lentils prepared this way are served as a side dish to *cotechino* and *zampone.*

PANIZZA
Chick-pea Pie

9 oz. chick-pea flour   scallions
4 Tbs. olive oil   salt
4 cups water   pepper

Pass chick-pea flour through a fine sieve.
Pour flour slowly in warm water and stir and cook slowly for about 1 hour, stirring frequently. The mixture will detach from the pot when ready. Season with salt and pepper. Pour in serving dishes, sprinkle with oil, chopped scallion, salt and pepper and serve hot.
VARIATION: Cook the *panizza* to a thick consistency; pour on to a pastry board, to about 1/2" thick, and let cool. When the *panizza* becomes very firm, cut into strips and fry in hot oil. Salt and serve.

PISELLI ALL'UOVO
Peas With Eggdrops

2 lb. fresh peas   1 onion
2 oz. pancetta   2 Tbs. grated pecorino cheese
2 Tbs. olive oil   3 eggs
4 Tbs. white bread crumbs   salt and pepper

Chop the *pancetta* and sauté with olive oil and the onion thinly sliced. When tender but not brown, add the peas, 1 cup water and cook for 30 minutes over medium heat. On the side, prepare a mixture with the eggs, bread crumbs and *pecorino* cheese. Pour this mixture over the peas just before removing from flame, toss gently to allow for the eggs to tighten slightly and serve.

FUNGHI E TARTUFI
Mushrooms and Truffles

Mushrooms and truffles belong to the same vegetable family (*funghi*); the main difference is that mushrooms grow on the surface, receiving their nourishment from the earth, whereas truffles grow underground, feeding themselves through the roots of trees.

Mushrooms are unanimously considered a gastronomical treat. Whether they are added to *fettuccine* or *risotti,* broiled or sautéed or simply eaten as a salad, mushrooms have a definite role in cooking.

Although it is true, they have very little to offer from a nutritious aspect. They are 80-90% water, the rest is mineral salts, potassium and iron. Therefore, we do not eat mushrooms for sustenance, but to please our palate.

Although some types of mushrooms are good eaten alone, such as *porcino* and *ovulo,* others are better when added to food preparations, such as *chiodino* and *gallinacci.* Finally, others are better when prepared and conserved — *sottolio* or *sottaceto,* pleurotus or hothouse.

There are many varieties of edible mushrooms in Italy which are concentrated in only a few regions.

We will not attempt here to teach how to distinguish poisonous mushrooms from edible ones. It is better to buy a good guide which can teach you how to differentiate them. The best education, however, is to go mushroom hunting with an experienced, qualified person. Buying wild mushrooms from a green-grocer is perhaps the safest way to purchase them. Beware of amateur mycologists or friends who claim to know a great deal about mushrooms.

FUNGHI
Mushrooms

PORCINI
Boletus Brisa

This well-known variety grows mainly in the Appenino Emiliano around Parma, in Valtellina, in the Appennino Toscano (particularly

PORCINI

the Garfagnana), Piemonte hills, Sila and Pollina in Calabria, but they can also be found in other mountain areas. There are several different types and qualities of *porcini* mushrooms. The best are the porcini picked in chestnut woods. They have a light-colored hat and a butter-white underhat. *Porcini* with dark hats are from the beech or fir tree and are more suitable to be preserved, but are less tasty. As the mushroom gets older, its underhat turns ocher or green. The hat must be big, round, fleshy and must be supported by a short round stalk.

Porcini can be eaten as a salad or can be braised, cooked in a sauce, grilled, sautéed or baked. They are also preserved in oil or dried for winter or commercial consumption.

OVOLO BUONO
Amanita Caesarea

This is considered by the experts to be the best of all edible mushrooms. When they are still young, they are closed, look like an egg and are completely white. As they bud (open up), the hat becomes a bright orange-yellow. Ovoli may be eaten as a salad, seasoned with virgin olive oil, lemon juice, salt and pepper. Once mature, they can be fried (with or without batter), grilled, sautéed or braised.

OVOLO

GALLINACCI
Cantharellus Cibarius

These are yellow mushrooms whose fragrance recalls the odor of a peach. The old ones must be dispensed with because their flesh is too fibrous and tough. They are cooked in sauces or preserved in oil. They are also known as *finferli*.

CHIODINI
Armillaria Mellea

These are tiny, dark mushrooms, with small heads and long thin stems. It is a mushroom easily found and grown in large spreads. They can be cooked like *porcini* mushrooms and, in addition, they can be preserved in oil. It is preferable to dispense with the lower half of the stem, which tends to taste woody.

CHIODINI   **RUSSOLA**   **FINFERLI**

PRATAIOLO
Psalliota Arvensis

This mushroom is white and meaty with a pleasant aroma. They are excellent in the kitchen for many preparations. They are found in open fields and are light-pinkish in color. *Prataiolo* is the classic mushroom used to prepare *trifolato*.

CEPPATELLI
Pleurotus Ostreatus

These mushrooms grow at the base of trees (rather than on the ground); that is why they are sometimes called *ceppatelli* (literally "little stumps"). They are light grey in color, have a large top and a very short stem. They are either breaded or simply fried.

FUNGHI COLTIVATI
Hothouse Mushrooms

These mushrooms do not grow spontaneously, but are the hothouse-grown version of several varieties of mushrooms (e.g. *prataioli, ceppatelli, pleurotus,* and others). They can be eaten raw, cut in thin slices and seasoned with oil, lemon juice, salt and pepper. All of them may be cooked in various sauces.

TAGLIATARTUFI

TARTUFI
Truffles

Italy is plentiful in truffles. The two most prized varieties are the white truffles from Alba (Piemonte) and Aqualagna (Marche) and the black ones from Norcia (Umbria). The white truffles are in season from October to December and have more flavor and a much more pronounced fragrance than the black ones. To find truffles, trained dogs or pigs are used to sniff out the prized tuber; it is then snatched away before the animal can devour it. White truffles are almost always eaten raw; when cut in very fine slices, they can be either used to top preparations that have already been cooked, such as *fettuccine, risotti, scaloppine,* and *fondute,* or simply seasoned with olive oil, salt and pepper. Truffles should be consumed within a week of picking and are best kept wrapped in paper towels or in a closed jar with raw rice, which should afterwards be used to make *risotto.*

White Truffles

The most prized white truffle of Alba (Piemonte) ripens from October to December. Its main characteristics are deep aroma and flavor. Its yellow/green skin is smooth, and its inside, whose color can vary from brown to hazel, is hard. It is also furrowed by thin white veins.

Quite popular now are also the white truffles from Acqualagna, a small town near Urbino (Marche), whose woods generate a large number of white truffles, very comparable to those from Alba.

Black truffles from Norcia have a delicate aroma and taste. They ripen from November to mid-March. The skin is black, thinly wrinkled, and the color of the pulp is a purplish-black. Black truffles are generally cooked and seldom eaten raw.

RICETTE
Recipes

OVOLI FRITTI
Golden Fried Ovoli

1 lb. ovoli	*lemon*
flour	*salt*
2-3 eggs	*pepper*
oil, for frying	

Clean, wash, dry the mushrooms and cut into quarters. Coat them with flour, dip in beaten eggs and fry in hot oil. When done, salt, pepper and serve very hot, garnished with lemon wedges.

PORCINI BRASATI
Braised Porcini

1 lb. porcini mushrooms	*⅓ lb. tomatoes, peeled, seeded*
4 Tbs. virgin olive oil	*and chopped*
2 garlic cloves, chopped	*1 Tbs. chopped parsley*
salt, pepper	

Slice the mushrooms (or cut into quarters if they are very small). In a saucepan brown the garlic with olive oil and remove when brown. Add the tomatoes, sauté for 5 mins., and add the mushrooms. Cook mushrooms till tender but still crisp. Salt, pepper, to taste and add the chopped parsley. Toss and serve.

CAPPELI DI FUNGHI CON ANIMELLE
Mushrooms with Sweetbreads

8 medium porcini	
mushrooms	*salt*
2 Tbs. chopped parsley	*pepper*
1 garlic clove	*4 slices white bread*
3 Tbs. virgin olive oil	*1 Tbs. parmigiano*
1 small onion	*1 egg*
1 salted anchovy	*breadcrumbs*
⅓ lb. sweetbreads, poached	

Clean the mushrooms, remove the stems and cut into very thin slices. Chop the parsley and the garlic. In a saucepan with 3 Tbs. oil, sauté the onions and the anchovy, add the mushrooms stems, the sweetbreads (or the calf's) thinly sliced. Salt, pepper and let cook for about 10 minutes, stirring frequently. When done, chop finely and place in a bowl. Remove the crust and add the white of the bread, softened in warm water, the cheese, egg, parsley and the garlic, and mix well.

Salt and pepper to taste, adding some breadcrumbs if the mixture is too soft. Fill each mushroom cap with the prepared mixture, level off the tops with a spatula, place them in a baking dish, sprinkle with breadcrumbs and a small amount of oil, and cook in preheated oven for 20 minutes at 400 F. Serve very hot.

FUNGHI ALLA GRIGLIA
Grilled Mushrooms

12 mushroom hats, ovoli or porcini are best, but
any type of meaty mushroom may be used
1 Tbs. chopped parsley
2 cloves garlic
3 Tbs. olive oil

Clean the mushrooms, reserve the stems for other use. Prepare a *battuto* with the parsley and the garlic and mix with 1½ Tbs. olive oil. Make a cross-like incision in the inside of the mushroom hat, place over the *battuto,* drizzle with the olive oil and grill with the inside up. Grill for about 5 minutes till tender but still crisp. Remove from grill, add the rest of the oil, salt and pepper to taste. Serve very hot.
VARIATION: The mushrooms may be grilled and the seasoning added afterwards.

FUNGHI TRIFOLATI
Sautéed Mushrooms

2 lbs. mushrooms
4 Tbs. olive oil   *2 Tbs. butter*
3 garlic cloves   *1½ Tbs. parsley, chopped*
1½ Tbs. mint   *Salt and pepper to taste*
(or nepitella)

Clean the mushrooms, slice the hat and chop the stem. Warm up the oil and butter and add the garlic. Remove garlic when brown. Add mushrooms and sauté briskly over a lively flame for 4 minutes. Make sure they are tender but still crisp. Add chopped mint and parsley, cook 1 more minute, add salt and pepper to taste. Serve over a slice of toast or by themselves.

Funghi trifolati are also served as a vegetable with a roast, meat, fowl, or venison.

TARTUFI WITH PARMIGIANO
Truffles With Parmigiano Cheese

1 oz. white truffles   *4 Tbs. fresh butter*

4 oz. thinly sliced parmigiano
salt and pepper to taste

Butter a small baking dish and shave the truffles into it in a layer. Cover with thin shavings of *parmigiano,* moisten with melted butter, and add salt and pepper. Repeat the operation two more times, using up the remaining truffles. Sprinkle with butter, cover and bake for 5 minutes at 375 F. Serve hot with lemon juice.

UOVA AL TARTUFO BIANCO
Eggs with White Truffles

1 Tbs. heavy cream	*8 fresh eggs*
4 Tbs. butter	*pinch salt*
1 Tbs. parmigiano	*4 small cocottes*
1½ oz. white truffles.	

Over a low flame, warm the cream, add 4 Tbs. butter. When melted add *parmigiano* and stir continuously — do not allow to reach a boil. Butter four 6-oz. baking dishes *(cocotte)* and divide the sauce evenly into each dish. Add 2 whole eggs and bake at 450° F. in a preheated bain-marie for 7 minutes. Remove from the bain-marie, add a thinly shaved white truffle, and serve immediately with toasted bread. If you have the bain-marie on top of the stove, cover the *cocotte* with tin-foil.

The cooking time may vary according to the size and thickness of the baking dish *(cocotte)* being used.

MINESTRE-MINESTRONE-ZUPPE
Soups

Italian cookery is very rich in soups of all kinds, because of the rich variety of our vegetables and the general use of leftovers from bread, starches, fish and shellfish. Unfortunately, people seem to shy away from anything that has to be eaten with a spoon, missing the flavors, the richness, the vitality and the fantasy employed to make and to eat a good soup.

MINESTRA

The term *minestra* refers to soups containing a liquid, either broth or simply water, always with the addition of a starch, a vegetable, or a legume.

Any type of pasta can be used for soups. In clear soups, usually small-sized fresh or dry pasta, dumplings or various other types of foods such as bread, eggs, or a combination of both may be used. Most leafy vegetables are suitable for clear soups.

RICETTE PER MINESTRE
Recipes for Soup

BRODO
Broth

Broth is a fundamental element to prepare a good soup. The following is the basic recipe:

1 lb. brisket of beef	1 onion
1 lb. shoulder	1 tomato
1 veal shank	$\frac{1}{4}$ bunch parsley
celery	$\frac{1}{2}$ Tbs. whole black pepper
carrots	2 garlic cloves
salt to taste	

Use 2 qts. of water for each pound of meat. Place the meat into the cold water with the salt and bring slowly to a boil. Add all the vegetables (diced or chopped) and the spices and cook for 3 hours at a slow simmer, skimming the fat that surfaces occasionally. When ready, remove the meats (these may have several uses), cool the broth so it becomes easier to skim off all the fat, and pass through a cheesecloth to further remove excess fat and other particles.

To make a chicken broth, the same recipe is used, replacing the meats with chicken. In this case, make sure to use an older bird because it will give more taste to the broth, a fowl would be the preferable choice. To clarify the broth with egg white, separate the yolks from the white and mix the white with a cup of the cooled broth and add to the pot with the broth. Bring to a boil, whisking continuously. The residue will float to the surface which you will remove after the broth has rested for 20 minutes. At this point, the broth should be very clear. Broth may be used for most soups or as a moistening agent for numerous preparations.

PASSATELLI IN BRODO
Bread and Egg Mix in Broth

3 eggs	*3 Tbs. finely grated bread crumbs*
salt	*6 Tbs. grated parmigiano cheese*
nutmeg	*1¼ qts. lean beef broth, seasoned*

Prepare a soft mixture with the eggs, a pinch of salt and a pinch of nutmeg, then, little by a little, add the bread crumbs and 3 Tbs. *parmigiano*. Bring the broth to a simmer. Place the bread mix into a potato ricer and, as the broth simmers, rice the mixture into the broth. Cook for 3 minutes and serve adding the remaining *parmigiano*.
NOTE: Use the larger holes when passing the mixture through the ricer.

STRACCIATELLA ALLA ROMANA
Egg Drop Soup

2 qts. beef broth, seasoned	*½ cup grated parmigiano*
4 eggs	*Salt and pepper to taste*

Beat the eggs with 2 Tbs. *parmigiano,* and salt and pepper. Bring the broth to a slow simmer, drop the egg and *parmigiano* mixture into the broth while whisking vigorously so that the egg becomes solid drops. Add the remainder of the *parmigiano,* mix well and serve immediately.

CICORIA, CACIO E UOVA
Chicory, Pecorino, and Egg Soup

1 lb. green chicory	*3 eggs*
2 onions	*1 qt. broth*
¼ cup olive oil	*4 Tbs. grated pecorino cheese*

Green chicory has a fairly bitter taste, therefore wash it and let it stay in cool water for one hour. It will then lose some of its bitterness. Boil the chicory, chop and squeeze all the water out and set aside. Cut the onions in julienne and sauté with olive oil. When tender, not brown, add the chicory and mix well. Add the beaten eggs which have been previously mixed with the *pecorino* cheese, sauté briskly and place into a pre-heated, large soup tureen, pour the piping hot broth over, stir well and serve.

MINESTRA CON FIORI DI ZUCCA
Soup with Zucchini Flowers

1 lb. zucchini flowers
¼ cup olive oil
1 small onion, diced pepper
1 garlic clove, minced

1 small celery stalk, diced
salt
1 qt. chicken broth

Wash the zucchini flowers and set aside (if they are too large, cut them up). Sauté onion, garlic, and celery with the oil and continue to cook until nearly tender. Add broth, already hot, then add the zucchini flowers. Continue cooking at a simmer for 30 mins. Add salt and pepper to taste and serve.

MINESTRA DI RISO CON ASPARAGI
Soup of Rice with Asparagus

1 lb. fresh, green and thin asparagus
2 qts. lean beef broth
3 oz. short or medium-grain rice, rinsed
2 Tbs. fresh butter
3 Tbs. grated parmigiano
salt

Clean and wash the asparagus ends, starting from the tip, breaking them into pieces about 1" long (do not use a knife). When you reach the point at which it is not possible to break the asparagus any further, discard whatever is left.

Bring the broth to a boil and then add the rinsed rice. Cook with the pot covered for 12 mins. When the rice is almost ready*, add the asparagus. Cook for 3 minutes. more, leaving pot uncovered. Remove from heat, mix in the butter and *parmigiano* and serve.

*NOTE: When cooking rice, just like pasta, it should be tasted for doneness. The cooking time depends on the quality, the water and the altitude.

LA MARICONDA
Soup with Bread Dumplings

7 cup bread crumbs
(2-3 day-old-bread
at the most)
1 cup milk
4 Tbs. butter
6 Tbs. grated parmigiano

pinch nutmeg
2 eggs
salt and pepper to taste
2 qts. beef broth

Moisten the bread crumbs with 1 cup warm milk in a bowl and then let stand for about 20 minutes. Squeeze out excess milk. Melt the butter in a small saucepan, add the bread crumbs, stir constantly with a wooden spoon and cook until the bread crumbs are entirely dry. Put the bread crumbs in a bowl to cool, then add 3 Tbs. *parmigiano,* a pinch of nutmeg, 2 eggs, and salt and pepper to taste. Mix the ingredients. Should the mixture be too soft to make dumplings, add some more bread crumbs and let it sit in a cool place for about an hour. Shortly before serving, divide the bread crumb mixture into small dumplings (each about the size of a nutmeg) and coat lightly with flour. Bring the broth to a boil, gently add the dumplings, lower the flame and, stirring carefully, let cook 5 mins. over a low flame. Serve with the remaining *parmigiano.* Variation: White meat from a boiled chicken or cooked ham (both finely minced) may also be added to the bread crumb mixture for the dumplings.

PASTA E FAGIOLI
Pasta and beans

1 lb. shelled, fresh	*2 Tbs. chopped parsley*
Borlotti beans	*1 ripe tomato, quartered*
3 Tbs. olive oil	*⅓ lb. mixed dry pasta*
1 small onion	*(maccheroncini, rigati,*
salt, white pepper	*or maltagliati)*
1 clove garlic	*2 Tbs. lard*
	5 Tbs. grated parmigiano

Put 2 qts. water in a pot — use very little salt since, as the water evaporates, the salt will intensify. Add the beans and let cook (with pot covered) at a simmer till ready. Finely chop the lard, onion, garlic, parsley and tomato. Sauté it in the oil over medium heat until the lard has melted and the vegetables begin to get tender. Set aside. When the beans are cooked, add the soffritto, bring to a boil and add the pasta, stir and let it cook until the pasta is *al dente* (about 8 mins.). Add more hot water or broth if you feel it is getting too dense. When the soup is ready, add a pinch of freshly ground pepper and 2 Tbs. *parmigiano.* Serve with the remaining *parmigiano.*

Variation 1: Before adding the pasta, pass about half the beans through a food mill and return resulting purée to the broth. (See other variations).

Variations 2: The *soffritto* may be eliminated. When cooking the beans add crushed garlic clove, onion, tomato, parsley and the fat (olive oil) when the beans are almost cooked.

NOTE 1: Other types of beans may be used, i.e., *cannellini,* navy beans, etc.

NOTE 2: When using dry beans they must always be soaked overnight.

NOTE 3: Practically every region of Italy has its own version of *Pasta e Fagioli.*

FAGIOLI CON CAVOLO NERO ALLA TOSCANA
Beans with Black Cabbage, Tuscan style

⅔ lb. dry cannellini beans	*2½ oz. pancetta*

⅔ lb. black Tuscan cabbage
⅔ lb. carrots
1 large onion
2 leeks
2 celery stalks
handful of basil leaves

⅔ lb. ripe tomatoes
pinch of thyme
black pepper
salt
½ cup extra virgin olive oil
1 oz. parsley

Soak the beans in a generous quantity of water overnight. The following morning, drain, put them in a pot with 2 qts. of lightly salted cold water, and let cook for 1½ hours. Clean, wash and slice the cabbage, carrots, onion and the leeks. Make a *battuto* with celery, basil and parsley. Thinly slice the *pancetta*. Put a pot on the stove with the oil, adding everything you have cut and minced (except the cabbage). Sauté over a low flame until the vegetables begin to get tender. Then add the cabbage and continue to cook over a low flame so that the vegetables can stew well. Add the tomatoes (peeled and chopped), a pinch of thyme and a pinch of pepper, and continue to cook over a low heat, stirring frequently.

Pass about half the beans in a food sieve and add the resulting purée to the vegetables. Add this to the beans and their broth, stir well and let cook for one more hour. Offer extra virgin olive oil on the side.
NOTE: Black cabbage may be replaced with Savoy cabbage. Always add more broth if soup gets too thick.

PASTA E PATATE
Potatoes with Short Pasta

1 lb. potatoes
¼ cup olive oil
1 onion cut in julienne
4 ripe tomatoes

salt and pepper
6 oz. short pasta
4 Tbs. grated parmigiano

Peel and dice the potatoes and simmer in 2 qts. of water until they are done.

Prepare a *soffritto* with olive oil, onion and the chopped tomatoes. When the vegetables are tender, not brown, add to the potatoes. Salt and pepper to taste, bring to a boil, add the pasta and cook till pasta is *al dente*. Remove from fire, add 2 Tbs. *parmigiano,* let it rest for a few minutes and serve with the remaining *parmigiano.*
NOTE: Always add more water or broth if soups get too dense while cooking.

PASTA E LENTICCHIE
Lentils with Pasta

10 oz. lentils
2 garlic cloves
1 celery stalk
salt and pepper to taste

1 ripe tomato, coarsely chopped
5 oz. spaghetti
1/2 cup olive oil

Check the lentils for dirt particles. Soak the lentils for at least 12 hours, discard all those that float. Cook the lentils starting with 2 qts. cold water, add crushed garlic cloves, the tomato, the chopped celery stalk and let cook slowly until lentils are ready. Add salt and pepper and broken up spaghetti (about 1"-1½" long) and cook till *al dente.* Remove from fire, add olive oil, mix well season and serve.

OPTION: Start cooking the lentils by themselves and halfway through the cooking, discard the original water and replace with piping hot water or light broth. Then add the garlic, celery and tomato. This operation must be done quickly so as not to interrupt the cooking process.

GRAN FARRO E FAGIOLI
Spelt* with Kidney Beans

1 lb. 6 oz. fresh kidney beans	*3-4 sage leaves*
3 Tbs. olive oil	*1 Tbs. marjoram*
½ onion, sliced thinly	*½ tsp. nutmeg*
4 oz. prosciutto, finely	*8 oz. tomatoes, peeled*
chopped	*seeded and finely sieved*
1 celery stalk, chopped	*salt and pepper to taste*
1 clove garlic, chopped	*5 oz. raw spelt or raw*
	hard wheat

Boil the fresh beans in water until tender (approx. 1 to 1½ hours). Drain and put through a food processor reserving the water and about ¼ of the whole beans. Heat the olive oil in a large saucepan and add the onion, *prosciutto,* celery, garlic, sage, marjoram and nutmeg.

Sauté gently and when the onion starts to brown add the tomatoes, salt and pepper. Simmer for about 15 minutes, until the mixture is well blended. Add the bean purée with a little of its own water. Mix well before adding the wheat. Simmer for about 40 minutes., adding more bean water as the soup thickens. Add the whole beans and allow to simmer for 10 more minutes.

Serve with extra virgin olive oil drizzled on top.

NOTE: If fresh beans are not available, you may use dry beans. Soak the beans overnight, rinse in fresh water and boil for 45 minutes.

* Spelt: See *FARRO* in Glossary.

MINESTRONE
Vegetable Soups

These are soups made with at least three or four kinds of vegetables. Their preparation may also include dry or fresh pasta, rice, legumes, or dumplings.

Grated *parmigiano* is always used to season *minestrone* that contains a starch. In some Italian regions pecorino (an aged sheep's milk cheese) is substituted for *parmigiano*. Grated cheese is never added to *minestrone* that contains only vegetables. Minestrone may be served at room temperature — especially in summer — but never just out of the refrigerator.

RICETTE PER MINESTRONE
Recipes for Vegetable Soups

MINESTRONE MILANESE
Minestrone with Rice and Vegetables

⅓ lb. pork skin (cotenne)	3 oz. pancetta, cut in little
1 lb. fresh peas (shelled)	strips
2 firm zucchini, diced	salt
2 celery stalks, diced	1 lb. shelled, fresh beans
2 carrots, diced	(Borlotti)
8 oz. ripe tomatoes	3 potatoes, diced
6 Tbs. lard	½ lb. Savoy cabbage, sliced
6 Tbs. parsley	⅓ lb. rice, short or
6 sage leaves	medium grain
2 garlic cloves	4 Tbs. parmigiano
1 large onion, sliced	

Scrape the pork skin with a knife to clean the surface and remove any bristle that might still be attached to it. Blanch the pork skin and let cool. Cut into strips and set aside. Rinse and dice all the vegetables (*zucchini,* celery, carrots). Peel, seed and dice the tomatoes, then let cool. Finely chop the lard, parsley, sage, garlic and onion. Sauté the *pancetta* over medium heat together with the lard and herbs, stir until the lard melts and the onions get soft, but not brown. Combine all the vegetables, except the beans, potatoes and cabbage, together with 3 qts. of hot water and a little salt. Cover the pot and let cook. When the water boils, add the beans and the pork skin strips, cook at low temperature for 1½ hours, then add the potatoes and the cabbage cut in julienne. When the beans are cooked, add the rice. Continue to cook on a medium flame, stirring frequently so that the *minestrone* — which has thickened by now — does not stick to the bottom of pot, when the rice is cooked (approx. 12 minutes.) Remove from fire and mix in the grated *parmigiano*. If *minestrone* gets too thick, add some broth. Let the *minestrone* rest for 15 minutes and serve. It may be served either hot or at room temperature.

NOTE 1: If using dry beans, remember to soak them for a few hours.
NOTE 2: Rice may be substituted with a short pasta.

MINESTRONE
Vegetable, Beans and Pasta

1 lb. cannellini or Borlotti	2 small tomatoes
beans	2 Tbs. olive oil

2 lbs. vegetables (zucchini,   4 Tbs. lard
spinach, leeks, turnip, chards,   2 oz. pancetta cut in julienne
curly chicory, escarole,   8 oz. tubettini (short pasta)
carrot, celery, Savoy cabbage)   1 Tbs. chopped parsley
2 potatoes   1 Tbs. chopped basil
2 onions   4 Tbs. grated parmigiano
1 garlic clove

Soak the beans overnight in 3 qts. of water and cook for about 1½ hours. Keep warm. Wash and chop all the vegetables, peel and dice the potatoes. Chop the onion, garlic and tomatoes in a large pot and make a *soffritto* with the oil, lard and *pancetta*. Add the onions, garlic and tomatoes. When tender, not brown, add the rest of the vegetables, potatoes, and beans with its water. Cook till all the vegetables are soft adding more water or broth if the soup gets too thick.

Next, add the pasta cooked for 7-10 minutes according to type of pasta used. Remove from fire, add chopped parsley and basil and let rest for 10 mins. Serve with grated *parmigiano* on the side.

NOTE: Add 3 Tbs. of pesto just before serving for *minestrone Genovese*.

MINESTRONE DI VERDURE
Minestrone of Vegetables

1½ lbs. fresh fava beans   handful of basil leaves
1½ lbs. fresh, unshelled   2 Tbs. minced parsley
green peas   1 head of lettuce
⅔ lb. ripe tomatoes   1½ qts. olive oil
⅔ lb. white or golden onions   1 qt. beef broth
1½ lbs. zucchini   salt, pepper

Shell the *fava* beans and the green peas (keep them separate). Peel, seed and chop the tomatoes. Slice the onions. Wash and slice the *zucchini* without peeling them.

Clean, rinse and mince the basil and parsley. Place all the vegetables in a pot in the following order: first, place the tomatoes at the bottom of the pot, cover them with the onions, place the *zucchini* over them, then the lettuce and the green peas; sprinkle half the parsley and add the *fava* beans. Sprinkle the vegetables with the oil.

Cover the pot and let cook over medium flame. Do not stir for about 10 minutes., that is, until the vegetables at the bottom of the pot release their water. Add the beef broth, a pinch of salt and a pinch of pepper. Stir, cover the pot and let cook on a very low flame for about an hour. (Do not add any water while the *minestrone* is cooking.) When ready, add the remaining parsley and serve. Neither rice nor pasta is to be added to this *minestrone*.

MACCA
Fava Beans and Pasta with Peperoncino

7 oz. dried fava beans	*3 oz. spaghetti*
1 onion, finely sliced	*peperoncino*
1 large tomato	*6 Tbs. olive oil*
salt	

Let the *fava* beans soak in water for at least 24 hours, 48 if possible. Drain and remove the skins.

Put 1 qt. of water in a pot with the *fava* beans, the onion and the peeled, seeded, chopped tomato. Salt, cover and cook over low heat for about 2 hours or until the *fave* begin to fall apart.

Break-up the spaghetti into 1" pieces. In a separate pot cook the pasta in plenty of salted water. When al *dente,* drain and add them to the *fava* beans. Add *peperoncino* and olive oil, mix well and serve.

This soup is also good at room temperature.

ZUPPE
Soups with Bread

Zuppe have a semi-liquid consistency achieved by cooking meat, fish, shellfish, seafood, legumes, or herbs in water and thereafter pouring the broth over slices of bread. At times, bread is toasted and served on the side, or it may be baked in with the vegetables and broths.

Bread meant for the *zuppa* must be crusty country-style, cut into slices. It is preferable to use slightly stale bread (3-4 days old). The slices of bread may be used as they are, or may either be toasted in the oven or fried in oil or butter before pouring the *zuppa* over them. The slices should not be very dry − the inside should still be a little soft; otherwise they will not properly absorb the broth.

ZUPPA VALDOSTANA
Cabbage and Cheese Soup

1 small Savoy cabbage	*3 oz. butter*
(about 1 lb.)	*salt*
8 oz. fontina cheese	*slices of country bread*
1 qt. beef broth	*(about ½" thick)*

Clean and wash the leaves of the Savoy cabbage well, cook them in boiling water for 10 mins. Drain and cut in julienne. Cut the fontina cheese in thin slices. Bring the beef broth to a boil. Melt the butter over a low flame. In an oven-proof casserole (preferably *terra-cotta*) arrange in layers all the ingredients in the following order: bread, cabbage, *fontina,* continue until all ingredients are used

up, making sure to finish with slices of bread. Drizzle the top layer
of bread with melted butter. Gently pour the boiling broth over it
and bake in a low oven (about 325 F.) for about half hour, until the
top layer becomes crisp. Serve hot.

ZUPPA PAVESE
Egg and Bread Soup

4 large ($\frac{1}{2}$" thick) slices   4 Tbs. grated parmigiano
crusty country bread   1 qt. beef broth
4 Tbs. butter
8 eggs at room temperature

Fry the slices of bread in butter on both sides. Break one egg on
top of each of the bread slices without breaking the yolk. Cover
with plenty of *parmigiano* cheese. Bring the broth to a boil and
pour it slowly over the eggs. The eggs will cook quickly. Serve immediately.
VARIATION: Fry the eggs in butter before placing them on the
bread slices, then cover with hot broth.

ZUPPA DI CARDONI
Soup of Cardoons

4 large cardoons $\frac{1}{2}$ cup grated parmigiano
$\frac{1}{2}$ lb. lean veal, chopped   2 Tbs. olive oil
$\frac{1}{4}$ lb. chicken livers, chopped $\frac{1}{4}$ cup white wine
2 eggs   2 qts. chicken broth
6 slices of country bread

Clean, remove the outer leaves and chop the cardoons. Cook in 2
qts. water with the juice of $\frac{1}{2}$ a lemon. When done, remove from
water and set aside.

Combine the veal, chicken livers, eggs, and *parmigiano,* mix
well and prepare small dumplings the size of a nutmeg. Sauté them
with the oil and sprinkle with the white wine. When they have
cooked through set aside.

Next, combine the cardoons with the dumplings and pour over
the boiling broth and bring the broth to a boil. Arrange slices of
country bread in 6 rimmed plates and pour over the boiling soup.
Serve immediately.

RIBOLLITA
Bean Soup Baked with Bread

Ribollita, literally translated, means "reboiled". This does not
refer to an actual re-boiling of the soup, but to the use of the leftover soup in the following way.

leftover Fagioli con cavolo nero alla Toscana
10 slices day-old country bread

1 qt. beef broth
2 onions, sliced
extra virgin olive oil

Arrange the soup and bread in layers in a baking pan. Add broth as necessary to moisten. Cover the upper layer with thinly sliced onions. Sprinkle generously with olive oil and heat in the oven until hot. Serve hot, with additional extra virgin olive oil to be added by each guest according to taste. The addition of the oil gives the dish a silky, smooth texture.

ZUPPA VALPELLINENSE
Cabbage soup

1 Savoy cabbage
3 oz. pancetta
2 Tbs. olive oil
12 slices country bread
1 cup juice from a roast
(or a strong beef broth)
¼ lb. prosciutto, sliced

pepper to taste
pinch cinnamon
pinch nutmeg
½ lb. fontina cheese
2 Tbs. butter
1 qt. broth

Clean the Savoy cabbage, remove the outer leaves and the stem. Sauté the cabbage in a saucepan with oil and chopped *pancetta,* making sure not to break the leaves. Toast the bread and place in a large, flat baking pan. Drizzle with the juice of a roast or a strong beef broth. Place a layer of the cabbage leaves over the bread, topped with slices of *prosciutto.* Add a pinch of pepper, cinnamon and nutmeg. Next, add thin slices of *fontina* cheese. Repeat layers until all ingredients are used up. Make sure the top layer is *fontina* cheese. Dot with butter and cover generously with broth.

Bake for 30 minutes. There are several variations to this soup depending on the village of Val D'Aosta the recipe is from.

PAPPA AL POMODORO
Tomato and bread soup

6 Tbs. extra-virgin olive oil
4 cloves chopped garlic
2 bunches chopped basil
3 lbs. ripe, peeled and seeded tomatoes, cut in large pieces
2 loaves day-old peasant bread, cubed
1 pt. beef or chicken broth
salt and freshly ground black pepper

In a saucepan, heat 4 Tbs. olive oil, 3 cloves of garlic and half the chopped basil at low heat. Do not brown the garlic. Add the tomatoes and cook for 20 minutes and set aside.
In a baking pan, mix 1 Tbs. oil, and the rest of the garlic with the

cubed bread. Salt and pepper to taste, and bake until golden. Add stewed tomatoes to the bread and the broth; cook for 10 more minutes. Serve on individual rimmed soup plates with the rest of the basil and a touch of extra virgin olive oil.

CACIUCCO LIVORNESE
Fish Stew Livornese

Caciucco is made with various types of rockfish, most of which are not found in the U.S. However, many kinds of fish would most likely be used such as red snapper, rock cod, halibut, tilefish, bass, or any other firm fleshed fish.

3 lbs. mixed fish (dog-fish,	*1 Tbs. chopped parsley*
seatoad, scorpion fish,	*1 whole peperoncino*
conger eel, gobies,	*3 garlic cloves*
star-gazer etc.)	*3 oz. extra-virgin olive oil*
⅔ lb. octopus and squid	*1 cup dry white wine*
1 medium size onion	*1½ lb. ripe tomatoes*
1 carrot	*salt, pepper*
1 celery stalk	*8 jumbo shrimp*
2 pt. fish broth	*6 slices bread, about ½" thick*

Clean and wash the fish well. Cut off the heads of the big ones, but leave the small ones whole. Cut the octopus and the squid into medium-size pieces. Make a *battuto* with onion, carrots, celery, parsley, *peperoncino* and 2 garlic cloves. Put it in a saucepan together with the oil and sauté until the onions are golden and the vegetables begin to get tender. Add the squid and the octopus and cook over low heat, occasionally moistening with white wine. When the wine is evaporated add the tomatoes (peeled and seeded). Add salt and pepper to taste, finish cooking the octopus and the squid. It will probably take about 45 mins. for the octopus and the squid to get tender, the best way is to test it (it should be tender to the fork). Then, remove them to another pot and hold them on the side. Add the pint of fish broth, all the small fish, the heads of the large fish and let cook 30 minutes, stirring now and then, and moistening with more broth as necessary. Pass through a sieve. Return the resulting strained broth to the pot (if the broth is too thick, add more fish broth).

Fillet all remaining fish and place it in the pot together with the shrimp. Let cook for a few minutes, moistening if necessary. Then add the octopus, the squid and remove from the heat. Use a rimmed soup plate and pour the fish broth over the slices of bread that have been toasted and rubbed with garlic. Then, distribute the fish evenly onto each plate and serve.

ZUPPA DI VONGOLE
A Stew of Clams

6 lbs. very fresh clams	*4 slices bread, about ½" thick*

2 Tbs. chopped parsley
2 garlic cloves
3 oz. extra-virgin olive oil

1 lb. ripe tomatoes, peeled,
seeded, and chopped
salt, pepper

Clean the clams, rinse thoroughly, then keep in cold, lightly salted water for 2-3 hours without touching them, so that they can open, releasing any possible remaining sand.

Chop the parsley. Pound in a mortar 1 garlic clove. Toast the bread. Lift the clams out of the water and let them drain through your fingers (do not drain with a colander, to avoid picking up the sand as well). Crush the remaining garlic and brown it with the olive oil in a large pan. When the garlic is lightly browned, remove with a slotted spoon and discard.

Add the tomatoes and a pinch of *peperoncino*. Let cook for about 5 minutes and add the clams, cover the pot and cook until all the clams open. Add the chopped parsley and remove from the fire. Place the bread in individual dishes. Pour the broth with the clams over the bread and serve hot.

NOTE: This *zuppa* can be prepared without tomatoes. Replace tomatoes with 1 cup of white wine, reduce for 2 minutes. and add the clams. Proceed as above.

ZUPPA DI AGNELLO
Soup of Lamb Innards

1 lb. lamb innards (including
liver and heart)
3 Tbs. chopped parsley
1 celery stalk
2 garlic cloves

1 small onion
5 Tbs. extra-virgin olive oil
1¼ qts. beef broth
4 slices of bread, about ½" thick
salt

Rinse the meats and slice them thinly. Make a *battuto* with parsley, carrots, celery, garlic and onion. Put the battuto with the oil in a saucepan (preferably a ceramic one) and sauté lightly for a few minutes.

Add the meats (except the liver) and brown over a low heat stirring frequently. Add the broth, stir and let cook over a low heat for about 40 minutes.

About 5 minutes before everything is ready, add the liver. Salt to taste. Toast the slices of bread and distribute them in individual dishes. Ladle *zuppa* over the slices of bread and serve.

SOPA COADA
Squab Soup

6 squabs
6 Tbs. butter
1 cup white wine
1 qt. chicken broth

6 thick slices bread
4 Tbs. grated parmigiano cheese
1 Tbs. salt

Clean the squab, split in half and season generously with salt. Sauté on both sides in 3 Tbs. butter. When they start to get golden brown add the white wine, cover the pot and cook slowly over low heat until the squabs are cooked. Remove from heat, cool and bone completely, trying to keep the meat as whole as possible. Using the same pot that the squab was in, add the broth and simmer slowly for 15 mins. Skim off any excess fat and keep warm.

Toast bread slices and spread with remaining butter. In a baking dish arrange the buttered toasted bread and drizzle with the broth. Top with squab meat and the grated *parmigiano,* add another layer with the same ingredients and pour over the rest of the broth. Bake for 1 hr. at 325 F.

NOTE: Squab may be replaced with chicken and sometimes with tripe.

BUSECCA
Tripe Soup

2 lbs. tripe, curly part (foiolo)	2 celery stalks
4 Tbs. lard	3 sage leaves
2 Tbs. butter	1 qt. vegetable broth
2 onions	6 slices bread
1 carrot	3 Tbs. grated parmigiano

Cut the tripe and into a thin julienne. In a pot, sauté the onion and sage with the lard and butter. When the onions are wilted, not brown, add the tripe. Sauté for 5 minutes. then add the chopped carrot and celery. Add the vegetable broth and cook for 3-4 hours or until the tripe is cooked. Place a slice of bread into a rimmed soup plate and pour over the soup.

Serve grated *parmigiano* on the side and offer freshly ground pepper.

NOTE: In other versions it is possible to add sliced potatoes and beans, white spanish beans variety would be best. These are best when cooked separately then added to the soup.

PASTA E RIPIENI
Pasta and Stuffings

PASTA

Cereals have always been the primary dietary source of people throughout the ages. In Italy, the daily diet, since ancient Rome, consisted mostly of *pultes* (flours) made of ground barley, rye or *farro* (spelt).

The introduction of wheat, which originally came from the highlands of Ethiopia, and the discovery of yeast, allowed the creation of bread as we know it today. Later, development of this culture allowed for the growth and usage of soft and hard durum wheat, which enabled the individual and later the industrial production of pasta. Through the centuries, the habit of eating pasta has consolidated itself so much that it has become the fundamental characteristic of the Italian diet. *Spaghetti* and *maccheroni, penne* and *cavatelli, ravioli, tortellini, fusilli* and so on, belong to an immense family of ingredients all of poor origins but all having in common the characteristic of offering a surprisingly balanced diet.

It is legendary that pasta was brought to Italy by Marco Polo on his return from China. This is a totally incorrect assumption. The first to ascertain proof of this is Massimo Alberini, a noted historian still living in Milan. A few years back, he gathered material for a *spaghetti* museum and, as he researched the city archives in Genoa, found a will, attested and signed by a public notary dated February 2, 1279, in which the soldier Ponzio Bastone lists as part of his belongings *"una bariscella plena di macaronis"*, a barrel full of macaroni. The document is important for two reasons: First the date is long before the return of Marco Polo from China, and second, for the first time the word "macaroni" is used, obviously to indicate dry pasta, as one cannot imagine that he would leave his heir a barrel full of fresh pasta.

PASTA SECCA
Dry Pasta

Dry pasta — that is, the pasta which is available commercially — must be made with hard wheat flour, regardless of size or shape. If the pasta contains a percentage of soft wheat flour, it will cook in a shorter time, will appear sticky, and the water in which it has been cooking will appear cloudy. Pasta made exclusively with hard wheat flour is compact and translucent; its surface feels slightly coarse to the touch. It will snap when it breaks, as if it were made of glass. It will take a longer time to cook, will increase considerably in size when cooked, will not stick (although it must be stirred occasionally), and the water in which it has cooked will remain relatively clear.

The quality of pasta, however, is not solely measured according to how much hard wheat flour it contains. The millstone employed in grinding it, the water used, the skill of the manufacturer, the kind of extruder used, the form, and last, but not least, a careful and thorough drying process, which must be carried out in separate stages over a long period of time, in the appropriate environment — are all important factors in determining the quality of a pasta.

PASTA ALL'UOVO
Egg Pasta (Dry)
This is dry pasta which contains 7 ozs. of egg for each 2.2 lbs. of wheat. This kind of pasta usually comes in short forms and is cooked in beef or vegetable broth; longer pasta like *tagliatelle* is served with sauce or *ragù*. Pasta cut into large squares is used for *pasticci* (*lasagna*) and timballi (baked pasta).

PASTA GLUTINATA
Gluten Pasta
This kind of pasta is particularly recommended for children, convalescents, and elders. Gluten is added to enrich the pasta. This is a substance rich in proteins, present in quantity in hard wheat flour: it is a tenacious, elastic substance, which gives cohesiveness to the starch particles of wheat flour. This kind of pasta is only available in small forms suitable to be cooked in beef or vegetable broth.

How to Cook Dry Pasta
In cooking pasta it is advisable to use a heavy pot, which allows the water to retain heat longer, with a wide bottom to allow the heat to spread evenly, and high sides to avoid the danger of boiling over. A pot like this allows the water to boil quicker and to reach the boiling point again more rapidly once the pasta has been added. This is important: if the water takes a long time to boil after the pasta has been added, the pasta may become sticky.

For each $\frac{1}{4}$ lb. of pasta, 1 qt. of water and about $\frac{1}{4}$ oz. of coarse salt are necessary. When the water reaches a full, rolling boil, add the pasta. When cooking short pasta, add it all at once. With long pasta it is better to add it in two or three batches, one right after the other, taking care to spread it out so that it does not stick. If you are cooking *ziti* or *bucatini,* fat *spaghetti* with a hole, make sure the pasta is fully immersed into the boiling water so that the hole is soaked immediately. After adding the pasta to the water, stir, cover the pot and increase the heat so that the water can return rapidly to a boil. When the water returns to a boil, remove the lid immediately. (This is crucial: pasta cooked in a covered pot will become sticky.)

While cooking, stir short pasta with a large wooden spoon and long pasta with a long wooden fork. It is necessary to stir now and then to prevent the pieces of pasta from sticking to each other and to the bottom of the pot. Adding a little oil to the water to prevent the pieces of pasta from sticking to each other is useful only for large home made pieces of pasta like those used for *lasagna*.

Cooking time will vary according to quality, form and thickness of the pasta, or even to the hardness of the local water and the altitude. To discover whether the pasta is cooked, taste it more than once as it approaches readiness. Remove from water when still al dente, which means when the pasta has a slightly chewy texture.

It is good habit to drain the pasta when it is still a bit underdone; drain it thoroughly, but reserve some of the water as you may need it later. If you plan to use a fairly liquid sauce, the warm sauce will provide the necessary moisture to complete the cooking process. If a heavier sauce is used you may need to add some of the cooking water you have set aside.

The standard way to strain pasta is to use a colander or a strainer, it depends on the amounts and size of the pasta being cooked. As you do so, the pasta will lose a lot of the starch coating on each pasta strand or piece. The optimal way to remove the pasta from its cooking water is with a long fork, a skimmer, or any other appropriate utensil. The pasta is then put into a pan already containing the sauce, which will allow the pasta to be tossed over the hot sauce, or in a tureen with a few tablespoons of the condiment at the bottom.

Whether or not to add a ladle of cold water to the drained pasta to stop the cooking process is a questionable practice. One might do so only if the pasta had been allowed to cook longer than necessary.

When the pasta is ready, put it in a warm tureen and pour on the designated sauce, add *parmigiano* if the recipe calls for it, mix well and serve.

NOTES: Most times pasta is *"mantecata"* before serving, that is, sautéed briskly in a skillet with the desired sauce and *parmigiano*.

Most seafood sauces for pasta are served without cheese, in many cases it is a grave error to do so.

It is a mistake to think that well-done pasta is more digestible. Indeed, the contrary is true. If the pasta offers some resistance to chewing, one will instinctively chew longer, hence producing more saliva and more gastric juice to make digestion easier.

While one might think that some gourmets overdo it when proclaiming that each style of pasta favors a particular type of sauce, it is true that not all kinds of pasta are compatible with a given sauce. In many cases the form of the pasta dictates the type of sauce to be used. Rule of thumb: lighter sauces for thin pastas, heavier sauces for short pastas.

Most common types of dry pasta

PASTA LUNGA
Long Pasta
TYPE: Capellini, capelli d'angelo, capelvenere.
Form: thread-like (very fine) and round; about .04 to .06 inch. in

SPAGHETTI

PENNE

CONCHIGLIE

FUSILLI

RIGATONI

TAGLIATELLE

diameter. Can be also found packaged in bundles or «nests».*
Use: with very delicate sauces and as pasta in soups.
Cooking time: 2-3 minutes, according to thickness.
Preferred Sauces: can be cooked in beef broth, or seasoned with butter, cream and *parmigiano*.
* When vegetable coloring is added, these may be found in different colors: green or red.
TYPE: spaghettini, spaghetti, vermicelli Form: long, round (from .065" to .08" in diameter).
Use: for pasta dishes with sauces.
Cooking time: 5-8 minutes, according to thickness.
Preferred Sauces: *spaghettini* are best with sauces containing oil, garlic and *peperoncino,* or with light fish sauces, while *spaghetti* are suitable with heavier sauces such as tomato, *carbonara,* fish *ragù. Spaghetti* may also be tossed with just oil or butter and grated cheese.
TYPE: Bigoli, vermicelloni Form: long and round (from 0.8" to .10 in diameter).
Use: for pasta dishes seasoned with sauces.
Cooking time: 10-12 minutes.
Preferred Sauces: meat and game sauces.
TYPE: trenette, linguine.
Form: long, flat, ribbon-like; varying from 0.8" to .10" wide.
Use: vegetable and fish sauces
Cooking time: 5-7 minutes
Preferred sauces: *trenette* with pesto or other vegetable sauces, *linguine* with either oil and vegetable combinations or, light fish sauces.
TYPE: lasagne, lasagne festonate, tagliatelle, reginette, tripolini.*
Form: long, flat; can vary from $\frac{2}{8}$" to $1\frac{1}{2}$" wide. *Tripolini* are 3/8" wide. *Lasagne festonate* are called *festonate* because of the peculiar rippled edges. The larger types of *lasagne* can be used also for *pasticci.*
Use: For baking with various sauces and other ingredients.
Cooking time: 7-10 minutes according to size.
Preferred Sauces: game and any type of *ragù.*
*Note: *Tagliatelle* may also be called *fettuccine.*
*TYPE: bucatini, maccheroncelli, perciatelli *.*
Form: long, tubular, hollow (*bucatini* are a bit thinner).
Use: for all sauces; they can also be used in vegetable soups (*minestra* and *minestrone*) but they have to be broken up. Cooking time: varies from 8 to 11 minutes, according to thickness.
Suitable sauces: *amatriciana* calls for *bucatini* or *perciatelli,* but other sauces containing various meats and vegetables; also suitable for baked preparations.
* The name *perciatelli* finds its origin in the dialect spoken in southern Italy, from Rome down where the word for hole is *"pertuso"*; *"perciato"*, pierced through. While from Rome up the word *bucatini* derives from *buco,* «hole», pasta with a hole.

PASTA CORTA
Short Pasta
TYPE: rigatoni millerighe, penne, sedani, maniche.
Form: these are all tubular in shape, varying in size and can either be straight or curved, smooth or grooved; grooves are sometimes in spiral patterns.
Use: The smaller type are suitable for soups, larger variety with sauces, or may also be baked.
Cooking time: 14-16 minutes, according to size.
Preferred Sauces: the smaller varieties are suitable for light sauces; the larger varieties with tomato and beef ragus.
TYPE: fusilli, conchiglie, farfalle. Form: *Fusilli* look like short, spiral-like *spaghetti. Conchiglie* look like a shell, whereas *farfalle* look like bow ties (*farfalla* means "butterfly" in Italian; *cravatta a farfalla,* bow tie).
Use: with vegetable sauces, also as cold pasta salads
Cooking time: varies from 10 to 13 minutes, according to size.
Preferred Sauces: light sauces with tomatoes and vegetable soups.
TYPE: stelline, anellini, alphabeto, risone.
Form: *stelline,* little stars; *anellini,* rings; *alphabeto,* A-B-C shapes; *risone,* rice shaped.
Use: mostly for clear soups
Cooking time: 5-7 minutes, according to type.
Sauces: Liquid sauces and broths, occasionally for molds.

PASTA FRESCA
Fresh Pasta

How to Make Fresh Pasta: Basic recipe

Fresh pasta is made with 1 lb. 2 ozs. of flour and 5 whole eggs. In many regions of Italy only 4 eggs are used and a little water; in others, 2 eggs and more water. In other regions only the egg yolks are employed and a little oil. Regardless of these regional variations, the dough must be well kneaded — that is, until little bubbles are visible — before being stretched with the rolling pin.
Procedure: pour the flour on a pastry board, (spianatoia) in a cone-shaped, mound. Break the eggs into the center of the cone and blend the yolks with the whites, using a fork or fingers; then begin gradually mixing the egg with the flour.

When the dough reaches a thick consistency, so that it is no longer possible to use a fork, the egg will no longer be liquid and about 1/2 the flour will be incorporated; continue to work with your hands, pushing the dough up from all sides, incorporating as much flour as possible; continue kneading for about 15 minutes.

The dough must be thick and rather stiff, otherwise it will be difficult to roll out, though it might seem to be the other way around. Wrap the dough with a cloth and keep it under a weight for half an hour.

This allows the dough (particularly the gluten in the dough) to relax; it will be less elastic and much easier to roll out after a short rest. Green pasta: wash and cook till soft $\frac{1}{2}$ lb., 2 oz. of spinach. When ready, squeeze it very hard between your palms, so that the spinach is as dry as possible; then pass through a fine sieve or blender. Add the spinach to the flour and eggs as in basic recipe. You may add or delete an egg according to the wetness of the spinach.

Red pasta

Substitute a teaspoon of concentrated tomato paste for spinach in instructions for basic recipe.

How to Roll and Cut the Dough

Put the dough on a pastry board that has been lightly dusted with flour, flatten the dough with your palm and begin rolling it out with a floured rolling pin. To roll it out evenly, start from the center of the dough, rolling in all directions, extending the pressure evenly toward the outer edges of the dough, turning the dough over occasionally, without pushing too hard with the rolling pin. In the end, the dough should form a large, flat circle of equal thickness throughout. Sprinkle with a little flour and fold the pasta into a roll. With a very sharp knife, starting from one end, cut throughout the width in ribbons as wide as desired. When finished cutting, unravel the ribbons on the board, tossing with more flour. Let the pasta dry for about an hour before cooking.

Most Commons Type of Fresh Pasta

Paglia e fieno; $\frac{1}{16}$" wide and long, best with light sauces or vegetables.
Trenette; $\frac{1}{8}$" wide and long, best with pesto or fish sauces.
Tagliatelle; $\frac{2}{8}$" wide and long, best with tomato sauce and meat *ragu.*
Pappardelle; $\frac{1}{2}$" to 1" wide, 6-8" long, best with game sauces
Lasagna; 1: to 2: wide, as long as desired, best baked with *ragù* and other ingredients.

LASAGNE

Maltagliati; irregular cuts of leftover sheets of pasta, used with *minestra* and *minestrone* or with light sauces.
Quadrettini; little squares used for clear soups
Note: *Tagliatelle* may also be called *Fettuccine*

Fresh Pasta Cut in Shapes

Farfalle, strichetti; these are names used to describe the same shape of pasta, the only difference being the size. *Farfalle* the Italian word for «butterfly», is the smaller of the two. *Strichetti* means "pinched", in this case in the center, therefore achieving the same result. Both types are cut from a flat sheet of pasta, approximately 2" long and 1" wide for *farfalle* and 3" long and 2" wide for *strichetti.* Pinch the dough in the center of the longer side and you have formed a bow. Make as many as necessary for your use. Both may be used with light, fluid tomato and vegetable sauces, while the smaller ones may also be used in broths and *minestrone.*

NOTE 1: All fresh pasta can be made with the addition of a vegetable purée for coloring, following the method explained in this chapter.

NOTE 2: Cooking time varies from 2-3 minutes for *paglia e fieno* to a longer time for the bows. A rule of thumb is that when the pasta starts to float, it is probably cooked. As always, the best way is to test it.

NOTE 3: The addition of grated *parmigiano* to the basic dough recipe, 1 Tbs. for each pound of flour, and the pasta, then cut 1/8' wide, is called *tajarin* a speciality from Piedmont.

How to Cook Fresh Pasta

All types and shapes of home-made pasta are cooked in abundant boiling, salted water, or broth.

When adding the pasta, add it all at once, making sure the water or broth, is boiling rapidly so that it can return to the boiling point quickly after the pasta has been added.

After adding the pasta increase heat under the pot (if possible) and then as soon as the water boils, decrease the heat to avoid a too-rapid boil. After adding the pasta, stir; use a wooden fork if cooking long pasta, or a big wooden spoon if cooking short pasta. When the pasta starts to float, test it, if it requires more cooking, push it down with a skimmer, so that it stays constantly immersed in water. Fresh pasta without stuffing cooks faster than stuffed pasta. As with dry pasta, fresh and stuffed pasta must be drained while still *al dente*, because the heat of the sauce will allow it to cook thoroughly. Add sauce or *mantecare* following the same procedure as for dry pasta.

TORCHIO
PER
BIGOLI

Other Types of Fresh Pasta

BIGOLI
Whole wheat spaghetti

Bigoli, whole wheat thick *spaghetti,* is a traditional pasta from Veneto. To make bigoli, a special kitchen utensil called *torchio* (see glossary) is used. Mix whole wheat flour with 2 eggs, ½ cup milk and 2 Tbs. melted butter for each pound of flour. Obtain a hard dough. The dough is then passed through the *torchio.* The thick *spaghetti* will come out without a hole. The traditional way to serve *bigoli* is with a sauce of slowly cooked onion in olive oil and a couple of fillets of anchovies. The preparation is called *bigoli* in salsa.

CIRIOLE
Twisted pasta

Knead wheat flour with the necessary amount of warm water and a pinch of salt. The dough is then cut into thin strips and each piece is pulled and wound by hand until it becomes about 6" to 8" long and fairly thin, about twice as large as spaghetti. *Ciriole* are usually served with a *amatriciana* sauce or with garlic, oil and *peperoncino*. The cooking time is 12-15 minutes.

GARGANELLI
Fresh quills

The dough for garganelli is prepared with flour, eggs and grated *parmigiano,* then rolled out very thin and cut into 2 inch squares. The dough is then rolled over a comb-like utensil, called *pettine,* with a wooden stick, the result is a quill shaped pasta. A meat *ragù* is their traditional sauce. The cooking time is 4-6 minutes.

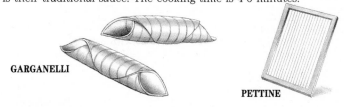

GARGANELLI

PETTINE

MACCHERONI
Macaroni

These can be found in almost all regions of southern Italy. They are made by kneading together 11 oz. of wheat flour with one egg, a pinch of salt and the required amount of water. Knead and roll the dough shaped into rounded strips $\frac{1}{3}$ inch thick and 1 inch long, then wound around a well floured knitting needle, and rolled back and forth on the pastry board until the dough closes around the needle. It will look like a small tube. The needle is pulled out delicately, so as not to close the hole. You now have a small tube about 2 inches long with a hole in the middle. They must dry for a while before cooking. Traditionally they are served with pork *ragù* and cook in 12-15 minutes.

MACCHERONI ALLA CHITARRA
Freshly cut spaghetti

A rustic form of pasta, a specialty of Abruzzo, cut in rather thick, long and squared strips on a device called a *chitarra*. This consists of a wooden frame across which a great number of thin wires stretched an equal distance apart. The pasta, rolled out thicker than usual (it should be approximately as thick as the distance between any two wires of the *chitarra*), is laid over the wires, and cut by passing a rolling pin over the pasta, pressing it through the wires. The preferred sauce for this pasta is a ragù of lamb, but it may also be served with other condiments such as tomato with basil and peperoncino. The cooking varies according to thickness.

CHITARRA

MALLOREDDUS
Tiny dry dumplings

In Sardinian dialect *malloreddus* means small bulls or calves. Make the dough with wheat flour, warm water, salt and a pinch of saffron, and knead. Stretch dough to ⅓ inch thickness and cut strips of the same thickness. Pinch off pieces of dough the size of a bean, roll them against a non-metallic sifter so that the pasta bean will curl when pressed. They will look like tiny dumplings. The pasta must be dried for at least two days and is usually served with a sausage *ragù* and cooks in 12-15 minutes.

ORECCHIETTE
Hat shaped pasta

To make *orecchiette:* Knead wheat flour with water to make a stiff dough; roll the dough into ½" thickness, cut into strips ½" wide, and cut in pieces the size of a kidney bean. Each piece is pressed down and rolled along the pastry board, either with a round, pointed knife or the thumb, going from left to right.

In doing so, the dough will stretch first and then roll up, forming a little shell-like shape with a thin edge. It is then turned inside out over the tip of the thumb. *Orecchiette* may be boiled in water along with vegetables (e.g., *cime di rape, rucola, broccoli* etc.), drained and sautéed in a frying pan together with oil and garlic, tomato and *peperoncino*. The cooking time is approximately 12-15 minutes.

PIZZOCCHERI
Whole wheat tagliatelle

Mix ⅔ lb. whole wheat flour with ⅓ lb. white flour, add warm water and knead. Roll the dough out to about ⅛-inch thick and cut into strips ⅓-inch wide. This pasta is characteristic of Valtellina and is served with vegetables, fresh cheese (Toma) and plenty of butter.

Variation: Eggs may be added to the dough just as in the basic recipe for fresh pasta and a cup of milk may be a substitute for water.

TESTAROLI
Pasta triangles

A pasta typical of Lunigiana, an area between Liguria and Tuscany, its roots being Etruscan, testaroli is one of the most elementary examples of food preparation which comes to us from our ancestors. *Testaroli* are in fact simple disks of pasta made with water and flour, cooked on a *testo,* or a hot flat surface of either terra-cotta or cast iron.

Pour 1 lb. of flour into water which contains $\frac{1}{2}$ oz. of salt and mix well till you achieve a fluid consistency (like a pancake mix). Heat up a *testo* or any type of greased flat surface, and make as many flat thin disks as you can, until you finish the mixture.

As the disks of dough are prepared they are set aside, each separated by a sheet of oiled paper, and stood to rest for 12 hours.

When ready to use, cut the disk in triangular shapes (or any shape will do). Bring a pot of salted water to a boil, turn off the flame, immerse the *testaroli,* cover the pot, turn the fire on again, to maximum flame, and cook for 6-7 minutes.

Remove the cooked *testaroli* with a strainer, place into a serving platter and use a classic *pesto* as condiment. Serve immediately.

TROFIE
Twisted gnocchi

This is a speciality from Liguria. Mix together 1 lb. of flour, $3\frac{1}{2}$ oz. of bran, a pinch of salt and water. Knead the mass to obtain a smooth, compact and elastic ball of dough. Roll to $\frac{1}{3}$-inch thick and cut into $\frac{1}{3}$" strips. Pinch off pieces of pasta the size of a chick pea and, with the palm of your hand, rub them across the pastry board one at a time forming elongated twisted *gnocchi* about $1\frac{1}{2}$ "to 2" long. *Trofie* are cooked in plenty of boiling, salted water together with a finely sliced potato and a handful of very thin string beans cut 1" long and served with *pesto.* The cooking time is 8-10 minutes.

PASTA RIPIENA
Stuffed Fresh Pasta

Cappelletti, tortellini, ravioli, and *tortelli* are always made with dough containing eggs and stretched thinner than that used for *tagliatelle.* The dough, once rolled, is cut at once into desired size, either squares, circles or rectangles, lightly brushed with beaten egg, or water. A little ball of stuffing is placed on each piece, the dough is then tightly sealed with the fingers into the desired shape, or some-

ROTELLA DENTATA

times the stuffing is placed on a stretched dough previously brushed with a beaten egg or water, in an intermittent sequence, and another sheet of pasta is placed above it. It is then pressed down with your hands all around the stuffing, so that the little packets are formed. It is then cut with a cutting pasta wheel into the desired shape.

The stuffing may be made of various meats, vegetables, fish, or ricotta cheese and is usually bound with eggs and *parmigiano*.

While the following stuffings are traditional to Italian cookery, they may be readily adapted to include ingredients favored by individual cooks. Using the basic elements — *parmigiano,* bread crumbs and eggs, meat may be interchanged with vegetables, a purée of beans, *ricotta* or *mozzarella*. The range of possibilities are limited only by the cook's ingenuity.

Stuffed fresh pasta is classified in types and varieties, according to the different ways of folding and sealing the pasta. Often, the same variety goes under different names in different regions of the country.

AGNOLINI
Stuffed Rings

Prepare the pasta following the basic recipe, roll it a little thinner and brush with egg or water. Cut in small squares with sides of 2 inches. Size may vary according to how the pasta will be served — whether with a sauce or in beef broth. Place a little ball of stuffing in the center of each square of pasta, using enough so that the finished piece will be plump.

Fold one edge of the pasta over to cover the stuffing and to reach the opposite edge of pasta. Press the folded edges around the stuffing with your fingers. Then, pinch together the two far corners of the resulting triangle around the end of your index finger. This will form an *agnolino* with a hole in the center.

CANNELLONI
Stuffed pasta roll

Cannelloni are squares of fresh boiled pasta stuffed and rolled with a desired filling covered with a preferred sauce dotted with butter, grated *parmigiano* and baked.

The basic method is to prepare the pasta dough as in basic recipe. Stretch it to $\frac{1}{2}$" thick and cut into 4" squares. The squares are cooked in plenty of salted boiling water, with 2 Tbs. of oil added. Cook till *al dente*, strain, cool with cold water to stop the cooking process and grease with olive oil so that they do not stick together and they will be easier to work with.

Stuff and roll in the desired stuffing and arrange in a greased baking pan. Add sauce, bake in oven at 375 F. until golden brown on top. Serve

NOTE 1: All stuffings for *ravioli* are suitable for *cannelloni.*

NOTE 2: The stuffing for *cannelloni* has to be more firm than those used for stuffed pasta, which is sealed on all sides, otherwise the stuffing will run out of the two open ends.

NOTE 3: The sauce for *cannelloni* must be more fluid, and abundant, as some of the liquid will evaporate while baking so that the *cannelloni* will remain moist.

CAPPELLETTI
Alpine Hats
These look somewhat like an Alpine hat. With a fluted pasta wheel cut the thinly rolled and brushed pasta in small squares, $1\frac{1}{2}$ inches. Place a bit of stuffing in the center of each square, fold a corner edge over and press around the stuffing. Then, keeping the stuffed area against (rather than around) your index finger, pinch together the two far corners of the resulting triangle. This type will not have a hole in the center. While pinching the ends together, lightly push the stuffing upward. Again, the resulting *cappelletti* should not have a hole in the center, but should look like an alpine hat.

CRESPELLE
Thin stuffed crêpes
These are thin pancakes (crêpes) prepared with flour, milk and eggs to obtain a fluid mix. To prepare *crespelle* use an 8" round iron pan. Heat the pan to the degree that would make a drop of water sizzle, then pour in 3 Tbs. of the mixture, rotate the pan so that the mix spreads evenly to cover the entire bottom of the pan. The crepe will form very quickly. Make as many as you may need to use. The fillings may be similar or more delicate that the stuffings used for pasta, but they should definitely be softer. The stuffing is placed on the *crespella* evenly. They are then folded twice to form a triangle, and served with a desired sauce.

RAVIOLI
Stuffed pasta
Ravioli are filled with stuffing made of vegetables, *ricotta,* meat, fish and so on. They are stuffed squares of pasta. Roll a 12" sheet of dough, brush with water or egg. Pipe the stuffing onto the dough in small bits, evenly separated in 2" distances from one another. Place a second sheet of dough on top of the first; press down gen-

RAVIOLI

tly in order to allow air to exit. Use an appropriate cutter to make 2" square *ravioli*. They are almost always served with light sauces, a ragu' or simply with melted butter, sage leaves, and *parmigiano*.

ROTOLO DI PASTA
Rolled Stuffed Pasta
This is a fresh pasta prepared as in the basic method, stretched out to make 2 sheets, $\frac{1}{8}$" thickness and cut into a rectangular form, approximately 10" wide and 20" long. Once this dough is in sheet form, a filling is spread on one sheet, making sure to leave an unfilled border of at least $\frac{1}{2}$". There may be various types of fillings such as meats, vegetables, cheeses, or any combination of one or more of these ingredients.
The second sheet is then placed on top of the first and both are

rolled and then wrapped in a cheesecloth with both ends of the cheesecloth tied. The cooking is very unusual because the rolled stuffed pasta should be cooked floating in boiling, salted water. For this, it is best to use an oval pot or a pot that resembles a fish poacher, so that the ends of the cheesecloth can be tied to the handles of the pot — this way, the *rotolo* will be floating and not sitting in the boiling water. The cooking time can be as long as 2 hours. The *rotolo* is then removed from the water, the cheesecloth discarded, and the *rotolo* is cut into $\frac{1}{2}$" thick slices. The slices are now arranged into a baking pan and served with melted butter and *parmigiano*.

TORTELLINI
Stuffed straight hats with a hole

Legend has it that the man that invented *tortellini* was a cook from Castelfranco, not far from Bologna. It was in his inn that Venus, the goddess of beauty, had stopped for a night's rest. The good cook, curious to see the naked beauty of Venus, spied from the keyhole,

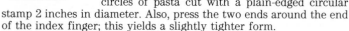

and afterward remembering the Venus belly button, he attempted to re-create it with the dough! Hence, the *tortellino!*

In reality, all stuffed pastas were born from the necessity to use the leftovers from the table of the masters.

Tortellini are like *cappelletti,* except that the edges are straight, not fluted, and there is a hole in the center. *Tortellini* may also be made from circles of pasta cut with a plain-edged circular stamp 2 inches in diameter. Also, press the two ends around the end of the index finger; this yields a slightly tighter form.

TORTELLINI

NOTE: The stuffing for *agnolini, cappelletti* and *tortellini* is generally made with beef, pork or veal.
Tortelli are like *tortellini,* but larger.

How to Cook Stuffed Fresh Pasta

Stuffed fresh pasta that is to be served with a sauce is cooked in boiling salted water. Add the stuffed pasta all at once, then gently stir with a spoon, or a skimmer. It is important that the water begins boiling again very quickly after adding the pasta. When the water begins boiling again, decrease the heat, because rapid boiling can destroy the pasta (remember that here the pasta is thinner than in other preparations). As the pasta floats to the top, test it, if it requires more cooking time, push it down with a skimmer. Cooking times vary according to the thickness of the dough. Stuffed pasta must be cooked *al dente*. The heat of the sauce will complete the cooking process without danger of overcooking. Drain the pasta well with a skimmer (do not use a colander), arrange in layers in a bowl and top each layer with hot sauce and *parmigiano*. If the pasta is to be cooked in broth, you can follow the same procedure outlined above, using a rich beef or poultry broth in place of the water.

RICETTE
Recipes

RIPIENO PER AGNOLINI ALLA PARMIGIANA
Stuffing for Agnolini Parmigiana

1 lb. round ground beef	1 stalk celery
2 oz. pancetta	1 small carrot
few cloves	pinch cinnamon
olive oil	3-4 cloves garlic
2 oz. butter	4 Tbs. tomato sauce
1 large onion, sliced	1 cup parmigiano
salt, pepper	6 Tbs. bread crumbs
1 pint beef broth	2 eggs

Spike the piece of beef with *pancetta* and some garlic cloves. Place in a heated casserole with 4 oz. oil, butter and onion. Add salt and pepper to taste and let cook on low heat for 10 minutes, turning to brown the meat. When the meat is browned on all sides, add the broth, celery, sliced carrot, a piece of cinnamon and three or four garlic cloves. Add tomato sauce, cover and let it cook very slowly for 4 to 5 hours till tender. Remove meat and keep on the side to be used as a main course or for any other use. Strain the remaining sauce. Add the grated *parmigiano,* bread crumbs, two whole eggs and regulate the density of the stuffing by adding other cheese and bread crumbs as needed. Refrigerate stuffing for 24 hours before using. *Agnolini* are stuffed following the same technique as in ravioli, but are cut in half-moon shape, so you need the proper utensil.

Stuff the *agnolini* and serve in a capon broth or just simply sauteed with butter and *parmigiano*.

NOTE: Agnolini are also called anolini.

RIPIENO PER TORTELLINI
Stuffing for tortellini

4 oz. loin of pork	5 oz. grated parmigiano
2 oz. turkey breast	2 eggs
2 Tbs. butter	nutmeg
¼ lb. mortadella	salt
¼ lb. prosciutto	pepper

Cut the pork loin and the turkey breast in thin slices. Melt the butter in a large saucepan, add all the meat and let brown over very low heat for about ten minutes, stirring thoroughly. Then grind the meat finely with the *prosciutto* and the *mortadella*. Put the mixture in a bowl, add the *parmigiano,* eggs, a pinch of nutmeg, pepper and salt to taste. Let it cool and keep well covered in a cool place for a few hours before using. The most suitable sauce for *tortellini* is beef ragù *bolognese*.

ANATRA/ANITRA
Duckling

1 lb. duck breast with skin	2 chopped scallions
1 oz. chopped spinach	½ oz. bone marrow
4 slices stale bread	1 small bunch of parsley,
1 cup milk	chopped
1 oz. chopped mushrooms	1 oz. heavy cream
1 Tbs. oil to sauté	salt, pepper

Chop the duck breast in small pieces. Cook the spinach in a pot without water, over low heat until the liquid has evaporated. Remove from pot, cool and chop very fine. Trim crusts and dip the white of the bread in the milk, squeeze out the excess liquid and mix with the spinach. Sauté the mushrooms, scallions and duck breast mixture for a few minutes, stirring well. Next, chop the whole very finely and add to the spinach, and bread mixture. Add bone marrow, parsley and cream. Salt and pepper to taste and mix well. This stuffing is suitable for ravioli and tortelloni. Sauces may vary from melted butter, sage and *parmigiano* to a reduction of duck sauce.

CACCIAGIONE
Game

1 squab or other type of game	3 Tbs. oil
salt, pepper	1 Tbs. butter
sage	2 oz. grated parmigiano
rosemary	2 eggs
5 oz. bacon, diced	nutmeg

Clean the squab, salt the inside and insert the sage, rosemary, and diced bacon. Heat the oil and butter in a pan and sauté squab, finish it in the oven. When the squab is cooked, bone and skin it and put it through a food mill. Mix together with *parmigiano*, eggs, nutmeg, salt and pepper. Keep in a cool place until ready to use. This stuffing is used for *tortelli* or *ravioli*, which should be served in capon broth or, if a sauce is desired, an herb sauce is best suited.

CARNE
Meat

2 Tbs. butter	1 bay leaf
¼ lb. lean ground veal	salt, pepper
¼ lb. ground loin or fillet	⅛ lb. prosciutto
of pork	⅛ lb. mortadella
¼ lb. lean ground beef	½ cup fresh bread crumbs
1 cup strong, dry red wine	6 Tbs. parmigiano
1 clove garlic	1 egg

In a large casserole with a heavy bottom, brown the butter and the finely chopped fat of the *prosciutto*. Add the meats, let brown, then add wine, clove, bay leaf, and a little salt. Cover and let cook on a very low heat for about 3 hours (it should not boil). Stir occasionally while cooking. If necessary, add some boiling broth, or water, in spoonfuls. The sauce should be quite concentrated and the meat well-cooked.

Drain the mixture and grind together with the lean *prosciutto* and *mortadella* in a food mill. Strain the leftover liquid and use to moisten the bread crumbs. Without squeezing the bread crumbs, add to the meat mixture. Add the egg, *parmigiano,* a pinch of freshly ground pepper and salt according to taste and mix well (using your hands is the best method). The stuffing is now ready. The stuffing will be more flavorful and easier to handle if allowed to let stand, covered, in a cool place for a few hours. This filling is suitable for all fresh stuffed pasta, particularly for the small sized types. Pasta with this filling may be served in broth, with tomato or beef *ragu*, or with just butter and *parmigiano*.

FEGATINI DI POLLO
Chicken Liver

4 oz. spinach	*1 chopped scallion*
2 oz. butter	*1 egg*
4 oz. chicken livers	*nutmeg*
½ oz. chopped black truffles	*salt, pepper*

Place the spinach in a pot without water after being washed and cook until the liquid has evaporated.

Cut chicken livers into very small pieces and sauté in 1 Tbs. of butter with the truffles and scallions for about a minute. After it has cooled, pass through a food mill with the spinach, add the egg, the remaining butter, nutmeg, salt and pepper to taste. Mix well and stuffing is ready, suitable for *ravioli, tortelli, tortelloni.* The accompanying sauce can vary from butter and sage to a very light tomato sauce. Remember, the sauce must always highlight the stuffing, not overpower it.

NOTE: The spinach may also be cooked in water, provided it is well strained. This method allows the greens to maintain their natural vivid color. Spinach cooked without water, has a tendency to make the finished stuffing look grayish-green.

FORMAGGIO
Cheese

⅔ lb. ricotta cheese	*pinch of nutmeg*
(Roman style)	*(optional)*
3 eggs	*salt*
3 Tbs. parmigiano	*pepper*

Push the *ricotta* through a sieve. Beat the eggs in a bowl and, while beating, mix in the *ricotta,* the *parmigiano,* nutmeg, salt and

pepper. If stuffing is too soft, add some bread crumbs. Keep the stuffing in a cool place, for a few hours. This stuffing can be used for all
types and shapes of stuffed pasta. The sauces vary according to the
recipe used.

PESCE
Fish

For court bouillon:

1 cup dry white wine	*1 very small onion*
1 lemon	*a few peppercorns*
	salt

For fish stuffing:

1 lb. spinach	*1 lb. fish fillets, one type*
1 very small onion	*or several*
2 Tbs. butter	*1 egg*
	pepper, salt

Make a court bouillon. Clean and cook the fish in a court bouillon
made with water, white wine, thinly sliced onion, 2-3 slices of lemon,
3 peppercorns and salt. Let it cool in its broth.

Clean, wash and cook the spinach, then, after having squeezed it
well, chop finely. Finely mince the onion. Heat the butter in a
saucepan. Add the onion and cook till browned. In the meantime,
drain the fish, bone it, cut the flesh in small pieces and add to the
onion. Add the spinach, mix well and cook over very low heat for a
few minutes. Pour the resulting mixture into a bowl and let cool.
After it has cooled, mix in the egg and a pinch of salt and pepper to
achieve a smooth mixture. Keep the stuffing in a cool place until
needed.

This stuffing is best for ravioli. A suitable condiment would be a
very light and fluid fish sauce.

SPINACI
Spinach

2 lbs. spinach or Swiss	*salt*
chard leaves	*½ lb. ricotta cheese*
1½ oz. parsley	*(Roman style)*
1 garlic clove	*8 Tbs. parmigiano*
1 very small onion or leek	*1 egg*
⅛ lb. pancetta	*nutmeg*
2 oz. butter	*pepper*

Wash the spinach carefully. Cook the spinach in a pot with very
little water. When the liquid has evaporated, remove from fire and
cool, then squeeze well and chop finely. Wash the parsley and mince
it finely with the garlic, onion and pancetta. Lightly brown the resulting *battuto* in a saucepan with the butter, stirring frequently, for
about 5 minutes. Add the spinach, salt, mix well and let cook over low

heat for about 10 minutes, stirring frequently. Let cool.

Push the *ricotta* through a sieve into a bowl. Add the spinach mixture together with the *parmigiano,* egg, a pinch of nutmeg and pepper (and some salt, if necessary). Mix well and let stand in a cool place for several hours before using.

If desired, 2 ozs. of sausage may be added to the *battuto.* This stuffing is suitable for *tortelli, tortelloni, ravioloni.* The most suitable sauce is a strained tomato sauce.

ZUCCA
Pumpkin

3 lbs. peeled, seeded and diced pumpkin	*grated nutmeg*
	4 oz. fruit
4 oz. Amaretti di Saronno, crushed	*salt*
	crushed black pepper
5 oz. grated parmigiano	

Bake the pumpkin at 500° F. until cooked, approx. 25 minutes. Remove from oven and purée, preferably by hand. Let cool, add half of the *crushed amaretti,* and all other ingredients, chop and mix until you achieve a smooth mixture. If necessary, pass mixture through a sieve. Place the stuffing in a cool place for one day. This stuffing is suitable for large *tortelloni.* The sauce most suitable is butter and *parmigiano.* When serving the pasta, add the remainder of the crushed *amaretti* over the *tortelloni* after they are plated, so that the *amaretti* remain crunchy.

NOTE: in some cases the crushed *amaretti* are mixed with the grated *parmigiano.*

PASTICCI/TIMBALLI
Baked Pasta & Molds

Pasticci and *timballi* are prepared with either dry or fresh pasta, which may be either stuffed or not. The pasta is cooked, then mixed with a ragu' and *parmigiano.* Up to this point the two preparations are similar; what differs is the way in which the recipes are completed and the way in which they are served.

To make *pasticcio,* place the desired pasta* in a greased, shallow baking pan, cover each layer with the desired ingredients and sauce, and bake until a crust forms on top. Serve in the same baking pan.

To make *timballo,* the *pasta* is placed in a mold with rather high sides, which has been lined with savory flaky pastry (*pasta frolla*) (although occasionally, to simplify the recipe, the flaky pastry is omitted). The pasta is covered and sealed with a top crust of the pastry dough and then baked. When it is ready, after having let it stand for about ten minutes so that the pasta consolidates, the *timballo* is turned upside down on a serving dish and served. You may also use a spring-form mold, so that the mold need not be turned upside down.

If there is some dough left over, it may be used to decorate the top of the *timballo* by cutting it into various decorative shapes (small stars, leaves and so on) with a pastry cutter.

Lay the pastry designs along the outer edge or in the center of the *timballo,* brush them with beaten egg and bake. Of course, in this case the *timballo* should be baked by using a spring mold, so that the decorations are visible.

* Refer to recipe for type of pasta to use.

RICETTE
Recipes

CAPELLINI CON SALSA VERDE
Capellini with Green Sauce

1 lb. capellini	2 garlic cloves
2 Tbs. chopped basil	4 Tbs. grated parmigiano
2 Tbs. chopped parsley	2 oz. olive oil

Combine into a food blender, basil, parsley, garlic and *parmigiano.* Start the blender and add olive oil, obtain a dense but fluid sauce and set aside.

Boil *capellini* in plenty of salted water, be careful as these will cook very quickly. Drain while still al dente, toss with the prepared sauce at room temperature and serve.

NOTE: If too dry, add 2 Tbs. of the pasta water.

LINGUINE ALLE VONGOLE
Linguine with clam sauce

1 lb. linguine	1 pinch peperoncino
2 lbs. little neck clams	4 cloves garlic
4 Tbs. olive oil	1 Tbs. chopped parsley

Let the clams drain in cold water for at least one hour. In a large pot steam the clams until they are just open. Do not overcook or they will get chewy. Remove from heat and cool. Remove the clam from the shell. Pass the broth, which has formed, through a fine sieve or a cheesecloth. Put the shelled clams into the strained broth and set aside.

In a sauté pan warm the oil, add the crushed garlic and a pinch of *peperoncino,* and remove the garlic when browned. Add $\frac{2}{3}$ of the clam broth, reduce by one third and add the remainder of the broth with the clams, the chopped parsley and remove from fire.

Cook *linguine* in plenty of salted water. When *al dente,* strain the pasta and toss with the clam sauce over a high flame for 2 minutes and serve.

SPAGHETTI ALLA PUTTANESCA
Spaghetti «Harlot's Style»
Serves 6:

1 lb. spaghetti	*1 peperoncino*
3 oz. anchovies	*1 lb. ripe tomatoes*
3 oz. very good olive oil	*3 oz. pitted brown olives*
1 crushed clove of garlic	*(preferably Gaeta or Nicoise)*
salt	*1-½ oz. capers*

Chop the anchovies. Peel the tomatoes, dispense with the seeds and cut in little pieces. Pour the oil in a heated skillet and add the garlic and *peperoncino* cut in little pieces. Cover. Cook over medium heat until the garlic browns. Discard the garlic and add the anchovies. Add the tomatoes, olives and capers (well washed). Stir and let cook for about 7 minutes. Taste the sauce for seasoning. Pour the sauce over the *spaghetti* in a skillet with the sauce, toss well and serve.

NOTE: Spaghettini may be used instead of spaghetti.

PASTA CON LE SARDE
Bucatini with Sardines
Serves 6:

3 bunches wild fennel	*1 Tbs. raisins*
1 Tbs. olive oil	*1 Tbs. pine nuts*
1 onion, diced	*saffron threads*
4 boned, salted anchovies	*1 lb. bucatini*
1 Tbs. tomato paste	*salt*
1 lb. cleaned, boned sardines	*pepper*

Clean the wild fennel and boil in salted water. Drain carefully, retaining the cooking water, then chop the fennel coarsely and brown in a small amount of oil. In another pan brown the onions, cleaned and coarsely chopped, in plenty of oil. Add the anchovies and the tomato paste then stir briskly until the mixture becomes homogeneous.

Add the sardines, the browned fennel, raisins, pine nuts, and a few threads of saffron. Let cook lightly for 5 minutes, adding some of the reserved fennel water if necessary. Salt to taste.

Bring the remaining reserved fennel water to a boil and use it to cook the pasta. When the paste is al dente, drain, mix in the sauce and serve hot.

PASTA ALLA NORMA
Pasta with Eggplant and Basil
Serves 6:

1 eggplant	*pepper*
1 clove garlic	*olive oil*

10 ripe, peeled, seeded	1 lb. penne
and diced tomatoes	3 oz. grated aged salted ricotta
salt	10 basil leaves

Cut the eggplant into slices and place on a cutting board propped on a slant, cover with salt and leave them under a weight for one hour until the bitter water seeps out.

Brown the garlic in oil, add the tomatoes and salt. Bring to a simmer over medium heat and continue cooking, stirring occasionally, until the sauce has reduced by one third. Add pinch of pepper, remove from heat and set aside.

Wash and pat-dry the eggplant slices, fry in hot oil, put on paper towels to dry, then chop coarsely, and set aside. Cook the spaghetti in a large pot of boiling salted water until just *al dente,* drain and quickly toss in a large skillet, over a brisk flame, half of the tomato sauce, the eggplant, a few basil leaves and half of the grated cheese. Then put the pasta in the serving dish, cover with the remaining half of the sauce, the rest of the grated *ricotta* and sprinkle with a few more basil leaves over it and serve.

TAGLIATELLE CON I FUNGHI
Tagliatelle with Mushrooms
Serves 6:

4 Tbs. olive oil	½ cup beef broth
8 oz. porcini mushrooms	1 lb. tagliatelle
½ onion	4 Tbs. butter
1 Tbs. chopped parsley	2 Tbs. grated parmigiano

Prepare a *soffritto* with olive oil and very finely chopped onion. When onion are just tender, add the sliced mushrooms, sauté for 2 mins., add the broth, reduce by one third, add salt and pepper to taste. Remove from fire. Cook the *tagliatelle* in plenty of boiling salted water. When *al dente* toss in a large skillet with the mushroom sauce and the butter. Add a few Tbs. pasta water if they get too dry. Dish into a serving bowl and serve with *parmigiano* on the side.

FETTUCCINE ALLA CARBONARA
Fettuccine with a sauce of Pancetta and Onion
Serves 6:

1 lb. fettuccine	3 egg yolks
4 oz. pancetta	4 oz. grated pecorino cheese
2 Tbs. olive oil	salt and pepper to taste

Chop the *pancetta,* and sauté both with the olive oil on low flame. When the *pancetta* is golden brown, remove from heat and set aside.

Separate the egg yolks, and mix well with cheese, salt and pepper, mix well with a whisk and set aside.

Boil the *fettuccine* in plenty of boiling salted water. When *al dente,* strain and pour, in a large skillet. Over a low flame, add the *soffritto* of *pancetta,* add egg and cheese mix. Toss thoroughly and serve immediately.

NOTE 1: The original recipe calls for *guanciale* (smoked hog jowl).

FETTUCCINE ALFREDO
Fettuccine with Double Cream

This recipe is an adapted version by Alfredo of Rome of *fettuccine alla doppia crema* (with double cream), a classic recipe prepared throughout Italy. The following is the original recipe:

Serves 6:

1 lb. fettuccine	*5 oz. grated parmigiano*
10 oz. double cream	*freshly ground white*
	pepper to taste

Have all your ingredients at hand before you start this preparation. The original version would be finished at table side.

Cook fettuccine with more salt than usual, strain and remove when *al dente.* Put fettuccine into a large skillet with a few Tbs. of the pasta water, add the double cream and the *parmigiano.* Toss well. The final result should be a smooth, velvety sauce. It should not be dry. Add freshly ground pepper and serve immediately.

VARIATION: Mascarpone may replace heavy cream for *fettuccine al mascarpone.*

NOTE: Alfredo Di Levio calls his double cream − *doppio burro* − (double butter).

PAPPARDELLE AL SUGO DI LEPRE
Pappardelle with Hare Sauce

Serves 12:

2 lbs. pappardelie	*2 oz. pancetta*
1 wild rabbit (hare)	*nutmeg*
4 Tbs. olive oil	*2 Tbs. grated parmigiano*

Marinade:

1 cup red wine	*1 celery stalk*
1 onion	*thyme*
1 carrot	*bay leaf*

Prepare the marinade, cut the hare into pieces and marinate for 12 hours. Keep in a cool place. Prepare the sauce in a casserole with the olive oil and *pancetta* over a brisk flame, drain and add the hare from the marinade. Cook till browned on all sides, add the marinade, a pinch of nutmeg and continue to cook until the meat falls from the bone. Add beef broth if necessary while cooking. (The stewing can be done on the stove over a low flame or in the oven at 375 F.) When done set aside and cool.

Remove the meat from the bones. Pass the cooking liquids through a fine sieve. Put into a saucepan, add the hare meat and keep hot. Boil the *pappardelle* in plenty of boiling salted water. Toss with the hare sauce and serve with *parmigiano* on the side.

NOTE: Instead of hare, rabbit can be used or any other type of game bird or venison. Hare can also be referred to as wild rabbit.

FARFALLE AL POMODORO FRESCO
Fresh Pasta Bows with tomato and herb sauce

1 lb. farfalle (3 colors)	*pinch of oregano*
4 Tbs. olive oil	*1 qt. chicken broth*
1 clove garlic, crushed	*1 Tbs. fresh chopped parsley*
pinch of peperoncino	*2 Tbs. butter*
2 Tbs. fresh chopped basil	*4 Tbs. parmigiano, grated*
4 ripe tomatoes, peeled, seeded and cubed	

Prepare fresh pasta as in basic recipe (see "Fresh Pastas Cut In Shapes").

In a sauté pan heat the olive oil. Add the garlic, *peperoncino,* basil, parsley and oregano. Sauté on low heat then add the tomatoes and half the broth. Add fresh pasta and stir continuously adding the remaining broth until the pasta achieves the desired doneness. Finish with butter and *parmigiano.*

PASTICCIO DI PIZZOCCHERI
Baked whole wheat tagliatelle
Serves 8:

½ *lb. peeled and cubed potatoes*	*5 oz. grated parmigiano*
1 lb. cabbage	½ *lb. butter*
1 lb. pizzoccheri	*4 cloves garlic*
10 oz. fresh cheese (Toma)	*pepper*
fresh sage	

Bring a large pot of salted water to a boil. Put in the potatoes, and the cabbage leaves cut into strips. When the potatoes are cooked, add the pasta and cook until just *al dente.* Drain, place into a heated bowl in layers, alternating layers with the toma cut into strips, the *parmigiano* cheese and the butter browned with garlic and sage. Pepper to taste and serve immediately.

NOTE: Toma cheese may be replaced with *parmigiano.*

CANNELLONI RIPIENI DI VITELLO E SPINACI
Cannelloni Stuffed with Veal and Spinach
Serves 6:

12 cannelloni	*2 Tbs. flour*
1 lb. veal chuck	*½ cup milk*
2 lbs. spinach	*salt, white pepper*
¼ lb. ham	*pinch nutmeg*
2 eggs	*4 Tbs. grated parmigiano*
2 Tbs. butter	*1 cup meat ragù*

Follow the basic technique to make and cook the *cannelloni.*
Prepare the stuffing, roast the veal and cook the spinach, squeezing out excess water.

Chop and mix the veal and ham together with spinach, eggs, salt, pepper, pinch of nutmeg and 2 Tbs. *parmigiano.* Use a food mixer to achieve a smooth stuffing.

Prepare a bechamel by combining butter with flour, then adding the milk slowly, add a pinch of salt, pepper and nutmeg.
Prepare a meat sauce as in *ragù bolognese.*
Roll the stuffing in the *cannelloni* and arrange into a buttered baking dish.

Pour over first the bechamel, then the beef *ragù,* sprinkle with grated *parmigiano,* dot with butter and bake at 375 F. for 20 minutes.

CRESPELLE CON RIPIENO DI POLLO
Crespelle with Chicken Stuffing
Serves 6:

12 crespelle	*6 Tbs. butter*
6 oz. boneless chicken meat	*salt and pepper to taste*
2 oz. mozzarella	*1 cup tomato sauce*
1 Tbs. chopped parsley	*2 Tbs. grated parmigiano*

Prepare *crespelle* as in basic method.
Prepare the stuffing by chopping the white meat (use a food mill) with chopped *mozzarella,* parsley, 2 Tbs. butter, and salt and pepper. Obtain a smooth stuffing.

Divide the stuffing evenly on the *crespelle* and roll them like a *cannelloni.*

Arrange the crespelle into a buttered baking dish, spread the tomato sauce over the top, sprinkle with *parmigiano* and dot with butter. Bake for 12 minutes, remove from oven and serve.
NOTE 1: Because the stuffing is fairly solid, the *crespelle* are rolled, rather than folded — a process used with a softer stuffing.
NOTE 2: The variety of stuffings are numerous, the cook may use his imagination here.
NOTE 3: Crepes can also be covered with bechamel and glazed under a salamander.

ROTOLO DI PASTA RIPIENO
Stuffed Rolled Pasta
Serves 6:

2 sheets of dough	2 oz. fresh mushrooms
(6" x 12")	2 lbs. spinach
½ lb. lean veal, diced	4 eggs
½ lb. chicken livers, diced	4 Tbs. grated parmigiano
4 Tbs. butter	salt to taste
¼ lb. fresh sausage, crumbled	2 cups tomato sauce
	(see basic recipe)

In a saucepan sauté 4 Tbs. butter with the veal, chicken livers, mushrooms and sausages. Add a few Tbs. of broth if the mixture becomes too dry. Cook for about 30 minutes. Remove from heat and set aside.

Wash and clean the spinach, squeeze out excess water, chop and sauté with 2 Tbs. butter for 5 minutes and set aside.

Combine meat and spinach mixtures together with 4 eggs, and salt and pepper. Grind finely using a food mill to obtain a smooth stuffing.

Take 1 sheet of dough and spread the stuffing, leaving an unfilled ½" border. Take the other sheet, place on top and roll. Wrap with cheesecloth and cook as explained in the basic method of preparation.

When cooked, slice and arrange the rotolo in a buttered baking dish, pour tomato sauce over, sprinkle with 2 Tbs. *parmigiano,* dot with butter and bake for 12 minutes at 375 F.

PASTA 'NCASCIATA
Baked Rigatoni with Eggplant
Serves 6:

2 eggplants	2 oz. salami
1 lb. rigatoni	2 oz. mozzarella cheese
2 oz. lean veal	2 eggs
1 clove garlic	grated pecorino cheese
2 oz. olive oil	basil
1 lb., 2 oz. plum tomatoes	oil for frying
2 oz. chicken livers	salt
2 oz. green peas	pepper

Cut the eggplant into slices and place on a cutting board propped on a slant, cover with salt and leave them under a weight for one hour until the bitter water seeps out. Wash, drain, pat dry and fry in 2 tablespoons of olive oil and set aside.

Brown the veal with the chopped garlic in oil (remove garlic when golden brown). Add the chopped, seeded plum tomatoes and cook for 10 minutes. Salt and pepper to taste. Add the livers chopped into pieces and the peas, cook for half an hour. Dice the *salami* and *mozzarella* cheese. Hard boil the eggs and slice. Cook the pasta just until *al dente,* mix with three quarters of the sauce, then add the *salami* and *mozzarella,* and toss well.

Make layers of pasta mixture in a greased baking pan, alternating with layers of fried eggplant, slices of eggs and more sauce. Sprinkle the top layer with chopped basil and grated pecorino cheese and bake until a golden crust forms. Let the baked rigatoni rest for 10 minutes and serve.

PASTICCIO DI TAGLIATELLE
Baked Tagliatelle

$\frac{1}{2}$" *wide tagliatelle*
tomato sauce
1 lb., 2 oz. mozzarella
5 Tbs. butter
$\frac{1}{2}$ *cup grated parmigiano*

Cook the *tagliatelle* very al dente. Heat the desired meat or tomato sauce. Cut the *mozzarella* in thin slices (if it is too wet, pat it with clean napkins and dry it well).

Mix *tagliatelle* with $\frac{1}{3}$ of the tomato sauce. Butter a shallow baking pan.

Arrange the *tagliatelle* in thin layers in the baking pan, top each layer with the sauce, cover with *mozzarella* slices and sprinkle with *parmigiano.* The top layer should be *mozzarella* lightly covered with the remainder of the sauce. Dot with butter and bake for 20 minutes at about 350 F. The top should show the melted *mozzarella* lightly browned.

Remove from oven, let rest for 10 minutes and serve.

VARIATION: Dry pasta (e.g., *penne,* or *ziti*) may be substituted for the *tagliatelle.*

LASAGNA DI CARNEVALE
Lasagna of Meat Ragù with Ricotta and Mozzarella

Ingredients for Sauce:

2 oz. strutto	*1$\frac{1}{2}$ lb. lean pork meat*
2 Tbs. olive oil	*1 cup red wine*
1 oz. prosciutto fat, chopped	*1 oz. tomato paste*
2 onions, finely chopped	*2 lbs. peeled tomatoes*
	salt and pepper to taste

Ingredients for Meat Dumplings:

$\frac{1}{2}$ *lb. lean veal*	*1 Tbs. parmigiano*
3 oz. white bread crumbs	*1 tsp. chopped parsley*
1 egg	*salt and pepper to taste*

Other Ingredients:

8 oz. sausage	*6 oz. mozzarella*

1 Tbs. strutto   8 oz. grated parmigiano
1 cup ricotta cheese   2 lbs. lasagne*

Lasagne should be made with 3 eggs for each pound of flour so that it will be a bit stiffer. Cut lasagne into 3" wide, 12" long ribbons, or the length of the baking pan you will be using.

The sauce:

This pork *ragù* should be made the day before it is used so that it becomes easier to remove excess fat which will float to the surface. Place *strutto,* oil and *prosciutto* fat in a saucepan, together with onion. Let onion get tender (not brown) and add pork meat. Brown on all sides and add the wine and let reduce by half. Add tomato paste previously diluted in a cup of water, then peeled tomatoes and bring to a simmer. Cook for at least 4 hours with the pot covered. Add some water if the sauce gets too thick. Stir occasionally to make sure it does not stick to the bottom of the pot.

The Dumplings:

Chop the lean veal, add white bread crumbs which have been previously soaked in water and squeezed. Add 1 egg, 1 Tbs. grated *parmigiano,* chopped parsley, salt and pepper. Mix all ingredients to achieve a smooth compound. Make dumplings the size of a nutmeg and fry in hot oil. Place on paper towel to rid of excess fat and set aside.

Sauté the sausage with the strutto and cook till well browned. Remove from pan. Chop and combine with the meat dumplings, place into a small casserole with a cup of the pork ragù. Pass the *ricotta* through a fine sieve and add 2 Tbs. of pork *ragù,* mix well and set aside. Slice the *mozzarella* thinly and set aside. Boil the *lasagne* in plenty of salted water, remove when *al dente* and strain. Cool with cold water to stop the cooking process and add a little oil so that pasta ribbon will not stick to one another and will be easier to work with.

The Baking:

Butter a large baking pan. Place a little *ragù* on the bottom of the pan. Next, place a layer of *lasagne,* a thin layer of *ricotta,* layer of *mozzarella,* dumplings, sausage, another layer of *ragù,* and a generous amount of *parmigiano*. Continue with at least 3 layers and make sure the ingredients prepared are evenly used throughout the layering. The top layer should be the pork *ragù,* grated *parmigiano,* and dots of butter. Bake for 30 minutes and let the *lasagne* rest for 10 minutes before serving.

TIMBALLO DI TORTELLINI
A Mold of Tortellini

Flaky Pastry (pasta frolla):
$\frac{2}{3}$ lb. bleached flour   grated peel of 1 lemon
$\frac{1}{3}$ lb. butter   a pinch of salt
3 eggs (yolks only)
1 lb. tortellini
To be mixed with the tortellini:

2 cups ragù Bolognese	⅓ lb. grated parmigiano
1 white truffle	4 oz. butter
	1 egg

Prepare *tortellini* according to basic recipe. Heat the *ragu'*. Cook the *tortellini al dente,* drain, and place in a bowl. Add the ragu', 3 ozs. of butter (cut in pieces) and 2 ozs. of *parmigiano*. Mix well and let cool. Make the flaky pastry (*pasta frolla*) and divide into two batches, one twice the size of the other. Roll out the bigger batch with a rolling pin, making a disk large enough to line a buttered spring mold sprinkled with bread crumbs. Arrange the *tortellini* in layers in the mold, sprinkling each layer with the remaining *parmigiano* and covering with very thin slices of the truffle. Roll out the second batch of pasta frolla, making a top crust large enough to cover the *tortellini;* lay on top and seal the edges by pinching all around. The top may be decorated with pastry leftovers. Brush the pastry with beaten egg, and bake the *timballo* for 40-50 minutes at 375 F. Once cooked, let stand for about ten minutes before serving.
Anolini, cappelletti may be substituted for the *tortellini.*

TAGLIOLINI AL TARTUFO BIANCO
Green and White (Straw and Hay)
Tagliolini with White Truffle

In Piedmont, *tajarin* are especially made to be used with white truffle. Sometimes a spoonful of *parmigiano* is added to the pasta dough. *Tagliolini* are cut so thin that they cook very fast. Therefore, prepare the sauce before cooking the pasta.

1 lb. green and white	pinch of nutmeg
tagliolini	salt and white pepper
4 oz. butter	1 oz. white truffle
2 Tbs. grated parmigiano	

Melt the butter, add *parmigiano,* nutmeg and salt and pepper to taste. Boil the pasta, which will take only 2-3 minutes to cook. Strain and pour over the sauce. Toss quickly and very thinly slice the white truffle over the pasta. Use a truffle slicer.
NOTE: Another name for green and white tagliolini is *paglia* e *fieno,* which means straw and hay. This phrase was coined in Tuscany.

SFORMATO DI ANELLINI
Baked Ditali with Ricotta
Serves 6:

1 lb. anelli or ditali	salt
2 oz. butter	pepper
3 oz. caciocavallo or grated	olive oil
parmigiano	slightly toasted bread crumbs
8 peeled, seeded tomatoes	1 lb. ricotta cheese, passed
	through sieve
	1 onion

Cook the pasta in a large pot of boiling salted water until just *al dente,* drain and add butter and a few spoonfuls of *caciocavallo* or *parmigiano* cheese. Cook the chopped onion with the diced tomatoes, salt and pepper in a dry pan. Cook until the sauce becomes thick then purée it in a food mill and return to the pot. Add a bit of olive oil, and let sit for a few minutes over low flame.

Butter a mold and sprinkle with bread crumbs. Alternate layers of pasta with layers of *ricotta,* and grated *parmigiano.* Spread a spoonful of tomato sauce on each layer. The last layer should be pasta. Sprinkle the top with bread crumbs and put into a hot oven for half an hour. Turn the mold out onto a plate and serve hot.

GNOCCHI

In the Italian tradition *gnocchi* are always meant to be dumplings. They are generally made with a potato - base with the addition of flour. The proportions of potatoes and flour may vary from one region to another, according to local customs and traditions, as well as to the type of potatoes used. In addition to potato based *gnocchi,* there are also other types of *gnocchi* made with flour, *semolina, ricotta* cheese, spinach, or bread crumbs.

Gnocchetti are usually smaller than *gnocchi*.

NOTE: Idaho potatoes are the best to use. Do not choose early potatoes, as they are too watery.

GNOCCHI DI PATATE
Potato Gnocchi
Basic Recipe:

Wash about 1 lb. baking potatoes and cook in lightly salted water (without peeling). It is best to start with cold water. The potatoes should all be about the same size. The cooking time will depend on the type and size of the potatoes. A rule of thumb to check when they are ready is to stick a fork into one or two potatoes and if it enters easily, the potatoes are ready. When the potatoes are cooked, drain, peel and mash them through a potato ricer, (do not use a food mill; it will make a sticky purée impossible to work with) and place on a pastry board or a marble surface. Should the resulting purée be too watery, put it back over the stove over moderate heat and let it dry well, stirring constantly.

It is important to have a dry purée, otherwise it will be necessary to add too much flour, which will result in heavy, doughy *gnocchi.* Add a small amount of salt and as much white flour as necessary to have a soft dough that does not stick to your fingers. It is not necessary to mix the dough for a long time; it is sufficient just to blend the ingredients. Cut a piece of the dough and, coating your hands with flour, roll the dough into a long cylinder about the thickness of your index finger. Then cut the cylinder in pieces about 1-inch long. By pressing with the tip of the finger against the board, sweep the dough lengthwise, toward you. This will cause each piece to curl up, taking the shape of a little shell. You may also use other utensils for this purpose such as the back of a cheese grater. In this case, the *gnocchi* will be ridged and curled. It is not absolutely necessary to give it one shape; they may be simply cut into nuggets of any desired size.

Handling the *gnocchi* as little as possible, quickly continue this operation until all the dough is used. Place the finished *gnocchi* in a flat pan sprinkled with flour without putting one on top of the other. Cook as soon as possible. A variation to this basic method is to add one or two eggs to the potatoes and flour dough. The eggs will make the mix harder, more consistent. In some cases this is a desired result, especially if large amounts have to be prepared or if they have to be made long before the final cooking. In this case the *gnocchi* will not be as soft, they will have more of a bite.

How to Cook Gnocchi

Gnocchi should not be prepared too far in advance before cooking. To cook *gnocchi* it is preferable to use a large pot with a wide bottom, so that the heat underneath can spread well, allowing the water to return quickly to the boiling point again after the *gnocchi* have been added. This is important because, if allowed to stay in the water for too long, the *gnocchi* can break up and absorb too much water.

Add the *gnocchi* to the boiling water all at once and stir gently. Let cook until the *gnocchi* float to the top (a few minutes are enough), then lift them out of the water with a skimmer (do not use a colander). Place in a preheated bowl. Toss with the desired sauce, add *parmigiano,* if necessary, and serve immediately.

Sauces for Gnocchi

They are many sauces for *gnocchi,* and they vary from region to region. You may use melted butter flavored with sage, tomato sauce, mushroom sauce, *bolognese ragu',* pesto, or one of a variety of meat-based sauces such as lamb, veal, beef or pork, as well as the juice resulting from roasting or braising beef or with *Gorgonzola, Fontina,* etc.

Sprinkling the gnocchi with grated *Parmigiano* is a must, except for a preparation with cheese, regardless of the type of the sauce used.

RICETTE
Recipes

GNOCCHI DI PATATE ALLA BAVA
Gnocchi with Fontina Cheese

1 lb. baking potatoes	*8 oz. fontina cheese,*
4 oz. flour	*thinly sliced*
salt to taste	*4 oz. butter*

Prepare the *gnocchi* as in basic recipe. In this case, no egg is required in the dough. Also, this *gnocchi* should be prepared right before use.

Cook *gnocchi,* and strain. In a buttered baking dish, prepare alternate layers of *gnocchi,* and *Fontina,* making sure you have at least 3 layers. The top layer should be of cheese. Dot with butter and bake for 5 minutes. Let it rest 5 more minutes and serve.

STRANGOLAPRETI
Potato and flour gnocchi

This is the Neapolitan recipe. Although the same name is used for certain *gnocchi* preparations in Trentino and Alto Adige, they have entirely different results.

3 lbs. potatoes	*3 eggs*
1 lb. flour	*salt to taste*

Boil the potatoes, peel and when still hot pass through a potato ricer. Using a wooden board work the flour into the potatoes, the quantity depends on the level of humidity of the potatoes. Add the eggs and the salt. Achieve a soft and homogenous dough.

Strangolapreti should be cooked as soon as they are ready, if they stand too long they harden. Cook in plenty of salted, boiling water. When ready remove with a strainer, do not dump into a colander. Add a tomato sauce or a *ragù* and serve with *parmigiano*.

GNOCCHI DI PANE
Bread Gnocchi

These are the classical knodel, it is a regional recipe from Trieste.

1 lb. crustless white bread	*3 spoonfuls flour*
2 eggs	*(more flour if necessary)*
2 Tbs. grated parmigiano	

Soften the bread in water or milk. Squeeze it dry. Add the beaten egg, flour, *parmigiano* and salt to taste. Work the whole into a smooth and soft dough. With wet hands and using a teaspoon, form the dumplings the size of a walnut. Dip them in flour and place on to a floured sheet pan.

Boil the *gnocchi* in plenty of salted boiling water and remove with a strainer from pot when they come to the surface. The cooking time is 4-6 minutes depending on the size of the dumplings. The preferred sauce is melted butter with the addition of bread crumbs and grated *parmigiano*. The sauce is poured over the *gnocchi* and served. Several variations are possible for the sauce. Sometimes, bread gnocchi are served as an accompaniment to dishes with a rich sauce.

GNOCCHI DI SEMOLINO
Gnocchi of Semolina

$\frac{3}{4}$ *qt. of milk*	*9 oz. finely ground semolina*
5 oz. butter	$2\frac{1}{2}$ *oz. grated parmigiano*
salt	*2 egg yolks*

Bring the milk to a boil in a little saucepan with 1 oz. of butter and a pinch of salt. Add the *semolina* little by little, stirring all the while. Continue to stir and cook for about half an hour. Turn off the heat, add 2 Tbs. *parmigiano,* the egg yolks and stir well. Wet a pastry board or a marble surface and pour out the cooked *semolina.* Spread with a wet spatula to make a layer about $\frac{1}{2}$ inch thick. Let cool.

Melt the remaining butter. Cut the layer of *semolina* in pieces, using a round mold about 1½ inches in diameter. Arrange the resulting disks in slanted layers in a baking dish, sprinkling each layer with melted butter and *parmigiano*. Then bake until the top layer is crisp. Serve hot.

MALFATTI
Spinach Gnocchi

1½ lbs. spinach	3 eggs (2 whole, 1 yolk)
1 small onion	nutmeg
5 oz. butter	salt
7 oz. fresh ricotta	pepper
⅓ lb. grated parmigiano	sage

Clean, wash and cook the spinach (using just the water which remains on the leaves after being washed). Drain, squeeze well and chop finely. Wilt the minced onion in 2 ozs. of butter, then drain the onion and add to the spinach. Cook at very low heat, stirring frequently to allow more water to come out from the spinach. Then let cool.

Sieve the *ricotta* into a bowl. Add the spinach, about 2 ozs. of *parmigiano,* two whole eggs and 1 yolk, a pinch of nutmeg, and pepper and salt to taste. Mix, adding little by little as much flour as necessary to obtain a firm but soft mix. Make dumplings using a teaspoon, each the size of a walnut. Lightly sprinkle the *gnocchi* with flour (the amount of flour used to dust the *gnocchi* will vary according to how well the spinach were dried), and set aside on a sheet pan.

In a large pot bring to a boil a generous amount of salted water. Meanwhile, brown the remaining butter in a saucepan, adding whole sage leaves to taste. Add the *gnocchi* to the boiling water, stirring gently. As they float to the top drain with a skimmer and arrange in a serving platter. Season with the sage flavored melted butter and *parmigiano*. Serve very hot. A light tomato sauce may be used instead of the sage flavored butter.

NOTE: To allow for the condiment to achieve its full flavor, keep the platter with the *gnocchi* warm over a bain-marie for 5 minutes before serving.

GNOCCHI DI RICOTTA
Ricotta Gnocchi

12 oz. fresh ricotta, well drained	4 eggs (2 whole, 2 yolks)
	flour
3½ oz. parmigiano	salt

Sieve the *ricotta* into a bowl. Add the eggs (2 whole and 2 yolks), half the *parmigiano* and a pinch of salt. Mix well with a wooden spoon, adding as much flour as needed to obtain a firm but soft dough so that the *gnocchetti* will hold their shape. The quantity of flour given in this recipe is only an approximation; more may be needed if the ricotta has not been properly drained.

By using a dessert spoon make dumplings about the size of a walnut. Bring a generous amount of salted water to boil in a large pot, add the *gnocchi* and stir gently. Cook until the *gnocchi* float to the top. Drain and arrange in layers in a soup tureen, seasoning each layer with the desired sauce and the remainder of the *parmigiano*. A preferred sauce for this type of gnocchi is a light tomato sauce, or melted butter and grated *parmigiano*. Serve very hot.

NOTE: As with malfatti, this preparation may be kept over a bain-marie for 5 minutes before serving.

POLENTA
Cornmeal

The ingredients to make *polenta* vary only slightly throughout Northern Italy. In some regions the yellow cornmeal used is very finely ground, while in other regions it is coarse, and in some others two kinds of *polenta* are blended. Sometimes yellow or white cornmeal mixed with buckwheat is used. The procedures employed to prepare *polenta* do not vary much. What varies is the thickness of the final product, according to how and with what *polenta* is going to be served. In order to maximize the taste, a harmonious balance in texture between *polenta* and other ingredients is necessary.

It is desirable to use coarsely ground *polenta* to make a rather thick *polenta*, while the finely ground type is more suitable for a thinner *polenta*. Medium ground cornmeal is suitable for most preparations.

Whatever kind of *polenta* is used, be sure that it is dry and without lumps. It should be recently ground; if stored for a long time, the *polenta* may taste bitter.

Basic cooking procedures

The best kind of pot in which to cook *polenta* is the classic *paiolo,* made of copper without a tin lining, and with a convex bottom. Stirring is done only with a wooden paddle. The *paiolo* should only be half full with water; otherwise, in adding the cornmeal the water might overflow. The water should be properly salted in the beginning in order to avoid having to add either salt or water later in the cooking process. For each pound of *polenta* use 2 quarts of water and ¼ oz. of salt. This ratio applies to a soft *polenta*, which are always served with a condiment or with other ingredients added. If *polenta* is to be used baked, grilled or instead of bread, use a 3 to 1 ratio of water to *polenta,* use the same amount of salt.

Bring to a boil the proper quantity of water, adequately salted, then lower the heat (be careful, because in the beginning, while adding cornmeal,

PAIOLO AND TARELLO

boiling water might easily splash) and add the coarsely ground cornmeal, little by little, stirring constantly. Do not pour directly from the container, but use your hands, pouring a handful at time. After adding all the cornmeal, increase the heat and let cook for 40-50 minutes, stirring constantly. While cooking, the heat should be high, to cause bubbles to rise and burst on the surface. While stirring, separate the *polenta* from the sides of the pot and from the bottom toward the top. When ready, the *polenta* should come away from the wooden spoon (*tarello*) and from the sides of the pot. It can be served hot immediately with the desired condiment, or it may be poured out of the *paiolo* onto a wooden board. To do so, smooth the surface of the *polenta* and with a brisk move, turn the paiolo upside down. The *polenta* will easily come away from the *paiolo*. Cut with a wooden knife and serve. *Polenta* is often cut with a piece of thick string stretched tightly between two hands.

NOTE: *Polenta* made with finely ground cornmeal forms lumps easily. In order to avoid this, add a fifth of the cornmeal to the salted water while it is still cold, mixing with a whisk. Once the cornmeal is blended with the water, cover, in order to prevent boiling *polenta* from splashing, and let boil for 10 minutes. Then, stirring constantly, add the remaining cornmeal following the procedures described in basic method.

How to serve polenta

Polenta is often served, as a starch instead of bread, especially in rural and mountain areas, together with tiny deep-fried fish, broiled *cotechino, salami,* or cheese. In this case it is not sauced but is served solely as a complement to meat, game and fish dishes cooked in sauces or gravies. *Polenta* is also served with cheese (*gorgonzola, toma, fontina*) or in bowls with cold milk.

It is delicious when served very hot, dotted with fresh butter and sprinkled with *parmigiano*. It is good when sliced, arranged in layers in a baking dish, covered with wedges of *parmigiano,* sprinkled with melted butter and baked for a few minutes. You may add thinly sliced white truffles, if in season.

Polenta leftovers may be sliced and fried in oil or lightly grilled over charcoal, then served either as a side dish or, better yet, covered with lard minced with parsley and garlic.

Polenta may also be prepared by cooking it with other ingredients like beans, cabbage, spinach, and potatoes. In this case, polenta is dotted with butter or browned lard, sprinkled with *parmigiano,* and thus served as a complete meal.

RECIPES

POLENTA CON FAGIOLI BORLOTTI E CAVOLO
Cornmeal with Borlotti Beans and Cabbage

7 oz. dried borlotti beans	*1 clove garlic, crushed*
salt	*4 oz. lard*
1 small Savoy cabbage	*9 oz. yellow, coarsely*
(about 1 lb.), shredded	*ground polenta*

Soak the beans overnight, then put them in lightly salted, cold water, and let cook over medium heat for 40 minutes. Clean and wash the cabbage, then blanch and immerse in cold water, cook till tender. Combine cabbage and beans. Cook for 1-2 minutes then begin pouring in the ground *polenta*. Follow the sauce procedure as in the basic recipe. You will need 40-45 minutes before the *polenta* is cooked. Add additional hot water if the *polenta* becomes too dry. When ready turn the *polenta* on a wooden board and let cool. Sauté the garlic with the lard, remove when brown and set lard aside.

Cut the cooled *polenta* with the cabbage and beans into strips (approx. 2×4"). Dust with flour and cook in plenty of oil till crisp. Dot with lard and serve very hot.

PASTICCIO DI POLENTA CON RAGÙ DI CARNE
Polenta with meat ragù

9 oz. yellow polenta	8 Tbs. grated parmigiano
1½ qts. water	1 oz. white bread crumbs
4 Tbs. butter	¼ oz. salt
meat ragù (see "Sauces")	

Preheat oven to 375 F. Prepare a *polenta* as in basic recipe. Once ready, pour into a large baking dish, previously moistened with water so that the *polenta* does not stick to the sides. Let cool, turn the casserole upside down, and turn out the *polenta*. With a long, wooden knife or a colorless string, cut the *polenta* horizontally in four equal layers. Butter the same baking dish, and pour in a few Tbs. of *ragù*. Place the first layer of *polenta* at the bottom of the baking dish; spread ragù over the layer of *polenta* and sprinkle with *parmigiano*. Repeat the operation with the remaining three layers of *polenta* in order to reconstruct its original form. Finish with the ragù, dot with butter and sprinkle with the remaining *parmigiano* mixed with a pinch of grated bread crumbs. Bake for about 40 minutes and then serve.

POLENTA CONCIA
Polenta with Butter and Fontina

13 ozs. yellow, coarsely ground polenta	8 oz. fresh butter
13 ozs. Fontina cheese	

Prepare a *polenta* following the basic procedure.

While the *polenta* is cooking, dice the cheese in small pieces. After the *polenta* has cooked for half an hour, add the butter, cut in small pieces. Five minutes before turning the heat off, blend in the cheese. Let sit several minutes, turn it on a wooden board, cut with a wooden knife and serve.

VARIATION: Substituting 7 oz. of yellow with whole wheat *polenta* cornmeal and *fontina* with *bitto* cheese (see Glossary) you will have a specialty of the Valtellina region called *polenta taragna. Bitto* may be substituted with *parmigiano.* The wholewheat cornmeal is mixed into the water when it is still cold. It is then brought to a boil and the yellow cornmeal is added following the cooking process as in basic method.

Polenta taragna is always served with good *salame,* sliced thick by hand or fresh pork sausage sautéed till brown.

RISO
Rice

Rice is a very old nutrient. We know for a fact that in India it was grown 4000 years before Christ. We do not know exactly when rice came to Italy. The only documentation we have is a letter dated September 27, 1475, in which the Duke of Milano, Galeazzo Maria Sforza, promises the Duke of Ferrara 12 sacks of rice seeds. It also indicates that cultivation of rice along the Po river was already considered viable. It should be noted that the acceptance of rice was not easy because it was felt that the stagnant waters necessary to grow rice would bring some health risks, such as malaria.

Today, however, rice is one of the basic elements of Italian cuisine. The more serious recipe books list innumerable recipes for rice and *risotti;* most of them, however, have their origins in main areas of consumption, such as Piedmont, Lombardy and Veneto.

It is in Piedmont that we start to discover *risotto,* where the basic preparation is onion sautéed with butter, finished with butter and *parmigiano,* and topped with the juice of the roast.

In some parts of Piedmont *risotto* is served with truffles, in other parts with sausage. Very common in Piedmont are also *risotti* with red wines, especially in the Barolo wine production area.

In the area of Pavia, Milano and Como, *risotti* with fresh water fish are very common because of the many lakes in that region. A lot of credit for several variations is attributed to the monks from Certosa because their diet called for only lean foods, such as frogs' legs and sweet water prawns, frequently enriched with mushrooms.

The most famous of the Italian *risotti* is risotto alla Milanese, with saffron. Various legends claim its illustrious beginning. One of them gives the credit to a master glassblower who, on the day of his wedding, added saffron (which he used to color glass) into the *risotto* he served. The reality is probably much simpler than that: *risotto* alla Milanese is none other than a simplified version of the Spanish paella because for a long time Milan was ruled by the Spaniards.

As we move east and south, the versions of *risotto* change according to regional ingredients. We find the risotto with black ink in Veneto, the sartù di riso from Naples, and the arancini di riso in Sicily. These are but a few of the many interpretations where the fantasy and ingenuity of the housewives and professional cooks came through triumphantly.

Italian rice can be divided into two major types: hard and soft grain rice — and four varieties: common, *semifine, fine* and *superfine.* Although the *superfine* extra-long variety is by far the most expensive one, it should be noted that the nutritive value remains constant for all kinds of rice. The difference in price is due to other factors, such as the size of the grain, productivity of the ears, response of the grains to cooking, vis-à-vis texture, and cost of production.

Rice is a most genuine and natural foodstuff and the most digestible of all cereals. It cannot be altered and does not undergo any process while cooking that might change its basic structure.

VARIETIES OF RICE

RISO COMUNE
Common, Short Grain Rice
This rice has small, round grains which tend to disintegrate in the cooking process. It is mostly used in broths (*minestra*). It is rich in starch, partly released in the cooking process, which enhances the flavor of the broth but causes it to be slightly cloudy. It is also suitable for desserts. It cooks in about 10 to 12 minutes.

RISO SEMIFINO
Semifine, Medium Grain Rice
This rice is medium size, with roundish grains. Its use is the same as for short grain rice. It cooks in 12 to 14 minutes and is suitable for *timballi, sartù* and *suppli.*

RISO FINO
Fine, Long Grain Rice
This rice has long, tapered grains. It is particularly suitable for *risotto,* since it has a medium starch content and absorbs seasonings well. It cooks in about 16 to 20 minutes.

RISO SUPERFINO
Superfine, Extra-long Grain Rice
This rice is fat and long. It can be used for *risotti* but is better suitable for pilafs. It is low in starch, absorbs less water and is therefore tastier when eaten plain. It cooks in 22-24 minutes.

DIFFERENT BRANDS OF RICE
AND THEIR USE

Kind of Rice	Group	Aspect	Use
Tondo Balilla	common	lightly pearled	soups and sweets
Lido Rosa Marchetti	semifine	shiny	Pilaf
Padano (Maratelli)	semifine	pearled	soups
Romeo	semifine	pearled	risotti
Vialone Nano	semifine	pearled	risotti
Ribe-Ringo	fine	lightly pearled	risotti and soups
S. Andrea (Rizzato)	fine	pearled	risotti
Baldo	superfine	lightly pearled	risotti and soups
Roma (Razza 77)	superfine	pearled	risotti
Arborio	superfine	pearled	risotti
Carnaroli	superfine	pearled	risotti

Advise about Rice

Rice must never be washed before being cooked. In cooking rice, the pot must be kept uncovered to avoid causing the grains to disintegrate. You must not forget that rice, like pasta, continues to cook after having been placed in a serving dish or saucepan. The residual heat of the rice continues the cooking process, even when drained and removed from the heat; therefore, it must be served immediately to avoid overcooking or it must be removed from the heat while still al dente if it has to rest for a few minutes, as is the case in most risotti.

Single portions of rice range as follows:

— 1½ oz. for a *risotto* rich in vegetables or other ingredients.

— 2 oz. for a regular *risotto* (one which does not contain a lot of ingredients).

— 2½ oz. for boiled rice cooked in water.

RICE COOKING METHODS

Boiled rice

The most suitable type of rice for this simple preparation is extra-long grain. Use 1 quart of water for each 3 ozs. of rice.

Bring an adequate amount of salted water to a low boil and add the rice. Let cook uncovered, stirring now and then with a wooden spoon. Turn off the heat when the rice is still *al dente*. Strain and retain some of the cooking water, in case the condiment used is too dry. Pour into a soup tureen previously warmed with boiling water, mix the condiment in and toss well, since the sauce itself will allow the rice to reach the final cooking point. If the rice is to be merely buttered, let the butter soften a couple of hours before adding it to the rice. *Parmigiano* cheese is most often used in all rice preparations except those with sauces containing fish.

Generally speaking, all sauces used with short pasta are suitable with rice. Other possibilities are egg yolk mixed with *parmigiano* and very fresh butter, or butter browned with a few sage leaves.

Risotto

The word *risotto* is meant to refer to rice which has been toasted briefly with a *soffritto* and then cooked by gradually adding boiling broth or water and *mantecato* (butter and *parmigiano* added). It should be remembered when cooking rice suitable for *risotto,* it absorbs a quantity of liquid three times the weight of the rice itself.
Procedures: To cook *risotto* it is preferable to use a heavy saucepan of medium height, with a rather large bottom so that the flame underneath can be well distributed.

4 oz. butter   6 Tbs. Parmigiano
1 medium onion, finely   1¼ qt. broth
chopped
12 oz. long grain rice.

Brown the onion in one oz. of butter. When the onion loses its crunchiness (do not let it brown) add the rice and toast gently over a medium heat, stirring frequently with a wooden spoon until the rice absorbs the fat and becomes flavored. Then pour a ladle of boiling broth into the pot. If the recipe calls for some dry white or red wine, add wine first, reduce by half, then add the broth. Continue to stir, but not too frequently, and gradually add more broth as the rice absorbs the liquids. It is important to maintain the simmering of the rice constant, so attention must be paid to the amount of broth as it is added to the rice. When the rice is cooked *al dente,* turn off the heat. Finish *risotto* by adding butter and grated *parmigiano,* let stand, covered, for a couple of minutes, so that the rice may become entirely cooked. Serve immediately.

NOTE 1: The *risotto* should not be too dry, but must be lightly creamy, and each grain of rice should be fluffy. The broth used for *risotto* should always be rather light and clear, most often made from chicken or veal. The ratio of broth to rice for *risotto* is 1 part rice to 3 parts broth, more broth or hot water for boiled rice. For *risotto* use only imported fine Italian rice, since it is less rich in starch and therefore more suitable for this preparation.

NOTE 2: Risotto can be prepared with one or more ingredient like meat, fish, vegetables, game, etc. Some of the most suitable are vegetables like asparagus tips, green peas, beans, *radicchio* leaves, artichoke hearts, leeks, *zucchini, fava* beans, and mushrooms; meats like chicken liver, and quails; fish and shellfish like mussels, clams, shrimp, baby cuttlefish, *scampi,* swordfish, crayfish and lobster.

NOTE 3: Types of *risotto* are named after the ingredients used — e.g., *risotto* with green peas, *risotto* with scampi, risotto with radicchio.

NOTE 4: parmigiano is never used for a risotto with fish or shellfish. There are exceptions, however, since it's a matter of taste.

Risotto Mantecato

Virtually any *risotto* can be made "*mantecato*", a term meaning butter and Parmigiano has been added and whisked in with a wooden spoon just before it is served.

This procedure allows for the *risotto* to achieve its smooth, creamy consistency. There are some exceptions. These are given by specific recipes. As mentioned in the prior chapter, it is advisable not to use cheese with fish *risotto,* because cheese has a powerful taste that would dominate the delicate flavor of fish. The term "*mantecare*" may also be used for a pasta that is finished with the desired sauce before serving. Butter and/or *parmigiano* may also be added if the recipe calls for it.

Risi

Most regions do variations on *risottis,* most notably in Veneto, where they are called *risi. Risi* are prepared in a similar fashion to risotto, with the difference that they are much more fluid. This is achieved by simply using more broth and removing from the fire while still very wet. Venetians used to say that *risi* must be *all'onda* (wavy), that is, when poured into the dish, the consistency of the *risotto* should be so fluid as to allow the rice to form waves.

RICETTE
Recipes

RISO IN CAGNON
Rice with Sage and Parmigiano

1 lb. extra-long grain rice	*1 garlic clove*
4 oz. butter	*4 Tbs. parmigiano*
2 sage leaves	*salt and pepper to taste*
1 sprig rosemary	

Bring 4 qts. of salted water to a boil, add the rice, and let cook uncovered, stirring now and then. Brown the butter in a large frying pan with the sage and garlic. Remove garlic when brown and re-move sage leaves. Drain the rice while still *al dente* and pour in a serving bowl, add the flavored hazelnut butter, and grated *parmigiano*. Toss well, place the sprig of rosemary in the center and serve.
NOTE: In the Piedmont version, diced *fontina* cheese is added instead of *parmigiano*.

RISOTTO ALLA MILANESE
Risotto with Saffron

12 ozs. long grain rice	*½ cup dry white wine*
3 oz. butter	*1¼ qt. of lean beef broth*
1" beef marrow (optional)	*pinch of saffron*
1 medium-size white onion,	*6 Tbs. parmigiano*
thinly sliced	*salt*

Dip the marrow briefly in boiling water. Chop the marrow. In a saucepan with 2 ozs. of butter, brown the marrow briefly, then add the onion. When the onion begins to get tender, add the rice and stir until it is lightly toasted and has absorbed the fat. Pour in the wine and let evaporate. Add a ladle of broth and, continuing to stir, let the rice absorb it. Continue to add broth, one ladle at a time, and stir until the rice is almost cooked. Allow each ladleful to be ab-sorbed before adding the next one.
Halfway through cooking, dissolve the saffron in a little broth and

add to the rice. Do not add in the beginning, since the saffron should not cook.

When the rice is ready, (*al dente*), turn off the heat and mix in the remaining butter and *parmigiano*. Add the marrow. Stir the rice well with a wooden spoon until the ingredients are blended thoroughly and the *risotto* is smooth. The rice grains should be fluffy, yet hold together and should not be too fluid.

VARIATIONS:

1. While cooking the onion you may also add a piece of sausage, sliced mushrooms, or chicken livers.

2. *Risotto* made without saffron is called alla *parmigiana.*

3. *Risotto* made using one-half red wine (Barbera or Barolo) and one half broth is a recipe characteristic of the Piedmont region.

4. *Risotto* made without saffron and covered with thin slices of *fontina* cheese then baked is another Piedmontese version.

NOTE: Of course each variation takes a different name.

RISI E BISI
Rice and peas

12 oz. long grain rice	*3 lbs. fresh peas*
2½ ozs. butter	*1 oz. parsley*
2 Tbs. olive oil	*6 Tbs. parmigiano*
1½ oz. lean pancetta	*1¼ qts. beef broth*
1 small onion	*pepper*
salt	

Shell the peas. Make a *battuto* with the *pancetta,* and onion: put in a saucepan, add half the butter and the oil, and lightly fry until the *pancetta* melts and the onion loses its crunchiness. Do not let it become brown. Add the green peas and a ladle of broth. Stir and let cook on low heat for about 10 minutes (if the peas are tough cook for 5 more minutes). When the peas are halfway cooked, add all the broth, bring to a boil and add the rice and cook over medium heat. Stir frequently, adding additional broth if necessary (especially toward the end). Remember that the final product should be fairly fluid so as to form a wave on the dish when served.

Once *al dente,* turn the flame off, mix in the remaining butter, the *parmigiano,* parsley, a pinch of pepper and serve.

VARIATION: In the Padova area this is prepared with goose meat preserved in its fat and is called *risi e bisi con l'oca in onto* (wet risotto with green peas and goose in its fat).

RISO E LATTE
Rice and Milk

10 oz. long grain rice	*2 oz. butter*
3 pts. milk	*salt*

Bring half of the milk to a simmer and add rice. Cook over medium flame, salt to taste and cook uncovered, stirring occasionally. When the milk is entirely absorbed by the rice, add more warm milk, a little at a time, until the rice is cooked. Mix in the butter and serve. The finished rice and milk dish should remain fluid.

RISOTTO CON CALAMARI
Risotto with Squid

2 lbs. squid	1 Tbs. chopped parsley
2 small onions	10 oz. long grain rice
1 clove garlic	1 qt. fish broth
2½ oz. olive oil	2 Tbs. butter
1 cup dry white wine	salt
pepper	

Clean the squid, setting aside 2 or 3 of the ink sacks, then cut squid into thin strips. Brown one onion and garlic in oil, remove garlic when brown, then add the squid. Sauté briskly then add the parsley and the white wine and continue cooking the squids for 15 mins. (the time of cooking depends on the size and quality of the squids) and set aside. Prepare a *battuto* with the other onion and 2 Tbs. butter. When onion is soft, not brown, add the ink sacks, stir well and add the rice. Proceed to make the *risotto* in the usual manner. When *al dente,* remove from fire and add the squids. Salt and pepper to taste and serve.

NOTE 1: No *parmigiano* is required for this *risotto.*
NOTE 2: If the *risotto* needs more binding, add 2 Tbs. of butter.

RISOTTO CON LE QUAGLIE
Risotto with Quail

salt	3 oz. butter
pepper	2 Tbs. brandy
6 quails, boned and ready to cook	1 cup dry white wine
	1 qt. beef broth
sage leaves	1 medium size white onion
4 very thin slices of lard or pancetta	10 oz. long grain rice
	6 Tbs. parmigiano

Salt and pepper the insides of the quail and insert a sage leaf. Wrap the quails with the *pancetta* or lard slices, fastening with toothpicks. Melt 1 oz. of butter in a saucepan and brown the quails, moistening with ½ cup of wine and brandy. When the wine evaporates, add salt and pepper and roast for 12 minutes., moistening with broth as needed. Cool the quail, strain, de-glaze the pan juices and set aside. Quarter the quails and remove the breast bone. Return pan juices to the saucepan and add the quail pieces. Finish the cooking for another 6 minutes on moderate flame.

In the meantime, prepare a *risotto* using half the remaining butter, the finely minced onion, the remaining wine, and the broth, following the basic procedures.

When the *risotto* is cooked *al dente,* remove from fire, add the remaining butter and the *parmigiano.* Pour the *risotto* into a serving dish, arrange the quails all around the dish, alternating legs and breasts, drizzle the border of the *risotto* with the pan juices, and serve.

RISOTTO CON COZZE
Risotto with Mussels

3⅓ lbs. of mussels	*1¼ qts. fish broth*
4 Tbs. olive oil	*1 oz. parsley*
1 small onion	*1 oz. butter*
2 garlic cloves	*pepper*
10 oz. long grain rice	

Wash and brush the mussels thoroughly, then let them sit in salted water for an hour. Drain and place in a large pan over medium-high heat, until the mussels open. Extract the flesh and check that they are all clean, taking care to remove the "beard". Strain the resulting broth through a very fine sieve or cheesecloth.

In a saucepan, cook the finely sliced onion, and the garlic cloves in oil. When the onion begins to get tender and the garlic is slightly browned, remove the garlic. Add the rice and let it toast and absorb the fats. Add the mussel broth and keep stirring the rice till the liquid is well absorbed. Add the additional fish broth as needed and proceed to cook as in basic recipe. When rice is *al dente,* add the minced parsley and the mussels, remove from heat, add butter. Rest it for a few minutes and serve.

TIMBALLO DI RISO CON PICCIONE
Rice Timbale with Squab

3 large squabs	*salt, pepper*
1 small onion or leek	*1 lb. medium grain rice*
4 oz. butter	*2 eggs*
1 cup dry white wine	*6 Tbs. parmigiano*
3 sage leaves	*small quantity of bread crumbs*

Quarter the squabs. Slice the onion and brown in a small saucepan with 1½ oz. of butter. When the onion begins to get tender, add the squab parts to the saucepan and brown, moistening with wine. When all the wine is evaporated, pour in ½ cup of water, add sage, a pinch of pepper, salt and let cook on a very low heat for 15 mins. Remove from heat, de-glaze and reserve the pan juices. Let cool and bone the squab completely. Set aside.

Cook the rice in boiling salted water, and, after 6-7 minutes, drain and put it in a large bowl. Add the squab pan juices, half the remaining butter, the eggs, 4 Tbs. *parmigiano,* and mix well.

Butter a baking pan and sprinkle with bread crumbs. Arrange the rice in layers, each topped with pieces of the squab. Sprinkle the top layer with the remaining *parmigiano,* dot with the remaining butter, and bake in a preheated oven (375 F.) for about 20 minutes. When it is done, let it rest for 4-5 minutes before serving.

SARTÙ DI RISO
Sartù of rice

1 oz. dried mushrooms	10 oz. medium grain rice
1 small onion, chopped	⅔ lb. ground beef
3 Tbs. olive oil	3 eggs
2 Tbs. tomato paste	2 oz. parmigiano
1½ quarts broth	bread crumbs
½ lb. fresh peas	salt, pepper
4 thin sausages	1 large mozzarella, diced

Reconstitute the mushrooms in lukewarm water and chop. Prepare a *ragù* in the following manner: Sauté the onion in 1½ oz. oil. When onion is soft, add the tomato paste diluted in 2 cups broth, the chopped mushrooms and the green peas, salt and pepper. Mix and cook for 2 to 3 minutes. Add the crumbled sausage and let cook for 20 minutes over low heat. Remove from fire and set aside.

In a bowl combine the ground meat, 1 egg, 1 Tbs. *parmigiano,* 1 Tbs. bread crumbs, salt and pepper to taste. Mix all ingredients well and make small dumplings the size of a hazelnut. Fry in the remaining oil, add to the *ragù* and set aside.

Pour the other half of the *ragù* into a large casserole. When it starts to bubble, pour in the rice, stir well, add broth as needed and cook rice till al dente. Add 2 ozs. lard (or butter), 4 Tbs. parmigiano and 2 whole eggs. Mix the ingredients well and let cool.

In a small skillet sauté the chicken livers with 1 oz. of lard. Sauté briskly for 2 to 3 minutes, salt to taste and set aside.

Grease a 2 qt. mold with the remaining lard and sprinkle the bottom and sides well with bread crumbs. Pour in about ¾ of the *risotto,* pressing it against sides and bottom of mold, leaving a well in the center. Place in it some *ragù* with the meat dumplings, a few chicken livers, pieces of *mozzarella* and sprinkle with *parmigiano.*

Add more rice and repeat the process. Fill the inside of the rice mold only three quarters full, cover with the remaining *risotto,* pressing lightly with your hands. Sprinkle bread crumbs over the top and dot with lard. Place in a preheated oven at 325 F. and cook for about 30 minutes. Remove from the oven and let stand for 10 mins. Turn the *timballo* upside down, on a serving platter to release the *sartù.* Serve immediately.

NOTE: Sartù may be sliced with a spatula when serving.

SUPPLÌ ALLA ROMANA
Supplì Roman style

1 oz. dried mushrooms	4 ripe tomatoes, peeled, seeded
2 onions, chopped	and diced
4 oz. butter	salt
8 oz. rice	¼ lb. mozzarella, diced
6 Tbs. parmigiano	2 eggs
2 oz. chicken livers, chopped	flour
3 oz. lean veal, chopped	bread crumbs
1 oz. prosciutto	frying oil
1 Tbs. tomato paste.	

Reconstitute the mushrooms in lukewarm water, chop and set aside. Sauté one onion in 2 oz. butter in a saucepan. When the onions are soft, add the rice and make a *risotto* as in basic recipe. Let *risotto* cool.

Make a *ragù* by sautéing one onion in the remaining butter. When onions are soft, add the chopped livers, veal, *prosciutto,* and mushrooms. Add the tomato paste diluted in 1 cup warm water, salt and let simmer over a low flame. Let the mixture cook and reduce to achieve a rather thick *ragù.* Remove from heat and cool.

Take a small amount of rice in the palm of your hand, flatten the rice and place in the center a teaspoonful of the prepared *ragù,* and few pieces of *mozzarella.* Close your palm and form a ball. Make sure the filling is securely closed in the center of the ball, twice the size of a walnut. Roll the rice ball into flour, beaten egg and bread crumbs, continue until all the rice is finished.

Fry the *supplì* in the hot oil until golden brown and crunchy. Serve immediately, plain or with a tomato or meat sauce on the side.

RISO AL SALTO
Crisp rice patty
The common version of *riso al salto* is just a way of utilizing leftover *risotto* by making rice patties. The leftover *risotto* is mixed with eggs and grated *parmigiano* and then fried. The result is a heavy unappetizing dish because the rice becomes soft and glutinous after a second cooking. Professional Italian cooks use this recipe:

Serves 6:

1 small onion	1 pinch saffron
3 oz. butter	4 Tbs. parmigiano
1¾ cups Italian rice	salt
1 qt. beef broth	pepper

Chop the onion and put in a saucepan with half of the butter. Let brown slowly, then add the rice and toast it until all the butter has been absorbed. At this point begin to make a *risotto* in the usual manner, adding hot broth as needed and stirring frequently. Add the saffron diluted in a ladleful of broth just before removing from fire. Stop cooking the *risotto* after 8 minutes. Remove it from the pan and spread it out on a large plate so that it cools.

Melt some butter in an 8-inch frying pan, add 2-3 spoonfuls of cooled risotto, and flatten into a patty that covers the bottom of the pan with a spatula. Cook over medium heat. As the rice patty cooks, the starch remaining in the grains of rice is expelled and makes the rice stick together perfectly. Shake the pan so the patty does not stick to the bottom of the pan, flip over the rice patty or use a plate if you are not an expert. Let cook on the other side and serve hot sprinkled with *parmigiano* cheese. Using this technique *riso al salto* need not cook more than six or seven minutes and should, therefore, be light and crispy.

PESCE
Fish

Italians throughout the centuries have retreated inland, building villages and towns on the higher hills to protect themselves from barbarian invasions from the sea. As a result, Italians developed a beef, vegetable, and dairy diet in their homes, relying heavily on farm products the land provided. This fact of life also affected the seashore populace who, perhaps because of an abundance of fish, considered it to be less nutritious than beef. This erroneous perception has changed in recent times, and today the Italian diet relies heavily on the richness of the Mediterranean sea, which surrounds the entire peninsula.

The origin of Italian cooking at seashores, however, was well established a long time ago. The Romans themselves started the first breeding of moray and gilthead bream for the table of the rich. From ancient times, the most prized Mediterranean fish have been caught and generally roasted or grilled. The seashore's inhabitants developed a fish cookery tradition which found its expressions in the rich array of the fish stews (*zuppe di pesce*), the cooking of various types of fish with a few vegetables and one common condiment: olive oil. It is curious to observe that the recipe books from the 15th to 18th century totally ignore fish cookery. It is only in the writing of Vincenzo Agnoletti in 1814 that we find the first hint of "fish broths to pour over slices of bread". *Zuppe di pesce,* the name of which changes according to regions, such as *caciucco, brodetto, ciuppin,* etc., does not have basic rules of preparation, but it is born by the obvious necessity of working with the least priced fish aboard fishing boats, or from customers who, at the last minute, bought whatever was left over from the daily catch. The consumption of fish has also increased considerably thanks to an extraordinary and perfect distribution network that allows for the merchandise to arrive at markets while still very fresh. The fish market in Milan, for example is the most important in Italy and one of the most important in Europe; therefore, it's relatively easy to find in Milan, Bergamo and other locations far away from the sea, restaurants that are well known for their fish cookery.

The fish in this chapter are the most common variety, and the recipes the most popular. *Caciucco, brodetti* and *zuppe* are all much the same although the names vary from one village to the other, each claiming its recipe to be the original. From the immediate consumption of the small fish along the shore to commercially organized fisheries in larger markets of Milan and Rome, today fish is one of the most important nutrients in the Italian diet.

The quality of fish is primarily determined by its environment: the cleaner and richer in nutritive elements the water is, the better the fish will taste.

All fish, shellfish included, must be eaten fresh or perfectly preserved by freezing, smoking, or salting.

How to Recognize Fresh Fish

Fresh fish have virtually no smell, or, if marine in origin, smell only of seaweed and seawater. The body of a fresh fish is rigid, the flesh firm. The skin should not be dry. The scales (if present) are shiny, tightly connected to each other and to the body. The eyes should be clear, shiny and not sunken. The gills should be red and wet. The stomach should be firm, neither swollen nor lacerated. The tail should be rigid, and the anal orifice completely closed. If you buy fish in fillets or steaks, check that the flesh is white or rosy, with iridescent reflections, and adheres firmly to the bone.

How to Clean Fish

Fish must always be thoroughly cleaned, regardless of how they are to be cooked. If the fish has scales, they must be removed: place the fish on a large sheet of paper, and, holding it by the tail (if it is slippery, hold the tail with a towel), lightly scrape the fish with the back of a knife or one with a dull blade, held at an angle, scraping from the tail to the head, until all scales are removed. The fins may also be removed. Gut the fish by making a small opening in the stomach to remove the intestines and black membrane (if present) which lines the stomach cavity.

To improve the aesthetic appearance of the fish, remove the guts by inserting your fingers through the gills and pulling them out through this opening. Wash the fish well and let drain, head down. This procedure is appropriate for most kinds of fish. With spiny fish it is a good idea to remove the fins first, because they are equipped with sharp points.

How to Fillet a Fish

Clean the fish and place it on its side on the cutting board. With a sharp knife cut the fish by following the line of the spine. Cut deeply into the flesh, releasing the fish from the backbone. Make a diagonal cut behind the head and gills and remove the fillet. Repeat on the other side.

How to Fillet a Sole

Slip the point of a knife under the skin near the tail and cut towards the tail to release the skin. Grab the skin in one hand, hold the tail down with the other and pull the skin toward the head, peeling it away from the flesh. Repeat the operation on the other side. Then, with a flat, flexible knife, cut the flesh down the center on either side of the backbone.

Going from the center, work toward the edge (along the bones). Remove the fillet with a knife. Repeat on the other side. A big sole will yield four fillets.

Poaching liquids for fish

2 carrots	*1 qt. white wine*
1 onion	*2 qts. water*
1 sprig parsley, chopped	*2 bay leaves*
1 celery stalk	*¼ oz. salt*
2 Tbs. butter	*8 peppercorns*
2 Tbs. oil	

Sauté the vegetables with butter and oil until they begin to get tender. Add dry white wine, water, bay leaf and salt. Cover and let cook over medium heat for about 45 minutes. Ten minutes before the end of the cooking time, add peppercorns. When the liquid is ready, let cool, filter, and place the broth in a poacher. Add the selected fish, bring slowly to a boil, lower the heat and cook, uncovered until fish is cooked through.

Poaching Liquid with Vinegar

Use same procedure and ingredients as in the preceding preparation, except that 2 cups of vinegar is substituted for the wine. The vinegar is boiled and reduced by half before being added to the water. Cooked in this way, the flesh of the fish keeps its pinkish color. One half cup of lemon juice may be substituted for vinegar.

Poaching Liquid with Milk

Use only water and milk (1 qt. milk to 1 qt. water) 2 bay leaves, 6 white peppercorns, ½ lemon (thinly sliced), 1 small onion and a sprig of thyme. Add salt to taste. If the poaching liquid is to be used for salt cod, no further salt need be added.

Simply bring to a boil and remove from heat. The poaching liquid is now ready. Bring the poaching liquids back to a simmer before adding the fish.

Poaching Liquid with Water

Mix only water and coarse salt together (½ oz. for every qt. of water), so that the very delicate flavor of the fish is not altered. In coastal areas the fish may be cooked in sea water.

COOKING TECHNIQUES
Poached Fish

Salt water fish is usually cooked in a wine or vinegar-based liquid, although it can be simply cooked in salted water.

Fish that require more than 20 minutes to cook do not need to be cooked in a specially prepared poaching liquid. Simply place vegetables and aromatic herbs on the bottom of fish poacher. Fish that are cooked whole must be started in a cold liquid. If the whole fish were immersed in boiling water, the skin would break and the fish would tend to break apart. Bring the cold water rapidly to a boil, then turn the heat down and cook slowly.

Fish fillets, however, must be started in a boiling liquid. If pieces of fish are begun to cook in cold water, flavor and juices will drain from the fish. A hot liquid prevents this by sealing the exposed flesh, thus keeping the juices in.

PESCE IN BRODETTO
Fish Cooked with Broth

Oil and cover the bottom of a saucepan with finely minced scallions, onion, carrot, celery. Sauté at medium heat for 5 minutes. Add salt and place the fish on top. Add enough poaching liquid to cover the fish completely. Bring to a simmer and cook till the fish has obtained the desired doneness. Remove fish and place it into a serving platter. Top with its broth and serve.

Note: The ingredients used to prepare the broth vary according to the recipe being prepared.

PESCE IN BLÙ
Quick Poaching

This preparation is for small live fish (not more that 20-24 oz.) and more suitable for fresh water fish. Hit the fish on the head to stun them. Gut and wash without removing the scales. Handle the fish with care to avoid removing the viscous substance. Place on a dish, sprinkle with white vinegar. Then immerse the vinegary fish in the desired simmering poaching liquid and cook over low heat. The skin of the fish will tear somewhat and become very blueish. Cook till it has achieved its desired doneness. The fish is brought at the table in its own broth, boned and served with steamed vegetables.

PESCE AL FORNO
Fish Prepared in the Oven

There are two ways to cook fish in the oven:

In umido
Moist-Baked

A sauce may be prepared in advance and the fish added, then baked or the cooking is started with the fish and the vegetables, herbs and spices lightly browned in a skillet on top of the stove. Then, a poaching liquid is added, and the cooking is finished in the oven. Oven heat and timing varies according to the fish and the recipe being prepared. This type of preparation can also be finished on top of the stove.

Arrosto
Roasted

Using a whole fish, if the fish is over 5 lbs., diagonal cuts are made along the body of the fish so that the fish can cook uniformly. The fish is marinated with oil, bay leaves, parsley and other herbs. It is lightly dusted with flour. Then, the fish is browned in a pan on top of the stove on both sides. The fish is placed in the oven at 450 F., basted with the juices released by the fish or a prepared juice. It is not necessary to turn the fish unless the heat is uneven and the fish is small enough to be handled easily. Remove from the oven when the fish has obtained the desired doneness, then, place in a serving platter. Present to guest, bone and serve.

NOTE 1: Moist-baked is suitable for most fish fillets, while roasting is suitable for whole fish.

AL CARTOCCIO
In Parchment or Tin-Foil
This method is suitable for small fish, fillets.
Grease a sufficiently large piece of parchment paper or aluminum foil and place the marinated, drained fish in the center. Fold up the paper or foil into a tightly closed, but fairly loose packet with the desired spices and herbs. Bake at 425° F. (about 15 minutes for fillets). The cartoccio should be presented immediately, the fish taken out of the paper and served.

PESCE SALTATO AL BURRO
Fish Sautéed in Butter
This cooking procedure is used with small and flat fish or with large fish cut in fillets. The fish is salted and lightly coated with flour, then cooked in hot melted -- not brown -- butter on both sides until golden brown.

Serve hot, topping the fish with desired sauce, or just sautéed.

PESCE IMPANATO
Breaded Fish
This is made in the same way as fish sautéed in butter, except you must first flour the fish, then dip in beaten egg and then in white bread crumbs. Pat the bread crumbs tightly to the fillets, so they will not form bubbles as they fry. Fry in oil until golden brown. Sometimes a mixture of oil and butter is used for frying.

PESCE FRITTO
Fried Fish
Olive oil is the best medium for frying fish. The temperature of the oil should vary according to the size of the fish being fried — the smaller the fish, the higher the temperature.

Fish for frying (either whole or cut in pieces or fillets) should not weigh more than 3 ozs. With the exception of whitebait, anchovies and other varieties of small fish which can be directly coated with flour before being fried, all other fish should be dipped in milk first.

After frying, drain off excess frying fat by placing fish on paper towels. Serve very hot with chopped parsley and lemon wedges. The very popular *Fritto Misto* is a platter with a variety of fried fish (see IL FRITTO chapter). The combinations of fish served varies from region to region and according to what is seasonally available at the market.

Never cover fried fish; otherwise it loses its crunchiness and becomes steamy.

PESCE ALLA GRIGLIA
Grilled Fish

Grilled fish is better if it is not scaled or seasoned but simply brushed with oil before grilling. When grilling fish without scales, coat the fish with flour before brushing with oil to prevent it from sticking to the grill.

If the fish is rather large, score the fish diagonally along its body (the cuts should be shallow), so the fish can cook through easier. Or the fish can be cut across into 1" thick slices or filleted. Certain types of fish are more suitable to be cut one way than another. For example, salmon and turbot are cut across, while bass are filleted.

When grilling a whole fish to facilitate the turning, it is better to use a hand grill that folds open like a book, so that the fish can be turned easily. The grill should be very hot and greased with oil in order to prevent the fish from sticking. The turning should be done only once to prevent too much handling.

When cooking is finished, brush the fish with condiments of oil, lemon, parsley, salt and pepper.

NOTE: The fire should be covered with a light film of ash before starting to grill.

SALT WATER FISH

ALICE
Anchovy

This is a saltwater fish from the family of *pesce azzurro*, blue fish. It has a short jaw and a tapered body. Anchovies are in season from March through September. They do not have scales. Their color is bluish-green, except for the insides and stomach, which are silver. They can be marinated, fried or baked. They can be preserved whole in salt or as fillets in oil, plain or with capers.

BACCALÀ
Salt cod

Fresh cod is boned and its sides salt cured and preserved in wood

BACCALA

barrels. The name "*baccalà*" is derived from the Flemish "Bakeljamo" which then became the Spanish "Bacalao". It was, in fact, the Hispanic Portuguese fishermen who first adopted the technique of preserving food under salt, one commonly used in Italian cuisine.

Before cooking, it must soak in cold water (either running water or water which is changed frequently) for at least 18 hours to soften the flesh and remove the salt.

It is then cut into pieces, skinned, boned and prepared in the desired manner.

BIANCHETTI
Whitebait

These are the newborn of both sardines and anchovy spawn. They are very small fish, which can be fried or cooked in *frittate* and in fritters. If the whitebait are really fresh, they can be marinated and eaten raw, as a salad, with oil, lemon juice, salt and pepper.

BRANZINO O SPIGOLA
Bass

This saltwater fish migrates up river in spring, living in fresh water until fall. Bass is in season in January, February, June, July and December. Its exquisite flesh is lean, firm, white, flaky and delicate, its scales small. It is gray on the back and silver on the sides. Smaller bass are cooked on the grill or baked *al cartoccio,* while larger ones may be poached or boned and filleted and moist-baked.

CERNIA
Grouper

This fish is available in spring and fall. Its back is dark yellow, becoming lighter in the belly area. The lower jaw is longer than the

CERNIA

upper one. The lower part of the body has dots, which disappear when exposed to the air. Grouper can be cooked whole or in slices, cutting them from the middle or towards the tail. It can be boiled, grilled or baked.

DENTICE
Red Snapper

This saltwater fish has a tapered body and oblique profile. It has four sharp pointed teeth and its color is purple and violet with silver overtones. The American species is similar but it is bright red. It is best roasted or baked.

MERLUZZO
Fresh Cod

This is a cold seawater fish that can grow very large. It has a broad body more or less elongated, well-defined head and fins, a large mouth with strong teeth and a kind of beard. Dorsal color ranges from brown to greenish or yellowish depending on its habitat.

The meat is white, delicate and flakes easily. Larger cod can be cut into slices. The most suitable ways of cooking cod are baked, poached, braised or in croquettes. It is better not to grill cod, because it falls apart easily.

MERLUZZO

MUGGINE
Grey Mullet

The mullet is in season year round, with the exception of January and February. Its back is dark grey, the stomach silvery white. On its sides there are silver and gold parallel lines. Its meat is white and delicious, though fatty. Its flavor varies according to season and geographical origin and to the food the fish has been eating.

Mullet can be boiled, stewed, sautéed, grilled or baked. Its liver is delicious. In many Italian regions its egg sac is salted and air-dried, and it is known as bottarga.

ORATA
Gilthead Bream

Gilthead brim is a saltwater fish which can be found on the market almost all year long. The small ones are available from October through January. Its body is sky-blue, with silvery reflections and vertical dark stripes. It has a dark violet spot near the gills. The belly is silver. It has a golden yellow line in the shape of a half-moon between the eyes. The meat is lean, white and delicate. It can be prepared in various ways. The small ones can be sautéed. The big ones can be cooked in a poaching liquid.

PAGELLO — SARAGO
Sea Bream
This is a beautiful, rather large salt water fish, at its best in spring or summer. It has a tapered oval shape, with a slightly oblique head. The mouth is tapered and the eye and teeth protrude. Its back is shiny blue, shading to silvery white in the belly area. Very large fish are reddish in color. Near the pectoral fins it has a black spot and light bluish dots. Its meat is very lean and delicious.

PESCESPADA
Swordfish
A very large Mediterranean fish found especially near Sicily. Its name is derived from the long thin bone which looks like a sword protruding over its mouth.

The flesh is delicious, compact and rosy. It is usually cooked in the same way as tuna.

PESCE PALOMBO
Dog-fish
This fish is from the same family as sharks (*squalo*). Its size can go up to 2' long. It is caught in the Mediterranean and is very good. To prepare in sauce or with fish stews, it must be skinned before it is cut in fillets or for the desired use. Preparations for tuna and swordfish are suitable for sea-squab.

RANA PESCATRICE
Angler or Monkfish
This fish is not particularly attractive, for its overly large head and mouth make it resemble a large toad. Its meat, however, is very tasty, similar in texture and flavor to lobster. It is most flavorful in the winter months. Since only the tail is eaten, the head can be used to make a poaching liquid. It may be boiled, stewed, grilled or baked, and may be included in a fish stew.

ROMBO
Turbot
This is a very large, oval-shaped saltwater fish. There are many varieties, but the best are those which have small, green or yellow bony plates that end in hooked points on its back. This variety is called *chiodata* (nailed) and has two eyes on the back. Its meat is white and tasty, though rather tough; therefore, it is preferable to tenderize the meat by keeping it on ice one or two days.

When purchasing turbot, check to see that its gelatinous external layer is soft; if not, do not use, since it will smell bad.

SAN PIETRO
St. Peter's Fish
A rather ugly salt water fish, dark yellowish in color, with thin threads attached to the fins and the back. It can be found in spring

and summer. Its name comes from the two dark spots on its sides, which are said to be St. Peter's fingerprints.

St. Peter's fish has a firm white flesh suitable for most preparations. It is usually cut into fillets, which can be cooked like those of a sole.

SARDINA
Sardine
A small saltwater fish with very fatty meat that belongs to the family of *pesce azzurro* (blue fish). An Italian proverb says that the sardine has 24 virtues, but loses one each hour, which is to say the fish must be cooked when it is very fresh. Sardines have firm meat, bright eyes and red gills.

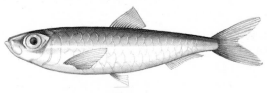

SARDINA

Sardines can be cooked fried or baked. To bone, cut open the stomach, gut and, using your fingers, pull out the backbone, together with the head (in some preparations the head is left on). Since the flesh is very fatty, avoid adding too much oil or butter to the sauce.

SCORFANO
Scorpion Fish
This fish is commonly found in the muddy seabed of the Mediterranean. Its meat is prized and especially good in *zuppa di pesce*. The larger specimens can also be baked. It is in season from June to October.

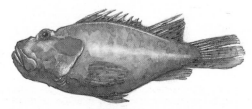

SCORFANO

SGOMBRO
Mackerel
This is a rather common fish inhabiting the Mediterranean. It is

inexpensive and fairly good when eaten fresh. The flesh of this fish is rather fatty. It is either grilled or baked al *cartoccio*.

SOGLIOLA
Sole
This is a choice saltwater fish, available on the market all year around. It is flat, the top-side skin is greenish-black and the belly side white. However sole is cooked, the skin must always be removed. Its meat is exquisite, lean and delicate. Sole can be cooked many ways, whole or in fillets, but it is best sautéed, simply coated with flour and sprinkled with melted butter.

STOCCAFISSO
Dried cod
Stoccafisso is a whole small cod which is cured in brine and air-dried. The technique goes back to the Vikings. The name derives from "stockfish", which in German means "fish as stiff as a stick". Dried cod is very commonly used in Italian cuisine and is frequently cooked in sauces with tomato or milk.

STOCCAFISSO

Before, cooking the dried cod must be softened by beating it with a wooden stick or a wooden pestle and then soaked in cool water (better is running water) for 4 or 5 days, even more if possible. The water should be changed at least twice a day. It is important to soak it for this period, otherwise the meat will be tough and woody, regardless of how long it is cooked. It takes about an hour and a half to two hours to cook depending on the recipe.

STORIONE
Sturgeon
This is a saltwater fish, caught in spring and summer when it swims up river to spawn. Its flesh is exquisite, but very fatty. It is almost always cooked in fillets or slices, either boiled, stewed or baked, occasionally being marinated in white wine first. Sturgeon eggs are a major source of caviar (*caviale*), and gelatin is made from the sturgeon's swimming-bladder.

TONNO
Tuna
Tuna can reach notably large dimensions — sometimes over 13

feet in length and up to 300 pounds. It has dark, compact flesh that may be a bit difficult to digest. The best part is the *ventresca,* the underbelly part of the tuna.

The most important Italian tuna-fishing areas are located along the Sicilian and Sardinian coast, where tuna pause during their mysterious migrations. Tuna is normally cooked sliced, either grilled, stewed, baked or sliced very finely and rolled with a filling and moist-baked. The egg sac of the tuna is used to prepare *bottarga.*

TRIGLIA
Red and white mullet

Mullet is among the most prized saltwater fish, despite its many thin bones. Some gourmets regard this as the "woodcock of the sea" in that, like the woodcock, the red mullet can be eaten (if fresh) with its innards. In this case, it is grilled without washing or removing the scales. There are two varieties of this fish: the red (or stone mullet) and white mullet. The red mullet is fished along the coast with rocky bottom. Red mullet are a brilliant red on the back, and a brighter red with golden stripes on the side. The breast, the throat and the belly are rosy-white. The lower jaw is equipped with two pendant barbells on the chin. The profile of the red mullet is oblique. White mullets are fished in deep waters with muddy bottoms. It has a rosy color with silvery reflections on the sides.

TRIGLIA

Red mullets are more prized than white ones. They are best from May to July, since in these months they are at their largest and their flesh is at its whitest. Mullet can be cooked in various ways — the smaller ones fried, the others moist-baked.

FRESH-WATER FISH

AGONE
Fresh Shad

This is a very common but not very prized lake fish. The best are those from Lake Como, which are fished in May and June, left to dry in the sun, then pressed into tin cans with bay leaves. *Agoni* conserved in this way are called *missoltitt* (derived from the name of the can *"missolta"*). They are grilled, then marinated in red vinegar.

ANGUILLA
Eel

This is a freshwater fish that lives in rivers, swamps or marshes. Eels go at sea to spawn during the month of January and February, then swim up river in the spring. The newborn eels are called *cieche*. For some unknown reason, in Italy they may be found only in *Versilia* (the coastline from *Forte Dei Marmi* to *Viareggio,* Tuscany) at the mouth of the river *Arno*. Legend has it that eels go to Sargassi, in the Caribbean, to spawn. This legend is supported by the fact that large schools of eels are seen crossing the strait of Gilbralter during the winter months. Eels are in season from October through May. Their meat, though fatty, is delicious. It can be cooked in many ways; roasting and stewing are the most suitable ones. It is also delicious when marinated. Large eels are called *capitone* and are part of the traditional Christmas Eve and Christmas day meals especially in southern Italy.

ANGUILLA

For some preparations, especially when it is too big, eel must be skinned. To do so, cut the skin of the eel right behind the head, hang the eel on a hook by the mouth and pull the skin down; it will peel off as if it were a glove. Then gut and clean. If the preparation requires that the skin be left on, the skin should be scrubbed with ash. If ash is not available, a rough cloth or a pumice stone may be used, making sure that the eel is well washed following these procedures.

CARPA
Carp

This is a common freshwater fish of a rather inferior quality. Its meat is rosy-white, its back dark, the sides golden yellow and the stomach greenish white.

CARPA

The best carp are found in clear, flowing waters (either in rivers or lakes). Those raised in swamps have a muddy after taste. Swamp carp are recognizable by their darker color and intense smell. If you buy a swamp carp still alive, you can purge it by keeping it in cold running water for three days, or by feeding the carp two spoonfuls of vinegar, then scraping and cleaning well, keeping it in running water for an hour. If the fish is purchased already dead, make sure that it is very fresh. Clean, rub with salt and let rest for half an hour. Rinse off the salt before cooking.

Small carp can be fried (and then perhaps marinated in vinegar with spices), while larger ones can be grilled or stewed.

COSCE DI RANA
Frog's Legs

Although not a fish, frogs are listed in this chapter. Only the legs are suitable for cooking preparations. Its meat is white, very tender and delicate. They may be sautéed, fried in batter, or added to *frittate*. Frog's legs are also excellent in preparing *risotto*.

LUCCIO
Pike

This is a big, freshwater fish, known as «the shark of rivers» for its voracity. Its body is covered with small, greenish scales, stomach and the sides white, with green gradations. The head is rather pointed, heavy and strong, the mouth is enormous.

The peak season for pike is September. Its meat is lean and flaky in texture. It can be cooked whole or sliced, either boiled, grilled or baked (with or without coating). Since the meat of the pike is rather dry, it is best served with a sauce.

LUCCIO

PESCE PERSICO
Perch

A freshwater fish, at its very best in May, perch has a golden, greenish back with 5-7 vertical stripes which shade off in the vicinity of the belly. The fins are rosy. It has two dorsal fins, one of which has very sharp points. Its meat is excellent — compact, white and delicate. It should be gutted immediately after it is caught.

One of the most exquisite varieties of perch is the perch trout found in the Lombard lakes. Another variety is the *persico sole* (sun perch), recognizable by a shiny black spot, partly surrounded by a bright red circle, near the gills.

The big ones may be boiled in a poaching liquid with vinegar or sautéed; the smaller ones may be fried, and the very big ones can be baked. Perch can also be filleted, floured and breaded, cooked in butter and sage or other delicate sauces and served with *risotto*.

TROTA
Trout
This is a freshwater fish of many varieties.

The brown trout lives in cold, clear mountain rivers or lakes. Its body is agile and sturdy and the color varies according to the environment. It always has red and black dots surrounded by a small ring of either white or pink.

Rainbow trout has a body more slender than that of the brown variety, and its head is slightly smaller. Its color varies, but its distinguishing marks are a rosy stripe on its sides and a thick concentration of black spots. It can be found in mountain streams as well as lowland lakes.

TROTA

Lake trout resemble the brown trout. Its back has a dark bluish color, which becomes paler blue on the sides and yellowish on the belly.

The salmon trout (*trota salmonata*) is not, contrary to what many people believe, a hybrid between a trout and a salmon, but a trout which has lived primarily on a diet of shrimp, so that it acquires a rosy flesh.

All these varieties of trout have lean meat. There are many ways of cooking trout. Smaller ones should preferably be sautéed or quick poached, fried or grilled. The bigger ones are poached in a poaching liquid, or baked. If poached, trout may be covered with aspic. Trout may also be stuffed with bread, mushrooms or other stuffings.

Trout are available all year round, since they are often raised in commercial hatcheries.

CROSTACEI E MOLLUSCHI
Shellfish and Mollusk

How to recognize fresh shellfish and mollusk
When you buy mussels, clams or other bivalves, always check to see whether the shells are tightly closed. If a shell is open, slightly

tap it, if it closes instantly, it means that it is still alive.

If the shell is closed, one may shake the mollusk to see if it is alive — you will hear nothing in a live mollusk, because the creature inside is tensed trying to keep the shell tightly closed. Shellfish should be immersed and kept in cold, salted water. Dispense with any floating mollusks, because they are either dead or empty. Lobster, crayfish and other crustacean must be bought and cooked while still alive.

Mollusks, if fresh, should not smell like moss. The flesh must be firm and have a shiny color, the skin should not be dry, and the tentacles should not break when pulled. Ideally crustaceans should also be bought while alive, but since one rarely finds them alive, they should at least be very fresh. The meat of fresh crustacean is firm and compact. If they have been kept for a long time on ice the flesh may become soft and flabby, the tail may break off from the rest of the body, and the head may smell strongly.

ARAGOSTA — Spiny Lobster
ASTICE — Maine Lobster

The spiny lobster belongs to the family of the Palinuridi. Its body can grow up to 22 inches and it has two antennas. Maine lobster belongs to the family of Nefropidi; the body is the same as the spiny lobster, but it has two strong claws. The spiny lobster is commonly found in the waters of the Mediterranean, South Africa, Australia and New Zealand. The type we identify as Maine Lobster is found from Newfoundland down to the Carolinas.

Both types of lobster are perhaps the most popular of the shellfish. If possible, choose a female lobster (its eggs are delicious). To recognize a female lobster, turn it upside down and observe the small fins on the abdomen which look somewhat like a fan. In the female these are larger and longer than in the male, since the female uses these fins to protect the eggs as they reach maturity. In the female lobster the fins on the abdomen largely overlap, while in the male they barely touch. Lobsters should not have holes in their shell nor broken-off limbs. It does not matter if the antennas are damaged because they are very fragile and can break during combat.

Lobster can be boiled, steamed or baked.

CALAMARO
Squid

Calamari are mollusks also known as *totani* although they are not exactly the same. The body of the *calamari* resembles a sac with a large and flat fin attached to it toward the middle. The extremity of the body has tentacles, its color when fresh is pinkish with brown/violet spots. The meat is more delicate than the totani. Totani are different, as the meat is tougher than *calamari*. The fin is attached to the bottom of the sac and has a triangular, spear-like shape. The color when fresh is violet. *Calamari* and *totani* are both cleaned by removing the fin, eyes, beak and all that is inside. They are then skinned and washed several times. The smaller examples are excellent fried, the larger ones may be moist-baked, with or without stuffing. If they are not fresh, the white color is predominant.

CALAMARO

CANNOLICCHIO
Razor clam

The shell of this mollusk is long and tubular, about 13 cms. long, and yellowish-grey of varying intensities in color. The «foot» protrudes from one end of the shell and the siphons from the other. These are excellent when eaten raw with lemon juice, but they can also be grilled or stewed in soup, by themselves or with other mollusks or fish.

CANNOLICCHIO

CAPESANTA
Scallop

This kind of mollusk has a very large and beautiful shell, and can be eaten either raw (with lemon juice) or cooked in various ways.

Those gathered in winter are particularly good.

As is the case with all shellfish, scallops must be alive when cooked. If there are any open shells, insert the tip of a knife; if the scallop is alive, the shell will close instantly. Otherwise dispense with the scallop. The meat inside is shaped like a large, flattened cork. This part is known as the *noce* (nut), and attached to it is the red half-moon of roe known as the *corallo*. Around the noce is a gray muscle or foot, which must be dispensed with. To open the shells, put them in a covered pot over low heat for a few minutes. Only the *noce* and the *corallo* must be cooked. Scallops may be cooked in a saucepan with anchovies or in a delicate sauce. It is preferable to serve them in their shells or in a pan with oil, chopped garlic and parsley, salt, pepper and lemon juice.

COZZA
Mussel

This bivalve can be gathered from either the sea or from commercial mussel beds. Mussels are available all year round, though in spring and summer the mussel is bigger. The shells are violet black, the flesh varies from pink to coral red. Before cooking the shells should be vigorously scraped under running water to remove all dirt and sludge.

Mussels are very tasty and can be used to prepare many dishes. They can also be used to garnish either hot or cold dishes (rice salads, boiled fish and so on). They may be cooked, with or without stuffing, alla *marinara* (see *SAUCES*) or baked. They may also be steamed with wine or garlic.

COZZA

The liquid should be filtered before serving and it may also be used for sauces or *risottos*. Be careful not to oversalt the liquid, because it is already quite salty. When buying mussels, check to see that the shells are tightly closed. Tap on any open one; if they are alive, the shells will close instantly.

DATTERO
Date shell

The shell of this mollusk looks very similar to a date, both in size

DATTERO

and color. They are more highly prized than mussels, and the best ones are medium-sized, about 2" long. They live in deep niches among rocks and are difficult to collect. They are sometimes eaten raw, if very fresh and well cleaned; otherwise datteri are used in soup, either by themselves or with other mollusks.

GAMBERO
Shrimp

The shrimp belongs to the family of decapodi because it has ten feet, five on each side, and does not have claws. Shrimp can reach a length of about 8 inches; the color varies from pink to bright red. Shrimp meat is very prized and very popular in the Mediterranean.

In the same family, we have *gambero imperiale*. This is a beautiful, rather large sea shrimp (whole, it can range up to 6 inches long). Its color is red and yellow, with dark spots on the tail tips. Its meat is delicious and delicate. All shrimp can be baked, grilled, fried or boiled.

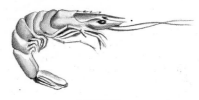

GAMBERO

GRANSEOLA
Mediterranean Crab

This exquisite variety of crab is commonly found in the Adriatic sea and the Mediterranean. It is also found in the oriental Atlantic and the British Isles. The scientific name is maja squinado and it belongs to the family of majidae. The body has a ovoid shape with an extremely hard shield, full of strong, pointed thorns. Its length can reach a maximum of 8-9" and it has 5 pairs of legs, the 2 forelegs have claws. The *granseola* is sold fresh and alive. It is generally boiled like lobster, then its shield is removed, the meat is taken out and the cartilage trimmed. It is then dressed with oil, lemon, salt and pepper and put back into the empty shell.

LUMACHE
Snails

Snails are considered to be a land mollusk. They are protected by a spiral shell within which they can remain for many months. The best variety are called *vignerole,* which live on grape vines, and are best from October through March. *Vignerole* are not easy to digest, due to the meat itself and because of the ingredients used to prepare them.

MOSCARDINO
Baby octopus

Moscardini should be boiled in salted water lightly acidulated with either vinegar or lemon. They may be served warm or cold with extra virgin olive oil, lemon juice and parsley, or they may be fried or used to prepare a very good condiment for spaghetti. (see polpo for description).

POLPO
Octopus

Octopus is a sea creature found in many varieties. The *polpo verace* (stone octopus) can be identified by the double line of suckers on its

POLPO

tentacles, the octopus with red and white dots, are known as *scorria* or *polpessa,* (the name varies from region to region). Octopuses are all cooked in the same way, boiled or stewed. The latter are particularly suitable for risotto or pasta dishes. Before cooking the larger octopus, it is advisable to remove the skin.

If you do not want to skin it, rub it vigorously with a very rough cloth under running water until no more foam is produced by rubbing. The skin can be removed after cooking, while still hot.

Very big octopus must be tenderized before being cooked. To do so, pound the body with a stone or a piece of wood to break down the tough fibers being careful not to crush the octopus. Octopus is available all year round, except in January, May and August.

SCAMPO
Prawn

Prawn is a prized crustacean with 2 long claws, 8 feet, 4 on each side, a fan-like tail, large head with white, firm and delicate meat. They can reach a length of up to 10 inches. Prawns belong to the nephropidae family, the same family that lobster belongs to.

Prawns may be cooked in boiling water with aromatic herbs, the cooking time varying according to size. They are served with olive oil, lemon juice and finely minced parsley. Oftentimes they are incorrectly called «shrimp scampi».

SEPPIA
Cuttlefish

SEPPIA

Cuttlefish are available year round. The large ones are best between January and June, but the medium or small ones are always preferred. The hood, or body, of the cuttlefish is shaped like a rounded sack, surrounded on each side by a fringe. Inside, underneath the skin of the hood, there is a large flat fin, which must be removed before cooking. Its mouth is surrounded by ten tentacles. When fresh, it has a greenish color, with luminous yellow highlights on the belly, and the hood is dark brown with light stripes.

The ink sac, which is inside the bag portion of the body, can be used to prepare *risotto nero,* or to season pasta.

Seppie can be cooked like squid.

VONGOLA
Clam

These are marine bivalves, but unlike mussels, their shells are light grey in color. As with all shellfish, clams must be cooked alive.

If you wish to cook them directly in a sauce (that is, without waiting for them to open first), keep them in lightly salted, cold water so that the shells will open, releasing any sand that might be trapped inside.

VONGOLA

Always drain them with your hands—do not use a colander; otherwise, you will get sand along with the clams. To open the clams, put them in a frying pan, turn on the flame, cover and shake now and then, so that they heat through evenly and open up.

Clams are cooked in various sauces, some of which go well with *spaghetti* or *risotto.*

RICETTE
Recipes

ORATA LESSA
Gilthead bream poached

2 — 2 lb. gilthead bream
4 qt. poaching liquids (see recipe)

Gut and wash the fish (if too big, it can be filleted). Use a fish poacher. If you cook the whole fish start by placing the fish in cold liquids, if cooking fillets, bring the liquids to a very light simmer (to the point where the surface «shimmers» or slightly moves) then add the fish fillets. Cook till done (whole fish should take 6 minutes each pound, fillets should take 5 minutes for 6/8 portions.)

Remove fish from poacher and serve with the desired sauce. The gilthead bream is a very delicate flesh fish, an appropriate sauce would simply be oil, lemon and chopped parsley. Other types of sauces may be appropriate also, such as tomatoes and vegetables.

Fish prepared in this manner may also be steamed, then, the desired sauce is added.

TROTA IN BLEU
Quick Poached Trout

4 trout, 20-24 oz. each
½ cup white vinegar
4 Tbs. butter

juice of 1 lemon
1 Tbs. parsley, chopped
salt to taste

Trout should be alive, stunned, gutted and cleaned. Using a fish poacher, add 4 qt. vinegar based poaching liquid (see recipe). Bring it to a simmer and pour the vinegar over the trout. Let it marinate for 5 minutes. Then, place fish (without the vinegar) in a poacher with simmering broth and cook till done. Cooking time will depend on the size of the trout. It should take no more than 10 minutes. Remove from water and serve one trout per person with steamed vegetable, with the sauce made with the browned butter and lemon.

NOTE: The poaching liquids may change according to the cooks skill and ingenuity.

ZUPPA DI PESCE
Fish Stew

3 lbs. assorted fish
(gray mullet, turbot, St.
Peter's, scorpion fish, squid,
octopus shrimps) or any
fish with a firm texture.
3 tomatoes, chopped

½ lemon
3 garlic cloves
2 sprigs parsley
salt
pepper
2 Tbs. olive oil

Gut and clean all the fish. Fillet the fish with bone and cut the squid and octopus into pieces while reserving the heads and the bone.

In a large pot bring 6 qts. water to a boil with the tomatoes, the fish bones and heads, including the head of the shrimps. Cook for 2 hours, then cool and pass through a fine sieve.

Bring this poaching liquid back to a simmer and start adding the fish, one at a time, in order of cooking time. First the squid or octopus, then the scorpion fish, the shrimps, turbot, St. Peter's fish and the mullets.

Cook till all fish has achieved the desired doneness. Prepare a *soffritto* with the garlic and parsley, add to the fish stew and remove from heat. Finish with lemon juice, place in a large serving platter and serve with toasted country bread.

NOTE: There are as many variations and as many names to this preparation as there are church bells.

Just to mention a few: *brodetto, caciucco, ciuppin.* The type of fish added also varies; some do not add mollusk, some add bivalve, some claim that at least 13 or 14 different types of fish should be used, others use only one type.

POLPO ALLA LUCIANA
Octopus alla Luciana

2 lbs. stone octopus
1/2 lb. ripe tomatoes, peeled,
chopped, and seeded
1 cup olive oil

1 handful parsley
1 garlic clove
salt, pepper

This preparation is called alla *Luciana* because it is a favored dish with the fisherman of Naples, particularly those from *Santa Lucia* point *(Luciana)*. Tenderize the octopus by beating with a mallet on a hard, preferably marble, table. Clean, wash and cut into quarters. Put the octopus into a baking dish or pot (a terra-cotta pot is preferable for this preparation), salt and pepper to taste and add the tomatoes, olive oil, parsley, garlic and salt to taste. Seal the pot with tin foil fastened by winding around with string, and place the cover on top. Cook over low heat or in oven at 425 F. for 1 ½ hours, shaking the pot occasionally, so that the octopus does not stick to the bottom. Remove from oven. It may be served in the same pot or dished out on a serving platter. Serve hot, warm or at room temperature, directly out of the cooking pot.

PESCE PALOMBO AL FORNO
Baked Dogfish

1 gilthead about 2 lbs.
parsley
2 cloves garlic
1 lb. potatoes

4 oz. olive oil
2 oz. grated pecorino
salt, pepper

Clean and fillet the dogfish. Finely chop a handful of parsley and garlic *battuto*. Peel and thinly slice the potatoes. Pour 2 oz. of oil into a baking pan and add half of the *battuto*. Make a layer of potato on top of the *battuto* and add half the cheese. Lay the fish fillets on top of the potatoes and cover with another layer of potatoes and cheese. Drizzle with oil, salt, pepper and bake in a hot oven for about 40 minutes. Shake the pan occasionally during baking so that the potatoes do not stick to it. Serve in the baking dish it has cooked in.

CALAMARI IN ZIMINO
Squid with Swiss Chard

2 lbs. Swiss chard
7 oz. tomatoes
1 medium size onion,
finely minced
1 celery stalk, finely minced

2 oz. olive oil
salt
pepper
1 lb. squid
1 oz. parsley

Remove the outer larger leaves, wash and cut into pieces the Swiss chard and set aside. Peel, seed and strain the tomatoes. Sauté onion and celery in 2 oz. of oil in a saucepan till tender but not brown. Add the Swiss chard, the tomatoes, salt and pepper, stir, cover and let cook over medium heat for 30 to 40 minutes. Then add the squid, and continue to cook for ten more minutes over medium heat. Sprinkle generously with the chopped parsley and serve directly from saucepan.

This recipe can also be used with cuttlefish.

CAPESANTE IN TECIA
Scallops in Tecia

16 scallops in the shell	*3 Tbs. dry white wine*
1 Tbs. chopped parsley	*2 oz. olive oil*
2 Tbs. bread crumbs	*salt*
1 clove of garlic	

Open the scallops, remove the mollusk with the roe and reserve the shells. Wash under running water and pat dry. Make a *battuto* of parsley and bread crumbs and coat the scallops with the *battuto*.

Sauté the garlic with oil in a skillet, remove when golden brown. Add the scallops, turning quickly, then add wine. Reduce briskly and finish the cooking in the oven for another 4 minutes. Season and serve immediately, either by returning the scallops to their own shell, previously heated, or by placing them on a serving platter.

TRIGLIE ALLA LIVORNESE
Red or white mullets, Livornese style

2 lbs. mullets	*4 oz. olive oil*
1½ oz. parsley	*1 lb. ripe tomatoes, peeled,*
1 celery stalk	*seeded and chopped*
2 garlic cloves	*2 Tbs. white flour*
salt, pepper	

Clean the mullets. Mince the parsley, celery and garlic and sauté in a saucepan with 2 oz. olive oil. When the vegetables are tender, add the tomatoes and cook for 10 minutes. Remove from heat and set aside.

Coat the fish with flour and brown them in a saucepan in oil till golden brown on both sides. Add salt and pepper to taste. Grease a casserole with oil, place the mullets in it, and pour the sauce in the casserole with the fish and bake for 5 more minutes at 450 F. Serve with a generous sprinkling of chopped parsley.

ALICI IN TORTIERA
Moist-Baked Anchovies

1½ lb. anchovies	*1 clove garlic*
2 oz. bread crumbs	*2 Tbs. parsley*

2 oz. grated pecorino   *salt*
1 Tbs. oregano   *2 oz. olive oil*

Remove the head and split open the anchovies. Remove the bone, wash and pat-dry. Prepare a *battuto* by mixing the bread crumbs, pecorino cheese, oregano and parsley, chopped garlic and salt. Grease a baking dish with oil and sprinkle with the *battuto*. Place the anchovies in rows, head to tail leaving no empty spaces. Sprinkle with more *battuto*. Make 3 layers, the top being the battuto. Drizzle with olive oil. Bake in a hot oven at 450 F. for half an hour.
VARIATION: Peeled tomatoes may be added to the top layer, or the juice of half lemon.

RANA PESCATRICE CON PISELLI
Monkfish with green peas

7 oz. tomatoes   *1½ oz. butter*
1¼ lbs. unshelled green peas   *salt*
1 small onion, thinly sliced   *pepper*
4 monkfish fillets, 6 oz. each *2 Tbs. white flour*
2 Tbs. olive oil   *½ oz. parsley*

Scald, peel, seed and cut the tomatoes. Shell the green peas. Sauté the onion with 2 Tbs. oil in a saucepan till tender but not browned. Add tomatoes and green peas. Season with salt and pepper and cook over very low heat for 25 minutes. Remove from heat and keep warm. Dust the monkfish fillets with flour, fry in butter till lightly browned on both sides, get rid of excess fat by placing on paper towels. Add fish to the prepared sauce with peas. Cook for 10 more minutes over very low heat, turning the fish only once. Add the chopped parsley and serve hot.

INVOLTINI DI PESCE SPADA
Involtini of swordfish

1 onion chopped   *1 Tbs. capers*
1 clove garlic, chopped   *3 oz. sharp provolone cheese*
olive oil   *2 eggs*
parsley, chopped   *salt, pepper*
basil, chopped   *3 oz. bread crumbs*
                                 2 lb. swordfish cut into very
                                 thin slices and trimmed

NOTE: Trimmings should not be less than 8 oz. in weight.

Chop and brown the onion, garlic and bits of the swordfish trimmings in 1 Tbs. oil. Add the parsley, basil, bread crumbs and capers. Let cook for 2 mins. remove from heat, cool, and pass through a food mill. Combine the diced cheese and the eggs with the mixture. Salt and pepper to taste and achieve a smooth filling. Flatten the swordfish fillets slightly with a mallet and place a spoonful of filling in the middle. Roll up the fillets and close with toothpicks. Cook the *involtini* by either grilling or sautéeing in olive oil and serve with *salmoriglio* sauce.

BACCALÀ IN UMIDO
Moist-baked salt cod

2 lbs. salt cod	1 Tbs. raisins, softened in
1 lb. onion	lukewarm water
4 anchovy fillets	1 Tbs. pine nuts
1 Tbs. capers	1 Tbs. chopped parsley
½ cup olive oil	

Follow the usual procedure to soften the salt cod and cut into 2 oz. pieces. Lightly dust with flour and fry in very hot oil. Remove excess fat by placing it on paper towels. Keep warm.

In a separate skillet sauté the onions with 1 Tbs. oil. When tender but not brown, add the anchovies, capers, raisins and pine nuts. Add the fried cod to the pan, mix well and cook for one hour over low heat. Occasionally baste the top of the cod with the cooking liquids. It it gets too dry, add a few Tbs. hot water. When ready, add the chopped parsley, remove from heat and serve.

NOTE 1: This preparation lends itself to several variations. For example, if 2 lbs. of peeled, seeded, chopped tomatoes and 1 cup of black olives are added and cooked for 20 mins. the fried cod is then added and baked in the oven at 450 F. for 1 hour.

NOTE 2: Some prefer eliminating the raisins and pine nuts from the recipe.

CALAMARÌ RIPIENI
Stuffed Squid

1½ lb. squid	1 Tbs. bread crumbs
2 garlic cloves	2 Tbs. grated parmigiano
2 Tbs. olive oil	pinch of oregano
6 pitted black olive,	1 lb. tomatoes, peeled, seeded
2 Tbs. chopped parsley	and chopped
2 Tbs. chopped parsley	1 Tbs. capers
pinch of peperoncino	salt

Clean the *calamari* by removing the eyes, the beak, the fin and all that there is in the sac. Wash until they become white. Remove the tentacles, chop and set aside. Sauté one garlic clove, olives, capers, parsley and *peperoncino* in olive oil. When everything becomes golden-brown, add the chopped *calamari* tentacles, sauté for 5 mins. over medium heat, remove from fire and cool, then add the bread crumbs and cheese mixed well to achieve a smooth filling. Stuff the *calamari* bodies with this mixture — do not overstuff or they will explode while cooking. Sew the opening of the sac with a needle and a colorless thread or close it with a toothpick.

Sauté the remaining garlic clove with oil, add the tomatoes, a pinch of *oregano,* salt and pepper. Cook for 10 minutes. Place the *calamari* in the sauce, cover and cook gently over low heat for another 30 minutes, adding poaching liquid if it gets too dry. When ready, place on platter and serve.

STOCCAFISSO ALLA GHIOTTA
Dried-cod with potatoes

1 onion	*parsley, chopped*
celery	*6 anchovy fillets, chopped*
2 carrots	*⅛ lb. pitted green olives, chopped*
3 oz. olive oil	*2 lbs dried cod*
1 oz. dried mushrooms,	*4 tomatoes, peeled, seeded*
soaked and chopped	*and diced*
1 oz. pignoli, chopped	*salt, pepper*
garlic clove, chopped	*4 medium-sized potatoes, diced*
	in small cubes

Chop the onion, celery, carrot, and sauté these with oil in a large pan. When these vegetables are tender but not brown, add the chopped mushrooms, pignoli, garlic, parsley, anchovies and olives. Add the dried-cod, previously soaked, skinned, boned and cut into pieces. Let the fish cook on both sides, then add the tomatoes, potatoes and salt and pepper to taste.

After 10 minutes add pepper and cover all the ingredients in the pan with warm water or a poaching liquid. Cover the pan and cook over low heat for 1½-2 hours. The liquids will be substantially reduced but make sure the dish remains moist, not wet. Dish out in a serving platter and serve.

BACCALÀ ALLA VICENTINA
Cod stewed in milk

2 lbs. dried cod parsley	*bunch of parsley*
1 lb. onions, chopped	*2 Tbs. flour/2 Tbs. grated*
2 cloves garlic, chopped	*parmigiano (mixed together)*
6 oz. olive oil	*1 pint milk*
8 anchovy fillets	*salt, pepper*

Soften the dried cod by beating with a mallet, then place cod in water for at least 3 days. When ready, prepare in the following manner. Make a *soffritto* with the onions and garlic browned in 2 Tbs. olive oil. Add the anchovies and parsley and cook on low flame for 5 more minutes. Remove from heat and set aside. Split open the cod and dust it with flour and parmigiano, then, spread ½ of the *soffritto* on it. Fold the fish closed and cut the cod across into pieces about 2" long. Roll the pieces of cod in the remaining flour and cheese then place in a baking dish (preferably made of terra-cotta). Sprinkle the remaining *soffritto* over the top, drizzle with remaining oil and cover completely with milk. Cover the pot and cook over low heat for 3 hours, shaking the dish occasionally.

Baccalà Vicenza Style is better if left to sit for a day after cooking and then reheated.

NOTE: In the *Veneto* region dried cod is called salt cod *(Baccalà)*, thus creating some confusion as to what type of fish to use. In this recipe, dried cod must be used.

PAGELLO IN CARTOCCIO
Sea Bream in Parchment

4, 6 oz. fillets of sea bream	*4 Tbs. olive oil*
2 ripe tomatoes	*6 sprigs basil*
8 oz. mushrooms	*½ cup white wine*
1 Tbs. chopped parsley	*4 parchment sheets of approx. 10" in diameter*

Prepare the sauce. Peel, seed and chop the tomatoes, chop or slice the mushrooms. Heat the olive oil in a pan add the mushrooms, sauté briskly over a lively flame for 2 mins., add the chopped parsley, the tomatoes and 2 sprigs of basil. Bring to a simmer then add the white wine, reduce for 5 minutes, remove from heat and set aside.

Grease the parchment with olive oil. Distribute the sauce evenly on each sheet, place the fish fillets on top, fold over the parchment paper and seal the packet securely. Place in a baking dish and bake in oven at 450 F. for 20 minutes.

VARIATION: Depending on the type of fish used, fish may be sautéed first before being placed in parchment.

TROTA RIPIENA
Stuffed Trout

4 trout, each 20-24 oz.	*1 small carrot*
2 shallots	*1 small onion*
3 oz. fresh mushrooms	*1 stalk celery*
parsley	*1 cup red wine*
salt to taste	*2½ oz. butter*
6 peppercorns, crushed	

Gut, clean and bone the trout. Wash, pat-dry and set aside.

Chop the shallots, mushrooms and parsley. Salt to taste, add peppercorns and half of the butter cut into pea size pieces, prepare a smooth mixture, then stuff the fish with it. Put the onion, the carrot and celery cut into pieces into a fish poacher, lay the trout on top and cover with red wine. Cook over low heat. When trout is cooked, remove from poacher, skin, place in a serving platter, and keep warm.

Filter the cooking liquid. Let it reduce a bit then add the butter whisking vigorously to prevent separation and cook until the sauce is very hot. Adjust seasoning, pour the sauce on the trout and serve immediately.

CUSCUS CON PESCE
Semolina and Fish Stew "Cuscus"

*1 lb. semolina (½ fine
  ground, ½ coarse ground)
pinch of saffron
4 Tbs. olive oil
2 cloves garlic
1 Tbs. chopped parsley
pinch nutmeg*

*2 qts. poaching liquid
(see recipe)
salt and pepper to taste
3 lbs. grouper or red snapper
fillets, each 3/4 oz.
1 bay leaf
pinch cinnamon*

Mix the *semolina* in a mixing bowl with 1 pt. of water and the saffron diluted with 1/2 cup lukewarm water. The *semolina* is worked until it becomes dry and granulated (add more water if too dry, or more *semolina* if too wet). Let these small kernels dry on a towel.

In a saucepan, warm the oil, brown the garlic, add the parsley, and onion. When tender, not brown, add 2 qts. poaching liquid, and salt and pepper. Bring to a simmer and add the fish. Cook till the fish is tender, but still crisp. Remove fish from broth, set aside and keep warm. Strain the fish broth, bring to a boil, place the *semolina* into a fine strainer and place suspended over the boiling broth. Care should be exercised so that the steam does not come out from the sides. This can be done by placing tin foil between the strainer and the sides of the pot. It will take at least 1½ hours for the *semolina* to cook in this manner.

Place cooked semolina in a large platter and add as much of the poaching liquid as it will absorb so as to be fairly humid and loose. Add the pinch of cinnamon, nutmeg and salt and pepper. Top with the fish, which should be warm and place on top of the *cuscus*. Serve.

FILETTI DI SOGLIOLA FRITTI
Fried Fillet of Sole

*4 fillets of sole, each 7/8 oz.
6 Tbs. flour
6 Tbs. butter*

*2 Tbs. olive oil
salt to taste
1 pt. water*

Pat-dry and lightly dust the fish fillets with flour. Melt 2 Tbs. butter and olive oil in a skillet. When hot, add the sole and fry on both sides until golden brown. Place the sole on a serving platter discarding frying fat. Wipe pan clean and add the remainder of the butter. When the butter has browned, add salt to taste and pour over sole. Serve.

SARDE A BECCAFICO
Stuffed sardines

2 Tbs. raisins	salt
5 Tbs. white bread crumbs	pepper
½ cup olive oil	2 Tbs. pine nuts
¼ lb. pecorino cheese	8 anchovy fillets
1 Tbs. minced parsley	laurel
4 oz. grated pecorino	2 lb. sardines
1 garlic clove	

Soak the raisins in warm water, then squeeze out the excess water. Brown 4 Tbs. of bread crumbs in 1 Tbs. oil, and mix all the ingredients except the laurel well to make a smooth stuffing. Remove the heads split open, bone the sardines and pat dry. Spread them open on a table and spread with stuffing. Fold them lengthwise and place on a baking dish . Drizzle with bread crumbs, olive oil, and the laurel and cook in the oven for 15 minutes at 450 F.

ANGUILLA ALLA BRACE CON ACETO BALSAMICO
Grilled Eel with Balsamic Vinegar

2 eels of approx. 1 lb. each	1 tsp. balsamic vinegar
3 Tbs. olive oil	salt to taste
2 sprigs rosemary	

Rub the eel skin with ash, or if not available, with a pumice stone or rigid cloth. Wash, gut, remove the head, split open and remove the bone. Marinate for 1 hour with olive oil and rosemary. Cut the eel across about 3'' long and place on the grill with the skin down. No other condiment is necessary as the fat of the fish will give its taste. Cook until done, remove from grill and brush with balsamic vinegar. Serve immediately.

SARAGO ALLA GRIGLIA
Grilled Sea Bream

4-20/24 oz. sea bream

Gut and clean, but do not scale the fish. Make a couple of incisions on the inside, along the bone in order to facilitate the cooking process. The size of the fish does not require to be scored on the outside. If the fish being grilled is large, then it is advisable to do so.
Light the grill, if possible with aromatic woods. The fire is ready

when the wood is completely burned and has formed a light layer of ash. Make sure the grill is clean and oiled before placing the fish on it. Simply place the fish on top of the grill. This is fine for small fish because they are easy to turn.

If grilling a large fish, use a folding grill (some are squares, others have the actual shape of a fish) this will make the turning a lot easier. Turn the fish only once with a large spatula. When the fish is ready it can be served with a variety of light sauces, mostly with an oil and lemon base.

RANE IN GUAZZETTO
Frog's legs in tomato sauce

36 frogs legs
4 Tbs. olive oil
2 garlic cloves, crushed
1 onion, chopped
2 celery stalks, chopped
1 lb. tomatoes, peeled,
seeded and chopped

flour for dusting
4 Tbs. butter
salt and pepper
1 Tbs. chopped parsley
6 croutons

Prepare a *soffritto* with the garlic, onion, celery and the olive oil. Remove garlic when brown. When the rest of the vegetables are tender, not brown, add the tomatoes and cook for 12 minutes at medium heat. In a separate skillet, sauté the frogs legs which have been lightly dusted with flour, in 4 Tbs. butter until just browned. Remove and add to the tomato sauce. Finish the cooking over medium heat for 5 more minutes. Adjust seasoning, add parsley and serve with a crouton.

COSCE DI RANE CON UOVA
Frog's legs with eggs

24 frogs legs, medium size
1 cup flour
6 Tbs. olive oil
6 eggs

1 Tbs. chopped parsley
2 Tbs. grated parmigiano
2 Tbs. butter

Wash the frogs legs and pat dry. Dust with flour and fry in 4 Tbs. hot oil until they turn golden. Remove from pan and place on paper towels to rid of excess fat. Cool, bone and set aside the frogs legs.

Break the eggs into a bowl, add the parsley and *parmigiano* and mix well (do not let the eggs form a foam). In a 12" iron pan, place the butter and the rest of the oil and pour in the frogs legs. When hot, add the eggs and mix well so that the frogs legs are well distributed throughout the pan. When the egg starts to coagulate spread it evenly in the pan and let it cook slowly with the pan covered. When eggs are set, serve from iron skillet.

LUMACHE
Snails. How to prepare snails

Snails are available frozen, but tradition demands that they be alive. Snails must be purged before they are eaten which requires a series of time consuming but not difficult operations.

Put the live snails into a wicker basket lined with grape or fig leaves (lettuce can be used) with some crustless bread which has been soaked in water and squeezed. Cover the basket with a towel wound round with string so that the snails do not escape, and let them purge for 3 days. After this time, remove the dead snails and put the live snails into a deep pot and cover with salted water, add a glass of wine vinegar. Move the snails around with your hands or a wooden spoon, leave them in this water for 2 hours. The top of the water will become quite foamy and viscous. Now, put the snails into another deep pot and repeat the operation. Continue changing pots and water until no more foam rises to the surface.

Drain the snails and rinse in running water. Put into a cooking pot and cover with cold water. Salt, add a glass of wine vinegar and bring slowly to a boil. Cook for about 15 minutes. Drain the snails, remove them from the shells with a fork, and cut off the black end. Wash the snails in vinegar and dry with a towel sprinkled with corn flour. Wash them again, then put in a cooking pot with equal parts water and white wine and bring to a boil.

Cook over low heat for 3 hours, then drain and prepare according to the recipe. To clean the shells, boil in water with baking soda then rinse very well and dry.

LUMACHE ALLA LIGURE
Snails, Ligurian Style

5 salted anchovies	*1 bottle dry white wine*
1 sprig rosemary	*salt*
2 garlic cloves, fully minced	*pepper*
2 oz. olive oil	*1½ oz. finely minced basil*
48 snails	*4 large croutons*

Fillet and finely mince the anchovies, and sauté them with rosemary and garlic in olive oil, until the anchovies disintegrate. Add the snails. Stir and moisten with white wine, 1 cup at a time. When the wine evaporates, add salt and pepper and continue to cook for half hour over low heat, moistening with more wine when necessary. Before serving, add the basil and serve snails on croutons topped with its own sauce.

VARIATION: Finely sliced mushrooms may be added after moistening with the wine.

GAMBERI E CANNELLINI ALLA TOSCANA
Shrimp and cannellini beans

20 large shrimp, cleaned	*½ oz. rosemary, chopped*

½ *lb. cannellini beans*
(boiled)
3½ *oz. of the water used*
to boil the cannellini beans

4 *Tbs. extra virgin olive oil*
2 *tomatoes, diced*
salt and pepper

After soaking the *cannellini* beans overnight, cook them in lightly salted cold water for 1 hour or until tender. In a casserole, heat 1 oz. of olive oil, brown and discard the garlic. Add the shrimp, cook for 90 seconds on each side. Add the rosemary, tomatoes, *cannellini* beans, water, salt and pepper and simmer for 3 more minutes, on medium heat.

Remove from the heat; place either in individual serving plates or a platter. Top with a spoonful of extra virgin olive oil and serve immediately.

CARNE
Meats

The diversity in the preparation of beef in Italian cookery is nearly endless and full of variety and imagination. These variations include the marvelous *bollito misto* or the more traditional preparation of *stufati, brasati,* and *stracotti,* which are subject to numerous interpretations. Meat cookery is full of surprises and, sometimes, contradictions. No dish is tied down to a basic recipe, but leaves a lot of room for improvisation and gives the cook an opportunity to use all that is left over, either raw or cooked. This can easily be seen in looking at preparations of *involtini, polpettone,* e *spezzatini,* in addition to unique ways to use variety meats, such as tripe, liver and other innards. Regardless of the recipe, it should be noted that herbs and spices are only used to highlight the basic taste of meat and to add the flavors so indispensable in Italian cookery. *Gabriele D'Annunzio* (1863-1938), a dramatist, novelist, and flamboyant political leader, was also a noted gourmand. He used to peek in the kitchen of his mansion and constantly remind his cooks of one thing, *«non dimenticate, i sapori! i sapori!;»* that is, do whatever you wish to the food but do not forget to highlight the basic flavors.

Beef, veal, pork and lamb are the most common types of meat sold commercially in Italy.

There are four categories distinguishing the various cuts of meat: meat classified as *primo taglio* (prime cuts), suitable for grilling and other quick preparations; meat classified as *secondo taglio* (choice cuts), suitable for longer cooking; meat classified as *terzo taglio* (select cuts), used for slow preparations, such as boiling, stewing, and braising; and, finally, *frattaglie* (varietal meats, including all innards, which are sautéed, stewed or grilled).

Recipes for cooking meat are practically limitless in number. Although the basic recipes should not be subject to much variation, one may still wish to vary some of the ingredients to achieve a more personal result.

COOKING TECHNIQUES

Boiling

Both beef and veal (as well as poultry--see POULTRY chapter) can be cooked in water. The following veal cuts are best for this type of cooking: brisket, flank, calf's head, calf's feet, and calf's tongue. The following beef cuts are best suited for boiling: shoulder, leg, round and rump cuts, brisket, oxtail, shoulder, arm and chuck, blade roast, neck, and shin.

Basic Cuts:

BEEF: brisket, flank, shoulder clod, tongue, neck, head

VEAL: hindshank, foreshank, neck, head, foot, tongue
PORK: shoulder hocks, head, foot
FLAVORING: Carrot, celery stalk, onion with a garlic clove spiked in it, several basil leaves, one bay leaf, and a ripe tomato add flavor and color. If, however, the vegetables will be served with the boiled meats, they should be added when the meat is half cooked or later, so that they will not overcook. You may choose among onions, leeks, radishes, carrots, celery and potatoes.
WATER: For 24-30 oz. of meat, use 2 qts. of water. In the beginning add 1 Tbs. salt (further additions can be made to taste). If too much water is used, the meat will be bland.
THE POT: The pot should be large enough to allow the meat to be covered with water while cooking. If the pot is too big, the water will not cover the meat; if it is too small, it may boil over.
COOKING PROCEDURE: Bring the necessary amount of water to a boil together with the vegetables. Add the meat, starting with the pieces that need longer cooking. Bring to a boil again and reduce the heat, add salt and continue to cook over a very low flame for 2-4 hours. If you wish to make a good broth, put the meat into cold water and slowly bring to a boil. If the cooking meat is too fatty, skim the fat occasionally. Often a marrow bone is cooked together with the meat (marrow is considered a delicacy). If marrow is used, wrap the bone with a piece of cheesecloth and tie with string to prevent the marrow from dispersing in the broth while cooking. Add the marrow bone halfway through cooking.

While cooking the meat, it is not necessary to remove the foam; indeed, some dieticians advise against it. If the foam is incorporated in the broth, the result will be richer in albumin. If however, a clear broth is desired it is better to skim off the foam. To obtain the clearest broth, after the meat and herbs have been removed, beat one egg white into the broth, return to a simmer and wait until it has coagulated and risen to the surface then remove. The egg white will have absorbed most or all of the fat residues.

Roasting
Basic Cuts:

BEEF: T-Bone, tenderloin, rib, rib-eye, strip loin.
VEAL: Chuck, loin, rack, rib-eye.
PORK: Loin, rack, leg, whole (when small).
SEASONINGS: Fresh rosemary, sage, and garlic.
UTENSILS FOR ROASTING: Roasting can be done on the stove, on a spit or in the oven. Roasting on the spit is preferable; in absence of a spit, roast the meat in the oven on a rack, using a roasting drip pan *(leccarda),* so that the juices from the roast can be collected for later use and the meat can cook without being immersed in its own fat.
THE OVEN: If using the oven, make sure it is preheated to the desired temperature before putting in the meat; the high heat will sear the meat, sealing in the juices. As soon as the meat is browned on all sides, lower the heat and continue to cook. If the oven is equipped

with a spit, do not preheat.

HOW TO PREPARE THE MEAT FOR ROASTING: When roasting, it is common practice to wrap leaner cuts of meat (except pork) with thin slices of lard or pancetta. * (*Pancetta* or lard provides the meat with the necessary fat for browning, enhances its flavor and protects it from extended exposure to high temperature.)

Secure the slices of fat with string. It is preferable not to add salt in advance, because salt draws out the juices. Salt may be added about ten minutes before the cooking is completed. It is also better to add pepper at the end. Sometimes the meat is rubbed with chopped herbs and left to sit for a while prior to roasting.

NOTE: * This procedure is not mandatory but it is common in Italy because meat is generally rather lean.

PROCEDURE: If using a spit, make sure that it goes through the center of the meat; otherwise the spit will not turn properly. If using the oven, place the roast on a rack, place the rack in a casserole or a drip pan large enough to catch the liquids coming out of the cooking meat. Baste occasionally with the drippings from the roast. Do not use liquids such as milk or wine, because the steam these produce prevents the meat from forming the desired outer crust.

About halfway through the cooking process basting should be stopped, since the «crust» now formed around the meat will prevent the fat from penetrating the meat.

If the piece of meat is too large, thus requiring a longer cooking time, cover with aluminum foil halfway through to prevent the outside of the meat from becoming too dry.

The roast is ready when, pricked with a fork, juices run pink.

PORK ROAST: The procedure for roasting pork is slightly different from the one outlined above. Pork should not be cooked wrapped with slices of fat because it is already fatty enough. Certain pork recipes allow for the roast to cook in its own fat. Remember that pork must be well done, but not dry.

ROASTING ON TOP OF THE STOVE: The meat should be seared and browned in oil (or other fat) together with a clove of garlic, sage and rosemary. Then cook over low heat, turning from time to time. If desired, after the meat has been browned, some white or red wine may be added.

How to Serve Roasts: Roasts may be served with grilled vegetables or roast potatoes, various raw salads, braised greens or onions.

BRASATO
Braising

The term *brasato* (braising) derives from the word *braci* (charcoal) because of an ancient cooking procedure in which the pot containing the meat was placed in, and covered with, the embers. Braising is very common in Italy, particularly in Piedmont and Lombardy. Meat for braising is often marinated in wine, herbs and spices. It is then browned on all sides with butter or other fats, then cooked in the liquids used for the marinade.

For braising it is necessary to use a deep pot with a heavy bottom, which can be made of stainless steel, aluminum, clay or copper lined with tin. The pot should be just big enough for the meat to fit. If the pot is too big, the liquid will evaporate faster. The liquid should only cover the meat halfway, never entirely. Never completely cover the pot, but leave the cover slightly ajar. Braising requires careful attention and long cooking time. Both white and red meat can be braised.

How to Serve a *Brasato:* When the *brasato* is cooked, strain the braising liquid and reduce it slightly. Arrange the meat (sliced or whole) on a preheated serving dish, top with the reduced liquid and serve with pureed or boiled potatoes, potato gnocchi or polenta. Brasato is more flavorful if let to stand overnight and reheated.

STRACOTTO
Over-braised Beef
This takes the same preparation as the braised beef, minus the marinating and browning of the beef, before the long cooking process starts.

STUFATO
Stewing
Stewing is a very popular preparation in Italy. The meat is cut in small or large chunks, and cooked slowly with or without the addition of other ingredients, such as potatoes, peas, and tomatoes. Stewing can be done on top of the stove or in the oven.

SALTARE
Sautéeing
Sautéeing is a method of cooking thin cuts of meat or poultry in as small amount of fat as possible. Since this cooking technique requires high heat, a pot with a heavy bottom is necessary. It should be shallow, to allow any steam to evaporate quickly. All the meat should be in direct contact with the bottom of the pan, so that no pieces overlap.

Fats: olive oil, butter or a mix of both. Usually olive oil is used for red meat, while butter is used for white meat.

Procedure: Heat a small amount of fat in a sauté pan. (The quantity of fat should be small; otherwise the meat would be fried and not sautéed.) When the fat is hot, arrange the meat in the pan and cook over high heat; the cooking time will vary according to how thick the slices or the cuts are. Turn the meat over and finish cooking. Salt and pepper should be added only when the meat is cooked. The meat should never be allowed to cook in the sauce; if so, the meat may become steamed and stringy.

GRIGLIARE
How to grill meat
If possible, grilling should be done over charcoal made from aromatic woods such as oak, juniper, chestnut or grape vine cuttings. Do not use resinous wood.

Commercial charcoal may be used if aromatic wood is not available. The fire is ready when the red-hot charcoal is covered with a light layer of ash (there should be a good quantity of charcoal in order to ensure adequate heat to complete cooking). The area of the charcoal layer should be bigger than that of the grill. These two points are important because one cannot add more charcoal midway. If the heat is too high, sprinkle the burning charcoal with some hot ashes. Do not use cold ash because it will extinguish the charcoal. Some sprigs of herbs (sage, rosemary, or bay leaves) may be added to the coals and the meat will absorb the aroma.

THE GRILL: It should be very clean, otherwise the meat will adhere to it. Before cooking, the grill should be greased with oil, then heated very hot. This will sear the meat and prevent it from sticking to the grill, or breaking up when turned.

COOKING PROCEDURE: The meat should be lightly marinated in oil and desired herbs before placing it on the grill. While cooking, baste the meat occasionally, using a brush or a rosemary sprig. This will prevent the meat from becoming too dry. If the outside dries too quickly, the heat will not penetrate the meat, resulting in uneven grilling. The meat should not be turned too often. Before turning, the side that has been exposed to the heat should be well cooked. Use a spatula to turn the meat; a fork would break the seared surface of the meat, causing it to lose its juices. Generally speaking, a slice of meat one-inch thick cooked rare takes about 5-6 minutes to cook on each side (of course, cooking time varies depending on the degree of done-ness desired). Add salt and pepper only when the meat is ready.

VITELLO
Veal

The term «veal» is used in Italy to refer to the meat of both the male and the female calf. Calves are butchered from one month old until one year. If the calf has been raised on proper food (milk and selected fodder), both its meat and fat will be very white. If it was fed badly and butchered at the wrong age, its meat will be darker in color and will be lean, watery, tasteless and low in nutritive value.

RECIPES

SCALOPPINE AL LIMONE
Scaloppine with lemon

3 oz. butter
2 lemons (1 squeezed, 1 thinly sliced into 12 slices)
12 veal scaloppine
flour
white wine
salt/white pepper
1 oz. dry white vine
1 Tbs. chopped parsley

In a shallow pan melt 1 $\frac{1}{2}$ oz. butter. Dust the veal with flour and sauté briskly, 30 seconds on each side. Remove from the pan, place in serving platter and set aside in a warm place. Using a clean skillet, melt the remaining butter. When hot, add a splash of dry white wine, let reduce quickly then add the juice of one lemon, salt and pepper to taste and parsley. While very hot and foaming, pour the sauce over the veal. Place $\frac{1}{2}$ slice of lemon with a pinch of parsley on each *scaloppina* and serve.

COSTOLETTA ALLA MILANESE
Veal chop, Milanese

4 *veal chops*	2 $\frac{1}{2}$ *oz. butter*
1 *pint milk*	*salt*
2 *eggs, beaten*	*pepper*
3 *oz. white bread crumbs*	

Use veal chops that have been pounded to about $\frac{1}{3}$" thick. Dip them in milk for 30 minutes and strain. Dip chops in the beaten eggs and bread them, pressing the crumbs onto the meat with the palm of your hand. Melt the butter in a frying pan and sauté the breaded chops for 3 mins. on each side over a medium heat. Turn only once. The crust should be a golden-brown and the meat should be pink. Salt and pepper to taste.

COSTOLETTA ALLA VALDOSTANA
Veal chop with fontina cheese

4 *veal chops*	1 *egg, beaten*
4 *oz. Fontina cheese*	*white bread crumbs*
salt	3 *oz. butter*
pepper	
white truffle (optional)	

Butterfly the veal chops, leaving them attached to the bone. Flatten slightly and place slices of *fontina* cheese in between the two pieces of meat, salt and pepper to taste and pound the edges together with a mallet. Then dip in the beaten egg and the bread crumbs. Melt the butter in a skillet. When hot, place the veal chops in and cook for 2 mins. on each side, then 3 more mins. in the oven at 450 F. Remove from oven and place in serving platter. Add a shaving of white truffles over and serve.

SALTIMBOCCA ALLA ROMANA
Involtini with prosciutto

1 *lb. top round of veal*	2 *Tbs. olive oil*
$\frac{1}{4}$ *lb. sliced prosciutto*	4 *Tbs. butter*
sage leaves	*salt, pepper*
1 *cup flour*	$\frac{1}{2}$ *glass white wine*
$\frac{1}{2}$ *cup beef broth (optional)*	

Cut the veal into thin slices and flatten with a wooden mallet. Over each slice of meat place a slice of prosciutto with a sage leaf in the middle. Roll them up and close them with a toothpick as you would a safety pin (it should not go across the *involtini* but make a stitch along the sides). In a saucepan, put the oil and butter. Lightly dust the *involtini* with flour and sauté over medium flame for 3 mins. Add wine and simmer for 2 more mins. Salt and pepper to taste. Arrange the *involtini* on a serving platter. In the skillet used to cook the *involtini*, let the cooking juices reduce for a minute, then pour over the *involtini*. Serve immediately.

NOTE 1: If there is not enough cooking juice in the pan add $\frac{1}{2}$ cup broth, reduce briskly by half, and pour over the *involtini*.

NOTE 2: Saltimbocca can also be sautéed flat, rather than rolled.

NOTE 3: Marsala wine may be used instead of white wine.

VITELLO ALL'UCCELLETO
Veal sautéed with sage

> $1\frac{2}{3}$ lb. top round or veal tenderloin bits
> 4 Tbs. butter
> 4 Tbs. oil
> 2 cloves garlic, crushed
> bay and sage leaves
> salt, pepper to taste
> 1 cup white wine

Cut the veal into irregular strips about 1-2" long. Put the butter and the oil into a casserole and add bay and sage leave and garlic. Remove garlic when brown and when very hot, add the meat. Sauté briskly over high flame for 4 mins., add the wine and reduce by $\frac{2}{3}$'s. Add salt and pepper to taste and serve.

SPEZZATINO DI VITELLO
A Stew of Veal

> 2 lbs. boneless veal shoulder   1 bay leaf
> or chuck   1 Tbs. parsley, chopped
> 3 oz. oil   1 cup white wine
> salt, pepper $\frac{1}{2}$ lb. ripe tomatoes
> 1 clove garlic   2 qts. beef broth

Cut the meat into large regular cubes. Heat the oil in a large heavy pot, add a smashed clove of garlic and then brown the meat. Salt, pepper and add the bay leaf and a little chopped parsley. Let cook for a bit then splash with white wine. When the wine has evaporated, add the peeled, seeded, chopped tomatoes. Cook for about 10 minutes, then cover the meat with hot broth. Mix the ingredients, cover the pot and cook over low heat for about 2 hours.

VARIATION: Stew is a very common dish in Italian cuisine and is also prepared with other meats, especially beef. Another variation is to cook the meat without the tomatoes. Frequently diced potatoes, artichokes, peas or other vegetables are added during the last half hour of cooking. Dried or fresh mushrooms may also be added for additional flavor.

NOTE: If potatoes are not already in the stew, it is usually served with mashed potatoes or *polenta.*

In Italy, meat for stew is sold in butcher shops already cut and prepared. «Stew meat» consists of bits and pieces of meat taken from various cuts of veal or beef and is sold at a low price. Generally the meat requires only trimming and is ready for cooking.

OSSOBUCO CON GREMOLATA
Ossobucco with gremolata

4 pcs. cross-cut veal shank	4 cups broth
flour	peel of $\frac{1}{2}$ lemon
2 oz. butter	1 clove garlic
4 oz. white wine	1 sprig rosemary
pinch of nutmeg	parsley (1 sprig)
salt, pepper	

Dust the veal shanks with flour and brown them in hot melted butter in a fry pan. When browned, splash the meat with white wine, let evaporate, salt and pepper to taste, and add a pinch of nutmeg. Braise over low heat, adding broth occasionally, until the meat begins to come away from the bone (about 2 hours).

To prepare the *gremolata:* Chop very finely the lemon rind, garlic, rosemary and parsley and sprinkle over the veal, when almost ready. Cook for another few minutes and serve. *Ossobuco* may be served with *risotto*, with saffron.

SCAVINO PER OSSOBUCO

VARIATION: After having browned the veal shanks, add about $\frac{1}{2}$ lb. of ripe, peeled, seeded, chopped tomatoes with some chopped celery and carrots. Then continue with the recipe.

NOTE: The best part of this famous Lombardian dish is the marrow of the bones which is removed with a utensil called *scavino,* in Milanese slang known as the tax man (see glossary).

VITELLO ARROSTO AL LATTE
Veal roasted in milk

6 Tbs. butter	$\frac{1}{2}$ qt. milk
3 oz. prosciutto, cut in strips	salt
1 $\frac{3}{4}$ lb. veal loin	flour for dusting

Spike the veal with a few strips of *prosciutto*. Melt the butter and the rest of the *prosciutto* in a saucepan. Dust the veal with flour and brown evenly on all sides. Warm up the milk and pour 2 cups of milk over the meat, then salt to taste. Lower the heat, cover, and when the milk has been absorbed, add more. Continue to do so as the milk absorbs. When all the milk is finished, the meat will be correctly cooked. Remove meat and slice it evenly. Place on heated platter, add the reduced cooking juices over and serve. Any kind of vegetable is suitable to serve with this roast.

VITELLO TONNATO
Veal in Tuna Sauce

2 lbs. butt tenderloin	6 anchovy fillets
3 cups white wine	2 hard-boiled egg yolks
1 celery stalk	2 lemons,
1 carrot	1 squeezed, 1 thinly sliced
1 small onion	$\frac{1}{2}$ cup oil
2 cloves	2 Tbs. capers
7 oz. tuna in oil	1 Tbs. white vinegar

Let the meat marinate in the wine, celery, carrot, chopped onion and cloves for one day. Remove the meat from the marinade, wrap and tie tightly in a cheesecloth and place in an oval pan just large enough to hold it together. Put back in the marinade and cook slowly for about one hour. Remove from heat and let the meat cool in its cooking liquid.

De-grease and filter the cooking liquid. Blend the liquid in a food mill with the tuna, anchovies, 1 Tbs. capers and egg yolks. Dilute the sauce with lemon juice, and vinegar, and whisk in the oil in a steady stream till a velvety sauce is achieved (similar to mayonnaise). Slice the veal and arrange in a serving platter in the following manner: Spread a few tablespoons of the sauce on the platter. Add the veal a layer at a time, with sauce covering each layer. Sprinkle capers over and decorate the rim of the platter with the sliced lemon. Serve.

CIMA ALLA GENOVESE
Stuffed flank steak Genoa Style

1 oz. dried mushrooms	1 oz. grated parmigiano
6 slices white bread (crust removed)	6 eggs, beaten
4 oz. lean veal	3 lbs. breast of veal with pocket
3 oz. meat from calves head	2 oz. shelled peas
$\frac{1}{2}$ calf's brain	marjoram
	1 clove garlic
	pinch nutmeg
	1 carrot

½ lb. veal sweetbreads	1 celery stalk
2 Tbs. butter	1 small onion
2 Tbs. shelled pistachio nuts	salt, pepper
2 Tbs. pine nuts	6 qt. beef broth

Soak the mushrooms in warm water for a few minutes. Chop the mushrooms. Soak the bread in cold water then squeeze to remove excess. Make an incision in the veal breast, creating a pocket closed on three sides. To prepare the stuffing: Brown all the meat, except the breast of veal, in butter, then grind the meats coarsely . Mix the meat with the pistachio, pine nuts, parmigiano and eggs. Add the mushrooms, peas, marjoram, chopped garlic and bread to the meat mixture. Salt, pepper, add a little grated nutmeg and mix well.

To stuff the breast: Fill the veal breast with the stuffing. It should not be more than two thirds full. Sew the opening closed with needle and colorless thread, and prick the meat with a large needle so that it does not break during cooking. If possible, wrap the meat tightly in a piece of cheesecloth and sew it closed. Place the celery, carrot and diced onion in a large pot with the broth.

Turn on the heat, but do not allow to boil. Add the meat to the pot and cook over low heat for about 3 hours. Salt when the cooking is halfway through. Remove the stuffed breast of veal and place on a cutting board. Place a plate with a heavy weight on top of the meat and let cool completely.

Let it rest for at least 2 hours. Serve sliced with a salad or other meat cold cuts. *Cima alla Genovese* can be kept for a few days when refrigerated.

VITELLO IN FRICANDÒ
Braised Veal

2 lb. round of veal	1 carrot (cut into pieces)
2 thick slices of prosciutto	1 bunch parsley
2 onions, thinly sliced	few celery leaves
few cloves	1 cup white wine
4 Tbs. butter	salt, pepper to taste

Remove the fat from the prosciutto, cut it into small cubes and set aside. Cut the lean prosciutto into strips. Spike the veal by making small cuts in the veal and inserting the cubed *prosciutto* fat. In a casserole, place the butter, lean *prosciutto* cut in strips, onions, and cloves. Let it lightly brown, then add the veal and brown on all sides. Add the carrots, and the parsley and celery leaves tied together. Pour a cup of white wine over the veal, salt and pepper to taste, cover the casserole and cook over low heat turning frequently. Add broth if it gets too dry. Cook for 1 hour. Serve thinly sliced, adjust the seasoning and serve with the drippings of roast passed through a fine sieve.

BUE/MANZO
Beef

Often the terms *bue* (ox) or *manzo* (beef) are employed in the same way. While they both refer to a castrated male of the same breed, the term *bue* describes an animal from one-and-a-half to four years old. Thereafter the term *manzo* is used.

Vitellone (baby beef) is an animal slaughtered between 14-16 months old. Its meat is tougher than veal and somewhat more tender than beef.

Torello (young bull) is an un-castrated male, raised for slaughter. Young bulls are usually slaughtered at two years. Their meat is excellent, leaner, but tender and flavorful like beef. It is butchered and cooked the same way as beef.

RECIPES

BOLLITO MISTO
Various boiled meats

A true triumph of Italian cuisine. The meats used to prepare a good *bollito misto* are fowl, beef, veal, and fresh sausage like *cotechino* and *zampone* (see *INSACCATI* chapter). The size or the types of meats to be used for bollito cannot be too small; otherwise you will achieve a poor result. The leftovers can be served cold in various preparations. The recipe given below is for minimum quantities and types of meat.

One can readily see that if the *bollito* is for more people, larger cuts of meats can be used; therefore more flavor results.

1 carrot	$\frac{1}{2}$ lb. calf's head
1 onion	1 pig's foot
1 celery stalk	1 fresh cotechino (sausage)
1 lb. brisket	$\frac{1}{2}$ capon
$\frac{1}{2}$ lb. breast of veal	$\frac{1}{2}$ lb. veal tongue
salt	

Begin with boiling water so the juices of the meats are sealed. If you start with cold water, you will obtain a good broth, not a good bollito.

In a large pot, bring the water to a boil with the chopped vegetables. Then add beef, veal parts (breast, tongue and calf's head) and the pig's foot. Add seasoning. Cover the pot, lower the flame and cook for 2 hours, then add the capon and cook for 30 minutes. In a separate pot, cook the *cotechino* in salted water, (pricking the sausage so the casing will not pop). When the *cotechino* is soft (it normally takes about 1$\frac{1}{2}$ hours), add to the other meats, cook for another 1/2 hour and remove from fire. Separate the fatty meats from the lean, skim the broth and keep the meats immersed into the broth, until ready to serve.

Ideally, boiled meats should be presented in its broth and, sliced at tableside.

NOTE: This is the original version but all the various cuts of meat may also be cooked separately.

Bollito misto may be accompanied by several types of sauces, *salsa verde* (green sauce), *mostarda di frutta* (preserved spiced fruit), or *cipolline in agrodolce* (spring onions in sweet and sour sauce), pickled vegetables or minced raw pepper with oil and vinegar, salt and pepper.

Leftovers from *bollito misto* may be served in various ways — as a salad with capers, anchovies, gherkins, aromatic herbs mixed in with oil and vinegar or with a condiment of tomato sauce and onions, in which case it is served hot. It may also be ground for *polpettone* (meat loaf).

BRASATO AL BAROLO
Braised beef with Barolo wine

salt	1 bunch aromatic herbs
pepper	spices
2 lb. top round	2 garlic cloves
2 carrots	2 Tbs. oil
2 onions	1 bottle Barolo wine
few celery stalks	flour for dusting

Salt, pepper and marinate the meat with the vegetables, aromatic herbs and spices and the wine for 12-24 hours at a cool temperature, but not in the refrigerator.

Drain the meat. In a large pan, heat the oil, dust the meat with flour and brown the meat over high flame on all sides. Add the marinade. Cover and cook gently in oven at 375 F. for 3-4 hours. Remove the brasato from its cooking liquid, set aside and keep warm. Pass the cooking liquids with the vegetable through a fine sieve. Adjust seasoning. Reduce a bit, slice the *brasato*, arrange in a pre-heated platter and serve with potato *gnocchi,* soft *polenta,* or mashed potatoes.

NOTE: The meat can also be larded or spiked with herbs and *pancetta* before marinating.

STRACOTTO
Over-braised beef

6 small garlic cloves	2 lbs. thinly sliced onions
2 lb. lean beef round	1 lb. ripe tomatoes, washed,
2 Tbs. olive oil	peeled, seeded and chopped
1 celery stalk	1 cup red wine
3 small carrots	salt and pepper to taste
1 bunch basil	broth

Spike the meat with the garlic, salt and pepper. Tie it with a color-less string to keep it in form. Place in a casserole with the olive oil and roast for 20 minutes turning frequently so that is browns evenly on all sides. In a separate pot, sauté the carrots, onions, celery and basil and cook over low heat for 30 minutes. Then, add the red wine and the tomatoes and cook for 15 minutes more. Remove from heat, pass the whole through a fine sieve.

Place the beef in a terra-cotta pot, add the strained vegetable purée and cook over low heat for 4-5 hours turning occasionally. Add broth in small quantities if beef gets too dry. Adjust seasoning and serve sliced with its own sauce over it.

NOTE 1: As a side dish beans or polenta may be served.
NOTE 2: Stracotto is a *brasato* without the marinating.

RUSTISCIADA — STUFATO
Stewed meats with onion

2 lbs. various lean meats:	*3 medium sized onions*
beef, veal, pork, sausages	*1 cup white wine*
6 Tbs. butter	*6 oz. veal liver*
2 cloves garlic	*salt, pepper*

Coarsely dice the various meats. In a casserole melt the butter and brown the garlic. Remove garlic when brown, add the finely sliced onion. When tender but not brown, add the meat and let it brown evenly. Add half of the white wine and let it reduce. Continue to cook for 10 minutes. Add the liver and continue to baste with more white wine as the meats get dry.

Cook for 3 more minutes, add salt and pepper. Remove from heat and serve with *polenta*.
NOTE: This dish can also be prepared with leftover meats of any type.

CODA ALLA VACCINARA
Stewed oxtail with celery
This dish is called *alla vaccinara* which in Roman dialect means, «butcher style», supposedly because originally it was prepared in the trattorie near the slaughter houses.

2 lbs. oxtail	*salt*
3 oz. lard	*1 peperoncino (optional)*
1 head of celery finely diced	*1 cup red wine*
1 clove garlic	*1 lb. peeled tomatoes*
1 onion	*1 bay leaf*
1 carrot	*pepper*

Cut the oxtail across into pieces 1½" long, cover with cold water, let it rest for 30 minutes then, boil and simmer for 5 minutes. Drain and dry. Chop the lard, half of the celery, garlic, onion and carrot, salt, pepper and *peperoncino*. Cook until lightly brown then, add the oxtail and brown. Add the wine and tomatoes. Braise on top of the stove at medium heat for about 4 hours. Moist occasionally as it dries. When oxtails are tender remove them and hold on side. Strain braising liquid, degrease and adjust seasoning. Return oxtails to sauce and bring back to simmer. Clean and peel the remaining celery, dice finely and add to the oxtail. Serve with grilled or fried *polenta*.

NOTE 1: White wine may be substituted for red because the stew cooks for a long period of time and the sauce may become too dark using red wine.

NOTE 2: Celery has to be devoid of strings and some cooks par-boil it, as the celery has a tendency to become dark as it cooks.

INVOLTINI DI MANZO
Braised Involtini of Beef

1 lb. boneless round of beef	*8 oz. red wine*
1 carrot	*8 slices lean pancetta*
1 celery stalk	*2 oz. butter*
1 onion	*olive oil*
2 garlic cloves	*salt*
1 bay leaf	*pepper*

Thinly slice the meat and pound with a wooden mallet. Place in a baking pan. Marinate with the carrot, celery and onion. Add the garlic, and bay leaf to the bowl with the meat and cover with the wine. Marinate for a couple of hours in a cool place.

Drain the slices of meat, pat-dry and cover each with a slice of *pancetta*. Roll each slice, with the *pancetta* on the inside, and tie the involtini with string or keep in place with a toothpick. Drain the vegetables, put them in a saucepan and sauté with half the butter and two teaspoons of oil. When tender (but not browned) add the *involtini* and brown quickly.

In a separate saucepan reduce the wine by half its volume, pour it over the *involtini,* add salt and pepper, cover and cook over very low heat for 30 minutes.

When the *involtini* are ready, remove the string or the toothpick and place the *involtini* in a warm platter. Strain the cooking liquid, and reduce for a few minutes more. Add the remaining butter without allowing the sauce to boil. Pour the sauce over the *involtini* and serve hot with *polenta* or mashed potatoes.

POLPETTONE
Meat Loaf

1 lb. ground beef	*salt, pepper*
1 oz. chopped lard	*1-2 oz. milk*

2 eggs	*olive oil*
2 Tbs. grated parmigiano	*2 Tbs. butter*
½ cup bread crumbs	*1 onion*
1 lemon	

Mix the ground beef, lard, eggs, parmigiano, 2 Tbs. bread crumbs, lemon juice, salt and pepper. Add a few spoonfuls of milk and mix well. The mixture should be fairly solid but humid. Shape the meat into a loaf and coat with bread crumbs. Heat the oil in a large pan and brown the meat evenly on all sides.

Melt the butter in another pan and brown the chopped onion. Place the loaf over the onions and cook in a preheat oven at 475 F. for half an hour. Keep the bottom of the pan moist enough to prevent the onions from burning. This dish is excellent hot or cold, sliced.

VARIATION: *Polpettone* can be prepared with other kinds of meat, leftovers or a mixture of meats. Mashed potatoes, crustless white bread, or chopped greens can be added to the mixture. However the mixture is cooked, it should be browned in hot oil first so that is does not break during cooking. The same meat mixture can be used to make meatballs, or patties, which must first be browned, cooked halfway, then stewed with tomato sauce. The resulting sauce can be used for *pasta*.

FARSUMAGRU
Stuffed beef roll

This is the Sicilian version of *polpettone*. Many regions have their own version of this dish.

1½ lb. beef rib, blade meat	*6 slices crustless bread*
(or beef chuck shoulder)	*(soaked in cold water*
7 oz. prosciutto	*and squeezed dry)*
7 oz. sausage	*1 onion, chopped*
slice of pancetta	*bunch of parsley*
¾ lb. lean ground beef	*2 oz. strutto (lard)*
3 oz. fresh pecorino cheese	*1 cup red wine*
6 eggs	*½ lb. tomato pulp*
1 clove garlic	*1 Tbs. tomato paste*
	salt, pepper

Pound the meat flat until it is ¼" thick. Prepare the stuffing: Chop the *prosciutto,* sausage, and *pancetta,* and mix with the ground beef. Add grated *pecorino* cheese, 2 eggs, chopped garlic and parsley, bread, salt and pepper. Mix thoroughly to achieve a smooth mixture. Hard boil the remaining eggs and remove the shells. Spread the meat filling onto the pounded steak and place the whole hard boiled eggs on top end to end. Roll up the meat and tie, securely.

In a frying pan, brown the chopped onion in the lard, add the meat roll and brown on all sides. Splash with red wine. When the wine has evaporated, add the tomato pulp and paste diluted with 1 cup of warm water. Add salt and pepper, and cook in oven at 475 for 45 minutes basting occasionally so that the top does not get dry. Remove the meat from the roasting pan, let cool, strain the cooking liquids, adjust seasoning and serve over the sliced beef roll.

BISTECCA ALLA FIORENTINA
Grilled T-bone steak

2 T-Bone steaks, 2 lbs. each
olive oil
salt, pepper, rosemary

Marinate the meat for 1 hour, brushed with oil, salt, pepper and rosemary. Grill the meat on aromatic woods, which include olive tree wood. Follow the basic procedure for grilling meat. Cook 12 minutes on each side (turn it only once). Remove from heat, slice and serve. Each T-bone serves 2-3 people.
NOTE 1: The meat may also be grilled without marinating. Simply brush with oil before grilling.
NOTE 2: The meat may also be broiled in a kitchen broiler.
NOTE 3: The T-bone may be seared on both sides in an iron pan and the roasting finished in the oven at 550 F.

CARNE ALLA PIZZAIOLA
Beef Pizzaiola

1 lb. beef round
4 Tbs. olive oil
2 garlic cloves

1 tsp. oregano
1 lb. peeled, seeded
and chopped tomatoes
1 Tbs. chopped parsley

Slice the beef into $\frac{1}{2}$" thick slices. Brown the garlic in olive oil and remove when brown. Add the beef, brown on both sides, add tomatoes and oregano. Bring to a simmer then lower and cook for 15 minutes. Remove from heat and add chopped parsley. Arrange in serving platter and serve.
NOTE: Although sometimes chopped olives and anchovies are added the term *«pizzaiola»* means it is a sauce only made with tomatoes, garlic and oregano.

MAIALE
Pork

The pork sold commercially today in Italy is considerably leaner than that of the past, due to refined techniques for raising pigs. Pork is very tasty and has a rosy color, with iridescent reflections. There is always a great deal of fat (even if the hog was raised according to new farming methods). The meat of a young pig is rosier in color,

contains more water and less fat and is more digestible. The meat of
an older pig is tastier, since it contains less water and more fat.
Piglets or suckling pigs are only few weeks old and have been fed
only with milk, preferably from their mother. They are generally
roasted whole in the oven or on a spit. All the meat that the hog
yields is used one way or another. *Testa* (head) is used together with
other ingredients, to prepare *soppressata* (headcheese). The cheek or
the temple can be either boiled or stewed. The jowls are cured in the
same manner as *pancetta* and are called *guanciale*. It is sweeter and
used for preparation of *matriciana* sauce. The neck is preserved in
salt and, after adequate aging, made into sausage, called *bondiola*.

Piedini (feet), primarily boiled, pigs' feet may also be grilled, following the procedure described for the tail. Boning the front feet, up
to the ankle becomes the casing for zampone, a raw sausage for boiling and a specialty of *Modena*.

Coscia (leg) is a prime cut and can be roasted when it is from a
freshly killed pig. If the leg comes from a freshly killed young pig, it
may also be braised, boiled or cooked in slices. Through a special
curing process, it is made into *prosciutto,* which, together with *culatello* and *salami,* are the pride of *Parma's* farm products.

When taken from a freshly killed pig, *spalla* (shoulder) should be
cooked like the leg. The best part of the shoulder, boned, cooked and
cured, is used to make ham.

Lonza or *lombata* (side) is a long, large section of meat, rectangular in shape. It is located on top of the fillet in the lumbar region,
along the spine. It can be cooked in many ways, either whole or
sliced. When roasted it is called *arista*.

Cutting the top part of the *lombo* (loin) in chops yields choice
chops, and the terminal part extending toward the tail yields the
saddle. It can be roasted as a whole piece (either boned or with bone
in).

RECIPES

PORCHETTA
Roast suckling pig

Porchetta is always boned to make it easier to serve and eat.

1 suckling pig, 18-22 lbs	*4 cloves garlic*
olive oil	*salt, pepper*
2 Tbs. white wine	*coriander*
wild fennel seeds	*nutmeg*
4 sprigs rosemary	*peperoncino*

Chop and sauté the liver, heart and kidney in 2 Tbs. of olive oil.
When hot, add the white wine, reduce and remove from heat. The
piglet is seasoned with its own liver, heart and kidneys, plus wild

fennel seeds, rosemary, salt, pepper, a good quantity of garlic, coriander, nutmeg, and *peperoncino*. It is then rolled up like a large sausage, securely tied with colorless thread and roasted whole on a spit over charcoal made from aromatic wood for about 4 hours. The time of cooking varies according to the size of the piglet, which should be basted frequently with a rosemary sprig dipped in oil and with white or red wine.

The juice and fat that collects in the drip pan *(leccarda)* can be used to cook potatoes and onions, which may be served together with the *porchetta*. *Porchetta* can also be roasted in the oven.

ARISTA DI MAIALE CON CANNELLINI
Loin of pork with cannellini beans

3 lbs. pork loin center	*olive oil*
cut, with bone or without	*salt*
a few cloves	*freshly ground black pepper*
2 small sprigs fresh rosemary	*1 lb. cannellini beans*
1 whole garlic head	

Spike the meat in the very center with a *battuto* prepared with garlic, rosemary and cloves. Brush the meat with oil, salt to taste and set aside for one hour. Having soaked the *cannellini* overnight, cook beans in slightly salted water. Set aside but keep warm.

Place the pork in a greased baking pan, roast in oven at 450 F. for 2 hours, turning the meat frequently in its own fat. When the *arista* is ready, remove from the cooking pan, slice and arrange on serving platter. Serve with the warm beans dressed with olive oil, salt and pepper. The *arista* is also very good if served cold. Frequently the cooking liquids from the meat are used to cook bitter broccoli or black cabbage, which are then served with the arista.
NOTE: Arista can also be cooked on the spit.

CASSOEULA
A stew of pork ribs and sausages

1 pig's foot	*½ lb. pork skin*
2 Tbs. oil	*½ lb. diced carrots*
2 oz. butter	*½ lb. diced celery*
1 diced onion	*diced tomatoes*
1 lb. pork sausage	*3 lbs. Savoy cabbage*
1 lb. pork ribs	*salt, pepper*

Boil the pig's foot and cut in two, lengthwise. Make a *soffritto* with oil and butter, chopped onion. Add the pork meats, cut into pieces, and the pig's foot. When the meat is golden brown, add all diced carrots, celery, tomatoes. Cook over medium heat. After 30 minutes, add the cabbage, cut into strips. Salt and pepper to taste and cook for 45 minutes. The cooking liquid should be rather dense. If you wish to remove some of the fat from the *cassoeula,* do so before adding the cabbage.

VARIATION: Cassoeula is a Lombardian dish which has several versions. Sometimes, after the meats have been browned, a spoonful of tomato paste is added. Other cooks prefer to cook the cabbage in a separate pot, steaming it in the water remaining on the leaves after washing, and then adding it to the meat. The quality of the meat added to the *cassoeula* varies. The simplest version requires only ribs and sausages, while the most complicated includes the ears and tail. *Polenta* is the traditional accompaniment to *cassoeula.*

BRACIOLE DI MAIALE ALLA NAPOLETANA
Pork rollatine with garlic

1 lb. boneless loin of pork	*2 Tbs. olive oil*
4 garlic cloves	*1 lb. tomatoes, peeled, seeded*
2 Tbs. raisins	*and chopped*
2 Tbs. pine nuts	*salt, pepper to taste*
1 oz. capers	*1 Tbs. parsley*

Slice the pork loin and flatten slightly with a wooden mallet. Chop 2 cloves of garlic very finely, mix with the raisins, pine nuts and capers. Place a small amount of this mix on each slice of pork and roll the slices of pork. Tie with colorless string. Brown the remaining garlic in oil then remove. Add the pork *braciola,* brown on all sides, add tomatoes. Salt and pepper to taste and cook for 25 minutes over low flame. Add parsley, remove from heat and serve.

NOTE 1: Braciola can be added to a *ragù* sauce.

NOTE 2: In northern Italy, the word *braciola* can refer to sliced pork similar to a *scaloppina* and cooked flat, not rolled.

MAIALE AL LATTE
Pork roast with milk

2 lb. leg of pork (fresh ham)	*few sage leaves*
1 bottle white wine	*2 rosemary sprigs*
4 Tbs. butter	*1 qt. milk*
salt, pepper to taste	

Place the pork meat into a bowl, cover with wine and marinate for 2 days in a cool place. Next, remove the pork from the marinade, dry it and let it brown on all sides with the butter in a casserole. Add salt and pepper, sage leaves and rosemary, and cover with the milk. Cook slowly in oven for 1 hour at 375 F., remove pork from casserole and set aside in a warm place. Continue to reduce the milk over high flame on top of the stove for 10 more minutes, then remove from heat and strain. Slice the pork fairly thin and pour over the strained sauce.

SALSICCE CON I BROCCOLI
Fresh sausages with bitter broccoli

2 lbs. fresh sweet pork   1 small peperoncino
sausage   6 lbs. bitter broccoli
6 Tbs. olive oil
4 garlic cloves

Prick the sausages with a fork so they don't explode during cooking. Heat 1 Tbs. olive oil and sauté the sausages over medium flame. When they get a color add $\frac{1}{2}$ cup of water and continue to cook for 12 minutes. Remove from heat and set aside. Clean the broccoli discarding the stems and the larger leaves. Wash thoroughly but do not drip dry.

In a large casserole, heat the remainder of the oil, add the garlic and *peperoncino*. Remove garlic when brown and add bitter broccoli. Sauté over medium heat, for 20 minutes with the casserole covered, stirring occasionally. Add the sausage and continue to cook for another 5 mins. with the pot uncovered. Remove from heat and serve.

AGNELLO E CAPRETTO
Lamb and Goat

Lambs are domestic animals raised on the highlands or the spiral mountain chain called Appennines, which runs throughout most of Italy. From the typical *abbacchio arrosto* (roast baby lamb) to the *testina di capretto* (baked head of the baby goat), lamb and goat are considered a delicacy. In some areas lamb plays a large role in the Italian kitchen, especially in the spring.

The lamb sold commercially is classified in three categories according to age. Lamb killed in its fourth week is called *abbacchio,* which denotes a milk-fed lamb weighing 14-20 lbs. When killed at about three months old (while still suckling) it is called *agnello di latte* (baby lamb), weighing about 20-25 lbs. The meat is white and tender. More mature lambs (*agnelli*), weighing 25 lbs. and up at the time of slaughter, are also quite tender, though their meat is redder than that of the younger lambs. The *capretti* (male baby goats) are slaughtered between $1\frac{1}{2}$ to 4 months old; the females are usually kept for milk production. *Capretti* (baby goat, also called spring kid) are sold from March to May. The meat is very tender, has a delicate taste and is similar to the meat of milk-fed lambs. Its meat is redder in color and has a gamier odor and taste than lamb. Goat is generally roasted or prepared in any of the ways suitable for lamb.

Both lamb and kid do not need to age; they are best freshly killed.

RECIPES

ABBACCHIO ALLA CACCIATORA
Baby lamb, hunter style

3 lbs. baby lamb,　　　　　*4 salted anchovies*
combination of leg,　　　　*1 fresh rosemary sprig*
shoulder, ribs and kidneys　*¾ cup good white vinegar*
3 garlic cloves　　　　　　*salt*
4 Tbs. olive oil　　　　　　*pepper*
2 oz. lard

Cut the baby lamb in equal pieces, each about 2 oz., then, rinse them to remove bone splinters, and dry thoroughly. Sauté 2 cloves of garlic in 4 Tbs. oil and lard in a saucepan large enough to contain all the pieces of lamb in a single layer. Discard the garlic. Add the pieces of lamb, turning the meat until all sides are evenly browned.

In the meantime, wash and fillet the anchovies. Mince the rosemary leaves finely, together with the remaining garlic and the anchovy fillets. Pour the resulting mixture into 3/4 cup vinegar, mixing well. When the meat is browned, add pepper and a small amount of salt (remember that the anchovies are salty) moistening first with the vinegar mixture and then with water and continue to cook, over medium heat for 30 minutes. When the baby lamb is ready, arrange the meat in a preheated serving platter together with its cooking liquids and serve.

AGNELLO BRODETTATO
Braised lamb with eggs

2 lbs. shoulder baby lamb　*salt*
1½ lemons　　　　　　　　*pepper*
1 oz. lard　　　　　　　　*1 cup white wine*
2 oz. chopped prosciutto　*3 egg yolks*
1 chopped onion　　　　　*chopped parsley*
marjoram

Rub the lamb with half a lemon. Wash, dry and cut the meat into 2 oz. pieces. Melt the lard in a sauce pan, add the *prosciutto* and onion and brown the lamb. Add salt and pepper. When the lamb is evenly browned, splash it with white wine. Cook till tender, about an hour at low heat, adding a few spoonfuls of hot water if necessary. In a bowl beat the egg yolks with the chopped parsley and marjoram, a tsp. of grated lemon peel and the juice of a whole lemon. When the lamb has finished cooking turn off the heat and pour the egg mixture over it. Stir and let the eggs coagulate, but do not let them set too hard. Serve with a green salad.

CAPRETTO AL FORNO CON PATATE
Baked baby goat with potatoes

3 lbs. baby goat, leg, rib	parsley
6 Tbs. grated pecorino	2 lbs. potatoes
4 Tbs. white bread crumbs	6 Tbs. olive oil
3 garlic cloves	

Prepare a mix with *pecorino,* white bread crumbs, chopped garlic and parsley. Spike the baby goat with this mixture. Peel and slice the potatoes. In a baking pan, place 4 Tbs. oil and arrange the sliced potatoes in the pan. Place the baby goat on top of the potatoes and add more of the mixture. Add salt and pepper, drizzle with remaining olive oil and bake in oven at 450 F. for 1 hour.

TESTINA DI CAPRETTO AL FORNO
Roast head of baby goat

3 baby goat heads	6 Tbs. white bread crumbs
2 oz. pancetta	salt, pepper
3 garlic cloves	1 cup white wine
6 sprigs rosemary	½ cup olive oil

Clean and split the heads of the baby goats. Remove any visible cartilage. Prepare a *battuto* with the *pancetta,* garlic, rosemary, bread crumbs, salt and pepper. Spread this mixture over the heads, press lightly so the mixture adheres tightly and cover the brain portion with tin foil so it does not burn during the cooking process. Grease a baking pan and bake in oven at 475 F. for 2 hours basting occasionally with white wine. This dish is considered a delicacy, especially in *Calabria, Sicily* and *Sardinia.*

CARNE DI CAVALLO
Horse Meat

Horse meat is sold in special butcher shops since it is very delicate and subject to stringent sanitary regulations.

Horse meat must not be allowed to age for too long, since it spoils more quickly than beef. Today commercial horse meat is obtained from young horses that have been raised on farms and have never been used as work animals.

Horse meat may be used for braising and stewing and can be cooked like beef. Colt can be compared to veal, although it is more flavorful than the latter. In horse meat butcher shops donkey meat is also sold. If the mule is young, the meat is very similar to horse meat. Donkey meat is used to make *tapulone,* a Piedmontese specialty.

PASTISSADA DE CAVAL
Horseman stew

Legend has it that this landmark in *Veronese* cuisine dates back to the time of King Theodoric, in the early Middle Ages. Following a particular bloody battle in which a great number of horses were killed, the meat was given to the citizens of *Verona,* who had been starving because of a famine.

It was in these unhappy circumstances that, quite by chance, it was discovered how to cook this delicious dish, and since then the recipe has been handed down to us over the centuries. Even in those times, using horse meat aroused uncertain feelings (perhaps more so than today), in that men had developed a rather affectionate relationship with horses, so that it seemed unnatural to eat their meat.

2 lbs. aged horse meat	*salt*
4 Tbs. olive oil	*pepper*
2 oz. butter	*1 pint red wine*
½ lb. onions	*(preferably Amarone,*
1¼ lb. puréed tomatoes	*Bardolino or Valpolicella)*

Tenderize the meat by pounding it with the dull side of a heavy knife and cut into cubes. Heat the oil and butter in a pan and brown the chopped onions. Add the tomatoes and the meat. Salt and pepper and cook for about half an hour. Pour in the wine, cover and cook over low heat for at least 3 hours. Serve with *polenta* or with potato *gnocchi.*
NOTE: Pastissada is better reheated the next day.

FRATTAGLIE
Innards

The term *frattaglie* refers to the innards or organ meats of all animals, regardless of species. They are also called variety meats or edible by-products, by the USDA.

ANIMELLE
Sweetbreads

These are the thymus glands of veal and lamb. They are tender and delicate. Veal sweetbreads are divided into two parts: the choicest portion is round and full; often referred to as the nut or noix. The other less desireable has a more tapered shape and taken from the throat. They may be fried (either whole or cut into pieces), or cooked in delicate sauces. *Animelle* must always be purged and blanched first.

Place in a pot with cold water, changing water every hour. Put them in cold water again and bring the water slowly to a boil, simmer for 5 minutes and place again in cold water for another 20 minutes. Drain and remove all the fat and cartilage parts. Leave the skin on. Wrap it in a cloth and place under a weight for one hour. This method will allow for the meat to be more compact when it has to be sliced.

CERVELLA
Brain

This is a choice organ meat. Beef, veal, lamb and goat brains may be fried, cooked in a delicate sauce, or made into fried dumplings. Brains must also be purged and blanched before cooking.

Blanch by putting in cold running water for 2 hours. Remove from water and skin the brain. Put back in the cold water so that any residual blood is eliminated; otherwise the brain will become dark when cooked.

FEGATO
Liver

Liver will always vary in texture, size and color according to the size and feed of the animal it comes from. If a calf has been properly fed, the color will be a light pink, if not it will be redder. Liver must always be fresh. It may be fried, sautéed, cooked with wine, or either roasted or braised as a whole piece. Always remove the membrane that surrounds the liver. The membrane is tough and causes the meat to curl when cooking. To keep the liver from toughening, it should be cooked very fast on a brisk flame, only enough to make it change color.

RETE
Caul Fat

This is the fatty net, a membrane that encloses an animal's stomach. That of the pig is most frequently used to wrap meats for roasting or grilling. This method allows for the wrapped meat to absorb the fat of the membrane and therefore it becomes tastier.

ROGNONE/RENE
Kidneys

Veal and beef kidneys are the same shape, a knobbed oval shape, although they differ in size and tenderness. Pork kidneys are the shape of a large elongated kidney bean. Kidneys must always be cooked fresh, and must never smell like ammonia. They must be purged before cooking (unless they are from a spring veal). They can be grilled, sautéed, or thinly sliced and cooked in oil, garlic and parsley (*trifolati*).

The simplest method to purge the kidney is to remove the fat and slice the kidney or cut it in half and immerse it in hot water 3-4 times. Place it in a colander, add some salt and let it rest for 3-4 hours. Drain, rinse and dry.

CORATELLA
Mixed innards
This is a combination of all of the innards of lambs and goat (heart, kidneys, liver, etc.) and is cooked either stewed or sautéed by itself or with a vegetable.

LINGUA
Tongue
Both veal and pork tongues are sold commercially. They are either boiled or stewed. The beef tongue may also be pickled and preserved, and then boiled before consumption. Tongue may be eaten warm or cold.

TRIPPA
Tripe
Tripe is the stomach and the first parts of the intestine of cows, hogs and lamb. Tripe is divided into four parts:

Rumine: a thick, spongy tissue

Reticolo: a part which is shaped like a beehive and textured like a honeycomb.

Centopelle or *Foiolo:* the part that has thin, overlapping, parallel strips

Ricciolotta: the fattest, very curly part of the tripe.

Tripe is rich in protein and low in fats, minerals and vitamins. It is sold already cleaned and par-boiled, but requires about 2 more hours of cooking. Each region of Italy has different recipes for tripe. In most preparations, all parts are used; in others just one part.

RECIPES

ANIMELLE IN PANGRATTATO CON CARCIOFI
Breaded sweetbreads with artichokes

4 Tbs. white bread crumbs	1½ lb. sweetbreads
2 beaten eggs	8 baby artichokes
salt	2 garlic cloves
pepper	1 tsp. olive oil
6 Tbs. butter	1 sprig minced parsley

Sift the bread crumbs. Beat the eggs in a bowl together with salt, pepper, and 1 tsp. oil. Blanch the sweetbreads. Cut them in equal pieces, dust with flour, immerse them in egg and then bread crumbs In a very hot pan, fry the sweetbreads in 4 Tbs. of butter, drain on paper towels and arrange on pre-heated platter. Clean the artichokes, cut them in quarters and put in a saucepan with a little oil, 2 garlic cloves, parsley, salt, pepper. Cover the saucepan, cook over medium heat for 6-7 minutes. Remove from heat, add the remaining butter, stir and pour on top of the sweetbreads. Serve immediately.

CERVELLA IN CARROZZA
Fried Brains

1 lb. brains	1 egg, separated
4 Tbs. butter	12 slices stale bread, cut
½ cup olive oil	⅓" thick
1 small onion, finely sliced	oil for frying
1 cup milk	salt, pepper
6 Tbs. flour	1 Tbs. chopped parsley

Blanch the brains and slice evenly, ¼" thick. Heat up the 4 Tbs. butter and 2 Tbs. olive oil and add onion. When browned add the brains and sauté one minute on each side. Remove from heat and set the pan aside. Prepare a batter by placing milk in a bowl and slowly add the flour. Whisk well and add the egg yolk, salt and pepper. Whip the egg white and fold it into the batter. You should achieve a thick batter. Place a slice of brain with the onion on each slice of bread and dip into the batter. Fry. Drain the brains on paper towels, sprinkle with salt and chopped parsley. Serve very hot.

FEGATO CON CIPOLLINA DORATA
Liver with onions

1 lb. calf's liver	2 oz. olive oil
cut in ¼" slices	parsley
¾ lb. onions finely	1 oz. white wine
sliced	salt
2 oz. butter	pepper

Sauté the onion in 1 oz. butter and 1 oz. oil in a covered skillet over a low heat. When the onions are cooked and the liquid is reduced, add some finely minced parsley. Set aside and keep hot. Season the liver slices with salt and pepper. Sauté liver slices in 1 oz. each of oil and butter over high heat on each side very quickly, turning them with a wooden spatula to avoid pricking them with a fork. Sprinkle with the wine and remove from heat. Arrange the liver on a preheated serving dish, topping them with the *soffritto* of onions, and serve.

FEGATELLI DI MAIALE ALLO SPIEDO
Pork Liver on the spit

4 pork livers	olive oil
caul fat	salt
approx. 20 bay leaves	pepper

Clean the liver, remove skin and cut into 1 oz. pieces. Place the caul fat in water for about 1 hour so that it will soften. Then, cut into 5" x 3" rectangles. Wrap each piece of liver in the caul fat with a laurel leaf. Bring the olive oil to high heat and fry the livers so they become browned on all sides. Remove from pan and serve immediately.

ROGNONE AL MARSALA
Kidneys with Marsala

1 lb. calf's kidneys	*1 Tbs. dry Marsala*
3 ozs. butter	*chopped parsley*
1 Tbs. flour	*salt, pepper*
¾ cup broth	

Melt 1½ oz. butter in a saucepan. Add the ¼" sliced kidneys for 2 minutes. Remove kidneys and set aside. In a casserole wide enough to accommodate the kidneys in one layer, prepare a sauce with the remaining butter and flour. When it begins to color add the broth. Reduce for 1 minute and add kidneys and *marsala*. Cook for 2 minutes on lively flame. remove and add chopped parsley. Serve.

TRIPPA CON FAGIOLI
Tripe with beans

2 lbs. tripe «foiolo»	*½ lb. carrots, thinly chopped*
2 oz. olive oil	*7 oz. ripe tomatoes*
1 oz. butter	*pinch nutmeg*
1 onion	*2 sage leaves*
1 bay leaf	*1 cup broth*
3 oz. pre-soaked Borlotti beans	*4 Tbs. grated parmigiano*
5 oz. celery	*salt, pepper*

Cut the tripe into thin strips, about 3" long. In a saucepan brown the chopped onion in oil or butter, add the tripe and the bay leaf, and cook until the water from the tripe has evaporated. Add the beans, diced celery and carrot, the puréed tomatoes, a bit of grated nutmeg and a small bunch of sage leaves. Mix well and cover with broth. Salt and pepper to taste, and cook covered over low heat, for 2 hours. Blend in *parmigiano* cheese with tripe and serve.
VARIATION: In some regions a boiled de-boned and thinly sliced beef or veal hoof is added instead of beans, and the quantities of carrots and celery are reduced. In this case the hoof is par-boiled then diced finely and added to the tripe.

CORATELLA CON CARCIOFI
Stewed Innards with artichokes

2½ lbs. lamb innards	*2 oz. olive oil*
(heart, kidney, lungs, liver)	*salt*
6 artichokes	*pepper*
	juice of 1 lemon

Cut the liver into slices and cut the other organs into pieces. Blanch the artichokes, remove the leaves and beard and slice the bottom. Toss with a few drops of lemon juice and set aside. Heat the oil and add all the innards except the kidney and liver. When innards are well browned and tender (about 5 minutes), add the kidney, liver and sliced artichoke bottoms and cook 2 more minutes. Salt, pepper, add the juice of a squeezed lemon and serve immediately.

POLLAME E CACCIAGIONE
Poultry and Game

Throughout the centuries chicken has always been the bird used exclusively for man's eating habit. «A chicken in every pot» has been the motto of world leaders from Henry IV to Herbert Hoover. In the Italian tradition, farmyard animals, as well as game, have always been the food most consumed at the table, much more so than beef. We should not forget that Italy has always been a country with a strong farming tradition. With the exception of Piedmont, Maremma and Val di Chiana, the breeding grounds for beef, the rest of the peninsula has always considered the cow to be only good enough for production of milk and the ox a working animal. Cows were butchered and eaten only after they had exhausted their productive cycle for milk. Oxen were butchered when they had lost all their strength to work the fields. For normal eating habits however, farmyard animals were grown, such as chickens, ducks, geese, guinea hen, turkey, rabbit, etc. Recipes using farmyard animals are found in cook books of the Renaissance much more so than game because hunting was a sport practiced and reserved only for the nobility. Today, however, the situation has changed, and therefore large consumptions of farmyard animals have led to industrial farm breeding, which has given us a product, perhaps more nutritive but definitely less tasty than the chicken coop birds our fathers were accustomed to eating. With time and demands, the industrial production is getting better, while free-range poultry is once again available on the markets.

The same applies for all other feathered animals, such as roosters, fowl, capon, and turkey. Of domestic game, we should not forget rabbit. Its meat is white and tasty, but rather stringy if the animal is too old. Rabbit can be cooked almost always just like a chicken.

At one time wild game was the only way to save people from starvation; today its «gamey» smell and taste is only reluctantly accepted. As a growing number of game farms are starting to produce a milder tasting product, game with feather and game with fur will be much more accepted in the future, making game once again an interesting and noble gastronomic item.

MOST COMMON BIRDS AND GAME

ANITRA
Duck

Always give preference to young ducks, especially if they are to be roasted. Duck can be cooked in various ways: roasted, jugged, braised, stuffed, etc. Ducks can also be used to prepare excellent sauces for *pasta* or *polenta*. *Germano* (wild duck) is smaller and more flavorful than domestic duck and is usually stewed. The sauce is used as a condiment for *pappardelle* (fresh wide noodles).

TACCHINO
Turkey
Both tom and hen turkeys are available commercially. These are rather large birds and are cooked like chicken. They can be roasted in the oven, keeping the temperature low and basting frequently with the cooking juices because the meat tends to be dry. If cooked on top of the stove, it is necessary to divide the bird in pieces which will be suitable for different preparations, such as fried, stewed or cooked in a sauce. For these preparations, a young turkey is preferable. Breast meat can be used for preparations suitable for veal.

POLLO NOVELLO
Spring chicken
This is a three-month old, common bird (either male or female). Cleaned, it usually weighs between 1 $\frac{1}{2}$ to 1 $\frac{3}{4}$ lbs. It is suitable for grilling, roasting, or frying.

POLLO
Chicken (broiler)
A chicken 3-5 months old, usually weighing 2-3 lbs. It is suitable for roasting, frying in sauce, or boiling, with or without stuffing.

POLLASTRA
Pullet
A female chicken, 5-7 months old — that is, a chicken that has not yet started to lay eggs. Its weight varies roughly from 3 to 4 lbs. It should be boiled or poached, with or without stuffing.

GALLINA
Hen
This is a female chicken that has already laid eggs. It is allowed to mature, since it is kept to produce eggs and to brood chicks. It is usually used to make broth.

GALLETTO
Rooster
Young roosters are suitable for the same preparations that call for spring chickens. If the rooster has reached mating age, its meat will be tough; in this case, it should be used only to make broth.

CAPPONE
Capon
This is prized among poultry for its choice meat. It is a castrated male chicken, usually killed at about 10 months. It can weigh 4 lbs. or more, and the meat is exquisite. It can be either boiled, roasted, or braised, with or without stuffing.

FARAONA
Guinea Hen

This bird has delicate, exquisite meat, considered by some to be superior to pheasant.

If available, a 6-8 month old guinea hen is preferred. Cleaned, it will weigh 2 lbs. at the most.

If possible, remove the intestines right after the slaughter. Leave the feathers on and let hang by the beak, in a cool airy place, for about 2-3 days. It may be roasted, or cooked like a pheasant. If roasted, cover the breasts with thin slices of lard.

PICCIONE
Squab/Pigeon

These are farm-grown birds with delicate, lean meat. The best ones are those less than 7 months old with tender, almost white meat. Older birds have tough meat, which must be cooked at length. Pigeons may be cooked in various ways: fried, stewed, breaded like cutlets, roasted, grilled and baked. If roasted it is best to wrap the bird with slices of *pancetta*.

OCA
Goose

Geese are usually available in winter, particularly in December. Some are extremely fat (their liver is highly prized) and the average weight (cleaned) is about 9 lbs.

The best ones are less than 10 months old with white or faintly pink skin and underdeveloped breast bones. They are cleaned like chickens and can be roasted, or cooked in various other ways. In any event, they should be cooked with only a small amount of fat, since geese are rather fatty. To de-fat the bird, keep it in a warm oven (225 F.) for about an hour and discard the residual fat before cooking.

In some regions geese are cooked and preserved in their own fat.

CONIGLIO
Rabbit

The rabbits available on the market are domestic ones. In buying rabbits, give preference to those which still have the fur attached to the body: the air cannot cause spoilage, and the meat will maintain good color and texture.

There are many ways to cook rabbit. Rabbits 5-6 months old are the best for roasting. They should be larded with lard or *pancetta* to keep the meat moist. Rabbit can also be boned and cooked with stuffing, tied as a meat-loaf and served as a galantine. Usually the legs and thighs are roasted, while the front part (saddle), which has less meat, is either stewed or used to prepare a sauce for *pasta*. The liver is also used for *pasta ragùs*.

QUAGLIA
Quails

These are small birds whose meat is delicate and delicious. The best time for wild quail is October, although farms provide domestic quail year round. Do not hang wild quail. In buying quails, give preference to the fatter ones. In some Italian cities they are sold on skewers, wrapped with slices of *pancetta*, ready to be cooked. Wild quails are cleaned like chickens and can be cooked in various ways: baked, grilled, stewed with mushrooms, or sautéed. Quail can also be used to prepare exquisite *risottos*.

PERNICE
Partridge

There are many varieties of partridge. The most common are the common grey and the red-legged partridge. Baby partridges are hunted in the month of September. You can tell a baby partridge by looking at the first feather of its wing: it will be pointed with a red dot (in an adult partridge, the wing is rounded). The beak will be rather hard and almost black; the legs (which have not grown spurs yet) will be grey, and the eye surrounded by a small red circle. Partridge should not be hung for too long. If it is not a very cold day, it may be hung for one day (without removing the feathers); if the temperature is low, it may be hung for two days at the most. It is plucked like a chicken, always just before cooking. If you intend to roast it, it is preferable to cook the bird when freshly killed. If it is to be cooked in a sauce, it is best to use an adult bird. Partridge can be jugged, cooked in a casserole, roasted, etc. Partridge for roasting should be larded or cooked in vine leaves; it is frequently stuffed or served with grapes. A large partridge can serve two.

TORDO
Thrush

This is a small bird from the blackbird family. Various types are to be found in Italy. Thrush meat is very delicate and the taste varies according to what the bird has been eating. The smaller thrushes have the most delicate meat, while larger thrushes' meat is a little bitter. Thrush is usually cooked like quail — roasted, grilled, or used as an ingredient in pâtés and terrines.

PASSERO
Sparrow

These are the most common birds in Italy. The meat is particularly suitable for serving with *polenta* (*polenta e osei*). Usually they are not gutted, but cooked on the spit or in a pan, wrapped in pancetta, flavored with sage and broth, which can then be used together with the drippings from the roasting to prepare a sauce.

FAGIANO
Pheasant

This is regarded as the most delicious of the game birds. It is available on the market during the winter season. If possible, select a 12-14 month old pheasant.

Pheasant meat must be hung. In addition to making the meat more tender, hanging enhances the flavor of the bird. The unplucked bird must be hung by the beak from a hook, in a cool, airy place (there should be air flow around the bird), until it is well ripened. It is impossible to say how many days it will take, but no more than four days depending on the climate and the age of the pheasant. The bird is ready to cook when, if you blow on the feathers, the visible skin is a bluish (not greenish) color. Check the bird after it is hung for two days and each day thereafter. When cooking, do not use strongly flavored ingredients, since these would overpower the taste of the pheasant. The male pheasant has prettier plumage than the female. However, the meat of the female is more delicate. The male has rather pointed spurs; the bigger the spurs, the older the pheasant. Put into the refrigerator for a couple of hours before plucking. A good pheasant is always under 2 lbs.; the female pheasant will weigh a little less. Young pheasants can be roasted on the spit, or larded with pancetta, and roasted. The meat should be cooked until pink. The older and fatter birds can be cooked in salmì, fricasséed, or as ingredients for pâtés and terrines.

BECCACCIA E BECCACCINO
Woodcock and Snipe

The woodcock is a migratory bird that flies over Italy in late fall. Gourmets regard it as a most prized variety of game. Its meat is delicious — succulent and nutritive. It must be hung with the feathers on for about five days or until greenish shimmers appear on the abdomen (if the shimmers are violet the bird has been hung too long). Pluck only before cooking. Singe the bird and clean well with a wet cloth. Cut off the legs, turn the bird on its back, turn the head around, and tuck the beak inside the body. As a final step, wrap the woodcock with large slices of lard. The woodcock should only be either roasted on the spit larded with lard or pancetta, or jugged. The snipe is a marsh-like bird similar to the woodcock, just a little smaller. It is cooked like a woodcock.

CAMOSCIO, CERVO, DAINO
Chamois, deer, roe-buck and fallow deer

These are large animals, usually sold in pieces. The meat has a very gamey taste and requires about a week of hanging, preferably on a bed of mountain grass. It must also be marinated at length. If the meat is larded before cooking, it will be even better. Younger animals, not older than $2\frac{1}{2}$ years, are preferable for cooking.

CINGHIALE
Wild Boar

This is a sizable animal, related to the pig, with hard bristles and large tusks protruding from its snout. The meat of the wild boar is delicious, especially if the animal is young (about 6 months old). If it is rather old, the meat becomes tough and requires long marinating. Boar is usually sold in pieces, seldom whole. It should be hung for 4-5 days. The meat must then be marinated for 2-3 days at least. If the boar is less than 3 months old, it cannot be killed by hunters, but if it is between 3 and 6 months old the baby boar (or milk boar) need not be marinated. It can simply be rubbed with oil and kept in the refrigerator for 3-4 days.

Chops from a young boar should be simply seasoned with salt and pepper, sprinkled generously with lemon juice and left to marinate for a couple of hours before cooking. Wild boar can be jugged or cooked in *salmi* like hare, or roasted. The chops can be grilled. The leg can also be salted and dry-aged for *prosciutto*.

LEPRE
Hare

Hare is a wild rabbit. Winter is the best season for hare, the meat stays fresh 5-6 days before being cooked if kept in a cool place.

Mountain hare is preferable to lowland hare. Although the mountain hare is smaller, its meat is tastier, since it feeds on mountain herbs, which is more flavorful than that of the lowlands. The hare's meat is dark and flavorful, but may be heavy to digest. Hare that are 10-12 months old are best. If the hare's belly fur is white (instead of tawny brown), then it is a young hare, regardless of weight. The doe hare has tender meat, even up to 1½-2 years. If you shoot your own hare, marinate it while still warm-blooded (do not hang). If this is not possible, hang for 2-3 days in a very airy place (do not remove the fur, only the bladder). Hanging causes the flesh to relax, losing its initial stiffness and making it more suitable for cooking.

Hare should always be marinated before cooking, though the marinating should not be excessively long — from 12 to 24 hours. Hare can be cooked in many ways — jugged, in *salmi,* roasted. It is customarily served with *polenta.* The sauce can be used with *pappardelle.*

RICETTE
Recipies

POLLO ALLA DIAVOLA
Split roast chicken

1 young chicken (about 1½ lbs.)
olive oil
salt
pepper

Wash and dry the bird. Cut the bird open along its back and remove the breastbone. Turn it over and pound the breast with a meat mallet without crushing it. Cut two holes in the skin beside the chicken's tail and insert the end of the thigh bones into them, sprinkle generously with oil on both sides. Place on a grill or a metal griddle. Place a weight over the chicken to maintain it flat. Lower the heat to allow the chicken to cook thoroughly. Baste often with oil, using a brush or a rosemary sprig. Once it is cooked on one side, turn it and finish cooking (should not take more than 30 minutes). Salt and pepper on both sides and serve.

NOTE: This grilling may also be made by roasting the chicken on both sides in a heavy cast iron skillet and finishing the roasting in the oven.

POLLO ALLA CACCIATORA
Chicken, Hunter's Style

2 lbs. chicken parts	bay leaf
6 Tbs. olive oil	juniper berries
1 small carrot	1 glass dry white wine
1 stalk celery	1 oz. dried mushrooms
1 lb. tomatoes, peeled,	1 clove garlic
seeded and chopped	½ cup chicken broth
salt, pepper	1 Tbs. chopped parsley

Wash the chicken parts and pat-dry. sauté the carrot, celery, onion, and garlic in olive oil. When tender, but not crisp, add the chicken parts, salt and pepper, bay leaf, juniper berry and let brown over high flame. Add the wine and, when it has evaporated, add a few mushrooms, which have been previously re-constituted in warm water, the tomatoes and ½ cup broth. Cook for about 1 hour over medium heat. When ready remove from heat, add the chopped parsley and arrange in a pre-heated serving platter. Serve.

ANATRA ALLE OLIVE
Duck with olives

1 young duck (about 2½ lbs.)	1 medium sized onion,
1 bunch parsley, minced	thinly sliced
5 oz. black olives (Gaeta	rosemary
or Nicoise)	6 Tbs. white wine
2 oz. pancetta or prosciutto	1 bay leaf
celery	4 anchovy fillets
carrot	1 lb. ripe tomatoes
1 garlic clove	salt
olive oil	pepper

Clean and cut the duck in equal pieces. Pit the olives and mince half of them. Make a *battuto* made of parsley, *pancetta,* carrots, celery, chopped olives and garlic in a large saucepan with 3 Tbs. oil. Add the onion and rosemary and cook for 4-5 minutes. Add the duck parts and brown, moistening with wine. When the wine evaporates, add the bay leaf, anchovies and tomatoes. Add salt and pepper, cover the saucepan, and let cook over a very low heat, turning the pieces of duck occasionally, for about an hour. Ten minutes before the dish is cooked, add the whole olives. Serve in a heated dish, topping the pieces of duck with the strained sauce.

FARAONA AL CARTOCCIO
Bagged Guinea Hen

1 guinea hen	sage
1 piece caul fat	salt
1 garlic clove, crushed	3 oz. sliced pancetta
1 Tbs. olive oil	

Clean the guinea hen, then wash and pat dry. Put the garlic clove, some sage leaves and salt inside the bird. Scald the caul fat in boiling water, drain and spread on a kitchen towel to dry. Salt the outside of the hen and sprinkle with a few sage leaves, then wrap the bird in the *pancetta,* then in the caul fat. Grease with oil a sheet of waxed paper and wrap the bird, once again, in it. Seal by twisting the edges of the paper onto itself. Cook in a pre-heated oven at 450 F. for about an hour. Remove from heat, open the bagged hen, carve and serve.

CAPPONE CON LE NOCI
Capon with walnuts
This is a specialty of the *Lombardy* region prepared during the Christmas season. The excellent broth can be used to cook small *ravioli,* and be served as a first course.

1 4-lb. capon	4 Tbs. cream
½ cup cream	salt, pepper
2 Tbs. butter	nutmeg
20 chopped walnuts	1 celery stalk
4 Tbs. grated parmigiano	1 carrot
3 egg yolks	4 slices white bread, crust removed

Clean and bone the capon and leave it in its natural shape. Soak the bread in the cream. Soften the butter and mix with the walnuts, the *parmigiano,* egg yolks, and the bread. Beat the mixture well with a wooden spoon until it is soft and dense, adding more bread or cream if necessary. Salt, pepper and add a pinch of grated nutmeg. Insert the stuffing in the capon, sew and tie the bird closed. Bring a large pot of water to a boil, the pot should be just large enough to hold the bird, add celery and carrot, lower the heat and cook the stuffed capon in this broth over low heat for 1½-2 hours, salting halfway through. Serve the capon carved with some of the stuffing. This dish may be accompanied by preserved spiced fruits *mostarda di frutta.*

PICCIONE RIPIENO
Stuffed squab

4 squabs
¼ lb. top round of veal
¼ lb. pancetta
¼ lb. prosciutto, diced
¼ lb. cooked pickled tongue, diced
¼ lb. butter
½ onion, chopped

½ carrot, chopped
½ stalk celery, chopped
2 cloves
½ glass Marsala
2 Tbs. grated parmigiano
bay leaves
salt, pepper

Bone, wash and pat dry the squab.

Grind the veal and the *pancetta* and mix with the *prosciutto* and tongue, diced. Brown the vegetables in half the butter. Salt, pepper, add the ground and chopped meats, and cook for 15 minutes over medium head. Add *Marsala* and *parmigiano,* mix well and remove from heat. Cool.

Fill the squab with the stuffing and secure with caul fat in such a manner as to prevent the stuffing from falling out. Place them in a greased baking pan with the remaining butter, a few bay leaves and salt. Let cook in oven at 450 F. for about 45 minutes, turning them frequently. Remove from caul fat, slice and serve with roasted potatoes.

CONIGLIO IN UMIDO
Stewed Rabbit

1 to 2½ lb. rabbit
sage
rosemary
1 clove garlic
3 oz. olive oil

salt
pepper
6 juniper berries
½ cup wine vinegar

Cut the rabbit into pieces, wash and dry. Chop a few sage leaves, a sprig of rosemary and garlic. Salt, pepper and add the juniper berries (slightly smashed). Rub the pieces of rabbit in the herbs and place in a deep dish. Mix together vinegar and 6 Tbs. olive oil and pour over the rabbit. Let marinate for 24 hours, turning the meat occasionally so that it absorbs the flavors. Pour the marinade and rabbit into a saucepan and cook covered over low heat for about 45 minutes. Uncover the pot, raise the heat and cook for another 45 minutes or until the rabbit is tender and the liquid almost completely absorbed. Serve with roasted *polenta.*

CINGHIALE ALL'AGRODOLCE
Wild boar in Sweet and Sour Sauce

½ cup wine vinegar
1 pint red wine

4 Tbs. butter
2 Tbs. bitter cocoa

1 bay leaf	1 Tbs. sugar
1 sprig thyme	3 oz. dried prunes
3 cloves	(softened and chopped)
2 onions, chopped	1 tsp. peperoncino
1 carrot, chopped	2 Tbs. candied orange peel
1 stalk celery, chopped	1 Tbs. raisins
3 lbs. fillet of boar	1 Tbs. pine nuts
	salt

Prepare a marinade by boiling the vinegar and wine with the bay leaf, thyme, *peperoncino,* cloves, 1 onion, carrot and celery. Pour into a large pot and let cool. Place the boar fillet into the marinade and let sit for 48 hours. Chop the remaining onion and brown in butter, then add the cocoa, sugar, prunes, candied orange peel, raisins and pine nuts. Stir for a few minutes, then add the boar meat and let cook slowly for an hour, then add the filtered marinade, salt and continue cooking until the meat is very tender and the sauce dense. Serve with *polenta,* potatoes or potato *gnocchi.*

ANITRA SELVATICA CON PAPPARDELLE
Wild duck with pappardelle

1 wild duck	1 oz. white wine
1 celery stalk, chopped	1 lb. ripe tomatoes
1 carrot, chopped	salt
1 small onion, chopped	pepper
4 Tbs. oil	pinch of fennel seeds
2 Tbs. butter	1 lb. fresh pappardelle
3 oz. prosciutto in strips.	

Wash and dry the bird and cut into equal pieces. Chop the celery, carrot, and onion and brown in the oil, butter and *prosciutto* in a saucepan. Add the duck and brown well, then splash with wine. When the wine has evaporated, add the seeded, peeled, chopped tomatoes. Salt, pepper and cook slowly for 1½ hours. Add the fennel seeds and cook another 20 minutes. Remove the pieces of duck and keep them in a warm place. Strain the sauce, return it to the pan and add the duck. Heat through.

Cook the *pappardelle* in boiling water, drain and serve with the sauce. The duck can be served on top of the pasta or as a second course, in which case the duck is better cooked whole so that it can be served more attractively.

SCOTTIGLIA
Stew of various meats

This is a *Tuscan* specialty and is also called *cacciucco di carne.* The dish requires the widest possible variety of meats. The ones requiring the most time for cooking are added first.

1 onion	1 cup red wine

1 clove garlic
4 Tbs. olive oil
basil
parsley
3 lbs. (½ lb. each) of various
cuts of meat veal round,
beef chuck, chicken, rabbit,
pork shoulder, ½ squab, ½ hare.

1 ¼ lb. ripe tomatoes
salt
pepper
1 cup broth

In a large saucepan, brown the minced onion and garlic in the oil, then add chopped basil and parsley. Add the meats, one at a time, tougher meats first, so that they will all be ready at the same time. Splash occasionally with red wine and, when all the meat is in the pan, add the chopped, peeled, seeded tomatoes. Salt, pepper and continue stirring, add broth as needed. Serve with toast rubbed with a clove of garlic.

LEPRE IN SALMÍ
Hare in Salmí, Lombardy Style
Within the term *salmí* falls a wide variety of preparations that belong to the Italian tradition. It is always prepared with game. The best known *salmí* is with hare.

1 hare
Barbera wine
3 onions, chopped
1 carrot, chopped
1 celery stalk, chopped
1 garlic clove
peperoncino
juniper berries

2 bay leaves
thyme
marjoram
4 Tbs. butter
2 oz. pancetta
1 Tbs. salt and coarse salt
¾ oz. bittersweet chocolate
¼ cup grappa
4 Tbs. lard
hare's liver

Marinate the hare in wine, onion, carrot and celery, garlic, *peperoncino,* juniper berries, minced herbs, whole bay leaf, and coarse salt. The hare should marinate for 48 hours, turning the hare in the marinade, from time to time.

When it is time for the *salmí* preparation, heat the butter and *pancetta* in a pan and brown 2 minced onions. Add the hare and brown on all sides. Then add the marinade and cook over high heat until the liquid has been completely absorbed and the hare is dry. Cover with water, stir and cook slowly for another 3 hours. Then take the hare out of the casserole and keep warm. Sieve the liquid to a bowl. Add some of the hot juice to temper the liquid and add this warm mixture into the sauce. Do not boil. Salt, add the pieces of lard, the *grappa* and the chocolate and cook until blended. Put the hare in, let sit for 5 minutes, then serve with *polenta.* (If the sauce has to be used for *pappardelle,* serve the hare as a second course.)

FORMAGGIO
Cheese

Italy is very rich in cheeses. A catalog published in 1977 lists at least 451 cheeses. Therefore, to get into a detailed list of all the cheeses made in Italy would be extremely difficult. Throughout the peninsula, wherever there is a herd there is a copper pot to make the whey and a cellar where cheese, such as caciotta, robiola or caciocavallo, rest on wooden boards. This text will limit itself to a selection of cheeses which are the most important in terms of notoriety.

The following are basic facts to know about how cheese is made.

Skimming
According to how much fat content is removed from the milk, we will have:
WHOLE MILK FAT CHEESES: 42% fat content
SEMIFAT: less than 42% fat
SKIMMED: less than 20% fat

Curding
During the preparation of cheese, the curd can be brought to various temperatures; accordingly the results can vary.

RAW CHEESE: If temperature does not exceed 100 F.
SEMI-COOKED: If temperature is between 100 F.-120 F.
WHOLLY-COOKED: If temperature exceeds 120 F.

Aging
Aging is determined by the time the cheese is allowed to rest from the time it is done. Therefore we have:
FRESH: Cheese consumed immediately.
AGED: Those cheeses that must rest in proper storages for long periods, before they are ready for consumption.

Types
According to how a cheese is made, it can be categorized as follows:
FRESH: i.e., mozzarella, mascarpone
SOFT: i.e., gorgonzola, stracchino, taleggio
HARD: i.e., parmigiano, pecorino

How to Keep Cheese
It is best to keep cheese in a dark, humid, ventilated room, at a constant temperature of 45-50 F. If it has to be refrigerated, it is advisable to store in the vegetable section in perforated paper or cheese cloth to allow air to go through.

How to Serve

The basic rule is to serve cheese at room temperature at all times. Cheese can be served with fruit, or vegetables. For instance, *pecorino romano* is traditionally served with *fava* beans, and goat cheeses with radishes.

Bread, of course, is a most important element in serving cheese; large crusty country loaves, olive bread, walnut bread and bread with sesame seeds are all appropriate.

Many cheeses are suitable to serve cooked, especially the soft, fresh types such as: *mozzarella, ricotta, fontina.*

FRESH CHEESE

These are sent to market after a very brief period of ripening. Their nature and nutritional value have not, therefore, been significantly altered. They should be consumed shortly after they are purchased. Even though they are not «real» cheeses, *ricotta* and *mascarpone* can be included in this category.

CAPRINO

Despite the name (goat cheese), this is made with cow's milk. It is a soft cheese, formed in a cylindrical shape and weighs about 25 grams. It is sold rolled in paper.

CRESCENZA

This is a cheese from *Lombardy.* It is an uncooked cheese, soft in texture and high in fat content, made from whole, pasteurized cow's milk. It is ripened for 15 days, has a rectangular shape with no crust and no holes. The cheese is white and has a butter-like consistency.

MASCARPONE

This is not really a cheese but rather a very rich substance made from cream that has been soured with fermenting bacteria. It is a regional speciality of *Lombardy* and is produced almost exclusively during the winter. It is sold by weight and usually mixed with liqueurs, sugar, chocolate. *Mascarpone* is also often used as filling for sweets and cakes, like *tiramisù.*

MOZZARELLA

This cheese originated in Southern Italy but is now produced all over the country. It has a stringy consistency, is uncooked, high in fat content, and made with whole cow or *bufala* milk.

MOZZARELLA

The cheese is very white, soft yet solid. A *mozzarella* must be ripened 3-4 days and is sold in various forms: 10-12 oz. braid, 4-5 oz.

round ball, and 2 oz. bite-size pieces. Not long ago, *mozzarella* was sold without a wrapper, but a new law specifies that they must have one. Therefore, they are now sold in individual plastic bags containing a small amount of whey to keep the cheese fresh.

If it is necessary to store *mozzarella* without whey, it can be put into a covered cup in a salt and water solution. Whether in whey or water, it must be stored in an airy, cool place. It should not be refrigerated.

RICOTTA

Ricotta is technically not a cheese. It is a by-product of cheese: the remaining whey is cooked with additional rennet after the cheese has formed (though it is also made with whey from cow's milk). *Ricotta* is a soft white cheese without a strong taste. There are two types: *Romana,* granular and flavorful, which is formed in small wicker baskets in the shape of a flattened cone and often used in cooking; and *Piemontese,* very smooth and delicate, shaped into small pyramids. *Ricotta* is also sold smoked or salted. This last one is a product of the south, particularly *Sicily*. Salted *ricotta* is aged and used as grating cheese.

ROBIOLA

Robiola is made from whole cow's milk and formed into pieces weighing about 1 lb. The cheese is uncooked, high in fat and has a slightly piquant taste. It is yellowish in color with few little holes. *Robiola* is not really ripened but is kept in the factory until a light yellowish-red crust forms.

In *Emilia Romagna robiola* is also prepared with sheep's milk or mixed sheep's and cow's milk. It is eaten fresh or within a month of production.

SCAMORZA

This is an uncooked, high-fat content cheese. The consistency is stringy and soft. It is made with whole cow's milk. It is formed in a pear shape which leans slightly and weighs about 12 oz. It is aged for about 2 weeks.

SCAMORZA

STRACCHINO

This cheese is made with whole milk from «tired cows» *(stracche* means exhausted) who have traveled from the Alpine pastures down to the plains in autumn. It is similar to *crescenza* but a little more solid in consistency.

TOMINO
This is made with partially skimmed cow's milk. Its consistency is hard, compact, and white with practically no crust. It has a sweet taste. Each form weighs about 10 oz. It is ready 2 weeks after production. *Tomini* are sold fresh, wrapped in paper, but it is also possible to buy them marinated in oil with hot pepper or with other aromatic herbs.

CHEESE AGED
FOR LESS THAN A YEAR

These cheeses are made with the addition of special microbes (molds and bacteria). After the curdling, the mixture is cooked.

ASIAGO
A compact, yellowish cheese made from whole cow's milk; it is thus high in fat content. It has small-to medium-size holes, and a smooth, regular and elastic crust. The wheels weigh between 20-25 lbs. and are aged for about a year if the cheese is to be grated, or 6 months if the cheese is for normal consumption.

BITTO
This is a specialty of *Valtellina,* made of whole cow's milk, sometimes mixed with sheep's milk. The wheels weigh between 6-15 lbs. The cheese is cream colored with minuscule holes and has a very delicate taste when it has aged an average of 40 days. Sometimes it is left to ripen a little longer, in which case the color deepens and the taste becomes more marked.

This cheese is utilized in many regional recipes, but, given that it is difficult to find, *fontina,* which melts as easily as *bitto,* is frequently substituted for it.

CACIOCAVALLO
Originally from Southern Italy, this cheese is now produced all over the country. Its name («horse cheese») derives from the way it is aged. Two cheeses are tied together, then draped over a stick to age as if they were on horseback. It is made of whole cow's milk and has a soft stringy consistency. The cheese is compact and yellowish with a thin, smooth yellow crust. It is formed in the shape of a melon or a salami and weighs about 10 lbs. The aging process lasts 3 months for normal consumption, 6-13 if the cheese is to be grated.

CACIOTTA

This name is given to a wide range of cheeses produced both in-

dustrially and in dairies. Made of sheep's or cow's milk or a mixture of the two, sold in round wheels weighing less than one kilo and only slightly ripened, the cheese generally has a delicate flavor, few or no holes, and is white or yellowish in color. The crust is thin and ranges from light to darker yellows.

CACIOTTA

FONTINA

Fontina is a regional speciality of *Valle D'Aosta* and derives its name *(fondere* means melt) from the fact that it melts easily. It is a hard cheese made from whole cow's milk and is high in fat, semi-cooked, light yellow in color, elastic, with few holes. The crust is thin and compact and stamped with the logo *"Fontina della Valle d'Aosta."* The wheels weigh 4-8 lbs. and are aged for about 4 months.

GORGONZOLA

Gorgonzola is made from whole cow's milk, high in fat and un-cooked. The cheese is very soft, sometimes creamy (if there are thin stripes throughout the cheese it is not the best quality), white or yellowish in color with areas of green and

a strong taste. The crust is reddish, rough, uniform and is wrapped in aluminum foil with the producer's name on it. It is a speciality of the *Lombardy* region and is sometimes called *erborinato* (from erbor, parsley in the *Milanese* dialect). Its characteristic green color comes from specially selected mold cultures (Penicillin Glaucum) added during the production process. The wheels weigh about 20 lbs. and are ripened 3-5 months. After the first

GORGONZOLA

month the cheese is pierced with long copper needles to allow air to enter and favor the growth of the mold. Nowadays a sweeter version of this cheese called *panerone* is made, which has a softer consistency.

PECORINO

Pecorino is a hard, wholly-cooked, grayish white cheese made of whole sheep milk and having a strong taste. The crust is hard, thick and darkened with oil. The wheels are not uniform in size and can vary in weight from 12-40 lbs. *Pecorino* must be aged at least 8 months. The fresh variety is used for eating, the other for grating. There are many varieties of *pecorino,* almost all of which are produced in small dairies, but the *Roman, Sardinian* and *Sicilian* (made in a basket, which has grains of black pepper mixed into the curd) varieties are considered the best.

QUARTIROLO

This cheese is given this name because the milk used comes from cows fed with the fourth cutting of the grass (*quartirola* grass). *Quartirolo* is similar to *taleggio* but lower in fat content.

TALEGGIO

Taleggio takes its name from a valley in the *Bergamo* area. It is a raw cheese made with whole cow's milk and is high in fat content. The consistency is very soft, almost creamy when very ripe, white or yellowish in color and has a relatively strong taste. The crust is thin, soft and reddish. The forms are rectangular and weigh about 4 lbs. *Taleggio* is aged 40 days.

AGED CHEESE

PARMIGIANO REGGIANO

This is a *Denominazione di origine Controllata* (*DOC*) cheese. Its production is carefully controlled and regulated by the government to insure its quality. Produced in the provinces of *Parma, Mantova* and *Bologna,* it is made only from the first of April until the middle of November with whole milk from cows fed fresh grass. It is a hard, wholly-cooked, compact cheese, light yellow in color with a strong but not piquant taste. The crust is very hard, oily and pricked all over the surface. The wheels weight about 60 lbs. and are aged from 18 months-5 years. It is excellent grated, but is also eaten in

PARMIGIANO

chunks chipped off the wheel with a special little knife whose blade is shaped like a drop of water. *Parmigiano Reggiano* is used in a vast number of Italian recipes.

GRANA PADANO

This is similar to *parmigiano* but is produced year round in the area north of the *Po* river with skim milk from cows that are fed hay. It is a wholly-cooked, hard, semi-fat cheese, yellowish in color with a delicate taste. The crust is hard, occasionally dark and oily. The wheels weigh between 50-75 lbs. and are aged 1-2 years. It is used in the same way as *parmigiano*.

PROVOLONE

This cheese is made with whole milk, and must have a fat content of at least 45%. The cheese is shaped into cylindrical form, which is then immersed in brine and hung in warm, smoky chambers. The

time varies according to size which can vary from 10-80 lbs. or more. The cheese is aged for at least three months. *Provolone* has a fairly compact texture when young, slightly veined and sharper as it ages, the color is a light straw yellow. This cheese is produced all over Italy with the exception of *Piedmont, Tuscany, Umbria* and *Sardinia.*

PROVOLONE

RICETTE
Recipes

FONDUTA

8 oz. fontina cheese	*8 oz. butter*
2 cups milk	*white truffle (optional)*
salt	
4 egg yolks	

Cut the *fontina* in small cubes, drop it in a double boiler and add half the milk. When the fontina starts melting, add a pinch of salt and stir constantly.

In the meantime, in a second casserole, warm the rest of the milk, add the beaten egg yolks, the butter and stir. When the mixtures of fontina and milk are creamy enough, combine them together. Stir constantly to obtain a creamy thick mixture.

Fonduta can be used either by itself or as a dressing for fresh *pasta,* such as *tagliolini, tortelli* or rice.

Suggestion: Sprinkle the *fonduta* with sliced white truffles.

MOZZARELLA IN CARROZZA

8 slices of bread	*4 eggs*
(bread should be about	*bread crumbs*
2-3" in diameter)	*flour*
1 lb. mozzarella	*1 cup milk*

Moisten the bread with a small amount of milk. Cut the *mozzarella* into slices the same thickness as the bread. Insert a slice of *mozzarella* between two slices of bread. Coat with flour, dip in beaten eggs, then coat with bread crumbs and fry in hot oil. Repeat the process until all the mozzarella and the bread have been used. *Mozzarella in carrozza* is fried in a skillet with plenty of oil.

PROVATURA ALLA SALSA DI ACCIUGHE
Provatura with anchovy sauce

⅔ *lb. provatura romana or* *4 anchovy fillets*
mozzarella *2 oz. of milk*
6 slices Italian bread *salt*
8 oz. butter *pepper*

Slice the cheese and sprinkle with salt and pepper. Cut the bread in slices, the same size of the cheese slices. Place a slice of cheese over a slice of bread. Repeat the process until all the cheese has been used. Place them in a buttered baking dish and put in the oven for about 20 minutes, brushing them occasionally with butter. Meanwhile, sauté the anchovies with the remaining butter until they melt, then stir in the of milk. Season with salt and pepper. Remove the dish from the oven, transfer the slices onto a warm plate, pour the anchovy sauce over the mozzarella, and serve immediately.

FRIED RICOTTA

⅔ *lb. very dry ricotta* *frying oil*
2 eggs *salt*
bread crumbs *pepper*

Beat the eggs, adding salt and pepper. Slice the ricotta, dip in the beaten eggs and the coat with bread crumbs Fry in hot oil, on both sides, until golden. Season with salt and pepper. Can be served plain or with fresh tomato sauce.

DOLCI
Desserts

Italians are not great eaters of desserts. The consumption of sweets is very much tied to religious holidays and private festivities, such as name days, birthdays, weddings, and to certain local, specific dates and traditions. Although these traditions are slowly disappearing, the climate is probably the most singular reason why Italians have been such poor eaters of sweets. Italy is a Mediterranean country of mild climate, and these environmental conditions do not harmonize with the powerful caloric contents of desserts. But in the last 20-30 years, we have seen a radical change in the alimentary habits of the Italians and, consequently, the consumption of sweets has grown. In part, this is due to the fact that it has become less complicated to make desserts in a modern kitchen with machines, such as blenders and ice cream makers, and because there are ample amounts of raw ingredients, such as fruit pulp, which allow for the creation of desserts that are lighter and easier to digest.

Piccola pasticceria (small pastries), *panettoni* (sweet cakes), *biscotti* (biscuits), and *gelati* (ice cream) occupy center stage in the sweet section of Italian cookery. Perhaps this is because these desserts are consumed outside of the main meal, and are considered to be too heavy after a full dinner.

RICETTE
Recipes

AMARETTI
Almond cookies

1 cup sweet almonds
1 cup bitter almonds
½ cup granulated sugar
1 tsp. vanilla
2 cups sugar
5 egg whites

Blanch and toast the almonds. Peel and chop them very finely or crush them in a mortar with ½ cup sugar. Add the vanilla, beat egg whites till stiffened then fold into the almonds. Spoon the batter into a pastry bag fitted with a ½ inch plain tip. Pipe 2½" wide rounds about 1½" apart on a buttered baking sheet and flatten them a bit. Sift the confectioners' sugar over the tops and let stand at room temperature 1 to 2 hours. Bake in a preheated 350 F. oven for about 20 minutes.

Remove from oven and cool. *Amaretti* may be kept in a sealed box for several days.

AMOR DI POLENTA
Sweet Polenta Cake

1½ cups butter	*4 Tbs. white flour*
½ cup granulated sugar	*½ envelope baker's yeast*
for dusting	*1 cup finely ground cornmeal*
2 egg yolks	*1 envelope vanilla*
1 oz. Galliano liqueur	*6 whole eggs*
6 oz. ground almonds	

Butter and dust with granulated sugar a fluted or rectangular deep mold. Beat sugar and remaining butter to a creamy consistency. Add the two egg yolks, liqueur and almonds. Mix the white flour with the yeast, the cornmeal and the vanilla, then sift into a mixing bowl. Combine the sifted ingredients with the prepared mixture, add the whole eggs and knead till you achieve a smooth dough. Pour the whole into the prepared mold and bake at about 350 F. for 50 minutes. Let cool, remove from mold and sprinkle with sugar before serving.

NOTE: If wrapped in aluminum foil it will keep for several days.

BABA AL RHUM
Baba with rum

Ingredients for the dough:

1 oz. yeast	*3 eggs*
½ cup milk	*½ cup butter*
½ cup flour	*4 Tbs. raisins*
salt	

Ingredients for the syrup:

3 Tbs. sugar
½ cup water
4 Tbs. rum

Dissolve the yeast in ½ cup of warm milk and make into a dough with 4 Tbs. flour. Place dough in a bowl, cover, and let it stand in a warm place for 30 minutes or until it doubles in size.

Make a *fontana* on a pastry board with the remaining flour, a pinch of salt, the eggs, the sugar, the butter and the fermented dough. Soak the raisins in lukewarm water, then squeeze out the excess water and work them into the dough. Put the dough in a large buttered, sugar-dusted ring mold and let rise again, in a warm place, until it doubles in size (it should take approx. 1 hour). Bake for 45 minutes at 375 F. oven.

Prepare a syrup by dissolving the sugar in the water, over a low flame. Add the rum.

Unmold the *baba* while still warm. Soak with the rum syrup and serve.
NOTE: Small *babas* are made the same way by dividing the dough and cooking them in little molds.

BACI
Lady's kisses

1 cup chopped almonds	1 cup sugar
1 cup butter	2 oz. bittersweet chocolate
1 cup flour	1 oz. butter

Mix the almonds, butter, flour and sugar together to achieve a smooth mixture, and form small balls, about the size of a walnut. Bake on a greased cookie sheet for about 15 minutes at 350° F. Let cool. Melt the chocolate in a double boiler. Dip the bottom of one of the cookies in the chocolate then press it against the bottom of another so that they stick together. Do so with remaining cookies and let cool.

CALCIONI
Crescent cookies

1 cup flour	4 Tbs. butter
5 eggs	$\frac{1}{2}$ lb. grated Pecorino cheese
2 Tbs. olive oil	1 lemon
$\frac{1}{2}$ cup sugar	butter

Mix the flour with 2 whole eggs, 2 yolks, oil, 2 Tbs. sugar and 2 Tbs. butter to make a dough. Let the dough rest for one hour in a cool place. Mix the cheese with the remaining egg and egg whites, the remaining sugar and the grated lemon rind. Roll out the dough to a thickness of about $\frac{1}{10}$ of an inch and cut out circles 3" diameter. Put a ball of filling in the middle of each disk, wet the edges, then fold over and seal the edges. Mold the cookies into a crescent shape and make a small cut in the middle of each one with a pair of scissors. Bake on a buttered cookie sheet in a preheated 350 F. oven for 20 minutes. Serve hot or warm.

CANNOLI CON RICOTTA
Ricotta stuffed rolls

1 cup white flour	$\frac{1}{2}$ cup sugar
1 Tbs. unsweetened cocoa	2 Tbs. butter
1 Tbs. ground coffee	1 cup white wine
pinch of salt	

1 cup ricotta	2 Tbs. candied orange
1 Tbs. orange-flower	and citron (diced)
water or vanilla liqueur	1 oz. chocolate

1 Tbs. cocoa powder	*2 Tbs. candied cherries*
1 egg white	*2 Tbs. almond oil*
oil for frying	*1 Tbs. powdered sugar*

Mix 1 cup flour, cocoa, coffee, salt and granulated sugar on a pastry board. Make a *fontana,* add the butter and enough white wine to make a moderately firm dough. Knead for a few minutes, then shape the dough into a ball. Wrap it in a cloth and let stand for one hour in a cool place.

Sieve the *ricotta,* add ½ cup of powdered sugar, orange-flower water or liqueur, mix well and add diced candied fruit and the chocolate in chunks. Divide the resulting cream into two equal portions, add the cocoa to one half. Hold both in a cool place.

Coat a few tin pipes (cornet molds) 5" long and 1" in diameter with

CANNOLO SICILIANO

almond oil. Roll the dough to ⅛" thick and cut into 4" disks. Fold the dough around the cornet molds, overlapping the two ends and seal with a bit of egg white. Enlarge the two ends to give it an hourglass shape. Fry in hot oil. Gently drain them and place on paper towels. Cool the pastries for a few minutes, then gently remove the molds and let cool thoroughly.

Fill the *cannoli* with *ricotta* cream in one end, and cocoa cream in the other end. *Cannoli* shells can be prepared in advance, but the cream should be added just before serving; otherwise the shell will become soggy. Dust with powdered sugar and serve.

Cannoli shells are also known as *scorze.*

CASSATA ALLA SICILIANA
Sicilian cassata

This cake, a specialty of *Sicily,* should not be confused with the ice cream dish of the same name. In Erice *cassata* is made with a citron jam filling and is covered with almond paste.

sponge cake	*1 tsp. powdered cinnamon*
1 cup sugar	*1 oz. Maraschino liqueur*
2 cups ricotta	*1 Tbs. pistachio nuts*
4 oz. chocolate	*½ cup apricot jelly*
2 cups mixed candied fruit	*½ cup fondant*
1 Tsp. vanilla •	*1 oz. orange flower water*
1 Tbs. chestnut flour	*1 Tbs. grated orange zest*
4 Tbs. sugar	*4 Tbs. soaked squeezed raisins*

pinch of salt
3 Tbs. olive oil

2 Tbs. pine nuts
2 Tbs. coarsely chopped walnuts
milk, as needed

Line the bottom and sides of a cake mold 10" diameter with thin slices of sponge cake. Dissolve the sugar over low heat in a small amount of water. Sieve the ricotta and mix it with the sugar. Cut the chocolate in small bits, dice half the candied fruit and add them to the *ricotta*, together with the vanilla, cinnamon, liqueur and pistachio nuts. Put the *ricotta* in the mold, level off the top, cover with slices of sponge cake, and cool for several hours. Before serving, unmold on a dish. Spread the top with apricot jelly, cover with fondant dissolved in a little orange flower water, and garnish with various types of candied fruit.

VARIATION 1: Often the fondant used to glaze the top is colored light green.

CASTAGNACCIO
Chestnut crust

1 lb. chestnut flour
4 Tbs. sugar
pinch salt
3 Tbs. olive oil

1 Tbs. grated orange zest
4 Tbs. soaked squeezed raisins
2 Tbs. pine nuts
2 Tbs. coarsely chopped walnuts
milk, as needed

Sift the chestnut flour, add the sugar and a pinch of salt. Add 2 pints cold water in a thin stream, beating constantly with a whisk so that lumps do not form. Add 3 Tbs. oil, orange peel, raisins, pine nuts and walnuts. Add warm milk little by little until you achieve a stiff consistency. Pour the batter into a greased pan large enough so that the mixture is $\frac{1}{2}$" thick. Dribble on some oil. Bake in a preheated 400° F. oven for an hour. Serve warm or cold. It can also be served with whipped cream.

VARIATION: Fennel seeds can be used in place of walnuts.

CHIACCHIERE
Puffed pastry strips

1 lb. all purpose flour
5 Tbs. sugar
pinch of salt
1 tsp. vanilla
1 oz. confectioners' sugar

3 eggs
1 Tbs. white wine
frying oil
4 Tbs. butter

Mix the flour, sugar, salt, and vanilla on a pastry board, making a *fontana*. Break the eggs into the center and add the wine. Knead for about ten minutes, moistening with an additional spoonful of wine, if needed. Wrap the dough in a cloth and let stand in a cool place for about one hour. Knead it again for a short while, then roll it out to about $\frac{1}{8}$" thick.

Cut the dough with a pastry wheel into 3 in. wide and 4 in. long pieces, and make three vertical incisions on each piece with a pastry wheel. Heat the frying oil in a deep pan. When oil gets hot fry the pieces of dough. Rid of excess fat on paper towels. When fried, serve them warm or cold, on a napkin-lined serving dish, sprinkled generously with powdered sugar.

CIAMBELLA BOLOGNESE
Almond cake

2 cups flour	2-3 Tbs. milk
1½ lb. confectioners' sugar	6 Tbs. butter
1 tsp. vanilla	3 eggs, separated
zest of ½ lemon	2 Tbs. Sassolino or Maraschino
1 envelope baking soda	liqueur
1 Tbs. granulated sugar	1 oz. shelled almonds

Reserving 1 Tbs. flour, mix the flour with the confectioners' sugar, vanilla, grated lemon rind and a pinch of salt. Dissolve the baking soda and cream of tartar in 2-3 Tbs. of milk. Melt 5 oz. butter in a saucepan. Add 2 egg yolks, 1 egg white, the liqueur, the baking soda and cream of tartar to the flour. Add the butter and knead till smooth. Roll the dough into the shape of a large sausage to fit a 12" ring mold. Butter a ring mold and dust with the flour. Shape the dough into the ring and pinch the two ends together. Brush the top with the remaining egg yolk, dust with granulated sugar, and place almonds on top. Bake at 350 F. for about 30 minutes, let cool in the mold and remove *ciambella* from mold. Serve.

COLOMBA PASQUALE
Easter Dove

1 oz. baker's yeast	salt
1⅓ lb. flour	3 oz. milk
6 egg yolks	4 oz. candied lemon and orange
5 oz. confectionary sugar	rinds (diced)
1 tsp. grated lemon zest	3 oz. peeled almonds
1 tsp. granulated sugar	7 oz. butter

Dissolve the crumbled yeast in some warm water and mix it with 2 oz. of flour. Make a rather solid dough and cut a cross on the top. Roll the dough in flour and put it into a bowl with 1 cup warm water for half an hour. Turn the dough occasionally when it floats to the surface. Knead the remaining flour separately with 5 egg yolks, 4 oz.

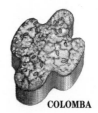

COLOMBA

softened butter, the sugar, the lemon zest, a pinch of salt and 3 oz. warm milk.

Add the yeasted dough and knead for 20 mins. until the dough is smooth and rather compact. Let the dough rise in a warm place until increased by a third in volume. Knead the dough once again, adding half of the remaining softened butter in pieces. Put the dough back in the bowl to rise until doubled in volume. Put the dough on the pastry board once again and knead in the remaining butter and the candied peel. Shape the dough into the form of a dove, or put it in a dove shaped mold, and let rise for half an hour. Brush the dough with the remaining egg yolk, distribute the almonds over the surface, pressing them in slightly, and then sprinkle with the granulated sugar crystals. Bake for 15 minutes in preheated 375 F. oven then lower the heat to 325 F. and cook for another 20 minutes.

COTOGNATA
Quince Preserve

1 lb., 2 oz. quince pulp
1 lb. sugar
1 lemon, squeezed

Remove the core of the quinces and cook in boiling water till tender to the fork. Drain and cool. Pass the pulp through a sieve. Add sugar and juice of the lemon.

Cook this mixture over medium flame for 10 minutes, stirring occasionally. Warm up a mold* and pour in the mixture. Let it dry in a cool and ventilated place. When a light film of sugar has formed on top, turn it in a dish so that it can dry on the other side.
*Cotognata is a typical Sicilian sweet and it is customary to make it in a small mold, such as fish and leaf shape.

CROCCANTE
Sugar and almond candy

1 cup shelled almonds   *1 cup sugar*
(lightly toasted) oil

Cook the sugar with one or two tsp. water in an unlined copper casserole until the syrup reaches a hard-ball stage. Mix in the almonds and continue to cook until caramelized.

Lightly coat a marble surface with oil and pour on the mixture of sugar and almonds, making an even layer. Score with a knife into squares or diamonds. Cool, then break into pieces along the scoring lines. *Croccante* will keep for a month if wrapped in aluminum foil.

CROSTATA DI FRUTTA
Fruit tart

1 cup flour   *3 egg yolks*
½ cup confectioners' sugar   *2 cups fruit preserve*
1 orange   *or marmalade*

| ½ cup butter | 2 Tbs. butter |
| 1 Tbs. honey | 1 Tbs. granulated sugar |

Mix the flour with the sugar and the grated rind of the orange. Make a *fontana* then knead in the softened butter in pieces, the honey and 2 egg yolks. Knead only long enough to mix thoroughly the ingredients. Use two-thirds of the pastry to line a buttered, sugar dusted tart pan. Spread the jam over the pastry. Brush the remaining dough with a beaten egg yolk and use this dough to make strips and lay them over the tart in a crisscross pattern. Bake in a 350 F. oven for about 35 minutes.

GUBANA
Pastry and candy roll

1½ cups white flour	4 Tbs. pine nuts
1½ oz butter	2 oz. candied lemon
3 egg yolks	and orange peel
2 Tbs. grappa	1 Tbs. bread crumbs
4 Tbs. raisins	1 lemon
1 cup Marsala	1 orange
5 oz. shelled, chopped	1 Tbs. sugar
walnuts	butter for greasing pan
4 Tbs. shelled, chopped	1 Tbs. flour
almonds	

Prepare a puff pastry with the flour and 11 oz. of butter, a whole egg and 2 Tbs. grappa. While the pastry is resting make the filling. Soften the raisins in the *Marsala* and squeeze out the excess.

Put the walnuts, almonds, raisins, pine nuts and candied peel into a bowl. Fry the bread crumbs in 2 Tbs. butter and mix it into the nuts, along with the grated rinds of the orange and lemon. Mix well, then add an egg yolk and a stiffly beaten egg white.

Roll out the puff pastry into a thin rectangle. Spread the filling on top of it. Roll and fold in the filling from the long side of the rectangle. Place rolled up dough into a spiral and set in a buttered and floured baking pan. Brush the remaining egg yolk and sprinkle with sugar. Cook in a 375 F. oven for about 50 minutes.

VARIATION: This specialty from *Friuli* can also be made with yeasted dough or depending on the province, with a simple crust made with melted butter, water and flour.

PAN DE MEI
Sweet Corn Buns

This is a *Lombardian* speciality. They should be eaten by dipping in a cup of thick cream.

¾ oz. baker's yeast	½ cup melted butter
½ cup white flour	2 egg yolks
½ cup finely ground cornmeal	4 Tbs. powdered sugar
6 Tbs. sugar	2 oz. dried Sambuco seeds

Dissolve the yeast in ½ cup warm water and stir in half the flour. Let rise for half an hour in a warm draft-free place till it has doubled in size. Punch down and mix in the remaining white flour, the corn meal, the sugar, butter and eggs. The dough should be very soft, add more warm water, if necessary.

Put the dough in a pastry bag and squeeze out 2-3 oz. mounds onto a buttered cookie sheet. Do not put them too close together. Let them rise in a warm place for about half an hour. Melt the powdered sugar in a little water, brush the liquid over the buns, and sprinkle with *sambuco* seeds. Bake in a 400 F. oven for 15 minutes.

NOTE: Sambuco seeds are gathered in spring and dried. Sometimes they are added to the dough itself, or they may also be omitted completely.

PANDOLCE

1 lb. flour	*½ cup sugar*
1 oz. baker's yeast	*2 Tbs. raisins*
salt	*2 Tbs. diced, candied squash*
½ glass Marsala	*2 Tbs. pine nuts*
½ cup melted butter	*2 Tbs. peeled pistachio nuts*
1 Tbs. orange flower water	*1 Tbs. anise seeds*
butter	

Mix the yeast into ½ cup of lukewarm water, add 4 Tbs. flour and mix till you achieve a smooth, elastic dough. Cover and place in a warm place until the dough has doubled in size. Make a *fontana* with half the flour. Put the risen dough and a pinch of salt in the middle. Knead together, adding as much warm water as necessary to achieve an elastic dough. Put the dough in a large, buttered and floured, sugar-dusted bowl and set in a warm place for about 18 hours. Make a fontana with the remaining flour. Put the Marsala, the softened butter, the orange flower water, and sugar in the middle and knead until it is elastic and smooth. Add the pre-risen dough, the raisins (previously softened in water), squash, pine nuts and pistachio nuts and anise seeds. Form the dough into a ball and place the dough on a buttered and floured baking mold and let rise in a draft-free, warm place for about 12 hours.

With a sharp knife cut a cross on the top of the cake and bake in a preheated oven at 350 F. for about an hour. Cool, slice and serve.

PANDORO

This cake is a specialty of Verona and is as famous as panettone.

2 cups flour	*pinch vanilla*
¾ oz. baker's yeast	*1 tsp. grated lemon peel*
½ cup confectioners' sugar	*3 Tbs. cream*
5 egg yolks	*4 Tbs. butter*
1 whole egg	*5 Tbs. sugar*
6 oz. butter	*vanilla-flavored powdered sugar*

Knead together 4 Tbs. flour, yeast, $\frac{1}{2}$ Tbs. sugar, and 1 egg yolk, adding some warm water if necessary. Let rise, covered, in a warm draft-free place for a couple of hours, or until doubled in size. Knead

PANDORO

the risen dough with $\frac{1}{2}$ cup flour, 1 oz. softened butter, 2 oz. sugar and 2 yolks. Knead energetically for 15 mins., then let rise for another two hours or until it has doubled in size again. Place on the pastry board the remaining flour, 2 Tbs. butter, 4 Tbs. sugar, 2 yolks, the whole egg and the fermented dough.

Knead again for 20 mins., then let rise for a third time for 2 hours. Once again take the dough and knead in a pinch of vanilla, the grated lemon rind and 2 or 3 tsp. of cream. When the dough is well

mixed, roll into a 12" x 8" rectangle, cut the butter into chunks, let soften and place in the middle of the dough.

Fold the dough back onto itself from both directions to make 3 layers and roll out again. Let rest for half an hour, repeat the folding and roll out two more times, letting the dough rest in a warm place in between. Butter and dust with sugar a deep mold, preferably a deep, star-shaped mold. Place the dough in the mold (it should fill it only halfway) and let rise in the same way as for panettone, until the dough reaches the upper rim of the pan. Cook in a preheated 375 F. oven.

Reduce the temperature after 20 minutes to 325 F. and bake 20 minutes more.

PANETTONE

Almost every region in Italy has its own holiday cake, but this *Milanese* cake is the most famous and certainly the most difficult to make. *Panettone* is available both in a high, dome shape or flat version. Natural yeast (that is, a piece of fermented dough) is essential to making a real *panettone,* because if the cake is made directly from brewers yeast, its flavor is less delicate. In addition, the process of letting the dough rise must be carried out according to very specific instructions so that the result will be a soft and airy texture. In any case, the time required for rising depend on many factors: the temperature of the room, the season, the length of the mixing process, etc. Therefore the periods of time given in the recipe can only be approximate.

1 oz. baker's yeast	*salt*
3 oz. flour	*$\frac{1}{2}$ cup melted butter*
2 cups flour	*6 Tbs. soaked, squeezed raisins*
7 Tbs. sugar	*2 oz. candied orange and lemon*
1 whole egg	*peel, diced*
5 egg yolk	*$1\frac{1}{2}$ Tbs. butter*

Mix the yeast with the flour and as much water as necessary to achieve an elastic dough, wrap in a towel and put into a warm draft-free place (an unlit oven for example) until it has doubled (should take approx. 30 minutes) in volume and the surface is uneven. Make a small *fontana* with 4 Tbs. flour. Crumble the dough cake on top of it, add ½ cup warm water and knead until you have a soft and elastic dough.

Let rise in a warm place for 3 hours. Punch down the dough, then, knead in another 4 Tbs. flour, with as much warm water as necessary. Place the dough in a warm place to rise for 2 hours. Combine the sugar, the whole egg and the yolks, mix well and cook in a double boiler for a few minutes, beating the mixture with a whisk so that it becomes light and airy. Let cool.

PANETTONE

Make another *fontana* with the remaining flour. Put in a pinch of salt, the risen dough, the butter and the egg mixture into the middle. Knead energetically for 20 minutes. When the dough is smooth and elastic, add the raisins and candied peel. Grease and flour a sheet of waxed paper and place the dough in the middle. Make a ring around it with a rectangular piece of cardboard and let rise in a warm place for at least 6 hours or until the dough has doubled in volume.

With a sharp knife cut a cross on top of the cake and put 1 Tbs. butter in the middle. Cook the *panettone* in a preheated 400 F. oven for 40-45 minutes. The cake is ready when a skewer inserted in the center comes out dry.

PANFORTE DI SIENA
Sienese Fruit Cake

This is a *Sienese* specialty usually eaten in the winter, especially for Christmas and New Year's Eve.

2 tsp. powdered cinnamon	1 oz. candied orange rind
6 oz. white flour	4 oz. walnut kernels
4 peppercorns	½ lb. toasted almonds,
½ tsp. cloves	shelled and skinned
1 tsp. coriander seeds	8 oz. sugar
pinch of nutmeg	juice of ½ lemon
½ lb. candied melon rind	3 oz. honey
wafer to line mold	

Mix 1 tsp. of cinnamon with 1 oz. of flour (a mixture known as *polverino*). Set aside. Pound the peppercorns, cloves, and coriander seeds, and mix the resulting powder with the remaining cinnamon and nutmeg (this mixture is known as *droghe*).

Dice the candied fruit and mince the walnuts. Mix the two with the whole almonds. Sift in 5 oz. flour and the *droghe* and mix the whole together. Set aside. Cook the sugar with 2 Tbs. water* in an unlined copper pan until it is browned and caramelized. Knead the previously set aside mixture into the cooked sugar until you achieve a smooth mixture.

Butter and dust with flour a 10" round cake mold. Cover the bottom with thin flat wafers and pour in the mixture, (it will probably be about $\frac{3}{4}$" thick) and sprinkle generously with the *polverino*. Bake at 350 F. for 30-40 minutes. Let set and cool in its mold. Remove from mold and *panforte* is ready to serve. *Panforte* may be kept for 2-3 weeks.

*: The 2 Tbs. of water may be substituted with the juice of $\frac{1}{2}$ lemon as the acid will prevent the sugar from lumping.

PASTA REALE
Royal almond pastry

$\frac{1}{2}$ cup peeled almonds	$\frac{3}{4}$ cup glucose
2 cups, 2 oz. sugar	1 Tbs. orange flower water

Pound the almonds in a mortar with a pestle, gradually adding $\frac{1}{2}$ cup sugar. Bring the remaining sugar and glucose to a boil until it reaches a soft ball stage of caramel. Pour the sugar syrup over the almonds in a thin stream while stirring. When the syrup is well mixed in add the orange flower water.

Turn the dough out onto a marble counter, let cool, then roll out, fold and roll the pastry as you would a simple pie dough, until it becomes smooth and homogenous. Refrigerate and use as needed.

NOTE: Almond paste is used to line molds and decorate desserts. It is also the basis for fancy almond pastry shaped as fruit, which are first dried for several days and then painted with food coloring by using arabic gum dissolved in water, brushed over the fruit.

PASTIERA NAPOLETANA
Easter Cheese and Grain Pie

This is a *Neapolitan* speciality, usually prepared around Easter.

Short Pastry:
1 cup, 4 Tbs. flour
5 oz. butter
$\frac{1}{2}$ cup confectioners' sugar
3 egg yolks

Knead the flour, butter, sugar and eggs together quickly. Make a ball of the dough and let rest in the refrigerator for at least one hour.

Filling:

1 cup whole-wheat grain	3 eggs, separated
1$\frac{1}{2}$ qts. milk	3 oz. candied orange
pinch cinnamon	and lemon peel
pinch vanilla	1 lemon rind

salt	1 Tbs. orange flower water
2 cups ricotta cheese	1 oz. butter
1 cup sugar	1 oz. powdered sugar

Soak the grain for about a week, changing the water every day. Drain and boil with fresh water for 15 minutes. Drain and put back in the pot with milk, lemon rind, cinnamon, vanilla, a pinch of salt, and 1 Tbs. of sugar. Bring to a boil, lower and cook over low heat until the milk is absorbed. Remove and discard the lemon rind.

Pass the *ricotta* through a sieve into a mixing bowl. Add the sugar and beat until creamy. Add the two yolks, the grain, diced candied fruits, grated lemon peel, and the orange-flower water. Fold in the beaten egg whites

Grease a 12" baking pan with butter and dust with sugar. Line with three quarters of the pastry. Roll out the remaining dough and cut into strips. Arrange the strips over the filling in a lattice design. Brush the strips of dough with egg yolk. Heat the oven to 375 F. and bake the cake for 1½ hours, until the filling sets and the crust is golden brown. Sprinkle with powdered sugar before serving.

NOTE: The *pastiera* is best if eaten a day after it is cooked, and it keeps in the refrigerator for a week. In Italy grain is sold pre-cooked and softened, sealed in plastic bags.

SBRISULONA
Crumbly cake

1 cup white flour	1 Tbs. orange-flower water or
1 tsp. ground coffee	vanilla liqueur
1 tsp. unsweetened cocoa	2 Tbs. candied orange and
salt	pinch citron, diced
1 Tbs. sugar	2 Tbs. candied cherries
2 Tbs. butter	1 oz. chocolate
1 cup white wine	1 Tbs. cocoa powder

Pour the flour and cornmeal on a pastry board and mix together with the sugar, ground almonds, grated lemon zest, vanilla and a pinch of salt. Break the egg yolks into the center of the flour, add butter and lard cut in small pieces and knead till all ingredients are mixed together. The dough should remain crumbly. Butter a 10" tart pan and pat in the dough, leveling the top. Bake for about 1 hour at 350 F. Let cool and sprinkle with sugar before serving.

NOTE: It is advisable to cut it into slices while still hot to avoid breaking, since it gets rather hard when it cools down. If tightly closed in a cake tin, this cake keeps for several days.

SFOGLIATELLA RICCIA
Shell shaped flaky ricotta pastries

| 1 cup water | ½ cup ricotta |
| salt | ½ cup powdered sugar |

½ cup semolina
1 cup, 2 oz. flour
6 oz. butter
2 oz. strutto

cinnamon
3 oz. diced, candied orange peel
1 egg yolk

Bring the water to a boil, add salt and pour in the *semolina,* stirring so as not to form lumps. Cook, stirring for about 8 minutes. Let cool. Make a *fontana* with the flour. Put half of the butter, a pinch of salt and as much water as necessary to knead the dough into a smooth and elastic consistency. Then, wrap in a towel and let rest for an hour. Pass the *ricotta* through a sieve, mix with the *semolina,* 6 Tbs. sugar, a pinch of cinnamon and the candied peel. Roll out the pastry with a rolling pin to obtain a 25" by 18" rectangle, ⅟₁₆" thick. Cut the pastry vertically into 4 strips and place one on top of the other, brushing each one with melted butter. Let rest for half an hour, then roll up the stack of dough. With a very sharp, floured knife slice the roll into 10 equal pieces. Place the pieces on the pastry board and roll them lightly with the pin, vertically at first in an upward direction and then in a downwards direction to give them an oval shape.

Turn the ovals over, place a bit of *ricotta* filling in the middle of each one, brush the edges with egg yolk, then fold the dough over and press to seal. Brush the *sfogliatelle* with melted *strutto* and place on a paper oiled with butter. Bake for 20 minutes in an oven preheated to 425 F. Remove from the oven, brush again with

SFOGLIATELLA

melted butter, lower the temperature to 350 F. and bake for another 20 minutes. Let cool, sprinkle with powdered sugar and serve.

STRUFFOLI
Honey balls

The dough:

2 cups flour
6 eggs
2 egg yolks
2 Tbs. butter

1 Tbs. sugar
grated zest of ½ lemon
pinch of salt
frying oil

The topping:

8 ozs. honey
4 oz. finely diced candied orange rinds

Make a *fontana* with the flour on a pastry board. Add 6 whole eggs and 2 egg yolks, butter, sugar, lemon and pinch of salt. Knead till you achieve a smooth but firm dough.

Cut and roll pieces of dough into long cylinders ½" in diameter, and cut each of these into ¼"-nuggets. Use all the dough and place the nuggets on a floured, surface. Fry the *struffoli* a few at a time in hot oil. When they are golden, drain well and dry on paper towels to rid of excess fat. Put the honey in a saucepan (preferably with a concave bottom) and bring to a boil, simmer until the foam subsides and the honey turns golden. Turn the heat down very low and add the *struffoli* together with the candied fruit and the grated peel. Mix well, coating all *struffoli* evenly. Place on a dish and, with wet hands, mold them into desired shape (flat, round, cylindrical). Always serve at room temperature, do not refrigerate this dish.

NOTE: Struffoli are very similar to Sicilian *pignolata,* though the latter are coated with a sugar and egg white glaze or a chocolate glaze instead of honey.

SUC
Red grapes pudding

3 lbs. red wine grapes
flour
sugar

Wash the grapes and remove the stems. Put the grapes in a large pot (not aluminum) and cook over low heat, stirring, until all of the grapes have popped. Pass the pulp through a sieve and cool. Weigh it to allow for proper proportions of flour. Add sugar to taste. Put 1 Tbs. flour for each 4 oz. of grape juice and, whisking constantly, add the flour to the grape juice. Continue to cook over low heat for 5-6 mins., then pour into small molds dampened with water and let cool and set. Unmold the *Suc* on dessert plates and serve.

NOTE: You may add a desired sauce under the pudding.

TIRAMISU'
Mascarpone and espresso cake

3 egg yolks	*3 oz. brandy*
6 Tbs. sugar	*3 doz. Ladyfingers*
⅔ lb. mascarpone	*1 oz. cocoa*
1 cup strong espresso	*3 oz. crushed amaretti*

Beat the yolks with ¾ of the sugar, add the *mascarpone* and continue to beat very well until the mixture becomes smooth. Separate the mixture into two equal portions. To one part, add ½ cup of *espresso,* and in the other part, the brandy. Moisten the ladyfingers with the remaining *espresso* and make a layer of them in a deep serving dish. Cover with the *Mascarpone* mixture and continue alternating layers of ladyfingers and the mixture of two different flavored *mascarpone.* The last layer should be *mascarpone.* Refrigerate for about 2 hours. Just before serving mix 1 oz. cocoa powder with the crushed *amaretti* and sprinkle evenly over the top.

VARIATION: Tiramisu may be made with sponge cake instead of ladyfingers. Ladyfingers can also line the side of the mold instead of being placed on the bottom and in between layers. *Tiramisu* may also be made into a large bowl with ladyfingers lining the bowl. All flavors and shapes can change according to the cook's desire.

TORRONE
Nougat

1 cup, 3 oz. honey	3 oz. candied orange and
1 cup, 3 oz. sugar	citron, or 1½ oz. pistachios
3 egg whites	2 lemons
1 lb. shelled almonds	large wafer sheets
1 cup shelled hazelnuts	6 Tbs. water
(lightly toasted)	

Cook the honey in a double boiler for about 1½ hours, stirring constantly. Cook the sugar and water until it reaches the hard-ball stage. Whip the egg whites till stiffened and fold them into the honey. When the mixture becomes a foamy mass, add the cooked sugar and continue mixing until the mixture begins to harden. Add the almonds and the hazelnuts, candied fruit and grated peel of two lemons, mixing thoroughly. Line a mold or a rectangular baking pan, with the thin sheets of unleveled wafer. Pour in the mixture making an even layer, top with another wafer, cover with a wooden board, and weight the board down. Let stand for half an hour, turn the baking pan over onto a cutting board, and divide the torrone in pieces as large as desired and keep at room temperature. *Torrone* may keep for a long time if it is wrapped in oiled paper or tin foil.

TORTA DI CAROTE
Carrot cake

½ lb. small carrots	1 lemon
salt	1 tsp. cornstarch
5 eggs, separated	1 oz. rum
1 cup sugar	butter flour
1 cup peeled almonds, ground	

Wash and peel the carrots, then grate them onto a cloth. Cover with another cloth and let stand for about an hour to let dry. Whip egg whites and sugar to a stiff meringue. Fold in the carrots, almonds, lemon zest, cornstarch, and the egg yolks, one at a time. Add the rum, stirring gently. Butter and dust a cake pan and pour in the mixture. Bake at 350 F. for about 40 minutes. Let cool before serving.

TORTA PARADISO
Paradise Cake

This is a *Lombardy* specialty from *Pavia*.

1½ cup butter
¾ cup potato starch
zest of 1 lemon
8 egg yolks
3 egg whites, stiffly beaten

1 cup, 3 oz. confectioners' sugar
¾ cup white flour
cornstarch
salt

Butter a deep cake pan (10" diameter) and coat with a small amount of potato starch. Beat butter till creamy. Add the lemon zest. Add the egg yolks one at a time, then the sugar, the flour, the sifted cornstarch and pinch of salt. Fold in the stiffly beaten egg whites. Blend the ingredients, stirring gently, and pour the mixture into cake pan. Bake at 350 F. for 40 minutes. Cool and sprinkle with powdered sugar before serving.

NOTE: It is best the day after baking. If wrapped in waxed paper or aluminum foil and stored in a cool, dry place, it will keep for a week; it should be heated for 5 minutes in a moderate oven to restore its freshness before serving.

TORTA SABBIOSA
Sandy Cake

2 cups, 6 Tbs. butter
1 cup, 6 Tbs. extra fine sugar
3 eggs, separated
½ cup, 3 oz. white flour

pinch of baking soda
½ cup, 3 oz. potato starch
salt
parchment paper, buttered

Whip the butter with the sugar until it reaches a creamy consistency. Add 3 egg yolks, one at a time, then sift in the flour, baking soda, potato starch and a pinch of salt. Beat the egg whites till stiff then add to the batter. Mix well and place in a 10" tart pan lined with buttered parchment paper, leveling the top. Bake at 350 F. for about 30 minutes.

If wrapped in aluminum foil, this cake keeps several days. It is best if eaten the day after baking.

TORTELLI DI CARNEVALE
Puffed Bignet

pinch of salt
4 oz. butter
½ cup, 2 oz. flour

4 eggs, separated
zest of 1 lemon
olive oil

Bring ½ pint of water to a boil in a small saucepan, then add salt and butter. When the butter is melted, turn the heat off and add the flour all at once. Mix well with a wooden spoon, turn on the heat again, and cook, stirring constantly for 10 minutes, until the resulting mix separates from the sides of the pan and begins to sizzle. Turn the heat off and cool.

When the mix has cooled off, beat the egg yolks into the batter one at a time. Add the grated lemon zest and the sugar, mix well. Beat the whites till they form stiff peaks and fold into the batter. Let stand for one hour.

Heat a good quantity of oil and drop the batter in by the teaspoonful; the resulting *tortelli* will inflate, and if there is enough frying fat they will turn by themselves. Once cooked, drain on absorbent paper and keep in a warm place. Arrange the resulting *tortelli* into a pyramid on a napkin-lined serving dish, sprinkle with powdered sugar, and serve.

ZABAGLIONE
Eggnog with Marsala

4 egg yolks
4 Tbs. sugar
4 Tbs. Marsala

Warm the eggs yolks and the sugar in a double boiler over low heat, then whip them with a wire whisk. Pour *Marsala* into the yolks, drop by drop, and keep beating.

The mixture will begin to foam and then swell into a light soft cream. Do not overcook or it will collapse.

Cinnamon and grated lemon rind may be added before pouring in the *Marsala,* and *Marsala* itself can be replaced with a high quality white, sweet, dry or sparkling wine. Brandy or cherry brandy may also be added.

ZUPPA INGLESE
Italian English trifle

8 eggs, separated $\frac{1}{2}$ *vanilla stick*
8 oz. powdered sugar   *sponge cake*
1 qt. milk   *1 oz. alchermes*
1 Tbs. flour   *1 oz. rum*

Prepare a vanilla cream with 8 egg yolks, $\frac{2}{3}$ cup sugar, the milk, the flour and the vanilla. Warm the milk, add the egg yolks, sugar, vanilla and flour. Keep mixing over low heat until you achieve a smooth cream, but do not allow the cream to boil. Cut the sponge cake into slices about $\frac{1}{2}$" thick and 1" wide. Arrange a layer of sponge cake in a deep serving platter, sprinkle with *alchermes* to moisten, then pour a layer of cream. Cover with another layer of sponge cake, sprinkle with rum, spread with cream, cover with a last layer of sponge cake and drizzle with *alchermes.*

Whip the egg whites, combine gently with remaining sugar and cover the cake. Brown the meringue with a burner or in the salamander.

NOTE: The shape can be round and flat, or egg-shaped. It may also be prepared in a bowl-like container. Also, the cream may be divided into two flavors, one vanilla, one chocolate. *Alchermes* is a liquor essential to this dessert, but it may be substituted with curacao or grand marnier.

GELATO
Ice cream

According to historians, *gelato* has very ancient origins. It is believed that the Arabs introduced *gelato* to the Western World through Sicily. The Greeks and the Turks were also known for preparing lemon-based mixtures that resembled *sorbetto* (sherbets).

It was *Caterina de' Medici* who brought a *Sicilian* ice-cream maker (whose name has been lost) to the court of Henry II in France in 1533. It was another Sicilian, *Procopio dei Coltelli,* who opened the famous Café Procope in Paris, opposite the Comedie Francaise, which was patronized by actors, nobles and scholars such as Voltaire, who made enthusiastic remarks about the sherbets served at the Café Procope. *Procopio's* specialties were made with fruit juice mixed with shaved ice and flavored with jasmine or rose.

Sherbets were thought to have a beneficial effect on the nervous and digestive systems, and were usually served between main courses, more precisely after the first few meat and fish dishes, at the sumptuous banquets of the 18th and 19th century. It was only later that richer ingredients such as egg yolks, sugar, milk and cream began to be used, to make what is now known as *gelati alla crema* (ice cream).

Gelati are classified according to the ingredients used in making them. They are categorized in the following way:

1) **Gelato** — ice cream made in an ice-cream machine and contains cream or milk, sugar and egg yolks.

2) **Sorbetto** — sherbets containing fruit juices or crushed fruit and sugar, with the occasional addition of wine or liqueur.

3) **Cassata & Bomba** — These are molds of gelati of two or more flavors frozen in a mold. Frequently the molds can be lined with ice cream and filled with chilled creams. Molds may also be shaped flat, round, heart shaped. Molds may also be called *«pezzi duri»*, when individual ice cream molds in small distinctive shapes of hearts, flowers, geometrical, etc. are used. The forms are filled with the desired ice cream, closed tightly and frozen. The dessert is removed from the mold when ready to eat. If a wooden palette is placed one-third into the mold, when one uses the individual mold, it can be held by the stick for easy consumption.

4) **Torta Gelato** — Ice-Cream Cake. Any round mold can be used to prepare ice-cream cakes, but it must first be lined with parchment paper and chilled in the freezer before using. Using a spring mold is easier. More than one flavor of ice-cream can be used as long as the flavors are complementary. Meringue disks, candied fruit, sponge

cake, or lady fingers *savoiardi* are often used in preparing these cakes, which must then be frozen for several hours. Once the cake is ready, remove it from the mold, place on a serving dish and garnish with whipped cream, candied fruit and chocolate shapes.

5) **Semifreddo** — Chilled Creams. *Semifreddi* are typical Italian desserts. They are prepared with an egg-based custard and whipped cream. No ice-cream machine is needed to make *semifreddi;* the basic mixture can be poured directly into the mold and put in the freezer for a few hours. Chilled creams may be used as filling for *cassate* and *bombe,* or can be prepared with fruits, syrups, chocolate, etc.

Semifreddo can also be called *spumone.* All *semifreddi* or *spumone* may be served with an appropriate sauce. These range from a simple fruit sauce to a vanilla cream.

6) **Granita** — *Granita* (ice) is a very light, slush ice made with sugar syrup and either fruit juice or coffee. Unlike ice creams or sherbets, *granita* must be frozen into a pan of plastic or stainless steel with the syrup not higher than 1-$\frac{1}{2}$" up the sides. It should be stirred from time to time to allow the sides and the top to freeze. Churn before serving, so as to yield a lightly granular texture. Liqueurs may be added if desired. The sugar and/or liqueur will not allow the *granita* to freeze solid, making it easier to churn before serving. *Granita* is served in a long-stemmed glass. Some go well with whipped cream.

GELATI ALLA CREMA
Ice Creams

GELATO
Basic Recipe

> *1 qt. whole milk*
> *1 cup sugar*
> *10 egg yolks*
> *grated rind of 1 lemon*
> *pinch of salt*

Bring the milk, less half a cup, to a boil in a stainless steel saucepan (do not use an aluminum container), adding the grated lemon rind and a pinch of salt. Remove from the fire. In a bowl whip the egg yolks with the sugar. Add the cold half cup of milk then add the hot milk a little at a time. Put the mixture in a pot on the fire and cook over very low heat for 20 minutes, stirring constantly. Do not allow to boil. When the mixture begins to thicken, pour it into a bowl and cool, stirring frequently. Strain through a fine sieve. Once entirely cooled, put the mixture in an ice-cream machine and churn until it reaches the proper consistency. Place in an ice cream freezer.

NOTE: The churning time varies according to the ice cream machine used. An ice cream freezer holds a temperature just below freezing.

CIOCCOLATO
Chocolate

1 qt. milk	12 egg yolks
1 qt. cream	1½ cups sugar
8 ozs. bitter chocolate	1 vanilla pod (in bars)

Break the chocolate in pieces, melt over low heat. When melted, add the milk, cream and vanilla pod. Stirring constantly, bring almost to a boil. Thoroughly whip the egg yolks with the sugar, add to the milk and cream and continue to cook as in the basic recipe. When the mixture is ready, pour it into a bowl and cool, stirring occasionally.
When the resulting mix is cool, strain through a sieve if necessary, put it in the ice-cream machine and churn.

VANIGLIA
Vanilla
Use the same ingredients and procedure as in the basic recipe, with the addition of a vanilla pod instead of lemon rind to the warm milk.

GELATI ALLA FRUTTA O SORBETTI
Sherbets

GELATO AL LIMONE
Lemon sherbet

1 cup, 2 oz. granulated sugar	1 cup lump sugar
1 qt. water	10 lemons
2 egg whites	2 oranges

Make a syrup with the granulated sugar in the water over low heat until entirely dissolved. Reduce by one third, remove from heat and set aside. Wash the lemons and rub them with the cube sugar until all cubes are thoroughly scented from the lemon rinds. Add the lump sugar to the syrup and cool. Squeeze the juice from lemons and the oranges. Add to the syrup, mixing well. Strain the resulting juice. Whip the egg whites thoroughly, gently fold them into the mixture, and churn. Keep sherbet in ice cream freezer till ready to serve.

GELATO ALL'ARANCIA
Orange sherbet
Use the same ingredients and procedure as in the preceding recipe, but the addition of orange liqueur or blood oranges juice may be used to give the *gelato* a brighter color.

GELATO AL MANDARINO
Mandarin sherbet
Use the same ingredients and procedure as in the two preceding recipes, substituting 10 mandarin oranges and 2 lemons for the 10 lemons. Halfway through, preparing the ice mixture, add 3 ozs. of mandarin liqueur.

GELATO ALLA FRAGOLA
Strawberry sherbet

8 ozs. water	*½ vanilla pod*
1 lb. strawberries	*½ orange*
1 cup, 2 oz. sugar	*½ lemon*

Bring the water to a boil in a stainless steel saucepan. Mix in and dissolve the sugar and the vanilla, and cool. In the meantime, wash the strawberries in ice cold water. Pass them through a non-metal sieve or a food mill. Mix the resulting puree with the strained juice of half a lemon and half an orange. When the sugar syrup has entirely cooled off, add the strawberry purée; mix well and churn the resulting mixture in an ice-cream machine.

GELU I MULUNI
Water melon sherbet

2 lbs. water melon pulp	*3 ozs. shelled and chopped*
4 Tbs. jasmine water (or	*pistachios*
orange-flower water)	*7 ozs. finely diced candied*
3 cups sugar	*pumpkin*
7 oz. finely minced chocolate	*1 Tbs. powdered cinnamon*

Sieve the melon, mix the resulting purée with the jasmine water and 1½ cups sugar. Pour the mixture into the ice cream machine and churn. Mix the resulting ice with the chocolate, pistachios, candied pumpkin, 1 tsp. of cinnamon and the remaining sugar. Stir gently and pour the resulting mixture into a round mold (preferably lined with oiled paper). Cover and freeze for at least two hours. Remove the sherbet from the mold and sprinkle with cinnamon before serving. If possible, decorate with jasmine flowers or lemon leaves.

CASSATA E BOMBA
Molds

To make molds it is necessary to have a special mold with removable top and bottom covers. *Bombe* consist of one or more varieties of gelati. In the past they were prepared and stored in spherical molds; today a semispherical mold is used instead. Generally, molds are made with basic ice cream on the outside and a light and fluffy, chilled cream or custard on the inside. Candied fruit, hazelnuts, pralines, and biscuits soaked in liqueur are often mixed into the filling.

To remove from the mold, immerse the mold up to its rim in warm water for a few seconds, shake out ice cream onto a serving dish and cut each into 2-inch large slices.

BOMBA FANTASIA
Southern ice cream mold

2 pt. vanilla ice cream	4 chopped figs
4 chopped dates	1 Tbs. pistachios
4 Tbs. chopped almonds	1 qt. sweetened whipped cream
	1 qt. curacao

Combine the nuts, dried fruit, and curacao and mix it with the whipped cream. Line a spherical mold with vanilla ice cream and fill the center with the whipped cream mixture. Freeze for at least 2 hours. Remove from freezer one hour before serving and place in refrigerator. Unmold just before serving. The *bomba* should be cut when serving.

CASSATA GELATO AL PISTACCHIO
Pistachio ice cream mold

1 lb. 5 oz. pistachio ice cream	5 oz. whipped cream
	1 egg white
3 oz. mixed chopped candied fruit	2 Tbs. caramel-covered almonds
rum	4 Tbs. powder sugar

Put a semi-spheric mold in the freezer to chill. Soften the ice cream just until spreadable and line the inside of the mold, leaving the middle empty. Put the mold back into the freezer. Soften the candied fruit in the rum, then drain. Whip the cream and stir in the candied fruit and the almonds. Beat the egg white and sugar until stiff and add to the cream. Fill up the center of the mold with this mixture and put the mold back into the freezer for at least 2 hours. Follow the same procedure as for southern ice cream mold.
NOTE: Cassata can also be in a round cake mold.

SEMIFREDDO CON FRAGOLE
Chilled cream with strawberries

2 cups wild strawberries	2 sheets gelatin
1 cup powdered sugar	1 oz. orange liqueur
1 qt. whipped cream	1 banana
4 slices pineapple	

Wash strawberries in cold water, dry them with paper towels and, select 2 ozs. of the best-looking berries for garnish. Pass the remaining berries through a non-metallic sieve. Sift the powdered sugar into the strawberry purée, and fold in the whipped cream. Soften the gelatin in a bit of water, then dissolve it in a saucepan with the liqueur over a low flame and let cool but not set. Gradually fold the gelatin into the strawberry and cream mixture. Wrap an 8"-soufflé dish with a collar made of cake cardboard (the collar should extend 2" above the edge of the dish). Pour in the strawberry and cream mixture and level off the top against the cardboard. Freeze the *semifreddo* for at least an hour. Remove the cardboard and garnish the dessert with the berries, *banana* and pineapple before serving.

SEMIFREDDO ALLO ZABAGLIONE
Eggnog chilled cream

8 egg yolks	1 pint whipped cream
1 cup sugar	10 ozs. dry Marsala
ladyfingers	

Beat the egg yolks with the sugar in a bowl. Add the *Marsala,* a tablespoon at a time. Place the saucepan over a very low heat or in a bain-marie and continue beating until the mixture becomes foamy. Pour it in a bowl and let cool. Fold in the whipped cream and pour the mixture into a mold lined with ladyfingers which have been moistened with *Marsala.* Freeze for at least 5 hours and serve.

ZUCCOTTO
Chocolate and curacao chilled cream

This is a Florentine specialty.

a large piece of sponge cake	3 oz. minced, roasted almonds
4 oz. chocolate	and hazel nuts
1 qt. whipped cream	1 oz. curacao
3 oz. powdered sugar	powdered sugar
1 envelope vanilla	cocoa

Cut the sponge cake in strips and use it to line a spherical mold. Finely mince the chocolate and, in a double boiler, melt half of it over medium heat. Pour the whipped cream in a bowl, add 3 oz. powdered sugar, the vanilla, the curacao and minced nuts. Lightly moisten the sponge cake in the mold with the liqueur and spoon in half he whipped cream. Mix the remaining whipped cream with the chocolate, and spoon this into the mold, filling it to the top. Seal with more sponge cake strips and moisten with the liqueur. Put the zuccotto in the freezer for about 4 hours. Make a funnel of wax paper and put the melted chocolate into it. Make small disks of chocolate on another piece of wax paper and let harden Remove *zuccotto* from the freezer one hour before serving. Unmold the *zuccotto* onto a serving dish, sprinkle with powdered sugar and garnish with the chocolate disks and cocoa powder (optional). Slice and serve.

GRANITE
Ices

GRANITA AL LIMONE (BASIC RECIPE)
Lemon Ice

2 cups lemon juice
1 cup water
2 Tbs. sugar

Blend all the ingredients, making sure that the sugar is completely dissolved. Strain the syrup into a flat pan and place in freezer. Scrape occasionally while freezing and churn before serving.

GRANITA AL CAFFÈ
Coffee Ice

2 cups espresso
small quantity of water
2 Tbs. sugar
whipped cream

Follow the basic recipe above. Top with whipped cream before serving.

GRANITA AL CIOCCOLATO
Chocolate Ice

1 pt. plus 6 Tbs. water
2 oz. cocoa
½ cup sugar
2 Tbs. chocolate liqueur
whipped cream

Bring 6 Tbs. water to a boil and stir in the cocoa. When dissolved, add 1 pint water and the sugar. Let cool.
Follow the basic recipe. Add the liqueur. Serve topped with whipped cream.

GLOSSARY OF WORDS AND EXPRESSIONS
Currently in Use in Italian cuisine

ABBACCHIO: Milk-fed baby lamb slaughtered before it is weaned.

ACCIUGATA: Raw anchovies seasoned with oil and lemon and left to marinate for an hour or two. Served as an antipasto.

ACETO BALSAMICO: Balsamic vinegar, a specialty of Modena, made from the fermentation of mosto (must) aged at least 10 years. In the past it was produced only on a small family scale with the recipe passed from one generation to the next. Today it is also produced in small quantities commercially.

ACQUA DI FIORI DI ARANCIO: An essence made from orange flowers and leaves used in making desserts, i.e., pastiera napoletana.

AFFETTATO MISTO: A term which indicates that many types of sliced salame and salumi are used in the same dish.

AGLIATA: Sauce made of pounded garlic, oil and crustless bread.

AGNOLOTTI: Disk or square-shaped pieces of pasta, filled and folded with meat and vegetables. They are either served in a broth or with a sauce.

AGONE: Another name for alosa, a fish quite common in the Northern lakes.

AGRESTO: Juice from green or unripe grapes used to make a sauce of the same name, widely used in the 14th-16th century.

AGRODOLCE: (Sweet and sour). A combination of sweet and sour flavors in the same dish. Also, a very old sauce made of vinegar and sugar or of any other 2 contrasting ingredients.

ALCHERMES: A liquor of Arab origins, perfected in Italy (it is also known as Alchermes of Florence). It is used almost exclusively in pastries, especially for Zuppa Inglese in which it is an indispensable ingredient.

AL DENTE: Pasta cooked al dente should have a somewhat chewy texture and should not break or become mushy when mixed with desired condiments.

AL FIASCO: Flask or a terra-cotta pot shaped like a flask, used to cook beans; «al fiasco», in a flask.

ALICE: Another name for anchovy.

ALOSA: See *AGONE*.

AMATRICIANA (ALL'): A spicy sauce for spaghetti or bucatini made with strutto, guanciale, white wine, tomato and peperoncino. It comes from the town of Amatrice in Lazio.

AL SALTO: A term used to describe a risotto alla Milanese cooked halfway, then cooled. It is then sautéed as thin fritters with butter over high heat. The starch expelled from the grains of rice allows the fritters to form a crunchy golden crust.

ALL'ONDA: A term used to describe risotto that is cooked until still creamy but semi-liquid in texture (wavy) when poured into a dish.

AL TELEFONO: A term used to describe fritters with cheese. When bitten into the fritters form long strings like a telephone cord.

AMARETTO: A cookie made of almonds, sugar and egg white, crunchy on the outside and soft and chewy on the inside. Also, a liqueur that tastes like almonds.

ANICINO: Hard biscuit made of flour, baking powder, eggs, sugar and anise seeds.

ANIMELLE (sweetbreads). The thymus glands of veal and lamb.

ANOLINI: Fresh stuffed pasta. In the Parma area these are made with the highly reduced cooking liquid of braised meats. They are usually served in broth.

ANTIPASTO: An appetizer or hors d'oeuvre. Antipasto literally means «before the meal».

APPIATTIRE: To flatten a steak or a piece of meat by pounding it with a mallet so as to break the tough meat fibers.

APPASSIRE: To sauté over low heat so that the vegetables soften but do not brown.

ACQUACOTTA: A peasant soup made of onions, celery and tomato browned in oil and diluted with water. It is served with hot pepper and toasted home-style bread.

ARANCIATA: Sardinian torrone made with orange peel, honey and almonds. It also means fresh squeezed orange juice.

ARANCINO: A rice ball filled with meat ragù, peas and cheese. These are served as antipasti, and in home kitchens are made with leftover risotto.

ARISTA: Saddle of pork. It is a term from Tuscany, where this meat is usually cooked on the spit. It can also be roasted in the oven in its own fat.

ARSELLA: A kind of small clam.

ARAGOSTA: Spiny lobster.

ARTUSI, Pellegrino: A banker and epicure from Emilia Romagna who wrote "La Scienza in cucina e l'arte di mangiar bene" (the Science in the kitchen and the art of eating well) in 1891 (see preface).

ASTACO: Maine lobster.

ANGUILLA: Eel. Eels live in fresh waters; they swim to the sea to spawn and then go back up rivers and lakes.

BABÀ: Neopolitan dessert made from yeasted dough, soaked in syrup and liqueur and topped with candied or fresh fruits.

BACCALÀ: Cod preserved in salt.

BACIO: (kiss). A cookie made from two smaller cookies stuck together with chocolate or cream. It is also a commercial chocolate candy with bits of almond.

BAGNA CAUDA: (hot bath). A sauce dip made of oil, garlic and anchovies.

BAGNET VERD: (green sauce). A sauce for boiled meats made of parsley, garlic, anchovies, crustless bread and oil used as a condiment for bollito misto.

BAGNOMARIA: (bain marie). A double boiler.

BAICOLI: Dry, crumbly biscuits; a Venetian specialty for dipping in wine or hot chocolate.

BALLOTTA: Chestnut boiled in its skin, flavored with bay leaves or fennel seeds. These are eaten by themselves or as a snack with wine.

BAMBORINO: Beef flank.

BARBA DE FRATI: (Monk's beard). Slightly acidic, long, thin string of a grass-like vegetable.

BARBAFORTE: See RAFANO

BARBAGLIATA: Milanese beverage made of milk and chocolate.

BATÙ DI OCA: Boned and salted goose preserved in its own fat.

BATTUTO: Finely chopped herbs, such as parsley, garlic added raw to a finished dish. When cooked it is called soffritto.

BAVA (ALLA): In dishes alla bava the cheese in the recipe melts, forming thin elastic strings when eaten.

BENSONE: Simple, unfilled sponge cake, covered with ground almonds.

BERLINGOZZO: Sweet anise-flavored cake in the form of a ring, a Tuscan specialty made during the Carnival Festival.

BIANCHETTI: Sardine and anchovy spawn.

BIANCHI DI SPAGNA OR SPAGNONI: Large white, kidney-shaped beans (much like U.S. Great Northerns).

BIANCO (IN): A term which generally indicates a boiled dish without, or with very little, condiment.

BIGOLI: Large, rustic fresh spaghetti originally made with a torchio.

BISATO: Term used for eel in the Veneto region.

BISCOTTATO: Said of bread re-baked to a crunchy consistence throughout. It may also refer to a biscuit being baked the same way.

BISTECCA ALLA FIORENTINA: A thick slice of young beef cut from the rib with the filet still attached. Similar to a T-bone steak; it should be at least 1" thick and large enough for 2-3 people. It is grilled, usually without greasing it.

BITTO: A soft, flavorful cheese from Valtellina. If aged, it can be grated.

BOCCONOTTO: A kind of pull pastry stuffed with chicken livers, sweetbreads and truffles. It is served as an antipasto.

BOERO: Liqueur-filled chocolate with a cherry in spirit.

BOLLITO MISTO: Various boiled meats, such as beef, veal, pork and fowl. It is traditionally served with green sauce or mostarda di frutta.

BOMBA: A semisphere-shaped ice cream mold, filled with two or more flavors.

BONDIOLA: See *COPPA*

BORLOTTI: Fat, pulpy medium-sized beans, light brown in color speckled with darker brown. Nearest U.S. equivalent: cranberry or pinto beans.

BOTTARGA: The whole ovary sac of either *TUNA* or *GRAY MULLET*. After removal from fish, the sac is placed under a weight to allow the discharge of its liquids. It is then hung and air dried. The finished bottarga is coated with wax to allow for a better preservation. Bottarga of gray mullet is considered much better than the tuna. Bottarga is eaten thinly sliced, coated with extra virgin olive oil, accompanied by greens or tomatoes as antipasto, or grated or chopped to flavor sauces for pastas.

BRACIOLA/BRACIOLINA: Pork involtino stuffed with pine nuts and raisins, used for ragù Napoletano.

BRASATO: Braised. A marinated cut of meat browned and cooked (covered) with herbs and spices in liquids or its own marinade for 3-4 hours.

BRESAOLA: Cured meat from Valtellina made of very lean salted, dried beef. It is served sliced very thin with lemon, oil and freshly ground pepper, as an antipasto.

BROCCOLETTI DI RAPE: A bitter winter green that grows in clusters of long, slender leaves with firm stems. This green becomes cime di rape when small yellow flowers or tiny green buds grow in the center of the leaf clusters.

BRODETTO: A fish stew from Venice and the upper Adriatic, made by cooking larger fish in a broth made from smaller fish.

BROS: Fresh Piedmont cheese preserved in a jar and fermented in vinegar, grappa or other spirits.

BRUSCHETTA: Slices of a large crusty loaf of toasted bread, rubbed with garlic cloves and seasoned with extra virgin olive oil, salt and pepper to taste. Chopped tomatoes may be added.

BRUTTI MA BUONI: (ugly but good). A type of very simple, flat amaretti made of almonds, sugar and egg whites.

BUCATINI: Thick spaghetti with a hole through the middle.

BUCCELLATO: A cake of yeasted sweet dough shaped like a round mold.

BUFALA: The female bufalo. This breed has been in Italy since the Roman Empire. Today bufala is being kept in the most advanced technological manner, in order to achieve the maximum production of milk for bufala mozzarella.

BURIDDA: Genovese fish soup.

BURRATA: Fresh cheese from Puglia with a stringy exterior like mozzarella but a mixture of creamy and stringy cheese on the inside. In Andria (Bari) the exterior is made from caciocavallo cheese.

BURRIDA: A Sardinian dish made from boiled Mediterranean catfish and covered with a walnut sauce. It should be prepared a couple of hours before serving.

BUSECCA: Tripe Milanese style, made with Spanish white beans and plenty of celery and carrots.

BUSECCHINA: Milanese dessert of puréed fresh chestnuts, combined with white wine and heavy cream, then baked.

BUSSOLÀ: Traditional yeasted sweet bread made with liqueur. There is also a richer version with candied fruit, almonds, pieces of chocolate and spices.

CACCIATORINO: Small finely ground pork and beef salami weighing from 31/2 to 10 ounces. It is aged for a short period and is suitable for snacks.

CACCIAGIONE: Game.

CACCIUCCO: A dense, Tuscan fish stew made up of several types of fish and shellfish, vegetables and garlic. Caciucco is served over slices of bread.

CACIOTTA: This name is given to a wide range of cheeses produced both industrially and in dairies. Made of sheep's or cow's milk or a mixture of the two, sold in round wheels weighing less than one kilo and only slightly ripened, the cheese generally has a delicate flavor, few or no holes, and is white or yellowish in color. The crust is thin and ranges from light to darker yellows.

CAFFÈ VALDOSTANO: Coffee served in a special short squat pot with at least four spouts. Coffee is put in the pot with lemon peel and grappa and is flamed, then drunk very hot from the spouts.

CAGNONE (IN): Term used to describe plain boiled rice served with butter and Parmesan cheese.

CALCIONI: Little cookies with fresh pecorino cheese filling. The dough is cut on the top so that some of the cheese seeps out during cooking.

CALDARROSTA: Hot roasted chestnut cooked in a special pan, preferably over coals. Before roasting, a cut is made into the curved side of the chestnut so that it does not explode.

CALZONE: One of the most famous Neapolitan specialties, calzone is a disk of pizza dough filled with prosciutto, mozzarella, ricotta and parmigiano cheese, folded over into a crescent shape.

CANNOLO: A Sicilian crunchy pastry shell filled with ricotta, sugar, and candied fruit.

CANNELLINI: Small, white beans, slightly elongated and arched in form. They are very common in Tuscany, where they are prepared al fiasco (see above).

CANNELLONI: Cylindrical rolls of fresh egg pasta, which are boiled, then filled. They are stuffed with meat, vegetables and/or cheese, then baked. Industrially produced cannelloni are now available on the market which generally do not require boiling before filling.

CANTUCCI: Crunchy Tuscan biscuits made of flour, sugar, eggs, almonds and pine nuts. They are eaten dipped in wine.

CAPELLI D'ANGELO: (angel's hair). Very thin spaghetti, usually cooked in broth. Fried and sweetened with honey, they are a Sicilian dessert.

CAPITONE: A term used in the south of Italy for a large fresh water eel.

CAPOCOLLO: see *COPPA*

CAPONATA: A combination of cooked vegetables, capers, olives and anchovies drizzled with oil and vinegar. It is a Sicilian specialty, served cold as an antipasto.

CAPPELLACCI: (ugly hats). Large ravioli filled with vegetables.

CAPPELLETTI: (little hats). Fresh egg dough pasta filled with meat or a combination of cheese, eggs and spices. They are rather small and shaped like an Alpine hat.

CAPPELLO DA PRETE: (priest's hat). A kind of sausage made of pork, skin, lard and spices stuffed into the lower part of the pig's foot, then sewn into a triangle. It must be cooked before eating. This term is also be used for a second choice cut of beef having a triangular shape from the forequarters.

CAPPONADA: Simplified version of cappon magro.

CAPPONE: (capon). Fattened, castrated male chicken.

CAPPON MAGRO: Elaborate Ligurian seafood and vegetable salad (see recipe).

CAPRESE: Salad made of tomatoes, mozzarella, basil and olive oil.

CAPRINO: Fresh goat's or cow's cheese having a cylindrical shape.

CARBONARA (ALLA): Spaghetti sauce made of browned pancetta, raw egg yolks mixed with parmigiano cheese, and cream.

CARPACCIO: Very thin slices of lean, raw beef seasoned with oil, lemon, salt and pepper or other sauces. This dish was served for the first time at Harry's Bar in Venice and named after a Venetian painter.

CARPIONE: Fried fish marinated in vinegar, oil, herbs and spices.

CARRETTIERA (ALLA): Spaghetti served with a sauce made of browned parsley, onions, garlic and bread crumbs.

CARROZZA (MOZZARELLA IN): Slices of mozzarella between two slices of bread. It is floured, dipped in egg, and fried.

CARTA DA MUSICA: (music paper). A Sardinian bread made of very thin, crunchy dough. It can be kept a long time.

CASALINGA (ALLA): Home-style cooking.

CASARECCIO: (pane casareccio). A traditional large-sized, thick-crusted bread.

CASSATA: An ice cream cake made with two or more flavors, sometimes they are filled with custard, cream or ricotta cheese.

CASONSEI: Ravioli made in Bergamo filled with a sweet-and-sour stuffing.

CASSOEULA: Pork ribs, small salami and other parts of the pig cooked with cabbage.

CASTAGNACCIO: Traditional Tuscan dessert made of chestnut flour, raisins, pine nuts and served with whipped cream.

CAVOLO NERO: A black cabbage with long, dark, narrow leaves. It is very diffuse in Tuscany, where it is used for ribollita and other soups.

CECI: (Chick peas). These are round, slightly dented, beige seeds only sold dried. Ceci can be used for soup, either whole or mashed as a side dish for pork, or simply boiled and seasoned with oil.

CENCI: Another name for chiacchiere.

CEPPETELLI: (Also known as orecchiette). Often found growing on tree stumps, these mushrooms are light grey in color with broad, flaring caps and slender stems. Those found in the market are often cultivated.

CHIACCHIERE: Dessert prepared during the Carnevale period, these are strips of sweet pastry dough, cut into various shapes and fried in oil.

CHIODINI: Small, brown mushrooms that grows in clusters. A common variety, they have tiny round caps and very fine stems.

CHISOLINI: Rhomboid-shaped pastry dough made of flour, strutto and baking powder. They are fried and served with salame.

CHITARRA: («guitar»). A rectangular, wooden frame with evenly spaced wires stretched across it; used for cutting sheets of pasta dough into thick spaghetti.

CHIZZE: Similar to chisolini, but the dough is cut and folded like ravioli and filled with slices of parmigiano cheese.

CIACCI: Fritters made of ricotta, flour and baking powder, made by using a utensil similar to a waffle iron. They are served with salame.

CIALZONE: Ravioli as made in Friuli. The simple version is made with meat, egg and cheese filling, the sweet-and-sour version with raisins, chocolate and candied fruit. Both versions are served with melted butter.

CIAMBELLA: A baked, round mold of sweet or savory dough.

CIBREO: Scalded chicken giblets, browned in butter and blended together with flour, lemon juice and broth.

CICERCHIATA: Umbrian dessert similar to struffoli.

CICCIOLI: The particles of fried pork meat left over in the process of making strutto. They can be either fresh or dried and can be eaten with bread or polenta.

CICORIA: (Chicory). Long, thin green salad leaves with a large white vein, chicory is known variously in Italy as catalogna, cicoria cimata or cicoriella.

CIECHE: Just-spawned eels, found in Versilia (the coastline from Forte dei Marmi to Viareggio, Tuscany) and Spain. They are usually floured and fried.

CIMA: Stuffed breast of veal, served cold.

CIME DI RAPA: See *BROCCOLETTI DI RAPE*

CIPOLLACI: See *LAMPASCIONI.*

CIRIOLA: A term used in Lazio for a small eel. Ciriole are also tagliatelle served with browned garlic,oil and peperoncino.

CIVET: Piedmont stew made of game marinated in its own blood, red wine, herbs and spices.

COLOMBA: (dove) Yeasted sweet bread baked in the shape of a dove and covered with sugar and almonds. It is traditionally prepared for Easter.

COLTELLO PER TARTUFO: Truffle slicer. A spatula-like cutting utensil with an adjustable blade to control thickness of truffle shavings.

CONCIA: Another word for «marinade.» The name concia is also used to describe a kind of polenta cooked with toma and fontina cheeses. Melted butter is poured on just before serving.

CONSERVARE: To save, to preserve.

CONSERVA DI POMODORI: Dried and puréed tomatoes. The mixture, which is very concentrated, is used in small amounts to add flavor to various dishes.

COPPA: Sausage made from deboned pork neck that is salted and marinated in wine. It is aged, but not allowed to harden.

CORALLO: Shellfish eggs, red in color. These are used to give color and flavor to both hot and cold sauces and to make buttery garnishes for fish courses.

CORATELLA: A mixture of the innards of a slaughtered lamb or goat.

COSTOLETTA: A chop pounded flat with the bone still attached.

COTECHINO: Fresh pork sausage.

COTENNA: Pigskin. Before it is cooked, it is scorched, scraped and scalded to remove the bristles and some of the fat.

COTOGNATA: A preserve of quinces.

COTOLETTA: A boneless cutlet of veal or pork, usually taken from the leg, pounded flat, breaded and sautéed in butter or a combination of butter and oil. They can also be prepared as involtini.

COZZE: Mussels.

CREN: See *RAFANO*

CREMOLATA: A kind of granita made like a sherbet.

CREMONA: a city in the region of Lombardia where one of the best fruit mustard is produced.

CRESCENZA: This is a cheese from Lombardy. It is an uncooked cheese, soft in texture and high in fat content, made from whole, pasteurized cow's milk. It is ripened for 15 days, has a rectangular shape with no crust and no holes. The cheese is white and has a butter-like consistency.

CRESPELLE: Thin pancakes made with flour, milk and egg. Prepared like crêpes.

CRISCO: A commercial vegetable fat product.

CROCCANTE: Caramel with almonds and nocciole, made by spreading the candy out onto a cold greased work surface and cutting it before it hardens.

CROSETTI/CORZETTI: A Ligurian fresh pasta made with flour and many eggs. The dough is cut and pressed into little molds with figures carved into them. The pasta is dried and then served with meat or cheese sauce.

CROSTINO/CROSTONE: Crustless slice of bread cut in different shapes — depending what it is intended for — either fried in oil or in butter, or toasted in the oven.

CRUMIRI: Dry biscuits made of flour and cornmeal. They are excellent with tea.

CUCCIA: A Sicilian dish, which can be either sweet or savory. The sweet version is made of softened, then boiled, wheat kernels mixed with ricotta, sugar, candied squash and chocolate. The savory version is simply wheat seasoned with oil.

CULATELLO: Highly prized salume. It has the same characteristics of prosciutto but is actually aged into a casing. Only the best part of the hog leg is used. For a detailed description, see the chapter on *SALAME* and *SALUMI*.

CUMINO: A plant typical of the Mediterranean. The seeds are very aromatic and are used to enrich the flavor of sweets and breads. These seeds are also used to produce a liquer called «kummel».

DIAVOLICCHIO: chili peppers, see: *PEPERONCINO*

DOLCEFORTE: A sauce with a base of mustard and sugar or any of two contrasting spices, e.g., peperoncino and honey.

DROGHE: A combination of spices used to prepare Panforte di Siena.

ERBAZZONE: Emilian savory pie filled with young chard or spinach, pancetta, eggs and parmigiano cheese. There is also a sweet version, made without pancetta in which the greens are mixed with ricotta, almonds and sugar.

ERBETTE: A tender chard-like green leaf.

ERBORINATO: This term is used to indicate the greenish streaks caused by the natural fermentation (mould) of certain types of cheese like Gorgonzola.

ESTRAZIONE: The extraction made from the actual pressing of the crushed olives to obtain olive oil.

FAGIOLI: Beans

FARINACEI: All food that contains starch such as pasta, rice, and dumplings.

FARINATA: Chick pea flour diluted with water and oil, then baked in the oven with rosemary. It is cut into triangles and eaten warm as a snack.

FARRO: A type of wheat that grows well in generally poor terrain and cold winters. For this reason it is grown in mountain areas. It has been used in Italy since the Romans; today it is grown in Liguria, Toscana and Puglia. It's kernal is used for soups, either shelled or unshelled (spelt).

FARSUMAGRU: A large roll of beef stuffed with chopped meat, whole hard boiled eggs, prosciutto, cheese and crumbled sausage, cooked in tomato sauce.

FAVE DEI MORTI: Cookies made of flour, sugar, almonds, pine nuts and egg whites.

FELINO: A type of salami that takes it name from a village just outside Parma.

FETTUCCINE: fresh ribbon like pasta.

FILASCETTA/FITASCETTA: Focaccia covered with onions browned in butter, fresh cheese and sugar.

FINANZIERA: A garnish or condiment of chicken livers and giblets, olives, sweetbreads, mushrooms and truffles.

FINOCCHIO: (Fennel). A celery-like vegetagle with a delicate anise flavor. May be eaten raw or cooked in various ways, such as braised, fried and boiled.

FINOCCHIELLA: Wild fennel seeds.

FOCACCIA: Cake or savory pie.

FOIOLO: The curly part of the upper intestine which falls into the tripe category

FONDUTA: A fluid and creamy cheese melt made by slowly melting fontina cheese in milk, then mixing in egg yolks.

FONTANA: A conical shape of flour with a cavity in the center in which eggs or other ingredients are mixed with the flour.

FONTINA: A rich, mellow, flavorful cheese from Val d'Aosta. It is a delicious melting or eating cheese.

FORMAGGIO: Cheese. See chapter for various types.

FRANTOIO: A machine to crush olives to extract olive oil. It consists of two large granite heels that turn on a large granite platter. Frantoio can also be the name given to the entire factory complex that makes olive oil.

FRAPPE: Another name for Chacchiere

FRATTAGLIE: Variety meat. The innards or organ meat of all animals.

FRICO: A kind of frittata made with potatoes and cheese.

FRISEDDA: A type of bread from Puglia shaped into a circle, baked, then cut in half and baked again till dry and crispy. It is served as a bread or is soaked in water and seasoned with oil, fresh tomato, oregano and salt. It keeps for a very long time.

FRITTATA: A flat omelet. It may contain vegetables, meat or cheese (particularly parmigiano). Frittate are often served at room temperature.

FRITTO (IL): An assortment of fried foods which may include vegetables, meats and fish. (See chapter)

FRUTTA ALLA MARTORANA: A Sicilian almond paste artfully molded into fruit shapes.

FRUTTI DI MARE: Seafood. The term refers to all types of shellfish only, e.g. insalata di frutti di mare (seafood salad).

FUGAZZA: A Venetian yeasted sweet dough enriched with many eggs, liqueur, vanilla, several spices, orange peel and (when available) iris root.

FUNGHI: Mushrooms. See chapter for various types.

FUNGHETTO (AL): A term used to describe vegetables cooked, sliced thinly or diced and sautéed. Parsley, garlic and tomato are usually added.

FUSILLI: Spaghetti or short pasta twisted into a long spiral. Short twisted pasta can also be called eliche (propellers).

GALANI: Venetian dialect word for chiacchiere.

GALANTINA: Cooked salame made with veal, pancetta, pistachios and spices.

GALLETTA: Sea biscuit. Made without yeast and shaped like a bagel, gallette are generally used in cappon magro.

GALLINACCI: (Also known as cantarelli). Pale yellow-ocher mushrooms with upturned, flared caps and slender, short stems.

GAMBERO: Shrimp. A crustacean without claws, it can reach a length of 10"; its shell can range from pink to bright red, the meat a delicate pink.

GARGANELLI: Small quills made of fresh pasta with some parmigiano cheese mixed into the dough. They are shaped by curling the fresh pasta dough around a special utensil made for this purpose called a pettine.

GARUM: A fish sauce very popular in ancient Rome. Its origins are Greek but in Turkey, even today, we find a fish sauce called «gharos». Samples have been found in the ruins of Pompei and the south of Spain or wherever there were salt beds. To make the sauce fat fish were used such as mackerel and sardines. They were cleaned and left to macerate in terra-cotta containers in alternating layers with spices such as mint, oregano, celery, fennel, dill, coriander and salt. The fish was left for 7 days in the sun, then it was mixed daily for 21 days. This mush was then saved to use as a sauce for suckling pigs on the spit. For home consumption it was diluted with water, wine or vinegar to prepare various condiments.

GATTÒ: Dish made of layers of mashed potatoes alternated with mozzarella, hard boiled eggs and salame, baked like a savory tart.

GELU I MULUNI: Sicilian watermelon ice cream made with watermelon pulp, chocolate and orange flower water.

GIARDINETTO: Plate of vegetables or sottoaceti laid out on a plate in such a way as to resemble a garden in bloom.

GIARDINIERA: A mixture of vegetables cooked in water and vinegar, then preserved in oil. It is served as a side dish for meats.

GNOCCHI: Small dumplings made of cooked potatoes, egg and flour.

GNOCCHI ALLA ROMANA: Semolina gnocchi, usually baked in round disks with butter and cheese.

GOLA: (Literally, «throat»). The tapered, less choice part of sweetbreads.

GRAMOLATURA: The process used to crush olives before the pressing to extract olive oil.

GRANA: See *GRANA PADANO.*

GRANA PADANO: A parmigiano-style cheese made outside the specified Parmigiano Reggiano areas. It can be made all year-round. It is used just like parmigiano and can be eaten on its own, for cooking or for grating.

GRANSEOLA: Venetian dialect word for spider crab.

GRANITA: Light slush-ice made with sugar syrup and either fruit juice or coffee.

GREMOLATA: A battuto made of garlic, rosemary, parsley and lemon peel, used on ossobuco.

GRISSINO: Breadsticks made of dough with butter or another fat added. The most traditional ones are those from Torino which are pulled by hand and are very long and irregular in shape.

GROLLA: A wooden bowl which may also have the shape of a calice, typical object of the Val D'Aosta artisans. A similar bowl is also known as coppa dell'amicizia (the friendship cup). Its shape is short and wide with a series of spouts circling its radius and with a cover. This bowl is used to pour in hot coffee with the addition of grappa and sugar, it is then flamed. When the flame has consumed a good amount of the alcohol, the bowl is passed from one person to the other with each one drinking the coffee from a different spout.

GUANCIALE: A type of fat (most often used in Central Italy) from the fattest part of the hog jowl. Used like pancetta, guanciale is said to have a better, sweeter flavor.

GUARDAPORTA: (doorman). Nickname given for ragù napoletano because a doorman, supposedly having nothing else to do but watch the main entrance, could watch the slow cooking of the ragù as well.

GUBANA: Friulian dessert made of sweet yeasted dough filled with mixed dried fruit, nuts and liqueur, then rolled and baked. It is served sliced and soaked in grappa.

IMPEPATA DI COZZE: Mussels opened by steaming them in a covered pan and seasoned with lemon juice, parsley and freshly ground pepper.

INSACCATO: Meat, fat and spices more or less finely ground in either natural or synthetic casings, then preserved. There are three kinds of insaccati: precooked (e.g., mortadella); those which must be cooked before eating (e.g., cotechino, zampone); and raw, which may be eaten dry-aged (e.g., salame).

INSALATA DI RINFORZO: («reinvigorating salad»). A Christmas salad from Southern Italy, made of cauliflower, olives, vegetables in vinegar, anchovies, and capers, then dressed with oil.

INTINGOLO: A sauce or a condiment in which bread, polenta or vegetables may be dipped.

INVOLTINO: Lean meat, pounded flat and rolled with a filling and/or spices, these are most often made from veal or pork. It can also be called rollatina. In the South, where this is made with pork, it is called braciola.

IOTA/JOTA: A Friulian bean soup from made with fermented turnips and polenta or with potatoes, sauerkraut, pork stew and ribs.

KNODEL: Classic bread dumplings from Alto Adige.

LAMPAGIONI/LAMPASCIONI: Small squat onions with a pleasantly bitter taste. They are commonly used in Puglia, usually boiled and served as salad, as a side dish for meat, in frittate or baked with potatoes.
LARDO: lard or back fat (see "condiments").
LASAGNE: Fresh pasta cut into wide strips.
LASAGNE FESTONATE: Lasagne with curly edges.
LATTE DI MANDORLE: The juice of almonds, made by pounding the almonds into a paste and then adding water.
LATTEMIELE: (milk honey). Lombardian name for whipped cream.
LATTERIA: Cow's milk cheese made in small mountain dairies.
LATTICELLO: The whitish, acidulous liquid reserved after cream has been clarified. This is also the name of the liquid in which mozzarella is preserved.
LATTONZOLO: An unweaned piglet.
LATTUGHINO: A lettuce that grows in small bunches with a few tiny, ruffled leaves. (Italian word for lettuce is lattuga).
LATTUME: The seminal liquid of a male tuna. The entire sac is removed from the fish and air dried. This is very rare and cannot be considered a common product. It is eaten in the same manner as bottarga, sliced very thin and accompanied by greens, with extra virgin olive oil.
LECCARDA: A dripping pan for roasts on the spit.
LIEVITARE: To leaven by adding either beer or natural yeast.
LINGUA: Tongue. Also a cooked salame made principally of calf's tongue.
LINGUA SALMISTRATA: Beef tongue preserved in salamoia. Before it can be eaten it must be de-salted and cooked.
LINGUINE: Long, flat,dried pasta about $\frac{1}{8}$" wide .
LUCANICA/LUGANICA: A long, thin sausage.

MACCHERONI: Dried, short, tubular pasta, smooth or ribbed.
MAGRO: Lean meat taken from the beef shoulder.
MALFATTI: («badly made»). Spinach dumplings made with cheese, spices and egg yolk. They are boiled and served with a condiment or may be baked.
MALLOREDDUS: Tiny Sardinian dry gnocchi made of flour, water, and saffron. Curled by hand, they are served with a ragù.
MALTAGLIATI: Pieces of leftover fresh pasta used in soup.
MANDORLATO: Nougat from Veneto made mostly with almonds.
MARGARINA: (margarine). A less expensive butter substitute (see condiments).
MANGIATUTTO: («eat-all»). Thin asparagus,all of which may be eaten, including the stems. Snow peas or taccole are sometimes given this name.
MANTECATO: A dish made with butter and cheese, added just before a rice or pasta dish is ready to serve.
MARICONDA (LA): soup with bread dumplings. See chapter on ZUPPE.
MARINATA: A marinade, used to preserve, flavor, or tenderize meat. The three basic types of marinades are: quick, raw and cooked. (See also *CONCIA/ CONCE*).
MARITATA: A Neapolitan cabbage, escarole and sausage soup.
MARITOZZO: A sweet bun filled with raisins, pine nuts and candied fruit.
MARRONE: A variety of large and tasty chestnuts obtained by grafting the chestnut trees.
MARZAPANE: Almond dough.

MASCARPONE: A rich, dense, fresh triple-cream cheese made from cow's milk. Very fresh mascarpone (seldom seen in the U.S). is vaguely sweet. It is used both in desserts and savory dishes.

MATTARELLO: Rolling pin. A heavy, cylinder-shaped wooden stick for rolling out any kind of dough.

MELOARANCIO: An old Tuscan dialect word for orange.

MEINO: A sweet bread made of cornmeal, white flour, baking powder and eggs. It is round and squat in shape and is served with heavy cream, into which it is dipped.

MESCIUA: Soup made of chick peas, beans and wheat seasoned with oil, salt and freshly ground pepper.

MESSICANI: Veal rollatine stuffed with sausage, eggs and parmigiano cheese. Two or three are skewered onto wooden sticks and cooked in butter, sage and Marsala.

MEZZALUNA: («half moon»). Crescent-shaped knife with one handle at each end, used for mincing vegetable, meats and other food stuff.

MIGLIACCIO: A special kind of baked, sweet blood sausage made into a cake. The ingredients are fresh pig blood, bread crumbs, lard, raisins and pine nuts.

MINESTRA: Broth served with the addition of fresh or dried pasta, rice, small dumplings, vegetables, or eggs and grated parmigiano.

MINESTRONE: A soup made of various vegetables, rice or pasta cooked in a broth.

MISSOLTA: A tin can in which agoni (see FISH chapter) are stored after drying.

MISSOLTITT: Dried and preserved agoni.

MISTICANZA: Mixed salad made of radicchio, watercress, endive, arugula and other field lettuces.

MITILI: Another name for mussels.

MOCETTA: Salame from the Valle d'Aosta, made with meat from chamois or deer.

MORTADELLA DI BOLOGNA: Large, cooked salame made of pork and usually mixed with other meats, seasoned with pepper and pistachio nuts. It is easily recognizable by its broad pink slices with chunks of white fat.

MORTADELLA DI FEGATO: A cooked salame made with liver, pancetta, spices and wine.

MORSA: A cradle designed to hold a hole bored in prosciutto to facilitate its slicing by hand.

MORTAIO: Mortar.

MOSTARDA DI FRUTTA: A piquant preserve of whole pieces of fruit in sugar syrup and mustard oil. It may include pears, peaches, apricots, watermelon and pieces of pumpkin. Intended for serving with boiled meats and the classic accompaniment to bollito misto, it is also mixed into the filling for sweet and savory tortelli.

MOSTO: Must. Grape juice not yet fermented into wine.

MOZZARELLA: A fresh cheese from Southern Italy, mainly from the Campania region. The best quality mozzarella is made with Bufala milk (a breed not to be confused with the American buffalo). In other parts of Italy this same cheese is made with cow's milk, generally known under the name «fior di latte.» The mozzarella produced with Bufala milk is higher in fat content and much more nutritious. Mozzarella has soft and elastic texture, oval-round shape, white color. Its taste is sweet and milky. It is sold in various shapes: braids, balls, bite-size pieces.

MUSCIAME: Musciame is filet of dolphin, cut in strips and air dried. It is eaten thinly sliced and is indispensable to prepare cappon magro a typical Ligurian fish salad.

NECCI: Sweet crêpes made with chestnut flour and served with fresh pecori no cheese and ricotta.

NERVETTI: Antipasto made of boiled calves' feet which have been de-boned and sliced into thin strips. It is seasoned with oil and raw onion and eaten cold.

NEPITELLA: Catmint. Belonging to the same family as mint, it grows wild and is commonly used in salads, to flavor white meats or roasts. The aroma is similar to mint with scents of sage. It should not be confused with wild mint.

NOCE: The eye of the round, a large single-muscle cut taken from the leg of either beef or veal. The choicest veal scaloppine are taken from this cut. It is also the literal translation for «walnut».

NOCETTA/NOCCIOLA: A portion-sized, de-boned saddle or rack of veal, lamb, or beef.

NOCINO: Alcoholic beverage made from green walnuts and aged for about a year.

NODINO: Loin chop, either veal or pork, cut from the saddle.

OFFELLE: Oval biscuits made of sweet pastry.

OLIVE ALL'ASCOLANA: Large pitted olives stuffed with cooked chopped meat, mixed with mortadella, prosciutto, parmigiano cheese, eggs, they are then breaded and fried.

ORCI: Containers to conserve olive oil made of terra-cotta with the inside glazed for smoothness.

ORECCHIETTE: Fresh pasta made of only flour and water and shaped into a curl.

OSSOBUCO: Veal shank cut across into thick slices, braised and customarily served with risotto Milanese.

OVOLI: One of the rarer varieties of mushrooms. Ovoli (still closed) are completely oval in form, pure white, often speckled with brilliant orange where the membrane was removed by checkers before the mushroom was sent to the market.

PAGLIATA/PAJATA: The upper part of beef and veal intestines.

PAIOLO: A heavy (unlined) copper pot with a convex bottom, used for cooking polenta.

PALA: An edgeless peel used to slide the pizza into the brick oven.

PALOMBACCIO: Wild pigeon.

PANCETTA: The salt-cured belly fat of a hog. Pancetta has deep pink stripes of flesh (similar to American bacon) and is used to lard meats and to flavor sauces, soups or other dishes. It may be cured in either a flat or rolled form.

PANPEPATO: (peppered bread). A sweet bread made of flour, sugar, almonds, pine nuts, orange peel and plenty of freshly ground pepper.

PAN DE FRIZZE: Friulian sweet buns made with cornmeal, white flour, ciccioli and sugar.

PANDOLCE: Genovese sweet bread that is densely packed with candied fruit.

PANDORO: Veronese sweet bread made with yeasted dough, eggs, butter and powdered sugar.

PANE: Breads. See chapter on BREADS for all types.

PANETTONE: Milanese sweet bread made with yeasted dough, raisins and candied fruit peelings. It can be dome shaped or flat.

PANE FRATTAU: Sardinian soup made of layers of carta di musica (thin layered crispy bread) sprinkled with grated cheese and covered with broth.

PANE SPEZIALE: A type of Emilian bread similar to panforte.

PANFORTE: A Sienese sweet bread made with flour, candied fruit, spices, almonds and sugar. It is baked on paper thin wafers and sprinkled with powdered sugar.

PAN GIALLO: Sweet bread from Lazio made with raisins, nuts, candied peel, honey and chocolate, and iced with chocolate.

PANISCIA: A thick soup made with sausage, rice, beans and plenty of freshly ground pepper.

PANISSA/PANICCIA: Polenta made with chickpea flour seasoned with oil and chopped onions.

PAN MOLLE: See PANZANELLA

PANSOTTI: Genovese ravioli stuffed with cooked greens, ricotta, borage, eggs and cheese. They are served with a walnut sauce.

PANZANELLA: A salad of stale bread softened in water and vinegar with various types of vegetables (often coarsely chopped) and dressed with oil and vinegar.

PANZEROTTI: Disks of yeasted dough stuffed with mozzarella and a little tomato sauce, folded in half, sealed and fried, served as an antipasto. The term also means potato croquettes with a piece of mozzarella in their centers.

PAPERO: Florentine word for duck.

PAPPA AL POMODORO: Tuscan soup made of stale crusty country bread, fresh tomatoes, garlic, basil, pepper and oil.

PAPPARDELLE: Long, wide strips of fresh pasta.

PARMIGIANA (alla): A food term which refers to preparation that always contain parmigiano cheese. In Southern Italy the term refers to a a dish consisting of fried slices of eggplant layered with tomato sauce, mozzarella cheese and baked.

PARMIGIANO REGGIANO: A cow's milk hard cheese from the region around Parma, it is the choicest type of parmigiano. Reggiano is produced under the strictest regulations: it must be made with milk produced between April 1st and November 11th, in the provinces of Parma, Reggio, Modena, Mantua and Bologna. It is a hand-made cheese aged a minimum of 18 months before it is sold. Authentic Reggiano has the words «Parmigiano Reggiano» etched in a continuous pattern of small dots around the entire circumference of the rind. It is eaten on its own, used in cooking and for grating.

PARMESAN: A type of parmigiano cheese which can be made all over the world.

PAROZZO: An Abruzzese cake shaped in a loaf and made of flour, almonds, sugar, and eggs, then iced with chocolate.

PASQUALINA (TORTA): Savory Ligurian artichoke pie made with many very thin layers of pastry.

PASSATELLI: A mixture of eggs, bread and grated parmigiano passed through a ricer and dropped directly into a broth.

PASTA: Spaghetti and maccheroni, plume and cavatelli, ravioli, tortellini, fusilli and so on, belong to an immense family of ingredients all of poor origins and all having in common the characteristic of offering a surprisingly balanced diet. See chapter on *PASTA* for details on all types.

PASTA AL FORNO: Baked pasta with a ragù and the addition of other ingredients.

PASTA ALLA NORMA: Spaghetti with fried eggplant, tomato and grated salted ricotta cheese.

PASTA 'NCASCIATA: A timballo of maccheroni and meatballs seasoned with meat sauce and layered with hard boiled eggs, salami, caciocavallo, peas and other ingredients, covered with more meat sauce, baked till golden brown, then removed from mold and served.

PASTA PER SIGILLARE: Dough made with flour and water, it is used to seal the cover of a pot so as to avoid heat dispersion.

PASTA REALE: Sicilian almond paste, used to make frutta alla martorana or to wrap around cakes. It is made from pounded or finely chopped almonds and mixed with the same weight in sugar and a little glucose. It is colored with food coloring.

PASTELLA: A frying batter.

PASTICCIO: Pasta layered with ingredients and baked.

PASTIERA: A sweet short pastry filled with ricotta, cooked wheat kernels, candied fruit peelings and orange water. It is prepared during the Easter period.

PASTISSADA DE CAVAL: Horseman stew (see meats chapter)

PECORINO: A sheep's milk cheese (pecora is Italian for sheep), pecorino can be mild or sharp in flavor, and of hard (for grating) or soft consistency. In the U.S. the most common form of pecorino is romano, a typical Roman cheese. In Italy, two other types of pecorino are: pecorino sardo (from Sardinia), and the pecorino made in Tuscany.

PEOCI: Another name for mussels.

PEPERONATA: Dish made of sweet peppers sautéed with oil, onions and a little bit of tomato. Peperonata is an excellent side dish for meats and is better eaten warm or at room temperature.

PEPERONCINO: A thin, long and pointed pepper, either red or green, it varies in intensity from mild to very hot. It may be dried whole or coarsely or finely ground.

PEPOSO: Pork shank cooked with tomatoes, wine, herbs and freshly ground pepper.

PERCIATELLI: see bucatini.

PERSICATA: Solid peach preserves made in the same way as cotognata.

PESCE: Fish. For various types, see chapter.

PESCESTOCCO: Another name for stoccafisso.

PESTO: Cold Ligurian sauce made of basil, garlic, parmigiano and pecorino cheeses and oil. It is used on trenette, gnocchi and in minestrone.

PETTINE: A utensil used in Romagna to shape pasta dough into short quills (garganelli).

PEVERADA: Sauce made of bread, beef marrow, parmigiano cheese, broth, salt and pepper for boiled meats.

PEVERE: An old venetian word for pepper.

PEZZO DURO: A kind of molded ice cream.

PIADINA: Unleavened pizza dough made of water, flour and strutto. It is baked on a testo and served hot with salami and cheese.

PIATTO: plate or course as in "first course".

PICCAGGE: A Ligurian dialect word for fettuccine.

PICCATA: Veal scaloppina sauteed very quickly in a pan with butter and lemon juice, Marsala or other ingredients.

PICCHIETTARE: To insert spices such as cloves, cinnamon, and bay leaves in pieces of meat for better distribution of flavor while cooking.

PIEDINI: Calf's feet, boiled and used for a salad called nervetti it can be served as antipasto.

PIEMONTESE: Inhabitant of the region of Piedmont.

PIGNATTA: Another name for a large pot.

PIGNOLI: Pine nuts, also called pinoli.

PIGNOLATA: Oversized amaretti sprinkled generously with pine nuts

PINOCCATE: Tiny cakes with a base of sugar and pine nuts; they are commonly wrapped in colored paper.

PINOLI: see *PIGNOLI.*

PINZA: Cake made of white flour, cornmeal, fennel seeds, raisins, dried figs, and other dried and candied fruit.

PINZIMONIO: A dip for raw vegetables made of olive oil, ground pepper and salt. By extension, the raw vegetables served with this sauce are also called pinzimonio.

PISAREI E FASOI: An Emilian soup of tiny dumplings made from bread-crumbs, flour and milk. They are boiled, then tossed briskly with cooked beans with a soffritto of pancetta, onions and peeled tomatoes. Pisarei are the dumplings — fasoi are the beans.

PISSALADEIRA: A kind of pizza covered with onions, anchovies, black olives, and tomato.

PISTUM: Dumplings made of bread, eggs, herbs, sugar and raisins, boiled in pork broth.

PITTA: Calabrian name for pizza. Pitta chicculiata is covered with tomato sauce, oil and peperoncino while pitta maniata is two disks of dough stuffed with slices of hard boiled egg, cheese, salami and peperoncino.

PIZZAIOLA (ALLA): A term used to describe stews and sauces made with tomatoes, capers, oregano and anchovies.

PIZZOCCHERI: Tagliatelle made of whole wheat flour and cooked with po-tatoes, cabbage and other vegetables then sautéed with plenty of butter and slices of bitto cheese.

POLENTA: Yellow cornmeal, either fine or coarsely ground, cooked with wa-ter, and seasoned with butter and parmigiano, polenta may vary in consisten-cy from a soft to a solid form, according to its intended use. In some regions of Italy white cornmeal or buckwheat flour is used instead of yellow cornmeal.

POLENTA CONCIA OR PASTICCIATA: Polenta casserole layered with sauce, cheese and butter, then baked.

POLENTA TARAGNA: Polenta made with half whole wheat flour and half yellow corn meal with the addition of bitto cheese. Its name is derived from a Lombardian word, tarello, the stick used to stir the polenta.

POLPETTA: (meatball). A mixture of ground meat, bread, herbs, and cheese formed into balls and fried. Polpette are also cooked in a tomato sauce for pasta. Polpette are often made using leftover bits of meat and vegetables.

POLPETTONE: A meatloaf made of the same mixture as for meatballs.

POLVERINO: The floury mixture sprinkled over panforte before it is cooked.

PORCHETTA: Suckling pig. Also «in porchetta», the name given to all the dish-es prepared in the same procedure as cooking roast pig, and using the same basic dressings (salt, pepper, garlic, rosemary, wild fennel seeds). Roasts and fish, especially lake fish, are cooked this way. Very popular in Central Italy is the carp in porchetta, made with carps between 12-20 pounds, oven-cooking the whole fish, flavored with the same ingredients as for the roast pig.

PORCINI: Wild mushrooms with large, meaty, brown caps slightly rounded on top. The stems are fleshy and wider at the bottom.

PORRATA: a sauce prepared in the same manner as agliata, but substituting leeks for garlic.

POTACCHIO: Term used to describe food stewed with herbs, white wine and peperoncino.

PRATAIOLO: A white and meaty mushroom with a pleasant aroma. It can also be cultivated (hot house).

PRESCINSEUA: Ligurian dialect word for soured milk.

PROSCIUTTO: A hog's leg, salted, aged and dressed according to local usage. For various types of prosciutto see chapter on *SALUMI.*

PROVOLONE: A firm cheese with a pungent, somewhat salty flavor. It can also be mild.

PROVATURA: Fresh cheese from Lazio, very similar to mozzarella, eaten as it is, or breaded and fried.

PUNTA DI PETTO: Brisket of beef.

PUNTARELLE: Budding tips of a type of chicory cut halfway lengthwise and soaked in cold water until they curl up. They are served as salad dressed with oil, vinegar, garlic and chopped anchovies.

PUTTANESCA (ALLA): A pasta sauce made of tomato, black olives, anchovies, capers, peperoncino and basil.

QUADRUCCI: Fresh or dried pasta, usually made with eggs, cut into little squares, then added to soups or broth.

QUAGLIA: quail.

QUAGLIETTE: Little balls of leftover stuffing wrapped in scalded cabbage leaves and fried.

QUARTIROLO: Soft, sweet-tasting cow's milk cheese shaped into a square.

RADICCHIO: The red and white leaf chicory of the Veneto region. Radicchio di Treviso or trevigiano refer to the type grown in the Treviso area. It has tender, large leaves with white ribs and red edges. The radicchio of Castelfranco grows in small, tight heads with wide, tightly cupped leaves (similar to iceberg) having white ribs and red edges.

RAGÙ: A pasta sauce made of meat, either chopped or ground, cooked for a long time with tomatoes and herbs.

RAMERINO: See *ROSMARINO* (herbs and spices chapter)

RAVIOLI: Disks or squares of fresh egg pasta stuffed with vegetables, or cheese or meat. The larger ones are generally served with butter, sage and parmigiano cheese. Smaller ones (raviolini) are served with various condiments or in broths.

RETE: Caul fat. The membrane surrounding the interior organs of slaughtered animals. Usually veal and, especially, pig membrane are used to wrap lean meats for roasting.

RIBOLLITA: («re-boiled»). It is made by using leftovers of Tuscan bean soup baked with stale bread, thinly sliced onion and extra-virgin olive oil.

RICCIARELLI: Sienese oval-shaped cookies made of almonds, flour and sugar.

RICOTTA: A fresh white cheese made with whey. It has the texture and consistency of farmer's or pot cheese and is made in both sweet and savory dishes. Ricotta romana is made with sheep's milk. There is also a salted version which can be aged and used grated.

RIGAGLIE: Giblets from a chicken or any other bird in addition to its combs.

RIGATINO: A Tuscan pancetta made with the leanest part of the hog's belly, covered with black pepper and cured flat.

RIGATONI: Medium-sized ribbed maccheroni made of dried pasta.

RIPIENO: Stuffing.

RISI E BISI: Risotto from Veneto made with rice and fresh peas.

RISOTTO: A preparation of long-grain Italian rice. The basic recipe uses rice, onions, butter, broth and parmigiano. Risotto is cooked slowly, adding small amounts of liquid at a time, and finished by adding butter and parmigiano. Variations may add fish, shellfish, vegetables, sausage, prosciutto, herbs, saffron and other cheeses besides parmigiano. Yellow risotto, derives its color from saffron.

RISOTTO NERO: Risotto made with squid ink.

ROBIOLA: Fresh, soft cheese made with whole cow's milk with a very delicate taste.

ROCCIATA: A specialty of Assisi, similar to panforte, but shaped in a folded triangle.

ROGNOSA: A frittata made with salame and grated parmigiano cheese mixed with the eggs.

ROLLATINA: See *INVOLTINO.*

ROMBO: Turbot, a fish common in the Mediterranean and the North Atlantic. Its form is oval, almost rounded, and it may reach a length of 40.

ROSSETTI: The newborn of red and white mullet. They are excellent floured and fried.

RUSTISCIADA: A mixture of sliced sirloin and pieces of sausages cooked in sauce of tomato, wine and onion.

SABA/SAPA: Grapejuice and pulp cooked until very concentrated, used to make sweets and for some sweet-and-sour dishes.

SALAMA DA SUGO: A cooked salame made of ground pork, innards, wine and spices, stuffed into a pig's bladder. It must be cooked before eating.

SALAM D'LA DUJA: Salame from Piedmont, kept soft in a ceramic container (duja) filled with liquified fat.

SALAME: Ground meat, seasoned and packed into a casing.

SALAME DI MILANO: Aged, very finely grained salame.

SALAME NAPOLETANO: Aged sausage with plenty of peperoncino.

SALAMELLE: Little salami, similar to cotechino, which must be boiled or grilled before eating.

SALAMINI DELLA VERZA: Sausage links used to prepare the Milanese cassoeula.

SALAMOIA: Brine.

SALMÍ: A stew of wild game that has been marinated in wine, herbs, and spices, then cooked in the marinade. The sauce is strained and the dish served with polenta. Sometimes the sauce is used for pappardelle.

SALMORIGLIO: A warm sauce for roasted meats and grilled fish, especially swordfish. It is made with lemon juice, oil, parsley and oregano emulsified in a double boiler.

SALSICCIA: Pork meat in casing. It may be consumed fresh, pan fried or cooked in sauce. It may also be dry-aged (see chapter on SALAME).

SALTIMBOCCA: Veal scaloppine rolled with prosciutto and briskly sautéed in butter, sage and white wine.

SALUMI: Whole cuts of meat that are either cured in salt and dry-aged or cured in brine (salamoia), then cooked and preserved.

SALNITRO: Salt of potassium, used in food meant for long conservation.

SAN DANIELE; A village in *Friulli* near *Udine* where they produce *prosciutto di San Daniele*.

SANGUINACCIO: Cooked salami made of pig's blood mixed with other, sometimes sweet, ingredients.

SANSA: The solid part of the olives leftover after the first pressing through chemical process.

SAOR: A milder version of carpione, Saor is the Venetian dialect word for flavor. It is a sauce made of fried onions, vinegar, sugar, pine nuts and raisins used to marinate fresh fish, especially soles and sardines.

SARGASSI: Legend has it that eels come here from the Mediterranean to spawn. A portion of the Atlantic Ocean northeast of the Antille, Sargassi takes its name from a particular algae called sargasso.

SARTÙ: A rice preparation with a ragù in the center, baked in a mold.

SAVOIARDI: Lady fingers biscuit. Often used in preparing ice-cream cake.

SAVOR: «Flavor» in Venetian dialect. Also, a preserved fruit cooked in must. It is used to accompany some meats or used for some stuffings.

SBRISULONA: Mantua cake made with white flour, cornmeal, almonds, sugar and eggs.

SCACCIATA: A savory pie made of two layers of yeasted salted dough filled with meat, vegetables and cheese. There is also a sweet version filled with ricotta, sugar and coffee.

SCALOPPINA: Thinly sliced lean veal from the center cut of the leg, rib, loin or square cut chuck, which has been lightly pounded flat. One scaloppina may weigh 1-2 $\frac{1}{2}$ oz.

SCAMORZA: A stringy, semi-aged cheese similar to caciocavallo.

SCAMPO: A prawn measuring up to 10 inches.

SCAPECE: A vinegar, and mint marinade for vegetables and fried foods.

SCAVINO: The utensil used to remove the marrow out of the bone in ossobuco. It is a thin, elongated and narrow spatula also jokingly called «the tax man,» meaning it will scrape the marrow to the bone!

SCHIUMA DI MARE: Antipasto of small, just spawned anchovies seasoned with oil, lemon and pepper.

SCORZONERA: Bitter root.

SCOTTADITO/A SCOTTADITO: Meat or other food broiled quickly and eaten while still very hot.

SCOTTIGLIA: A mixture of various kinds of meat stewed together.

SCROFA: Sow. An adult female pig.

SCRIPELLE: Crêpes, cooked in broth or in a timballo.

SEADAS/SEBADAS: Large, sweet Sardinian ravioli filled with fresh cheese, fried and covered with honey.

SEMIFREDDO: Chilled Creams prepared with an egg-based custard and whipped cream. May be used as filling for cassate and bombe, or can be prepared with fruits, syrups, and chocolate.

SEPPIA: Cuttlefish. See FISH chapter.

SFINCIUNI: Rather thick focaccia covered with tomato sauce, anchovies, onions, cheese, oregano and oil. It can be served as an antipasto, main course or snack.

SFOGLIATELLE: Puff pastry made with many layers of curled pastry and filled with ricotta and candied fruits. It has a ridged look and the shape of a large sea shell.

SFORMATO: A savory mold bound with eggs and baked in a double boiler. Sformati may contain vegetables, meat or fish.

SOFFRITTO: Soffritto is the base of most preparations in Italian cuisine. One or more types of vegetables, herbs and spices are cut in julienne, diced and lightly fried in a fat (olive oil, pancetta or strutto) until they lose their crunchiness. The sauté of onions as the base for risotto is called soffritto.

SONCINO: Small, oval-leafed lettuce that grows in small bunches.

SOPA COADA: A Friulian soup consisting of boneless squab on slices of bread, covered with broth and baked.

SOPPRESSATA: Cooked and aged salame made from meat taken from the head of the pig, lard, spices and pistachio nuts.

SORBETTO: Sherbet, usually made with the juice and pulp of fruit.

SOTTACETI: Diced or whole vegetables, cooked in vinegar or water, then preserved in vinegar in jars. They are served as an antipasto or as a side dish for meat.

SOTTOFILETTO: The short loin of beef, minus the filet.

SOTTOLIO: Vegetables (sometimes fish), cooked in the same manner as sottaceto, but instead of vinegar they are preserved in oil.

SPALLA: Shoulder.

SPECK: Cured, dried, aged pork thigh as made in Alto Adige.

SPEZZATINO: Cubed or diced meat stewed or sautéed with or without tomatoes and/or other vegetables.

SPIANATOIA: A rather large, wooden pastry board, perfectly smooth and without knots.

SPONGATA: A roll of sweet pastry filled with honey, dried fruit, nuts and candied fruit.

SPUMA: A sweet or savory mousse.

SPUMONE: Spumone can also be called semifreddo. All semifreddi or spumone may be served with an appropriate sauce. These range from a simple fruit sauce to a vanilla cream.

STECCARE: To insert pieces of pancetta, lard or spices through the piece of meat ready to be roasted.

STECCHI: Ligurian brochettes of veal, brains, parmigiano cheese, vegetables and herbs that are breaded and fried. Stecco is also the name of the wooden skewer holding the meat.

STOCCAFISSO: Air-dried cod -- not to be confused with baccala', which is salt cod.

STRACCIATELLA: A soup made by rapidly mixing eggs beaten with parmigiano cheese into boiling broth.

STRACOTTO: Beef braised with herbs, vegetables and spices, cooked very slowly and for a long time on top of the stove, or in an oven.

STRANGOLAPRETI: («priests' chokers»). Dumplings made of potatoes and flour, cooked greens and ricotta, boiled and served with melted butter and parmigiano cheese or with a gorgonzola cheese sauce.

STUFATO: Chunks of meat cooked covered with wine and herbs over low heat for several hours.

STRUTTO: Melted animal fat, rid of all meat particles and preserved in soft-form. It is used as a fat for many preparations.

SUGNA: See *STRUTTO.*

SUPPLÌ: Rice balls with mozzarella, herbs and spices in the center. The rice is cooked like a risotto and it is then breaded and fried.

SVEZZATO: Weaned, baby lamb or pig just born.

TACCOLA: (snow peas). A kind of pea, also called mangiatutto (eat it all).

TAGLIAPASTA: Pasta knife in the shape of a small wheel made out of tin. It comes in different sizes and can either be grooved or not.

TAGLIATELLE/TAGLIATELLINE/TAGLIOLINI: Fresh pasta, between .08 of an inch and .02 of an inch wide.

TAGLIERE: Cutting board.

TAGLIO: («cut»). Cuts of meat; e.g.: 1° Taglio (primo taglio) refers to the choicest cuts; 2° e 3° Taglio (secondo e terzo taglio) indicate less choice cuts.

TAJERIN: Also taglialini with the addition of grated parmigiano to the dough. They are a specialty of Piedmont and are used mostly with white truffle.

TAPULONE: A dish of ground donkey meat cooked in wine.

TARAGNA: See POLENTA TARAGNA.

TARELLO: A wooden stick used to stir the polenta.

TARTUFO: A very rare aromatic tuber. White truffles are a great deal more aromatic, expensive and flavorful than black truffles. Also called Tartufo are rich chocolates or a vanilla and chocolate ice cream with candied fruits in the center shaped into a ball and covered with chocolate. It is also a kind of clam.

TELLINA: A tiny clam.

TENERUME: The piece of beef consisting of muscles and tissue where the ribs end.

TESTINA: Calf's head, used for bollito misto or served in a salad, cut in julienne and seasoned with oil, lemon, salt and pepper.

TESTO: A flat, round, edgeless cooking utensil with a handle on which testaroli are cooked. It can be terra-cotta or cast iron.

TIELLA: Large casserole dish for use in the oven. By extension, all of the dishes cooked in this pot take the same name.

TIGELLA: Similar to a piadina, it is served hot with lard, garlic and rosemary.

TIMBALLO: Baked pasta, rice or polenta, with the addition of other ingredients such as sauce, meat, vegetables and cheese.

TIRAMISÙ: A cold dessert made with layers of sponge cake or ladyfingers soaked in coffee and covered with a mascarpone cream.

TOMAXELLE/TOMACELLE: Veal rollatine stuffed with meat, mushrooms, pine nuts and herbs, cooked in sauce.

TOMA: A soft-ripened cheese, creamy in texture and high in fat content, shaped round and flat. It can be eaten fresh or preserved in oil with herbs or hot pepper.

TORCETTO: Sweet ciambella made of curled-up puff pastry.

TORCHIO: Utensil used to prepare bigolo. It is used to wind, pull, or stretch pasta.

TORCOLO: Sweet ciambella with candied citrus, raisins, pine nuts and anise seeds mixed into the dough.

TORRONE: Candy made of sugar, honey, almonds and hazelnuts cooked on top or in between very thin wafers. In addition to traditional crunchy variety from Cremona there are also chewy, chocolate-covered versions.

TORTA PASQUALINA: See *PASQUALINA.*

TORTELLI: Sweet fritters or ravioli stuffed with vegetables, pumpkin and/or cheese.

TORTELLINI: Stuffed pasta, similar to cappelletti, but shaped into a closed ring.

TORTELLONI: Large ravioli, usually stuffed with vegetables and/or cheese.

TORTIERA: A cake pan, round and of varying sizes, either simple or spring-form. The term tortiera is also used to describe something cooked in this pan.

TOSCANELLI: Small brown beans used in dishes such as pasta e fagioli. The same beans are also called fagiolini all'occhio in Tuscany.

TOTANO: A mollusk from the same family as squid (calamaro), the fin is a triangular shape which is attached to the bottom of the sac.

TRATTORIA: A rustic restaurant that serves traditional regional cuisine.

TRENETTE: Long, flat dried pasta.

TRIFOLARE: A way of preparing mushrooms or certain variety of meats, such as sweetbreads or kidneys. It refers to the method of slicing the meat or mushrooms very thinly, and sautéeing briefly, most often in butter.

TRIPPA: (tripe). The stomach and the first part of the intestines of cows, hogs and lamb. This is part of the frattaglie (innards) and is sold already cleaned and par-boiled.

TRIPPATI: Egg frittata cut into thin strips and served with tomato sauce. The name derives from trippa (tripe).

TROFIE: Little twisted pieces of pasta made only of flour and water. They are a Ligurian specialty and are served with pesto.

TRUSCELLO: Layers of beef meatballs alternating with a mixture of ricotta, parmigiano cheese, and eggs. It is a specialty of Messina.

UCCELLETTO (ALL'): Diced or julienne of veal or beef browned rapidly in oil and sage, then splashed with white wine and served immediately.

UCCELLETTI SCAPPATI: Skewers of rollatine of pork or beef wrapped in pancetta and sautéed in oil and sage. They are served with polenta.

UOVA: Eggs

VACCINARA (ALLA): A Roman dish usually containing ox tails.

VALDOSTANA: A veal chop sliced open like a pocket and stuffed with fontina, then breaded and fried in butter.

VALIGINI: («little suitcases»). Cabbage rolls stuffed with meat or vegetables.

VALTELLINA: An Alpine valley by the river Adda in the province of Sondrio, in Lombardy. It borders with Switzerland to the north, the province of Como to the west, Bergamo to the south and Bolzano to the east.

VENTRESCA: Another name for pancetta. Ventresca may also refer to the fatty belly flesh of a tuna, considered a choice cut.

VERMICELLI/VERMICELLONI: Long, dried rounded pasta between .08 of an inch and .07 of an inch thick.

VINCISGRASSI: Fresh lasagne made with flour and semolina, boiled, then drained and layered with stewed giblets, sweetbreads, brains, prosciutto, herbs and béchamel sauce. It is baked for 30 minues in a 375° F. oven.

VINO COTTO: (cooked wine). Must (just pressed grapes) cooked for many hours until it is as dense as honey. It can also be made with figs and water instead of grapes. It keeps for a long time sealed in jars and is used instead of honey in some Puglian desserts.

VIRTÙ: An Abruzzese soup made by cooking dried legumes left over from the winter and adding fresh spring vegetables.

VITELLO TONNATO: Cold dish of veal with tuna sauce. The lean veal is marinated and cooked in white wine, then sliced and covered with a tuna, anchovy and caper sauce.

ZABAIONE/ZABAGLIONE: A mixture of egg yolks, Marsala and sugar beaten in a double boiler until fluffy. It is served warm, in dessert cups or cold with fruit.

ZAFFERANO: Saffron is the stamen of a flower from Asia Minor. It is used for coloring and flavoring.

ZAMPETTO: Pig's trotter (hooves). They are usually stewed, either by themselves or with other parts of the pig. They can also be boiled as part of bollito misto or by themselves and served with green sauce.

ZAMPONE: A de-boned pig's shank stuffed with pork, pork fat, skin, and herbs. It is traditionally eaten on New Year's Eve with lentils for good luck.

ZELTEN: Yeasted Christmas bread made with rye and white cake flour mixed with candied fruit and iced with honey.

ZEPPOLE: Fritters made of flour, eggs and yeast. They can be used plain, sprinkled with sugar, or filled with cream.

ZIMINO: Sauce made of very finely minced greens or spinach, parsley and garlic blended with oil. It is usually served with fish.

ZIMINO DI CECI: Soup made of boiled chick peas, flavored with browned onion, garlic, celery, greens, tomatoes and dried mushrooms in oil.

ZITE/ZITI: Long, cylindrical, hollow dried maccheroni.

ZUCCOTTO: A semifreddo (chilled cream) made in a semi-spherical mold consisting of layers of sponge cake sprinkled with liqueur and filled with whipped cream and chocolate.

ZUPPA: A dense, semi-liquid soup made by cooking meat, fish, shellfish, dried beans or vegetables in water. Zuppe are usually served with slices or cubes of toasted or leftover country bread.

ZUPPA INGLESE: An Italian version of English trifle; sponge cake soaked in alchermes and layered with vanilla cream, chocolate and fruit preserve.

ZUPPA PAVESE: Hot broth poured over buttered or plain toasted bread with one or two eggs on top.

Bibliographic Note

In compiling this book, and in many years of work in the restaurant profession, I have used the knowledge acquired by reading and consulting a great number of published materials. The most relevant to the present work are listed below:

1300's

Anonimo Toscano del Trecento: *Libro della Cucina* (manuscript in the University Library of Bologna) published in Bologna, 1863.

1400's

Maestro Martino da Como: *Liber de Arte Coquinaria* (manuscript in the Library of Congress, Washington, DC) published in Venice, 1516, under the name of Giovanni de'Rosselli and the title of Epulario.

Bartolomeo Sacchi, known as Platina: *De Honesta Voluptate atque Valetudine*. Rome, 1474.

1500's

Bartolometo Scappi: *Opera,* Venice, 1570.

Cristoforo di Messisburgo: *Banchetti, composizioni di vivande et apparecchio generale*. Ferrara, 1549.

1600's

Bartolometo Stefani: *L'arte di ben cucinare* Mantua, 1662.

1700's

Jacopo Vittoreli: *I maccheroni*. Venice, 1773.

Vincenzo Corrado: *Il cuoco galante* Naples, 1773.

Francesco Leonardi: *L'Apicio Moderno* Rome, 1790.

1800's

Ippolito Cavalcanti, duca di Buonvicino: *Cucina teorico-practica,* Naples, 1837.

Pellegrino Artusi: *La scienza in cucina e l'arte di mangiabene,* Florence, 1891.

1900's

In our century, the gastronomic bibliography of Italy becomes so vast and complex that even a synthetic discussion of its major trends would exceed the purpose and scope of the present work. Among the works that I have consulted more often during the compilation of the present volume are:

Massimo Alberini: *4000 anni a tavola*. Milan, 1972, and *Storia del pranzo all'italiana* Milan, 1966.

Massimo Alberini and Giorgio Mistretta: *L'Italia gastronomica, Publisher,* Touring Club Italiano, Milano, 1984.

Vincenzo Buonassisi, *Il Codice della pasta*, Milan 1973, (English Edition, Pasta, Wilton, 1976).

Luigi Carnacina and Luigi Veronelli: *La Cucina regionale*. Milan, 1974.

Riccardo di Corato: *2214 vini d'Italia,* Milan, 1975, *451 formaggi d'italia,* Milan, 1977 and *928 condimenti d'Italia*, Milan 1978.

Fernanda Gosetti: *In Cucina con Fernanda Gosetti,* and «*il dolcissimo*» *Fabbri, Milan 1984*.
Waverley Root, *The Food of Italy*. New York 1977.
Luigi Veronelli: *Bere Giusto*, Milan, 1971.

GENERAL INDEX

BIOGRAPHY

Tony May is a New York restaurateur renowned for his efforts to bring authentic Italian cuisine to the attention of the American public. As owner of three restaurants — Sandro's, San Domenico and La Camelia — he has been responsible for bringing over some of Italy's finest chefs, and he has been invested as a Cavaliere dell'Ordine al Merito della Republica Italiana for his efforts on behalf of his native country's gastronomy.

He is also chairman of Gruppo Ristoratori Italiani, N.A., *and serves on the board of the National Restaurant Association and he is a member of the board of trustees of the* Culinary Institute of America, *where he was active in establishing the Caterina de Medici restaurant and a course of studies intended to teach authentic Italian cooking to American students. For years he ran New York's pre-eminent restaurant and night club, The Rainbow Room, and in 1986 opened the restaurant Palio which attracted critical acclaim throughout the world. In 1989 Tony May was chosen by a distinguished panel of his peers to be included in the prestigious "who's who of Cooking in America". In 1990 Mr. May was voted the recipient of the most coveted award in the hospitality industry in the United States "The Silver Plate Award" in the category of indipendent Restaurant Operator. Mr. May lives in Greenwich, Connecticut with his daughter, Marisa.*

THE ITALIAN WINE & FOOD INSTITUTE

The Italian Wine & Food Institute, headquartered in New York, is a non-profit organization which was created in 1984 to enhance the image of Italian wines and foods in the United States. The Institute's goal is to educate the consumer with special cultural events about Italian wines and food with participation of professional establishments and tradespeople. A broad range of activities is planned annually, such as vintage barrel wine tastings and wine and food tasting seminars. Moreover, the Institute serves as an information center for the wines and foods of Italy. The Institute performs valuable services for its members by fostering relationships with the government, the press, with businesses and consumers, and by disseminating information on market and production.

The members of the Italian Wine & Food Institute include the leading producers and connoisseurs in the field.

Roto-Offset S.r.l. - Funo (Bo) - Industria roto-litografica